YOU SAY YOU WANT A

REVOLUTION?

RECORDS AND REBELS 1966–1970

YOU SAY YOU WANT A

REVOLUTION?

RECORDS AND REBELS 1966–1970

EDITED BY VICTORIA BROACKES AND GEOFFREY MARSH

V&A Publishing

First published by V&A Publishing, 2016
Victoria and Albert Museum
South Kensington
London SW7 2RL
www.vandapublishing.com

In partnership with   Sound experience by

With additional support from

      SASSOON

Distributed in North America by Harry N. Abrams Inc., New York

Hardback edition
ISBN 978 1 85177 891 1

Paperback edition
ISBN 9781 85177 892 8

Library of Congress Control Number 2016930363

10 9 8 7 6 5 4 3 2 1
2020 2019 2018 2017 2016

Design: johnson banks
Copy-editing: Tamsin Perrett
Index: Hilary Bird

Michael J. Sandel's text (Epilogue, pp.304–5) has previously appeared in
What Money Can't Buy: The Moral Limits of Markets, first published in
the United States of America by Farrar, Straus and Giroux, 2012, and in
Great Britain by Allen Lane, 2012 (published by Penguin Books, 2013, pp.3–6).
© Michael J. Sandel, 2012, Reproduced by permission of Penguin Books Ltd.
Used by permission. All rights reserved.

New photography by Richard Davis and Paul Robins
V&A Photography by V&A Photographic Studio

Printed in Italy

V&A Publishing
Supporting the world's leading
museum of art and design,
the Victoria and Albert
Museum, London

Front cover and chapter openers
rebel cluster includes: John Lennon
by Larry Smart; Andy Warhol,
photograph by Greg Gorman, 1982;
Martin Luther King, Jr, photograph
by John Littlewood, 1967; Jimi
Hendrix by Joe Roberts, Jr, 1969;
Twiggy, photograph by Bert Stern,
1967; Che Guevara, photograph by
Alberto Korda, 1960; Germaine Greer,
photograph by Keith Morris, 1969;
Timothy Leary, 1966; Kathleen Cleaver,
photograph by Ted Streshinsky, late
1960s; Buckminster Fuller, 1967;
Stewart Brand, photograph by Bill
Young; Allen Ginsberg, photograph
by John 'Hoppy' Hopkins, 1965;
Chairman Mao poster, c.1969

Back cover: The crowd at Woodstock,
photograph by Barry Z. Levin

Endpapers: The crowd at Woodstock,
photograph by Baron Wolman
(see pl.171)

p.2: Caroline de Bendern holding
a Vietnamese flag on the Boulevard
Saint-Michel, Paris, 1968,
photograph by Jean-Pierre Rey

opposite: Emperor Rosko
(Michael Joseph Pasternak), newly
appointed DJ for BBC Radio 1, Paris,
1967, photograph by Reg Lancaster

p.6: Detail of *Grain of Sand* (see pl.271)
by Mati Klarwein, 1963–5

CONTENTS

8 Director's Foreword

12 Curators' Preface

16 **1. A Tale of Two Cities**
London, San Francisco
and the Transatlantic Bridge

Geoffrey Marsh

54 **2. Revolution Now**
The Traumas and Legacies
of US Politics in the Late 1960s

Sean Wilentz

98 **3. The Counter-Culture**

Barry Miles

136 **4. All Together Now?**

Jon Savage

166 **5. The Fillmore, the Grande
and the Sunset Strip**
The Evolution of
a Musical Revolution

Howard Kramer

194 **6. You Say You Want
a Revolution?**
Looking at the Beatles

Victoria Broackes

224 **7. British Fashion 1966–70**
'A State of Anarchy'

Jenny Lister

250 **8. The Chrome-Plated
Marshmallow**
The 1960s Consumer Revolution
and Its Discontents

Alison J. Clarke

276 **9. 'We Are As Gods...'**
Computers and America's
New Communalism, 1965–75

Fred Turner

304 Epilogue: Michael Sandel on
Where We Go from Here

306 Notes
312 Networks of Resistance
314 Index
318 Picture credits
319 Acknowledgements
320 Contributors

DIRECTOR'S FOREWORD

(opposite)
Bob Dylan 'Mister Tambourine Man'
poster, 1968, designed by Martin Sharp
V&A: S.28–1978

In 1970 I was a teenager living in West Germany. I was an avid reader of newspapers and followed current affairs on the radio and TV.

I can still remember that moment of dawning consciousness and conscience, of discovering that the way the world was presented via mainstream media was only one view. West Germany at that time was in a period of turmoil. In the wake of demonstrations that took place during the late 1960s, in which the contentious issue of America's role in Vietnam played a part, students sought to find out more about the role of their parents' generation in the Nazi era. Calling into question the actions and policies of government led to a new climate of debate. Emancipation, colonialism, environmentalism and grass-roots democracy were discussed at all levels of society. Don't forget that until 1977 a married woman had to have her husband's permission if she wanted to take a job or open a bank account in Germany.

Like most young people, I wanted to change the world. I still do. Now I run a national museum and have the opportunity to revisit the utopian vision and revolutions that took place in the latter half of the 1960s through an exhibition imbued with the innovation and spirit of the time.

You Say You Want a Revolution? Records and Rebels 1966–1970 investigates the seismic political, social and cultural changes that took place during this period and resulted in a fundamental shift in the mindset of the Western world. The exhibition explores these revolutions by focusing on particular spaces and environments that defined the cultural and social vanguard of the time, including Carnaby Street in London, clubs where the counter-culture thrived, the Paris protests of May 1968, World's Fairs including Montreal and Osaka, the Woodstock festival of 1969 and alternative communities on the West Coast of America.

Fifty years have now passed since 1966. While it is apposite to reflect on the period, it is just as important to consider how the revolutions of those five years have affected the way we live now. From the international relations we enjoy to the jobs we do, to the way our politicians behave – so many things we take for granted today came out of the changes of the late 1960s. But which developments from that time have perhaps not gone far enough? And what can we learn from those heady days when anything seemed possible?

These are just some of the questions we hope this exhibition will encourage visitors to consider and debate. To stage such spectacular and groundbreaking exhibitions, the V&A depends on the support of its sponsors, and I would like to thank Levi's, a brand that has always been associated with new ideas, rebellion and individuality, and Sennheiser, whom we are delighted to be working with on a major exhibition for the second time. Their generous support has made this exhibition possible. I would also like to offer sincere thanks to the Annenberg Foundation, Fenwick and Sassoon, and to acknowledge the support of the American Friends of the V&A. Finally, I would like to extend heartfelt thanks to our many lenders, without whom this exhibition would not be possible.

Martin Roth
Director, Victoria and Albert Museum

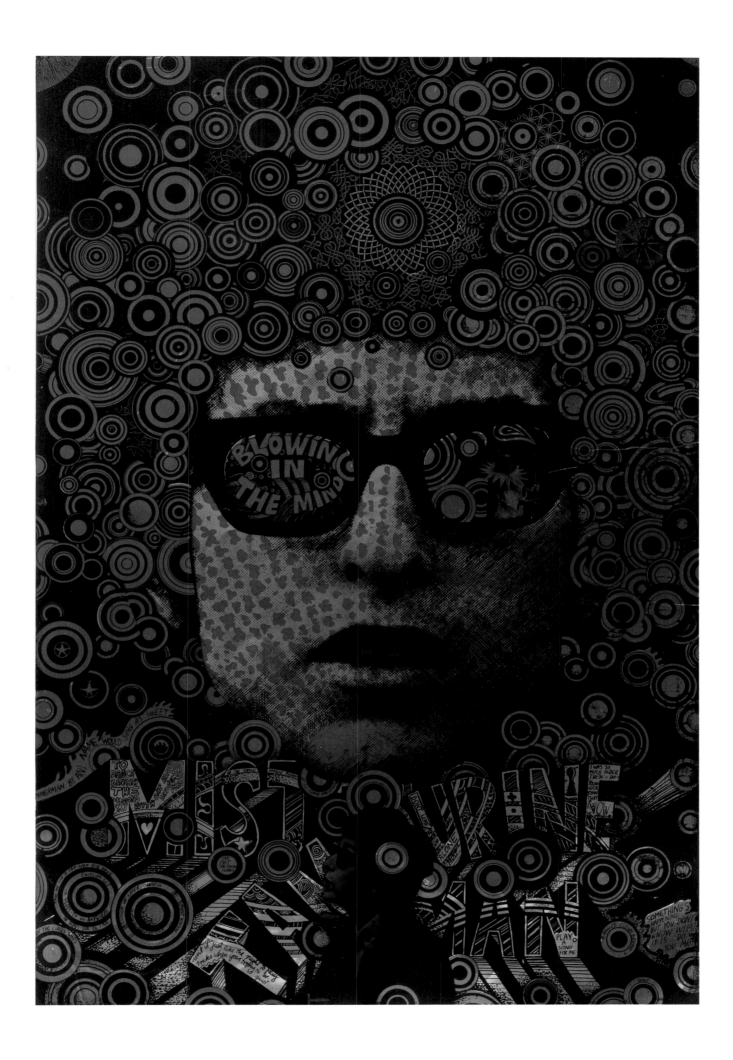

LEVI'S

The Levi's 501 has been the uniform of progress since 1873. From gold miners to cowboys, from rebels to rockers, Levi's have always found relevance in the centre of culture. A culture shaped over time by purpose, style, and the quest for authentic self-expression. In the 1960s, this quest positively clashed with the music scene to start a movement that would set the cultural stage for years to come.

It's because of this that we are extremely excited to support the V&A as the exhibition reminds us why this era was so significant. For Levi's, this was the moment when our jeans emerged from workwear into the outfit of choice for youth culture. With the addition of the Levi's 505 in 1967 a new style icon was born and rockers around the world made it their own. Then, as the scene shifted, Levi's continued to evolve to remain the uniform of progress. Years later, this relevance continues, but taking a trip down memory lane is always an inspiring way to celebrate the past and continue to create the future.

James 'JC' Curleigh
President of The Levi's® Brand

SENNHEISER

I would have loved to experience these pivotal times of transformation personally, but it was before my time. Even so, I strongly feel the powerful influence of this era on the way we live today.

At Sennheiser, we naturally have a strong affinity for all things music. It is therefore our joy and privilege to be the sound partner of the Victoria and Albert Museum for this fantastic exhibition.

You Say You Want a Revolution? Records and Rebels 1966–1970 artfully recreates the spirit and mentality of the late 1960s, exploring its rich musical heritage and impact on today's world. These times were equally eventful for Sennheiser, with many new ideas emerging that indelibly changed audio technology, such as the invention of the world's first open headphones, the Sennheiser HD 414, in 1968, which laid the foundation for music on the move.

A wealth of exhibits, lovingly compiled music, an unforgettable immersive soundscape – revisit and relive this unique experience with this book. And if you could not attend the exhibition in person, you can discover it in these beautifully photographed items and evocative, knowledgeable essays. Enjoy.

Daniel Sennheiser
CEO, Sennheiser

CURATORS' PREFACE

The years from 1966 to 1970, just 1,826 days, shook the foundations of post-WWII society and undeniably shaped the way we live today. They set the agenda that is at the heart of the current fierce struggle between Western liberal values and fundamentalism of all sorts: the rights of the individual and their relationship to the 'State'.

In the United Kingdom in 1965 society was in many ways unrecognizable. Homosexuality was illegal; police entrapment was common; abortion was illegal; you could be hanged for murder; a woman had to be married to get the pill; divorce was uncommon and rarely granted; racial discrimination was commonplace; women could be paid less than men for the same work; theatre performances were subject to official censorship. In sharp contrast, LSD was still legal. Similar value systems existed across most of the West, yet by 1970 much of this had changed in most Western countries. Revolutions of different kinds had taken place – in look, lifestyle, politics and beliefs – but which achieved real, permanent change, and which faded in subsequent decades?

In the exhibition and book *You Say You Want a Revolution? Records and Rebels 1966–1970*, we explore key subject areas and locations where these revolutions took place: fashion; drugs, clubs and counter-culture; human rights and street protests; consumerism; festivals; and alternative communities. From London's Carnaby Street to the hippies of Haight-Ashbury, tech innovators in the Bay Area Labs to protesters on the streets of Paris, and alternative communities across America to festival-goers at Woodstock and the Isle of Wight, these years saw an optimistic idealism that motivated people to come together and question established power structures across every area of society.

The people central to these changes were the generation born during and in the aftermath of World War II. In 1947 alone more than a million babies were born in the UK – a peak year in the post-war demographic cycle – becoming teenagers in 1960. The same was happening elsewhere: 50 per cent of the US population was under 25 in 1966, and 1 in 3 people in France were under 20 in 1967. This new generation wanted to escape the confines of the past and their parents' generation. Growing affluence and the erosion of traditional class-based societies led to an increasing emphasis on 'me'. There was a desire to be 'cosmonauts of Inner Space', to discover new ways of seeing the world – whether through recreational sex, drugs, eastern religions or esoteric thinking.

In a world without mobile phones or personal computing, music – alongside the burgeoning underground press – provided the connectivity for the late 1960s, linking similarly minded people thousands of miles apart with ideas, words, humour, images and, above all, a sense of community and common aspirations. From London to San Francisco and New York to Berlin, Bob Dylan, the Beatles, the Stones, Jefferson Airplane, Jimi Hendrix, Frank Zappa and the Grateful Dead (to name just a few) were the soundtrack, giving voice to millions who were inspired to change the world.

From action on civil rights, multiculturalism, nuclear weapons, colonialism, environmentalism, consumerism, computing and communality, there was not a single focus, but many, crossing causes and continents. That these revolutions were so extensive and groundbreaking is part of the era's ongoing appeal and cross-generational relevance. It also makes for a subject so sprawling yet surprisingly interconnected that no exhibition or book could cover it in all-encompassing fashion. We have attempted to move outside the linear story and highlight the often unexpected connections that underpinned these revolutions, but there are inevitably gaps, lacunae and omissions, even with such a broad approach.

The 1960s were not, of course, the first time that different ways of living were imagined or implemented, and the exhibition takes as its starting point four documents from the past five centuries that attempt to set out another vision. The year 2016 also marks the 500th anniversary of the publication of Thomas More's *Utopia*, in which inhabitants of a fictional island reject intolerance, personal gain and property, and instead find peace and contentment as part of a community. Three hundred years later, William Blake was still raging against the deadening effect on the imagination of 'mind-forg'd manacles' in 'London' and in *The Marriage of Heaven and Hell* commented, 'If the doors of perception were cleansed every thing would appear to man as it is, Infinite. For man has closed himself up, till he sees all things thro' narrow chinks of his cavern.' Similar sentiments were being expressed in the 1960s when the popularization of LSD in the counter-culture offered the hope of throwing the doors wide open.

At the start of the 1960s, a number of dissident currents from the 1950s merged into a torrent to challenge the status quo. 'The Port Huron Statement', published in 1962, has been described as 'the visionary call of the 1960s revolution'. This manifesto of the activist movement Students for a Democratic Society criticized the United States' foreign and domestic policies, and addressed the cold war, the nuclear arms race, partisan politics, social inequality and racial discrimination. It called for 'the establishment of a democracy of individual participation governed by two central aims: that the individual share in those social decisions determining the quality and direction of his life; that society be organized to encourage independence in men and provide the media for their common participation'. Finally, Alexander Trocchi's Sigma statements from 1964 prefigured the networked world

of today by demanding that millions link together to create a universal university of knowledge. This desire for transcendence, a utopia of the mind, was advocated by Timothy Leary in *The Psychedelic Experience*:

> [It] is a journey to new realms of consciousness. The scope and content of the experience is limitless, but its characteristic features are the transcendence of verbal concepts, of spacetime dimensions, and of the ego or identity ... Most recently they have become available to anyone through the ingestion of psychedelic drugs such as LSD ... Of course, the drug does not produce the transcendent experience. It merely acts as a chemical key — it opens the mind, frees the nervous system of its ordinary patterns and structures.

By 1966–67, the counter-culture had engaged significant numbers and the debate moved from 'if...' to 'how?' All action, however, was set against the increasingly bitter arguments about America's involvement in Vietnam. The sight of the world's most powerful democratic nation relentlessly bombing an underdeveloped country to support a widely disliked dictatorship united radicals of all types around the world.

THE
PORT HURON STATEMENT

. . . we seek the establishment of a democracy of individual participation governed by two central aims: that the individual share in those social decisions determining the quality and direction of his life; that society be organized to encourage independence in men and provide the media for their common participation . . .

Students for a Democratic Society

35¢

Looking back from today's viewpoint, long after this 'revolution' of utopianism fell into decline, a huge amount is still with us. Lines can be traced from the civil rights movement to multiculturalism, from the permissive society to feminism and gay liberation, from the hippy movement to environmentalism and communality. On the other hand, is personal computing, which evolved in the 1960s, the best or the worst influence on our lives? Here the same system that allows us to connect across the globe, regardless of physical location, is also responsible for surveillance culture and the dark web. Likewise, the environmental problems that began to be defined in the 1960s are still with us, though the emphases have changed, and the planet is in an ever more precarious state.

Despite political reaction in the 1980s, the Right has not undone the major changes that passed into legislation during this period, while the Left has failed to conjure anything as visionary or universal. Indeed, with the rise of fundamentalism democracies face external threats that now question their very right to existence, which may make such differences seem secondary. Despite the many forms of revolution that took place between 1966 and 1970, and their successes, failures and unintended consequences, the resulting change that stays with us, and underpins the way we all live today (at least in the West), is above all a change in outlook – a 'revolution in the head'.

Victoria Broackes and Geoffrey Marsh

MOVING TIMES THE MOVING TIMES

Comment

•

project sigma

William Burroughs
Robert Creeley
Alexander Trocchi
Uncle Tom Cobbley
. . . etc.

the moving times

general editor: A. Trocchi
associate editor: J. Nuttall

title by courtesy of W. Burroughs

price 2/- U.K.
25 Cents U.S.A.

'Art can have no existential significance for a civilization which draws a line between life and art and collects artifacts like ancestral bones for reverence. Art must inform the living; we envisage a situation imaginatively and passionately constructed to inspire each individual to respond creatively, to bring to whatever act a creative comportment.'

•

'. . . the cultural revolt must seize the grids of expression and the power-house of the mind. Intelligence must become self-conscious, realise its own power, and, on a global scale, transcending functions that are no longer appropriate, dare to exercise it. History will not overthrow national governments; it will outflank them. The cultural revolt is the necessary underpinning, the passionate sub-structure of a new order of things.'

•

'However imperfect, fragmentary, and inarticulate this new force may presently appear, it is now in the process of becoming conscious of itself in the sense that its individual imponents are beginning to recognize their involvement and consciously to concern themselves with the technical problems of mutual recognition and, ultimately, of concerted action. . . .'

The above quotations are taken from the sigma pamphlets: *The Invisible Insurrection* and *Sigma: a tactical blueprint*.* The concept of a poster-magazine was actually outlined in the latter. Well, here it is: the first number of THE MOVING TIMES. We take this opportunity of inviting you to move with them.

FROM NOW ON, you are invited to take part in a continuous international concordium concerning the future of things.

Actually dispersed as we are and will be until several self-conscious focal points are established (in each of which an experimental situation is in the process of being articulated) effective communications are vital. And so, THE MOVING TIMES. To borrow the Marlovian definition of hell (is it?), now and in the future our centre will be everywhere, our circumference, nowhere. No one is excluded. A man will know when he is participating without our offering him a badge.

THE MOVING TIMES is just one of many of project sigma's undertakings, both here in England and abroad. Look out for others.

martin's folly by William Burroughs

Now, look, boys, I'm going to say it simple-country simple. Martin is 'time.' Martin is 'reality.' Martin is blind. Mars Martin is a blind cave organism — old and evil presence from an old and evil cave. He orients himself by radar that is word lines. Shift cut tangle Martin's word lines and he can't find you. He can't find himself. Martin, you always tell your reporters to get the *address*. When you want to block someone out of present time you shift the address from Git-le-Coeur to l'Ile de la Cité or was it St Louis? the time say from August to October, or maybe you put something there that isn't there like the tables in front of 9 rue Git-le-Coeur or the universities in Morocco. Well, boys, shift cut tangle Martin's address. The Retroactive Kid is on stage, Martin, also known as Amnesia Allen. He is forgetting you right off stage, Martin. Such a lot of words and pictures, a whole warehouse full of garbage, no wonder you can't exactly remember and they all run together now. Your home office in Minnesota, wasn't it? — The Old Flatiron Building on Market Street only it wasn't Market Street then, it was just Mark Street named after the survey line run right through there and it turned out a heap of folks didn't own what they thought they owned after the Big Survey. . . . On this historic date, Monday, 25th May, 1963, twenty-fifth anniversary of *Word Picture Daily*, or was it weekly? or monthly? surely Mr Martin, you remember your *offices* — your *address*? Get research on the intercom. They can refresh your fading memory with a brief history of the World Picture story: Took over a defunct humour magazine known as *Ballyhoo* in 1929 and built it into a vast empire of word and image not in all respects candid or complete to be sure with branch offices in major cities of the world. Let me list a few of your branch offices, Mr Martin; always, of course, designed with a keen eye for local architectural styles, an unobtrusive but imposing appropriateness: In the flourishing Peruvian city of Shell Mara, oil capital of South America, and the bustling port city of Esmeraldas — on the outskirts of Mogador rising from the sheer cliffs of Imshallah — overlooking the exclusive Barrio Chino in Barcelona where the old movies come to die and 192 gangsters send tracer bullets flashing out across the Bay of Biscay from broken film — on the palm-fringed archepelago that stretches from Macao to the lovely tropical island of Formosa ruled by a hereditary sultanate — and the Paris office on the historic Ile de la Cité or was it St Louis? — the Seine glittering far away in the distance through the fashionable suburbs of Meudon — And remember the sidewalk cafés along Git-le-Coeur where you used to lunch with your staff? — and in London a discreet four-storey building located at 6 Cambridge Square — a stone's throw from the Crystal Palace — adjoining the editorial offices of *The Daily Observer*. Now the word and image horde, constantly shifted from one office to the other to accommodate the necessities of time, was guarded by a fleet of armoured trucks against possible hi-jackers — The truck routes were plotted by secret formulae and all the secret formulae had to be guarded of course like the formulae of Shitola so the staff went about handcuffed to briefcases and to each other — whole clusters of them often entrapped the unwilling passer-by into the service of time like a netted fish. This grew until the entire staff was handcuffed together and you conveyed your instructions by pulling the chains. However, this system tended to immobilise your staff and you saw fit to establish under each of them a chemical toilet. Time passed, and cesspools of the world groaned with word and image waste. Disposal was always your big problem, was it not? So you called in the technical department and they arranged a system of direct vein feeding for your staff from a central tank of nutrient fluid on the roof — the waste products being all unmentionable and your executives now housed over the trough. Breakdowns were frequent and despite the most modern artificial kidney provided for each cell block the silent portentious smell seeped out and blanketed the planet with a suffocating smog. There was no place for it to go. But you were busy perfecting the system and installed transmitters in all your executive brains controlled by one super efficient composite brain housed in a lead cylinder. The location of central intelligence was special top secret and the cylinder was guarded in your fleet of trucks now cruising round the clock like Strategic Air Command. But the disposal problem is not to be ignored. Scientists shook their heads and stated they could not answer for the consequences if the Earth's crust, already buckling ominously, were to give way under the accumulated weight of time, and this ocean of unmentionable matter were to flood the planet's molten core — And there were sullen mutters of revolt from the peasantry sloshing to work in rubber suits through shallow canals of the unmentionable not infrequently run down by the cruising lorries which were now amphibious. So Martin turned his blind visionary gaze on space. He took all the words and images and all his executives and technicians and processed them down to time meal under a cyclatron, a compact substance of crystalline hue. This was the answer. He would transport this time meal to another planet where it would hatch out the whole beautiful cycle of word and image. Of course, in the fullness of time he would have to move again, but there was always plenty of time in the bank. However, the board of health had got wind of his malodorous plan to move around through the cosmos, planets blowing up behind him like rusty boilers, trailing a nebulla of scalding unmentionable in his wake. And they moved with inflexible authority to forestall 'Martin's Folly' before he could, by any means at his disposal, carry out his unsanitary purpose. Martin, meanwhile, had procured a pack train of kangaroos and loaded the precious time meal into their pouches. His preparations were completed. It was time for the countdown. And then a goof on the launching platform panicked his kangaroos and they bounded away in all directions, scattering the time meal which hatched out every which way, clusters of sabre-toothed tigers, atomic physicists, reporters and centurions, savage tribes and Western gun fighters. Decent American youths were dragged from their TV sets and sacrificed by Aztec priests to the waltzes of Old Vienna while Ghengis Khan looted New York. General Lee clashed with Spartacus and Bolivar liberated everything in sight. Cross your cancelled skies, Martin, nothing nothing nothing at all. They all went away. You can look any place. No good. No bueño. Adios Meester Martin.

NO TIME.

TOP FIFTY **BOOKS & RECORDS**

24 Thornhill Road N1, NORth 1041
26 Powis Terrace W11, BAYswater 9661

We stock SIGMA publications

LEONARDO CARTOON

'Perhaps the most striking example of the wrongheaded attitude towards art in official places is provided by the recent scuffle to keep the well-known Leonardo cartoon from leaving the United Kingdom. The official attitude has more in common with stamp-collecting than with aesthetics. The famous cartoon could have been sold abroad for around £1,000,000. For a small fraction of that sum, *perfect replicas* of it could have been made and distributed to every art gallery in the country. It is small wonder that the man in the street has such a confused attitude towards art. This confusion of value with money has infected everything. The conventional categories distinguishing the arts from each other, tending as they do to perpetuate the profitable institutions which have grown up around them, can for the moment only get in the way of creativity and our understanding of it.' *(Sigma: a tactical blueprint)*

THE THEATER

From *The Theater and its Double*
(Evergreen Edition)

— To break through language in order to touch life is to create or recreate the theater. . . . This leads to the rejection of the usual limitations of man and man's powers, and infinitely extends the frontiers of what is called reality. We must believe in a sense of life in which man fearlessly makes himself master of what does not yet exist, and brings it into being. . . . Furthermore, when we speak the word 'life', it must be understood we are not referring to life as we know it from its surface of fact, but to that fragile, fluctuating center which forms never reach. And if there is still one hellish, truly accursed thing in our time, it is our artistic dallying with forms, instead of being like victims burnt at the stake, signalling through the flames.

the real climate

by Kenneth White

I am attached by a chord to the world, the material scope of my language; the world fights in me, dances, cries and laughs. In my person the world finds itself, and the generations. From the depression into the winter I have travelled, and in midwinter now I write, where all things are, trying to take the big view, at the centre of reality, the source, not hanging on the tip of a detail, not retailing.

There are two main localities in my mind: a white birch wood, and an iron-ribbed concourse. I have lived in a parish and a city, in another city and in a field within a city, in suburbs and country solitude. I know the ways of my mind and the world, my only wisdom. The core of my thought is man, and the core of the world is my need. I have seen the world as a home of hunger, and I have felt my mind as need undefined. I need the world to define my need and to satisfy it, and the world needs me to be fulfilled. Birch wood and iron-ribbed concourse are stations on the one same line. I refuse nothing, and I transform everything, from the core.

So many attempts to crystallise the flowing of my mind, to find the formula, the natural form, the living shape. My poems are the body of my mind. They form in me, and I give them birth. Poetry is nothing I say, if it is not a coming to life.

There are days when new patterns suddenly become evident, there are days full of realisation; there are days when rage twists in my belly and breaks out in spiritless violence, days when my mind stares dully and the world is transparent into nothingness. I claim no perfection, and fabricate none. I live my life, I try to give it room to breathe and move in, I know of too many men who died stifled. I am never concerned with essence, but with milieu. The essence can take care of itself, it needs no tampering from me. I shall live it when the milieu is right.

I live in a sounding world, full of wild rhythm. It is not music. It is a joyful noise. I have always associated it with popularity as against gentility. I am no gentleman poet. Mine is the poetry of joyance and pain, sudden and naked language, however long the process in the dark and the confusion and skill of the throes, the reality is sudden and naked. My poetry is like the prose of a seagull. It is direct speech, rather than indirect diction. Every vaguest idea conceived has an unsuspected materiality and words itself into evidence.

Suddenly to realise a living thing is marvellous, even with all its imperfections. It takes a high and wide view to see this, one not obnubilated by ideas of moral perfection, or intellectual perfection. It means seeing the living thing — the human being, to take the most complete example — against the background of, and implicated in, all other things. If you isolate the human being — say, in the face of God, or an abstract idea — he is miserable, but if you see him in reality, in movement, in communication, the outlook changes, you are aware of inner forces. You no longer have merely an outlook — you have an in-living.

Poetry is a shape of mind, it is nothing so abstract or sterile as a state. There is such a thing as state-poetry and poetry in state, and there are stately poets and statesmen poets — but they are not what I call poets. I call a poet a man with an active shape of mind; poetry is for me something natural and, being natural, necessary. When more people have come full circle, this natural necessity will come to be recognised. What seems an artifact at one stage of its process, a stage which some have isolated into absurdity, making artifact artificial and reserving the words artistic or scientific for their elucubrations, is in perpetual growth and development; the artifice is only apparent. We have tended to see things as states instead of process, and some isolate one state, some another, and we have a world of separate states, each one busily worked at and elaborated by its upholders, and all tending towards absurdity and sterility. Whereas if we see things as shape rather than state, as process rather than essence, our notion of reality changes, and our living. This change is becoming more and more evidently necessary.

Between accomplishments and endlessness, between product and process, the romantic stands with the question: what am I? and with the answer: I am nothing, what I seek is everything — I am what I seek. With romanticism, the idea of *investigation* enters literature — investigation of the past, of nature, investigation of the self, of the future. Art is no longer a talent to be exploited, it is a faculty of questioning; it is no longer stationary, but in movement. The romantic poet is not only an emotive poet, he is a poet in movement. The emotion should not be considered as an end in itself, but as the concentration of a movement, like a knot in wood, or like the light-point in a painting. The poem as product and process, simultaneously and indivisibly, that is the romantic idea of creation. Nothing is, but it is becoming. The key word is nature — not to be understood as mere external reality, an object to be looked upon, but as movement, dynamic. And the paradox at the source of romanticism is something that might be called: natural thought — a state and working of the mind free of intellectual schematics and closed terms, a state of vacancy even, of openness, a space in which new combinations of sense will occur apparently of their own accord — a vacuum which nature will fill in its own way, a space which itself will react on nature. The brain is not a storehouse, but a retort, a furnace, here things meet *in activity*.

The oriental idea of Spiritual Emptiness is united with western Concretion. That is essential romanticism.

Our age is concerned almost exclusively with production. I suggest it is essential to insist on what, liable to further definition, could be called: procession. I mean the flow of natural things, the interconnected forces. What we have today is the production (in series of isolated objects, though all alike) of goods which are then put into use, discarded, and simply make room for others; there is no continuity, only repetition. I say: procession, and I mean an interest in the how as well as the what, believing that the history of a thing is as important as its use, its function. I mean that history and function should not be separate, I mean that there should be awareness of continuity, evolution, that the history should be living and the functioning meaningful, not merely momentary and utilitarian. We tend to see only end-products, and we are blinded by the new (and, as a corollary, befogged by the old). Old and new are separate, both seen as end-products, neither in a process of being, they are results of fabrication, the new glorified for its newness, the old for its oldness, two sides of the same bad coin. History is for museums and art-collections, and newness for today's newspaper. Both are dead; the one with life choked within it (and the more choked, the more 'artistic'), the other stillborn. It is a world of art-dealers and connoisseurs, and producers and consumers. It is not a living world, there is little felt living. Heard a woman complaining yesterday that the olive oil she had bought had a smell; the new stuff is odourless, tasteless, lifeless, the perfect product for a senseless, gumptionless, lifeless people. It is the same with the bread — corpse bread (that pale, wheatless substance) is fit only for corpses. Why does perfection have to mean deadness? I want bread with some wheat-force in it (and with that force, sun, climate and a bread-making I know) — and so also I want men with some life-force in them, living men, not improved human products, or processed persons. I heard an American scientist announce the other day that, in his opinion, the perfect man would be a mixture of Einstein and Albert Schweitzer, and he was confident that one day soon he and his colleagues would produce (after due manipulation of nuclear acids) just such perfect men, as many as you like. Isn't that just dandy? Well, include me out.

(to be continued) reprinted from *Cleft* (Edinburgh)

the barbecue

by Alexander Trocchi

New York, 1960. The image of a grey man lying motionless on a white stretcher. Not a flicker of muscle on his face. It is rigid. The eyes are closed, the nose like a dumb finger, pointing; jaws clenched. He neither speaks nor reacts to the spoken word. He doesn't react to pin-pricks and other irritations. If food is put in his mouth, it stays, and decays, there.

The barbecue was executed at 4.45 pm, late on an August afternoon in a secret chamber somewhere in the bowels of the Institute. It was supervised by Dr Hare Q. Kildare, prominent medical telecaster, who headed the disciplinary board at the Institute, and who, at a recent general meeting of the AMA, was highly commended for a speech entitled: *The Health of the Citizen under Free Enterprise*, in which he stressed the importance in a democratic society of a man's paying his own medical bills, issued a warning against foreign bodies of all kinds, at the same time calling for a strict international ban on narcotics as a must for civilizationasweknowit. In their various official and unofficial capacities, the following ladies and gentlemen were present: the Reverend Filing Delinquent of Llareggub, Prof Horst Wesel, Doktor Mengele of Auschwitz Sanatorium, Lord Jeremy Stoppit, Mrs Remember Gomorrha, and the elegant Countess Dracula, sophisticated wife of the Enemanian Ambassador, which lady is herself a noted student of Science, and who studied under our own Commissioner Manslayer.

The jolt or brainbouncer was what is considered average in this kind of case, Rev Filing Delinquent said afterwards, slightly more than is ordinarily employed in current European practice, considerably less than that recommended in Ambassador Dracula's country. 'Enough,' concluded our distinguished cleric, 'to dissolve neural tissue without causing body odour.' Mrs Remember Gomorrha spoke afterwards, calling for the stimulation of public interest in the various modes of electrocution. 'This poor fellow,' she said, referring to the electrocuted catatonic, 'is now no longer a menace to himself or to others.' She concluded by insisting upon the urgent need for the immediate segregation of that portion of the population which was infected. In this she was eagerly seconded by Doktor Mengele who offered to place his sanatorium at the disposal of the committee. His engineers, he averred, were already studying the feasibility of chain-treatment.

At the third jolt the patient's body was seen to shudder like a tall jelly within the leather harness, and a wisp of blue smoke issued from his nostrils, a reaction generally regarded as a symptom of what, in technical nomenclature, is called 'reintegration'. The patient reintegrated slowly, the shuddering subsiding gradually over a period of two and a half hours, after which he was returned to the deepfreeze as a precaution against pong.

It was the practice, Dr Kildare pointed out to those present, to wait three days before attempting to estimate the results of the operation, since further changes not unlike those of terrestrial subsidence (earthquakes, volcanic eruptions, etc) were often met with during a period of up to forty-eight hours after the barbecue. The patient's eyeballs, which had been driven out of their sockets by the electric shock, had a vaguely cooked look which, explained the eminent telecaster, could have sinister implications, and this naturally made him reluctant to predict success or failure at the present time.

Later, when Dr Hare (Bunny to his friends) Q. Kildare returned to his study with the other members of the committee, the long grey gink on the stretcher was left alone within the thin clear bubble of his isolation. Up, down, north, south, east, west, from all angles his own grey reflection bounced back at him. Meanwhile, Kildare, extemporizing for his captive audience, was saying: 'Trouble was, though I'm reluctant to say it, the man failed to distinguish between two kinds of perspiration — the physical kind, and the mental kind. Science shows that in the glands of the mature male and in the glands of the mature female, perspiration caused by anxiety emits an offensive odour. For two thousand years man has sought to avert this embarrassment. Poor Cleopatra had to spend twelve hours a day in milk baths and having oils and expensive elixirs rubbed into her skin, particularly during political crises, and all to avoid what nowadays we very bluntly call BO. With our modern techniques, in this instance electric shock therapy, we have found ways to abolish all thought and thus, Ladies and Gentlemen, all anxiety and the resultant offensive odours.'

Applause, handclapping.

Read realnews in **MY OWN MAG** sez Kafka at sceance.
Homosap Inc. 37 Salisbury Road, Barnet, Herts. England.
why is Perfume Ja ck in the Casbah?
3d plus postage anywhere/early numbers antiques already

* Sigma pamphlets are obtainable at 1/– each (incl. postage) from 6 St Stephen's Gardens, W2, and in some bookstores.

VILLIERS LTD—LONDON

Your support is sought not only for this broadsheet but for the future evolution of the sigma experiment. Subscribe to the sigma portfolio and receive our various publications and informations throughout the year. £1 1s 0d to Trocchi, 6 St Stephen's Gardens, W2.

ECT SIGMA PROJECT SIGMA PROJECT SIGMA PROJECT

YOU SAY YOU GOT A REAL SOLUTION?

1

A TALE OF TWO CITIES

LONDON, SAN FRANCISCO AN THE TRANSATLANTIC BRIDGE

GEOFFREY MARSH

'It was the best of times, it was the worst of times, it was the age of wisdom, it was the age of foolishness, it was the epoch of belief, it was the epoch of incredulity, it was the season of Light, it was the season of Darkness, it was the spring of hope, it was the winter of despair, we had everything before us, we had nothing before us, we were all going direct to Heaven, we were all going direct the other way ... '

Charles Dickens, *A Tale of Two Cities*, 1859[1]

London and San Francisco. In 2016, two great thriving creative powerhouses. In 1966, 1967, 1968, 1969, 1970, two great port cities at the centre of upheavals in music, culture, politics, communication and living. Connecting them together a 'Transatlantic Bridge', looping through New York, allowing a cultural exchange of ideas, sensibilities, sounds and images. This essay centres on a hundred fictional diary entries written by two imagined journalists, fifty for each city, twenty from each year, to highlight the similarities and differences between the shifting psychogeography of both bridgeheads. London in the 1970s and '80s then experienced years of decline. In Silicon Valley, sprawling south from San Francisco, April 1976 and September 1998 saw the founding, 12 miles apart, of Apple and Google respectively – as of this writing the two most valuable public companies in the world. Yet London was to bounce back, a reminder that revolutions come in many forms.

Films such as *Blow-Up* (1966) portray a beguiling 'Swinging London' – fashion, beautiful models, trendy photographers, parties, pop, easy sex, dissatisfaction, uncertainty – that has tended to overshadow other contemporary representations. *Smashing Time* (1967) scripted by George Melly,[2] although largely forgotten today, offers an alternative view of the London scene. Its background is a traditional, largely working-class city of smoke-blackened buildings, greasy-spoon cafés and condemned slum terraces that seems little changed since the 1930s.[3] Yet, on close inspection, Melly's sly quips – 'Direct Action – the perfume with a provocative odour' – are set against a metropolis being transformed by 'the white heat of technology' promoted by the recently re-elected progressive Labour Government: the

new Post Office Tower, the construction of the 'modernist' Euston Station fit for 'electric' railways, contrasted with Victorian St Pancras Station[4] and grimy 'Camden' Street.[5]

The reality behind the headlines in London and San Francisco was poisonous. In both cities racial discrimination was legal at the beginning of the 1960s, as was discrimination against women in terms of expectations, educational opportunities, pay and working conditions; homosexuality was illegal in both Britain and the United States. While marijuana was illegal in both countries, LSD was lawful until late 1966. London experienced theatre censorship, while in San Francisco cross-dressing was banned.

The 'Transatlantic Bridge' was facilitated by the growing ease of air travel. In 1960, the British Overseas Airways Corporation (BOAC), the long-haul predecessor of British Airways, was flying Bristol Britannia turboprops from London Airport via New York to San Francisco International Airport on the way to Tokyo and Hong Kong. The change to Boeing 707s ushered in the intercontinental jet age, though only the rich or business travellers could afford the route – most people would only ever visit San Francisco through films, magazines and books. However, the counter-culture made new connections on the 'Transatlantic Bridge'. Records had always been sold internationally, but the rise of the LP meant that fans in the UK and US could increasingly buy their favourite group's newest release within a couple of weeks of its arrival in the 'home' territory.

On 1 June 1967, *Sgt. Pepper* became the first Beatles album to be issued simultaneously worldwide and the Monterey International Pop Festival was built to its sounds. This was paralleled by the shipping of underground magazines which, if they could avoid the attention of customs, would find their way into a network of radical bookshops and headshops in both the US and Europe.

And so, as 1965 turns to 1966 …

1966

Lyrics: from 'For What It's Worth' by Buffalo Springfield, 1966

Image: detail of pl.7

Sunday 30 January

Staff Sgt Barry Sadler debuts his patriotic song 'The Ballad of the Green Berets' on America's prime-time *Ed Sullivan Show*. It will reach number one on 6 March and stay there for five weeks, eventually selling over nine million records. Following the landing of America's first combat troops in Vietnam at Da Nang, on 8 March 1965, US military personnel in the country increase to 385,000 by the end of 1966; that year 6,143 are killed.[6]

Monday 16 May

The 72-year-old Chairman Mao issues a 'notification' that justifies the Cultural Revolution, with the aim of rooting out class enemies within the Communist Party of China. Young Chinese form Red Guard groups acting as paramilitary units to carry out the destruction of the 'Four Olds': old customs, culture, habits and ideas. The *Little Red Book* becomes the visible symbol of Mao Zedong's 'thought', both in China and, from 1966, through translations around the world.[7]

Friday 5 August

The Beatles issue *Revolver*, their seventh studio album, which shows the impact on the group of ideas drawn from Eastern philosophy and of mind-expanding drugs. It helps redefine the boundaries of pop and includes tape loops on 'Tomorrow Never Knows', classical strings on 'Eleanor Rigby' and Indian musical instruments on 'Love You To'. In the UK it was number one for seven weeks. LPs provide an instant communication/identification system between young people in a world before mobile phones.

here's battle lines
being drawn
Nobody's right if
everybody's wron
oung people spea
heir minds
Getting so much
resistance from be

LONDON 1966

Sunday 6 February: Central line to Shepherd's Bush, for *Dig*, an action/art 'happening' in a fire-gutted factory organized by Mark Boyle and Joan Hills, aka The Institute of Contemporary Archaeology (ICA). Excavated finds are to be exhibited at their new flat at 225 Holland Park Avenue.[8]

Thursday 31 March: General Election result. Harold Wilson's Labour Party has returned with a powerful majority of 96. Roy Jenkins to continue as Britain's youngest Home Secretary since Churchill.[9]

Friday 15 April: Walked to Oxford Circus then to Carnaby Street. Full of hipsters in the boutiques and posing on the pavements. American *TIME* magazine proclaims 'Swinging London'. Bought myself a striped Indian-cotton shirt for tomorrow's party celebrating Twiggy as the 'Face of '66'.[10]

Monday 16 May: Central line to Holland Park then walked to John Cowan's studio at 39 Princes Place. Michelangelo Antonioni shooting *Blow-Up* – Vanessa Redgrave and David Hemmings inside on set.[11] Then north to Ladbroke Grove tube. After 10 minutes found total devastation: entire streets in Notting Dale torn down for the new Westway.[12]

Wednesday 29 June: Financial journalist friend got a Barclaycard today – first credit card in the UK.[13]

Sunday 31 July: Writing after all-night celebrations. Yesterday took Metropolitan line to World Cup final at Wembley. Beautiful sunny afternoon, Union flags everywhere.

Thursday 13 October: Walked to Aldwych Theatre for press night of Peter Brook's new RSC production, *US*. Extraordinary critique of the Vietnam War.[14]

Friday 14 October: Cycled up through Camden to the Roundhouse for the launch party of the *International Times* newspaper. Poster promised Pink Floyd and Soft Machine, with a 'Pop/Op/Costume/Masque/Fantasy-Loon/Blowout/Drag Ball' and strips, trips, happenings, movies. Not disappointed.[15]

Wednesday 9 November:[16] Bus down Piccadilly to the Indica Art Gallery at 6 Mason's Yard. John Dunbar welcomed and we watched Yoko Ono (Fluxus) arranging her show *Unfinished Paintings and Objects* (opens tomorrow). Just as I was leaving John Lennon arrived.

Thursday 17 November: Press furore over last night's 'Wednesday Play' on the BBC – Ken Loach's *Cathy Come Home*, about the impact of homelessness.[17]

SAN FRANCISCO 1966

Friday to Sunday, 21–23 January: Trips Festival at the Longshoremen's Hall on North Point. Thousands of heads there for acid, multimedia projections, light shows, fantastic music including the Grateful Dead and Big Brother & the Holding Company, dancing, general chaos and each other.[18]

Monday 21 March: Supreme Court decision in *Memoirs v. Massachusetts* – trying to define obscenity in print and film.[19]

[Undated] April: Down to the bay, watched transporters crossing from Oakland, heading out to Hawaii and beyond to Vietnam. Looked over to Fort Mason where 1.5 million troops left during WW2 for the Pacific Theatre. Now derelict.[20]

Friday 27 May: To Fillmore to see Andy Warhol's Exploding Plastic Inevitable Show on tour from The Factory in New York.[21] Do I dig the Velvet Underground? Yes. Nico, possibly; Danny Williams's light show, great; Warhol's films, pass.[22]

[Undated] August: Heard about a riot at Gene Compton's Cafeteria, one of the few places transgender people can get served. Many of the street queens involved are members of Vanguard, a new gay and queer youth organization set up by ministers from Glide Memorial Church in the Tenderloin.[23]

Monday 29 August: Beatles at the Stick.[24] The Ronettes warmed up but seats were only half full when the Beatles came out. They played for 33 minutes and then left in an armoured (!) car. Got a flyer for a new TV show – *The Monkees*.

Tuesday 20 September: First edition of *The Oracle of the City of San Francisco*. Quality paper covering counter-culture ideas and spiritual interests.[25]

Tuesday 27 September: Matthew Johnson, 16-year-old black kid, shot in the back and killed by 51-year-old SFPD patrolman in the Hunters Point ghetto. Immediate protest against police tactics, National Guard called out.[26]

Thursday 6 October: To the Panhandle in Haight-Ashbury for Michael Bowen's Love Pageant Rally to mark the criminalization of LSD in California. Hundreds of freaks moving in from downtown and out of state. Acid everywhere and aggressive police. Popped in to Peggy Caserta's hip new boutique, Mnasidika.[27] Met a couple of 'Diggers' providing free food and welfare. They say everything should be free.[28]

Saturday 29 October: SNCC Chairman Stokely Carmichael spoke at the UC Berkeley 'Black Power' Conference, urging resistance to the draft. In Oakland they're setting up a Black Panther Party for Self-Defense to monitor the cops.[29]

Clockwise from top left, all 1966

5
Carnaby Street, London, photograph by Jean-Philippe Charbonnier

6
Set model for Peter Brook's play *US*, made by Sally Jacobs
V&A: S.84–2016

7
National Guard on the streets of Hunters Point, September

8
The Beatles walking to the stage before the last show of their final tour at Candlestick Park, San Francisco, 29 August, photograph by Koh Hasebe

9
Flyer for the three-day Trips Festival at the Longshoremen's Hall, designed by Wes Wilson

1966

Left to right from top:

The Seeds, *The Seeds*

Bob Dylan, *Blonde on Blonde*

Donovan, *Sunshine Superman*

The Who, *A Quick One*

The Seeds, *A Web of Sound*

Buffalo Springfield, *Buffalo Springfield*

Love, *Love*

Bert Jansch, *Jack Orion*

Pete Seeger, *God Bless the Grass*

The Butterfield Blues Band, *East–West*

Love, *Da Capo*

Mothers of Invention, *Freak Out!*

The Beach Boys, *Pet Sounds*

Gábor Sabó, *Jazz Raga*

Otis Redding, *Complete & Unbelievable, the Otis Redding Dictionary of Soul*

Small Faces, *Small Faces*

Donovan, *Mellow Yellow*

Cream, *Fresh Cream*

John Fahey, *Guitar vol. 4, The Great San Bernardino Birthday Party & Other Excursions*

Simon and Garfunkel, *Parsley, Sage, Rosemary and Thyme*

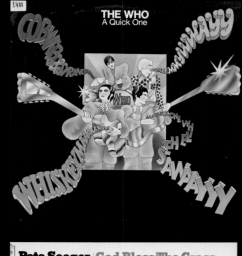

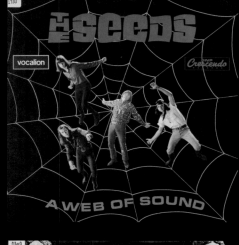

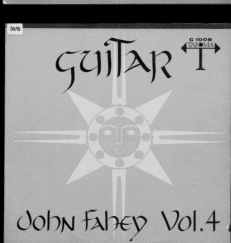

1967

Lyrics: from 'San Francisco
(Be Sure To Wear Flowers In Your Hair)'
by Scott McKenzie, 1967

Image: Buckminster Fuller's
geodesic dome for the US pavilion
at Expo '67, Montreal

Thursday 27 April

The 1967 International and Universal Exposition (Expo '67), opens in Montreal, Canada, through to 29 October. It celebrates the centenary of the Canadian Federation and the theme is 'Man and His World', taken from Antoine de Saint-Exupéry's 1939 memoir *Terre des hommes* (published in translation as *Wind, Sand and Stars*). A total of 62 countries take part in one of the most successful World's Fairs of the 20th century, with the most attendees to date – 50 million visitors.

Friday 28 April

Boxer Muhammad Ali refuses, as a conscientious objector, to be conscripted to fight in Vietnam. He had earlier declared, 'I ain't got no quarrel with them Viet Cong – no Viet Cong ever called me nigger.' Now he added: 'No, I am not going 10,000 miles to help murder, kill and burn other people to simply help continue the domination of white slavemasters over dark people.' On 20 June he is sentenced to five years in prison. He is also stripped of his world heavyweight title.[30]

Thursday 1 June

The Beatles release *Sgt. Pepper's Lonely Hearts Club Band*. The album has a huge impact around the world, spending 27 weeks at the top of the albums chart in the UK and 15 weeks at number one in the US. It goes on to win four Grammy Awards in 1968, including Album of the Year; *TIME* magazine calls it 'a historic departure in the progress of music'. David Bowie releases his first album, *David Bowie*, the same day, but it is a commercial failure.

Friday 27 November

French President de Gaulle vetoes UK entry into the Common Market.

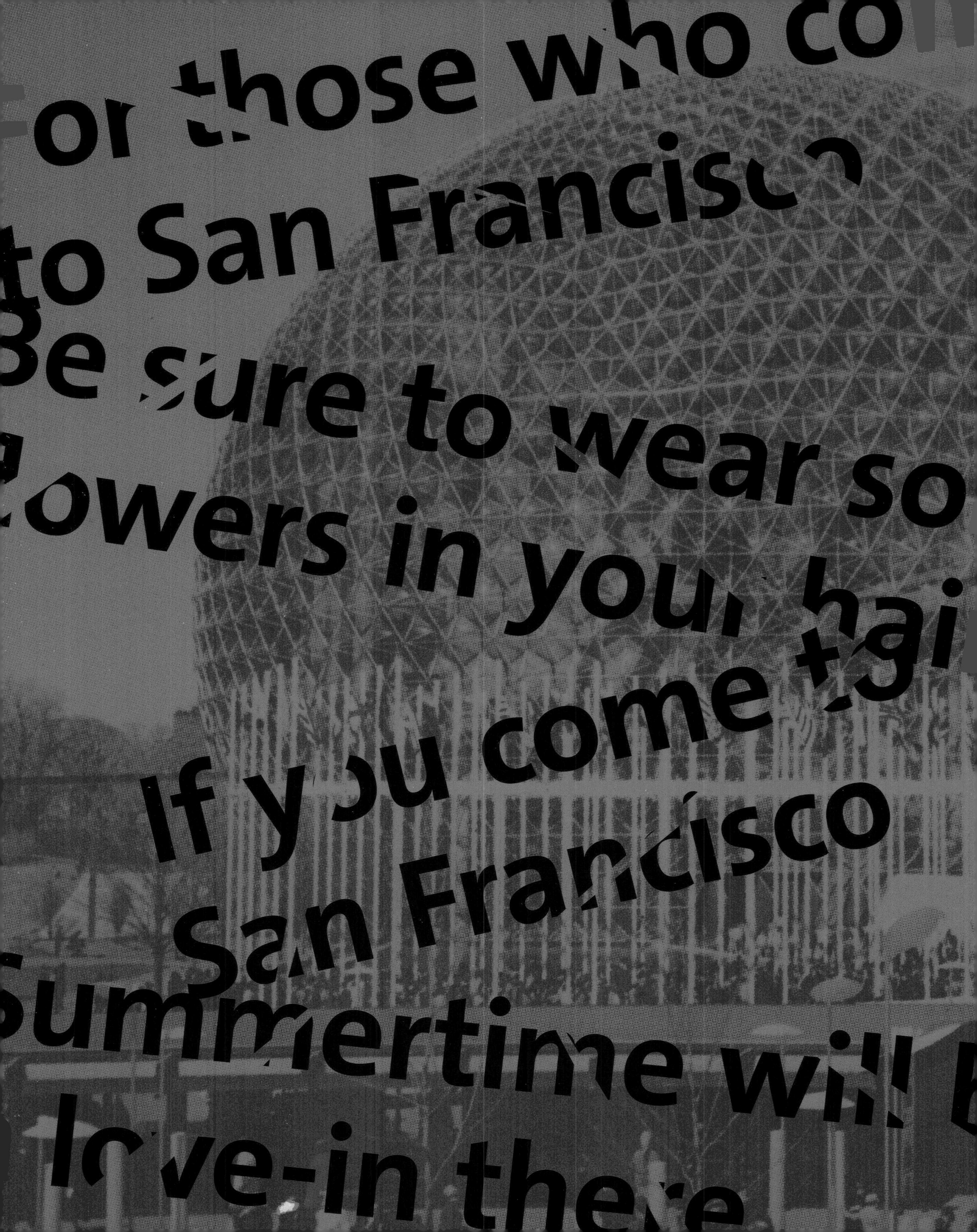

or those who come
to San Francisco
Be sure to wear so
flowers in your hai

If you come to
San Francisco
Summertime will b
love-in there

LONDON 1967

Friday 13 January: Having missed the two opening gigs at UFO, despite being five minutes from my flat, made it to this new 'psychedelic' club organized by 'Hoppy' Hopkins and Joe Boyd. Pink Floyd and The Sun Trolley played. Amazing light shows (Technicolor strobe and Fiveacre slides). Groovy vibe.

Saturday 25 February: New UK edition of *OZ* magazine at Miles's party. Cover line 'turn on, tune in, drop dead' – and a Playmate fold-out of LBJ!

Saturday 8 April: Watched the Eurovision Song Contest televised from Vienna. Sandie Shaw, barefoot, took a first win for Britain with *Puppet on A String*.

Saturday to Sunday 29–30 April: Drove to Alexandra Palace for the 14-Hour Technicolor Dream – London's own Human Be-In – a fundraiser for *International Times*. Everyone from the counter-culture was there. Two main stages for music inside the hall and a smaller space for poets, performance artists, jugglers and dancers. Massive helter-skelter in the middle, light shows and strobes; films shown on big sheets taped to the scaffolding. Last set at 5am: Pink Floyd.

[Undated] May: Wandered down to 182 Drury Lane to see Jim Haynes's new culture venture the Arts Lab. Gallery, cinema and good café. Eclectic mix of people but it works.[31]

15–30 July: Dropped in on the Congress on the Dialectics of Liberation (for the Demystification of Violence) at the Roundhouse. Met Julian Beck of the Living Theatre, Emmett Grogan of the Diggers, artist Carolee Schneemann and Stokely Carmichael from SNCC.

Thursday 27 July: Huge news – the Sexual Offences Act 1967 has finally decriminalized homosexual acts in private between two men, if they are 21. Only applies to England and Wales though and doesn't cover the military.[32]

Saturday 30 September: Up for 7am for first broadcast of new BBC Radio 1. Tony Blackburn opened with The Move's 'Flowers in the Rain' and then 'Massachusetts' by the Bee Gees. Good start. DJs include John Peel, Ed Stewart, Mike Raven, Jimmy Young, Dave Cash and Kenny Everett – the Pirates are taking over the Establishment![33]

Friday 27 October: Another major legal change coming – the Abortion Act 1967 will legalize abortions by registered practitioners from 27 April 1968.

Saturday 18 November: Government has devalued the pound from £1 = $2.80 to £1 = $2.40.[34]

SAN FRANCISCO 1967

Saturday 14 January: To the Polo Ground in Golden Gate Park for the Human Be-in – billed as a 'Gathering of the Tribes'. Haight streets packed with freaks. Timothy Leary was in the city for the first time – challenged us to 'Turn on! Tune in! Drop out!' Great Music. Apparently Owsley was handing out his special 'White Lightning' acid.

Sunday 29 January: Mantra-Rock Dance at the Avalon. Fundraising for a Hare Krishna temple in the city to match the SF Zen Center. A couple of thousand people in tribal robes, Mexican clothes, Indian *kurtas*, feathers and beads hanging out with Hell's Angels in jeans and boots.[35]

Saturday 15 April: My first demo: the Spring Mobilization Committee to End the War in Vietnam say there were 50,000 of us. In New York they say over 300,000 marched with Martin Luther King, Jr. His wife Coretta was here.[36]

Saturday and Sunday 10–11 June: At last minute decided to go to the KFRC Fantasy Fair and Magic Mountain Music Festival on Mount Tamalpais. Fantastic to see so many bands in one place. The Doors' 'Light My Fire' best song.[37]

Saturday 13 May: New song from Scott McKenzie – 'San Francisco (Be Sure to Wear Flowers in Your Hair)', written by John Phillips of the Mamas and the Papas. Going to be huge.[38]

Monday 12 June: Unanimous decision in *Loving v. Virginia* that all race-based legal restrictions on marriage are unconstitutional. Mildred and Richard Loving have been fighting Virginia's Racial Integrity Act of 1924 for a decade.[39]

Weekend, 16–18 June: 120-mile drive to Monterey. Whole festival great but Sunday's line-up was amazing: Ravi Shankar, Big Brother & the Holding Company, Buffalo Springfield, the Who, Grateful Dead, the Jimi Hendrix Experience (introduced by Brian Jones), Scott McKenzie, Mamas and Papas and more![40]

Friday 6 October: Death of Hippie demo today: they carried a coffin from the park to the Panhandle. The whole Haight-Ashbury scene is so depressing, all those stoned teenagers begging and gawking tourists with cameras. Crime going up too. Lots of people moving out to Berkeley or even farther.

Monday 16 October: First day of the Stop the Draft Week demonstrations. Joan Baez arrested, plus another 60 women protesters. Many injured by police.[41]

Thursday 9 November: First issue of *Rolling Stone*. Founder Jann Wenner says it's 'not just about the music, but about the things and attitudes that music embraces.' Looks great.

Clockwise from top left, all 1967

10
Mildred and Richard Loving,
13 June, photograph by Francis Miller

11
'Mantra Rock Dance' poster,
designed by Harvey W. Cohen
V&A: PROV.9162–2016

12
Sketch by Feliks Topolski of Stokely
Carmichael and Scottish psychiatrist
R.D. Laing at the Congress on the
Dialectics of Liberation

13
Spring Mobilization Committee
to End the War in Vietnam march
in San Francisco, photograph by
Ralph Crane

14
The crowd enjoying the 14-Hour
Technicolor Dream

15
First UK edition of *OZ*, February
Editor: Richard Neville
V&A: NAL

1967

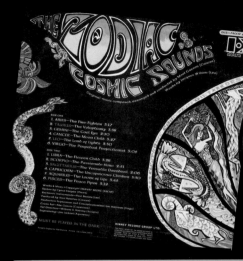

Left to right from top:

The Beach Boys, *Smiley Smile*

Bonzo Dog Doo Dah Band, *Gorilla*

Kaleidoscope, *A Beacon from Mars*

Ken Nordine, *Colors*

The Monkees, *Pisces, Aquarius, Capricorn & Jones Ltd.*

Big Brother & the Holding Company,
Big Brother & the Holding Company

The Zodiac: Cosmic Sounds

Arlo Guthrie, *Alice's Restaurant*

Procol Harum, *Procol Harum*

Rolling Stones, *Their Satanic Majesties Request*

Cream, *Disraeli Gears*

Jefferson Airplane, *Surrealistic Pillow*

The Doors, *The Doors*

The Kinks, *Something Else by the Kinks*

Timothy Leary, *Turn On, Tune In, Drop Out*

Jimi Hendrix Experience, *Are You Experienced*

Joe Harlott and John Mayer Double Quintet,
Indo–Jazz Fusions

The Who, *The Who Sell Out*

Moby Grape, *Moby Grape*

Grateful Dead, *The Grateful Dead*

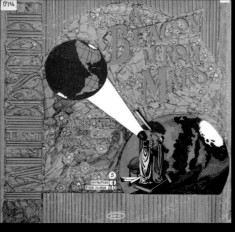

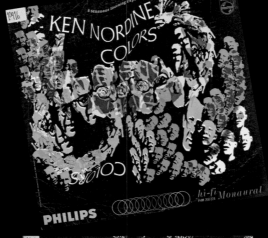

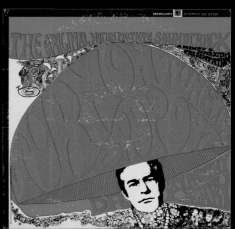

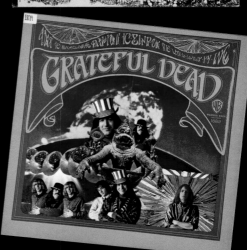

1968

Lyrics: from 'Revolution 1'
by the Beatles, 1968

Image: detail of pl.18

Tuesday 30 January

North Vietnamese and Viet Cong forces launch their surprise Tet Offensive, attacking 35 major cities in the South. Although these attacks are eventually beaten off, the 'instant' reporting on television, especially the assault on the US Embassy in the heart of Saigon, convinces many Americans that the Vietnam War is unwinnable.

Thursday 4 April

Martin Luther King, Jr is assassinated at the Lorraine Motel in Memphis, provoking riots in 100 cities. The previous evening he has given his 'Mountain Top' speech:

> Well, I don't know what will happen now. We've got some difficult days ahead. But it doesn't matter with me now. Because I've been to the mountain top. And I don't mind. Like anybody, I would like to live a long life. Longevity has its place. But I'm not concerned about that now. I just want to do God's will. And He's allowed me to go up to the mountain. And I've looked over. And I've seen the promised land. I may not get there with you. But I want you to know tonight, that we, as a people, will get to the promised land! And so I'm happy, tonight; I'm not worried about anything; I'm not fearing any man. Mine eyes have seen the glory of the coming of the Lord!'[42]

Wednesday 16 October

Jimi Hendrix releases *Electric Ladyland*, his third and last studio album, in the US. Tracks include 'Voodoo Child (Slight Return)' and his cover of Bob Dylan's 'All Along the Watchtower'. The double LP reaches number one in the US and is Hendrix's most commercially successful release. In 2012 it is ranked 55 in Rolling Stone's 500 Greatest Albums of All Time.[43]

Tuesday 24 December

Astronaut Bill Anders, on Apollo 8, is the first human to take a photograph of Planet Earth – the Blue Planet. The resulting 'Earthrise' image is later selected by *Life* magazine as 'one of the 100 most important photographs of the Twentieth Century'.[44]

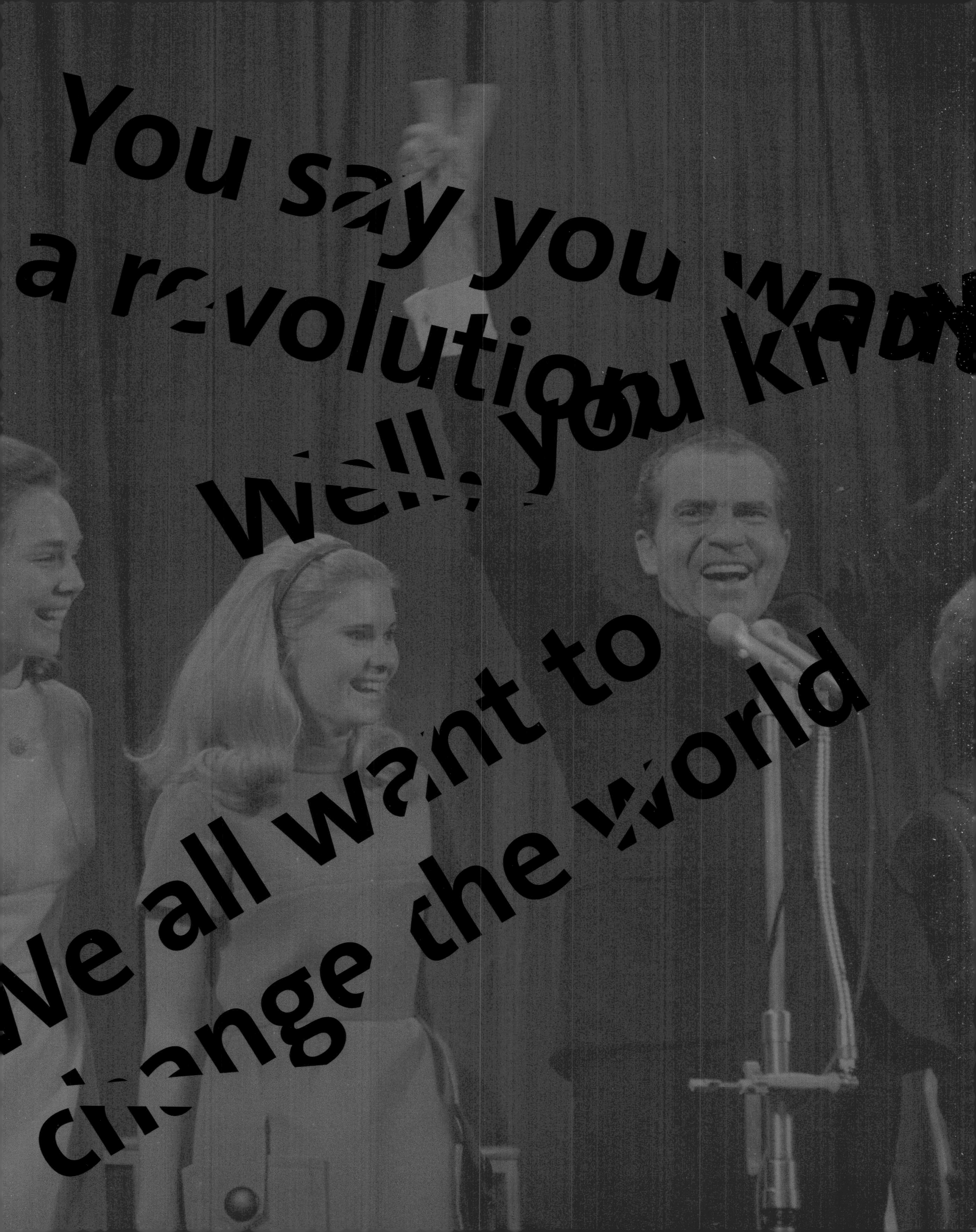

You say you want
a revolution, you know
Well, you know
We all want to
change the world

LONDON 1968

Thursday 25 January: Saw film version of *Up the Junction*. Poster says 'It's rough, raw and randy'. More like 'crude, dull but trendy' and not a patch on Ken Loach's 'Wednesday Play' adaptation on the BBC back in 1965. It's patronizing to Battersea and everybody who has to struggle to survive in this city. Mentioning abortion no longer shocks anyone.[45]

Sunday 17 March: Watched thousands gather in Trafalgar Square for anti-Vietnam War protest. Vanessa Redgrave and Tariq Ali led a march to the US Embassy in Grosvenor Square, where there were major fights with police – 200 arrested.[46]

Monday 13 May: Just got to Paris after taking cross-channel ferry. Fascinating to see the impact of a General Strike and join the enormous demonstration through central Paris.

Thursday 16 May: Heard that a gas explosion has caused the partial collapse of Ronan Point, a brand new 22-storey block of council flats in east London. Area completely sealed off.[47]

Friday 2 August: *Cybernetic Serendipity* at new Institute of Contemporary Arts (ICA) in The Mall. As tonight's *Evening Standard* puts it, 'Where in London could you take a hippy, a computer programmer, a ten-year-old schoolboy and guarantee that each would be perfectly happy for an hour without you having to lift a finger to entertain them?' With the opening of the Hayward[48] on the South Bank last month, London now has two great new spaces for modern art.

[Undated] August: Met Tony Elliott, in London on summer break from Keele University. He's made a one-sheet listings magazine called *Where It's At*. The underground magazine market is crowded but it's a good idea.[49]

Friday 27 September: To Shaftesbury Theatre for first night of the American 'love rock' musical *Hair*. Full-frontal nudity and songs about drugs and opposition to Vietnam. Afterwards celebrations of the abolition of the Lord Chamberlain's theatre censorship powers.[50]

Monday 14 October: Attended official opening of the new Euston Station by HM Queen Elizabeth II. First London terminus to be rebuilt – cool modernism – ushering in the new age of the 'electric' train. New Victoria tube line scheduled to open here in six weeks.

Friday 25 October: New version of the Race Relations Act in force, replacing 1965's unsatisfactory effort.[51]

Friday 22 November: Double album out today: *The Beatles*.[52] Best song 'Revolution 1'. All-white cover by Richard Hamilton.

SAN FRANCISCO 1968

Thursday 4 April: To see opening night of Stanley Kubrick *2001: A Space Odyssey*. Enjoyed it but a bit disappointed after all the hype.

Thursday 6 June: Terrible news – Bobby Kennedy assassinated in Los Angeles. Apparently shot while cutting through the kitchens of the Ambassador Hotel by 24-year-old Palestinian Sirhan Sirhan.[53]

Tuesday–Wednesday 27–28 August: Protests at Democratic National Convention in Chicago. Extraordinary scenes on TV of police beating up student protesters outside. No one can believe it.

Sunday 8 September: Black Panther leader Huey Newton convicted of voluntary manslaughter for killing a policeman last October in Oakland. Not guilty of felonious assault; kidnapping charge dismissed. Already in custody, sentenced to 2–15 years in prison.[54]

[Fall] 1968: Picked up a copy of the *Whole Earth Catalog* – fascinating guide to alternative living. Publishers are a husband and wife team in Menlo Park. It's a do-it-yourself guide to setting up your own community.

Friday 27 September: Went to see *Psych-Out,* a hippy exploitation movie. The poster screams 'These are the Pleasure Lovers. They'll ask for a dime with hungry eyes … but they'll give you love – for NOTHING!' Hilarious.[55]

Friday 1 November: Fourth day San Francisco State University is out on strike. Ugly atmosphere across town.

Wednesday 6 November: Disaster. Nixon has been declared winner of the presidential election by 512,000 – less than one per cent. How have the Democrats allowed this to happen?

Tuesday 3 December: Stayed in to watch the Elvis Christmas Special on NBC. A truly extraordinary 'comeback' appearance. He looks fantastic in black leather … where has he been?

Monday 9 December: A computer industry friend took me to a tech demonstration at the Fall Joint Computer Conference at the Brooks Hall by Douglas Engelbart from SRI. Didn't mean much to me – a 'mouse'? oN-Line? – but his 90-minute presentation got a standing ovation. Delegates clearly astonished by the technology on display.[56]

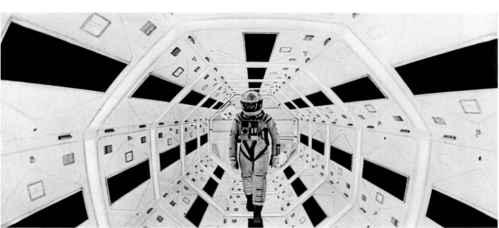

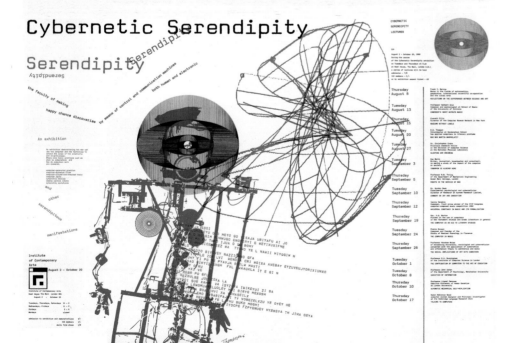

Clockwise from top left, all 1968

16
Paris protesters battling with police in the Latin Quarter, 6 May, photograph by Georges Melet

17
Poster for the London run of the musical *Hair*
V&A: S.25—1983

18
Richard Nixon and his family celebrating victory in the presidential election

19
Poster for the *Cybernetic Serendipity* exhibition at the ICA, London, 2 August – 20 October, designed by Franciszka Themerson

20
Film still from *2001: A Space Odyssey*, directed by Stanley Kubrick, released 18 months before the moon landing

1968

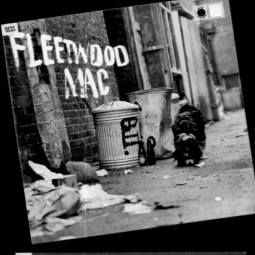

Left to right from top:

Fleetwood Mac, *Fleetwood Mac*

Canned Heat, *Living the Blues*

Joan Baez, *Baptism: A Journey through Our Time*

Soft Machine, *The Soft Machine*

Golden Dawn, *Power Plant*

Grateful Dead, *Anthem of the Sun*

Jimi Hendrix, *Electric Ladyland*

Mothers of Invention, *We're Only In It For the Money*

Diana Ross and the Supremes, *Love Child*

Steve Miller Band, *Children of the Future*

Rolling Stones, *Beggar's Banquet*

Pink Floyd, *A Saucerful of Secrets*

Van Morrison, *Astral Weeks*

Small Faces, *Ogdens' Nut Gone Flake*

Quicksilver Messenger Service, *Quicksilver Messenger Service*

Procol Harum, *Shine on Brightly*

Jimi Hendrix Experience, *Axis Bold As Love*

The Pretty Things, *S.F. Sorrow*

Family, *Music in a Doll's House*

Big Brother & the Holding Company, *Cheap Thrills*

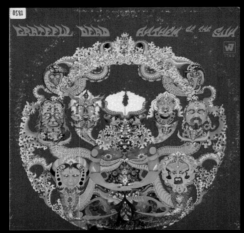

1969

Lyrics: from 'Woodstock'
by Joni Mitchell, 1969

Image: detail of pl.170

Monday 14 July

Easy Rider, written by Terry Southern and starring Peter Fonda (producer) and Dennis Hopper (director), and with Jack Nicholson in a break-out role, is released. The film is a massive financial success: made for only $360,000 it grosses $60m. It follows the story of two drug smugglers cruising on motorbikes through the fabulous scenery of the Southern US states only to be brought low by rural rednecks. A fantastic soundtrack includes the Byrds, the Jimi Hendrix Experience and Steppenwolf.

Sunday 20 July

At 21.18 UTC the Apollo 11 lunar module Eagle lands on the Moon and six hours later Neil Armstrong is the first man to walk on its surface, describing it to a worldwide television audience as 'one small step for man, one giant leap for mankind.' In 1961 President John F. Kennedy had put forward the challenge: 'before this decade is out, of landing a man on the Moon and returning him safely to the Earth.' Eight years later NASA achieves its goal, beating the Soviets in the space race. David Bowie's 'Space Oddity' and a Pink Floyd improvisation are played by the BBC during its special *Man on the Moon* broadcast.[57]

Friday to Monday 15–18 August

Woodstock Music and Art Fair – 'An Aquarian Exposition: 3 Days of Peace & Music'[58] – takes place at White Lake, in Bethel, upstate New York. An estimated 500,000 people descend on the site, causing massive traffic jams. Despite the limited services and rain, the star-packed line-up creates enduring and iconic images of the 1960s. Jimi Hendrix finally appears at 8.30am on Monday, entrancing the remaining crowd with an extraordinary rendition of the 'Star Spangled Banner' – caught forever on film.

By the time we got to Woodstock
We were half a million strong
And everywhere there was song and celebration

LONDON 1969

Monday 27 January: LSE students are now occupying the University of London, having smashed up buildings on Friday.

Tuesday 25 March: Reported on the BBC News that John Lennon and Yoko Ono have started a 'Bed-In' at the Amsterdam Hilton for their honeymoon. Their statement to promote peace and opposition to the war in Vietnam.[59]

Wednesday 9 April: Test flight of incredible 'Concorde' aeroplane at RAF Fairford in Gloucestershire today. Supersonic travel within our grasp![60]

Saturday 5 July: Walked to Hyde Park to see the Stones. Vast crowd – some say 300,000. Mick did great tribute to Brian Jones reading from Shelley. I don't know who schedules these events but seems crazy that the Who were playing the Albert Hall on the same date.[61]

Thursday 14 August: Troops have been sent onto the streets in Northern Ireland. Yet another Sterling crisis. Britain's position as a world power looking pretty shaky.

Friday to Sunday 29–31 August: Went in a packed car (and ferry!) to second Isle of Wight Festival. Amazing seeing Dylan – best thing ever and he did 17 songs. Leonard Cohen fantastic, too. Back to London exhausted.[62]

Friday 26 September: Bought the Beatles' *Abbey Road*, out today. Played it over and over again. Great, and brilliant cover.

Sunday 5 October: Watched new comedy programme called *Monty Python's Flying Circus* on BBC. Some jokes very funny others just weird. Loved the animations.

Thursday 25 December: Finally have my own copy (for Christmas, thanks to my sister) of Penguin's great poetry book *Children of Albion: Poetry of the Underground in Britain*, edited by Michael Horovitz. Dipped into this before at other people's flats but now can sit and read it at home.[63]

[Undated]: Formal announcement of creation of The Open University which will allow people to do a degree from home by watching lectures on television. First courses planned to start in 1971. Can't imagine many people wanting to study at home alone.

SAN FRANCISCO 1969

[Undated] April: Elvis's new single 'In the Ghetto' is number three in the charts, so a lot of people must be buying. Seems everybody is connecting with inner-city struggles.[64]

Sunday 20 April: We started construction of a 'People's Park' in Berkeley on waste ground owned by the University of California.[65] Many radicals having been crossing the Bay from Haight-Ashbury due to the spiralling crime there.

Thursday 10 July: Second issue of *Berkeley Tribe* out today – a new radical mag put together by about 40 disgruntled ex-staffers from the *Berkeley Barb* (splinter group upset by some sex advertising).[66]

Saturday 9 August: Gruesome murders in Los Angeles last night, five people including the actress Sharon Tate – pregnant wife of Roman Polanski. Everybody here is terrified.[67]

Wednesday 13 August (Friday to Sunday 22–24 August): The festival that wasn't! Huge three-day Wild West Festival was planned at Golden Gate Park. Janis Joplin, Jefferson Airplane, the Grateful Dead, Country Joe, Santana, Sly and the Family Stone and many more. Collapsed because of arguments whether it should be free or not (and some local protests). The idea was to turn the four-mile park, Kezar Stadium, Japanese Tea Garden, de Young Museum, and various lakes and meadows into one long-running carnival of free music and arts. Only this city could produce TEN headliners.

Tuesday 21 October: Beat author Jack Kerouac has died of cirrhosis in St Petersburg, Florida, aged just 47.

Thursday 20 November: Indians of All Tribes have taken over former Alcatraz prison island demanding recognition of Native Americans' rights. Looks to be a long occupation.[68]

Saturday 6 December: To Altamont Speedway for a free concert headlined by the Rolling Stones. Arrived late so was a long way back – saw Santana and Crosby, Stills, Nash & Young. Grateful Dead bailed out. Edgy vibe. Learned on way back that someone was murdered by security – a bummer.[69]

[Undated] December: A friend who works at Stanford Research Institute (SRI) told me in confidence that they have found a way of sending messages between computers that could survive a nuclear war.[70]

Wednesday 31 December: Waiting for the new decade with an advance copy of *Fire!: Notes from the Counterculture* edited by Paul Samberg, who lives around the corner. Not sure whether to feel inspired or depressed.

Clockwise from top left, all 1969

21
Leonard Cohen at the Isle of Wight Festival,
photograph by Charles Everest

22
Film still from *Gimme Shelter* (1970), directed
by Albert Maysles, David Maysles and Charlotte
Zwerin, showing Hell's Angels beating a fan with
pool cues at Altamont

23
Concorde, the fruit of an Anglo–French
design collaboration, on its maiden flight

24
Front page of *New York Daily News* Sunday
10 August after Sharon Tate was murdered in LA

25
Occupation of Alcatraz, demanding rights for
Native Americans, photograph by Ralph Crane

26
Mick Jagger at the Hyde Park concert,
wearing Mr Fish 'man-dress',
photograph by David Gahr

'1969

Left to right from top:

Free, *Free*

Captain Beefheart and His Magic Band, *Trout Mask Replica*

Quicksilver Messenger Service, *Happy Trails*

MC5, *Kick Out the Jams*

Neil Young, *Neil Young*

Creedence Clearwater Revival, *Green River*

Crosby, Stills & Nash, *Crosby, Stills & Nash*

Quintessence, *In Blissful Company*

Third Ear Band, *Alchemy*

The Stooges, *The Stooges*

David Bowie, *Space Oddity*

Grateful Dead, *Aoxomoxoa*

The Who, *Tommy*

Various artists, *Easy Rider* soundtrack

Elvis Presley, *From Elvis in Memphis*

Jefferson Airplane, *Volunteers*

Jethro Tull, *Stand Up*

Rolling Stones, *Let It Bleed*

King Crimson, *In the Court of the Crimson King*

Frank Zappa, *Hot Rats*

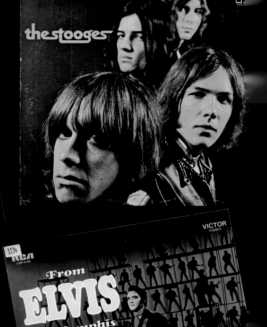

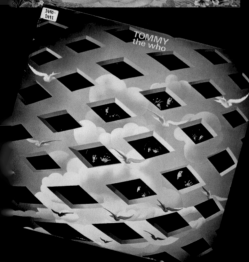

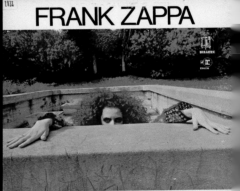

1970

Lyrics: from 'The End'
by the Doors, 1966/67

Image: detail of pl.32

Thursday 26 March

Documentary *Woodstock*, filmed during the festival 17–19 August 1969 by director Michael Wadleigh, is released in the US to huge commercial and critical success. It had cost $600,000 to make but grosses $50m in the US alone and receives an Oscar for Best Documentary Feature.[71] The film does much to spread the idealism of the counter-culture around the world. Six weeks later, on Monday 11 May, the triple-LP set *Woodstock: Music from the Original Soundtrack and More* is released.[72]

Wednesday 22 April

The first Earth Day is celebrated in the US by a claimed 20 million people.[73] During the late 1960s concern about environmental pollution had increased rapidly. On 20 October 1969, a signed *New York Times* editorial stated: 'Call it conservation, the environment, ecological balance, or what you will, it is a cause more permanent, more far-reaching, than any issue of the era – Vietnam and Black Power included.' On 1 January 1970 President Nixon signed the National Environmental Policy Act, making it his 'first official act of the decade', which led to the creation of the Environmental Protection Agency (EPA).

Monday 12 October

Germaine Greer's *The Female Eunuch* is published and is an instant hit. An international best-seller, it is translated into eight languages in six months, the bible of the '70s women's lib movement. Greer comments 'The title is an indication of the problem. Women have somehow been separated from their libido, from their faculty of desire, from their sexuality. They've become suspicious about it. Like beasts, for example, who are castrated in farming in order to serve their master's ulterior motives – to be fattened or be made docile – women have been cut off from their capacity for action. It's a process that sacrifices vigour for delicacy and succulence, and one that's got to be changed.'[74] The famous surrealist cover of the Paladin paperback edition, showing the skin of a female torso hanging on a garment rail, is designed by John Holmes (pl.78).

This is the end
Beautiful friend
This is the end
My only friend
the end

LONDON 1970

Thursday 22 January: First commercial 'jumbo jet' flight by Pan Am, from New York, landed at Heathrow. The Boeing 747, which can seat several hundred passengers, will bring transcontinental flight within reach of millions.[75]

Weekend 27 February to 1 March: Flatmate back from the first National Women's Liberation Conference at Ruskin College, Oxford. Reports that the four main demands are equal pay, equal education and job opportunities, free contraception/abortion on demand and 24-hour nurseries.[76]

Friday 8 May: Despite Paul's announcement last month that he is leaving the Beatles, their new LP *Let It Be* is out on schedule. 'The Long and Winding Road' is the best track.

[Undated] May: Picked up a copy of *OZ* no. 28 – apparently edited by a group of schoolkids. Wild.[77]

Friday 19 June: General Election result – surprise Tory win! Voted for Lena Jeger who retained Camden for Labour. Edward Heath and the Conservatives took a 4.5 per cent swing overall, giving them a majority of 31. Many pundits blaming England's defeat by West Germany in the World Cup.

Monday 27 July: Opening of *Oh! Calcutta!* at the Roundhouse, a nude revue produced by Kenneth Tynan with sketches by Samuel Beckett, John Lennon and others.[78]

Tuesday 28 July: To Paddington to see Michael Heseltine cut the ribbon to open the Westway, Britain's longest urban motorway. Heckled by residents: 'You drive over our lives'.[79]

26–31 August: Third Isle of Wight Festival – the biggest yet. Saw Joni Mitchell, the Doors, Sly and the Family Stone, the Who, Emerson, Lake & Palmer, Miles Davis, Melanie, Pentangle, Joan Baez, Leonard Cohen and Jimi Hendrix.[80]

Friday 25 September: Went round the new *Kinetics* exhibition at the Hayward Gallery. One piece is great fun, there are buckets of six-inch nails and you can throw them at magnetic targets creating your own work of art.

Friday 20 November: High drama at Miss World Contest. Evening interrupted by Women's Lib activists who heckled Bob Hope![81] Huge media coverage has probably done more to raise the profile of the movement than many marches.[82]

Friday 1 January 1971: Scanned *Radio Times* for TV tonight. Must-see programmes: *Top of the Pops* introduced by Jimmy Savile at 7.05 pm.

SAN FRANCISCO 1970

Monday 16 February: Twenty-six today – all my girlfriends came round to celebrate. 1965 seems so long ago. When is the war going to end?

Thursday 30 April: Nixon has announced a US attack on Cambodia. After all his promises of withdrawing from Vietnam! Everybody phoning to decide how to protest.

Monday 4 May: Horrific news tonight. Massacre at a university in Ohio. Four students shot dead and many injured by the National Guard at Kent State, protesting against the invasion of Cambodia.[83]

Friday 8 May: Now 450 campuses are on strike across the country – there is in effect a national student strike.

Saturday 9 May: 100,000 protest the war in Washington DC. Ron Young from the Mobe and Jane Fonda gave speeches.[84]

Wednesday 1 July: Xerox has opened their new multimillion-dollar computer research centre at Palo Alto (PARC), close to Stanford.[85] Many of my friends are deeply suspicious of the research work being done around the university campus. Some say all the bombing raids are planned there.

Friday to Sunday 3–5 July: Flew across to Atlanta, first time in Georgia, and then on to Byron for the Second Annual Atlanta International Pop Festival. Jimi Hendrix played an amazing set at midnight on Saturday.[86] Festivals just seem to get bigger and bigger – some say that there were 600,000 people present despite the heat.

Monday 20 July: Friends going to see Alex de Renzy's new film *Pornography in Denmark: A New Approach*. Apparently it shows pretty much everything that they get up to in Scandinavia.[87] No thanks. Adult movies seem to be taking over North Beach. Glad I moved to Berkeley.[88]

Wednesday 26 August: Went downtown to protest Women's Strike for Equality organized by the National Organization for Women (NOW). Celebrating the 50th anniversary of the 19th amendment in 1920 giving women the vote – but certainly not equality.[89]

Thursday 15 October: Heard Miles Davis live from the Fillmore West, broadcast on Berkeley's KPFA. Amazing, he's already moved on so far from *Bitches Brew*.[90]

Wednesday 20 January 1971: New Marvin Gaye single 'What's Going On' out. Understand it started as a response by the Four Tops to police brutality at the People's Park.[91]

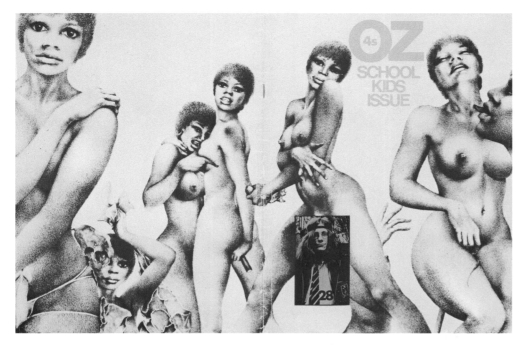

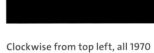

Clockwise from top left, all 1970

27
OZ no. 28, *School Kids Issue*, editor: Richard Neville
This issue led to the famous *OZ* trial in 1971. V&A: NAL

28
Miles Davis at the Isle of Wight festival,
photograph by Charles Everest

29
Nude dancers in *Oh! Calcutta!*, 29 July,
photograph by Leonard Burt

30
Xerox PARC researchers meet in the Computer
Science Lab Commons, *c*.1970s–80s

31
Nixon announcing US attack on Cambodia, 30 April

32
Student Jeffrey Miller was shot and killed by
guardsmen during an anti-war demonstration, Kent
State University, 4 May, photograph by John Filo

1970

Left to right from top:

Black Sabbath, *Black Sabbath*

Black Widow, *Sacrifice*

Jimi Hendrix, *Band of Gypsys*

The Temptations, *Psychedelic Shack*

The Last Poets, *The Last Poets*

Miles Davis, *Bitches Brew*

David Bowie, *The Man Who Sold the World*

Various artists, *Zabriskie Point* soundtrack

Traffic, *John Barleycorn Must Die*

Simon and Garfunkel, *Bridge Over Troubled Water*

Deep Purple, *Deep Purple in Rock*

The Stooges, *Fun House*

Santana, *Abraxas*

Lee Dorsey, *Yes We Can*

Free, *Fire and Water*

Grateful Dead, *American Beauty*

Various artists, *Performance* soundtrack

Syd Barrett, *The Madcap Laughs*

Various artists, *Woodstock* soundtrack

Crosby, Stills, Nash & Young, *Déjà Vu*

49

WHAT HAPPENED NEXT?

London and San Francisco entered the 1970s with much in common from their '60s experience, but the following years were to reveal distinct and critical differences. Both cities were battered by the global economic crises of 1973–5, beginning with the 'Nixon Shock' of 1971 and the oil crisis of 1973, which suddenly made the optimism of the 1960s seem far away.[92] During the 1973–4 stock market crash the New York Dow Jones and the London FT30 lost 45 per cent and 73 per cent of their respective values. The trust funds that had propped up many communes and other progressive social projects suddenly shrank. Unemployment in the United States had hit rock bottom at 3.6 per cent in 1968 but by 1976 it had doubled to 7.7 per cent – a level not seen since the US entered World War II in 1941.[93] Suddenly 'dropping out' for a couple of years looked a much riskier choice.

An equally acute factor in the economic downturn was the rapid decline in traditional dock work – the *raison d'être* of both cities – with the arrival of containerization and the shift to deep-water port facilities at Tilbury in Essex and Oakland across the Bay.[94] This had a knock-on effect on associated manufacturing industries. In San Francisco there were still 60,000 jobs in this sector during the 1960s but by the end of the decade most had gone.[95] Although some were replaced by the growing tourism and financial services industries, the haemorrhaging of traditional business names was a blow to the city's prestige and identity.[96] Many creatives also left for the booming artistic scene and cocaine-fuelled hedonism of Los Angeles, encapsulated in the Eagles' *Hotel California* (1976). The revival of the film industry with the new wave of Hollywood blockbusters led by *Jaws* (1975) and *Star Wars* (1977) created a new confidence across LA.[97]

London, as a capital city, always had the associated infrastructure of central and local government to keep rolling but the rest of the UK went into an economic slump. In 1967, following a series of takeovers, the General Eelectric Company announced the closure of the huge historic AEI factory in Woolwich, with the loss of 5,000 jobs.[98] This was followed by a string of related factory closures over the next decade particularly in riverside industries – which left large patches of east London derelict.[99] A total of 360,000 industrial jobs disappeared. Although these were replaced by 190,000 office jobs, the net loss of 170,000 traditional jobs was massive and the manufacturing base of London crashed.[100] The arrival of punk's 'no future' attitude in 1975–6 reflected the reality for a generation of working-class teenagers whose employment options had evaporated. Attempts in the 1970s to kick-start the economy were small-scale and fragmented. Nothing much happened for a decade until, in 1981, Margaret Thatcher took the controversial decision to create the London Docklands Development Corporation (LDDC), the full impact of which was not felt until the 1990s.[101]

There were significant social changes in parallel. In the 1960s and '70s the key economic indicators were jobs and output – not people, knowledge and ideas. The concept of a post-industrial society was emerging but had not yet been popularized.[102] Government policy focused on relocating people to the new towns; the Milton Keynes Development Corporation, aiming for the biggest yet, was set up in 1967. London's population continued to drop, sinking to its lowest point of 6.5 million in 1983, a loss of 25 per cent from its pre-war peak in 1939. The results were boarded-up houses, increasing dereliction and neglect of the public realm.[103]

The same fall in population and flight of the middle classes from city centres to the suburbs was a key feature of American cities including San Francisco. There, a series of gruesome crimes, the 'Zodiac Killer' 1968–9 and particularly the racially motivated 'Zebra' murders 1973–4, caused public panic. The reality was inflamed by media coverage and a wave of vigilante films set and filmed in the city – starting with *Dirty Harry* (1971), in which Clint Eastwood famously demands, 'You've got to ask yourself one question: "Do I feel lucky?" Well, do you, punk?'

However, while San Francisco and the Bay Area faced such problems, it had several crucial advantages. A useful guide is provided by *The Good Time Manual: 257 Places in the Bay Area Where People Under 30 Are Going (Or Should Be Going)*, published in 1972. It highlights an alternative city based around bars and clubs where people could meet, talk and network – a proto-model of contemporary Soho or Hoxton in London. San Francisco's liberal reputation for tolerance encouraged many gays to locate to the city, resulting in the rise of the Castro district where Harvey Milk – the first openly gay person elected to office in California – opened his camera shop in 1972. The two major universities at Berkeley and Stanford, both located a short distance from the city itself, were increasingly important economic powerhouses, driven by massive government research support during the 1960s.

During the first half of the 1970s the Bay Area was home to two men who would change the world: Steve Wozniak and Steve Jobs. In 1972–3 Jobs lived a hippy lifestyle, building computers and working on a commune at an apple orchard in Oregon, studying Zen Buddhism and experimenting with vegetable diets. In 1974 he went travelling in India for seven months and experimented with LSD, later stating that this was 'one of the two or three most important things' he had done in his life. In early 1975 he returned to San Francisco.[104]

In March 1975 a hobbyist meeting group – the Homebrew Computer Club – was established by Gordon French and Fred Moore, creating what has been called 'the crucible for an entire industry'.[105] Jobs and Wozniak were among the many famous members. On 29 June 1975 Wozniak achieved for the first time ever a character on a television screen controlled by a personal computer: the basis of the Apple 1. The rest is history. On 1 April 1976, they formed Apple Computer in Steve Jobs' parents' garage, and within a year made sales of $775,000. From 1977–80 Apple averaged an annual growth rate of 533 per cent, going public in December 1980 and creating around 300 millionaires. On 25 November 2014 Apple became not only the largest publicly traded company in the world by capitalization but the first US company valued at over $700 billion.[106] The 1960s ideal of sharing knowledge universally has now been achieved up to a point – but not in a way anyone imagined in the 1970s.

Despite ups and downs, the economic impact of Silicon Valley's technology industry on San Francisco has been phenomenal. The city now draws ambitious people from across the world, all seeking to realize their dreams, though the 'Golden Gate' is likely to be a specialist digital investor rather than the harbour entrance. The 1960s flop houses and communes of Haight-Ashbury regularly trade for $3 million plus, and young people have been forced out of the city across the Bay to regenerate/gentrify Oakland, where some properties have remained untouched since the riots of the late '60s. A rising population is the second most highly educated in the US after Seattle's, with 44 per cent holding a college degree. At 15 per cent, it has the highest proportion of gays and lesbians in the country.

In 2015 London's population finally reached and then passed that of 1939. It has fully regained its world city status. Digital industries are now booming, clustered around 'Silicon roundabout' near Old Street, an extraordinary sight for those who remember the 1970s when London's decline might have become terminal.

Lyrics: from 'Imagine'
by John Lennon, 1971

Image: detail of pl.265

The demise in 1990 of ICL, created in 1968, as the flag-bearer of the UK computer industry, seemed to have sounded a death-knell. Although the Greater London Council (GLC) abandoned its massive inner London motorway scheme after 1973, it was not replaced with a coherent plan to regenerate the declining inner boroughs. Indeed, the 1972 *GLC Covent Garden Action Area Plan* for replacing the relocated vegetable market (which was moved to Nine Elms, near Vauxhall) proposed demolishing 16 historic West End theatres. This scheme was supported by the Arts Council, even though it did not actually own or fund any of the threatened theatres.[107]

While London received a shot in the arm from the arrival of 27,000 entrepreneurial Ugandan Asians expelled by Idi Amin in 1972, generally the economy was in decline – a situation reflected as much by the bitter two-year strike in 1976–8 at the Grunwick film-processing plant in Willesden as the punks walking down the King's Road. While the two Steves were founding Apple in San Francisco, the British trade unions and government battled in the High Court over an industry that was to be swept away within 25 years by the invention of the camera phone. The eventual revival of London – through the impact of Big Bang and the deregulation of financial services in 1986, globalization and the LDDC, the details of which lie outside this essay – followed two decades of neglect only now being addressed.

AND THE FUTURE?

In R. Luke Dubois' 'emotional dating maps' of the US, published in *A More Perfect Union* (2011),[108] the ten words generated for central Los Angeles are:

ACTING, STYLE, FILM, HUMAN, FEMININE, URBAN, MONEY, WRITER, ENTERTAINMENT, DIRECTOR

and those for San Francisco are:

GAY, YOUNG, SPIRITUALITY, DRESS, ENERGY, LOVER, CREATE, INTELLIGENCE, ARCHITECTURE, SOFTWARE, SENSUAL

One wonders what the equivalent for London in 2016 should be? **GM**

Imagine there
no heaven
It's easy
if you try
No hell
below us
Above us
only sky

YOU SAY YOU WANT TO CHANGE THE WORLD?

2

REVOLUTION NOW

THE TRAUMAS AND LEGACIES OF US POLITICS IN THE LATE 1960S

SEAN WILENTZ

In the United States, the insurgent mood of the 1960s boiled over mid-decade, when President Lyndon B. Johnson rapidly escalated American involvement in the Vietnam War. Johnson's hawkish certainty about his intensification of the conflict, despite private doubts, almost immediately sparked dissent. Reinforcing the backlash against his Great Society and War on Poverty programmes, reactions split the Democrats, ruined his administration, and damaged liberalism's standing for two generations and more. The apparently solid political coalition that had elected him in 1964 crumbled.

The anti-war Left and the civil rights movement fractured, too. Protest turned to talk of resistance and then to calls for revolution. Time seemed to pass in exclamation points. Student activists, having started out in the early 1960s marching for racial equality and contemplating the soullessness of suburban middle-class life, began burning draft cards, blocking army recruitment and conscription centres, and shutting down universities to protest against both complicity in the war and racial oppression. The non-violent resistance methods developed by Dr Martin Luther King, Jr gave way to chaotic explosions of rage that set the black ghettos of Northern cities (Los Angeles, Newark, Detroit) ablaze and led to a new black nationalism demanding Black Power. Within two months during the spring of 1968, the assassinations of Martin Luther King, Jr and Robert F. Kennedy seemed to foreclose any possibility of ending the war or advancing social justice by working within the political system. New movements based on gender and sexual identity suddenly emerged. By the end of the decade, so-called 'second wave feminists' had moved from challenging the straightjacket of wifely domesticity to questioning the entire patriarchal order. In the summer of 1969, the refusal of the customers at a shabby gay bar, the Stonewall Inn in Greenwich Village, to submit to some routine pre-dawn police harassment precipitated a riot that led in turn to the formation of the Gay Liberation Front.

Amid these sensational events, there were smaller, human-sized, but just as telling signs of fragmentation and radicalization. One of these came in the form of popular singer-songwriter Phil Ochs (pl.33). Arriving on the Greenwich Village scene in 1962, Ochs made an impression as one of the most talented young performers following in the footsteps of Woody Guthrie (pl.65) and the left-wing folk revival of the 1940s and 1950s. Witty, passionate and prolific, Ochs, like his friend and rival Bob Dylan, wrote and sang dissenting songs about civil rights, war and peace, labour struggles and other polarizing issues of the day.

In 1965 and '66, when Dylan famously began to take his music in a more personal and poetic direction, Ochs continued to compose and perform topical songs. His output turned increasingly mordant and radical, indicting liberals and Democrats as shady cowards and finks, and advocating what he somewhat loosely called 'revolution'. During his concerts, Ochs poked fun at the generationally universal object of derision Lyndon B. Johnson, as well as reactionaries such as washed-up actor and aspiring California politician Ronald Reagan, before launching into his proletarian anthem, 'Ringing of Revolution':

And the soft middle class crowded in to the last,
for the building was fully surrounded.
And the noise outside was the ringing of revolution.

Not much time was left to Phil Ochs. He appeared at anti-war rallies across the country into the early 1970s,

performing new songs including 'The War is Over' and 'White Boots Marching in a Yellow Land'. Shaken into despair by the police violence at the Democratic National Convention in 1968, however, he gradually lost his artistic as well as political footing, succumbed to bipolar disorder and depression, and finally took his own life in 1976. Nor was time left to the stormier radical groups from the late '60s with which Ochs identified; some (like the largest of the campus groups, Students for a Democratic Society, or SDS) descended into ultra-leftism both destructive and self-destructive. Ronald Reagan, meanwhile, won his California gubernatorial campaign in 1966, and two years later, Richard M. Nixon won the White House.

The revolutions of the late 1960s ushered in a long era of conservative politics, carried forward by President Reagan in the 1980s, pushing the nation's politics far to the Right. Yet even so, 50 years on, many of the egalitarian hopes that at the time seemed either utopian or outrageous have come to define the way Americans live. Neither side emerged entirely triumphant: the paradoxes of those years of unstable conflict persist, and help to explain the sharp polarities within American politics today.

The fracturing of the 1960s began in March 1965, when – as sometimes happens in American history – dissent and mainstream politics dramatically converged. On 7 March, some 600 marchers in Selma, Alabama, demanding voting rights for black Americans, were brutally attacked by state and local policemen at the Edmund Pettus Bridge. Eight days later, President Johnson addressed a joint session of the House and Senate to call for sweeping federal voting rights legislation, and in doing so formally allied his administration with the civil rights movement, powerfully invoking the movement's rallying cry: 'We shall overcome'. Martin Luther King, Jr, who led a follow-up march and would lead another a week later, watched the speech on television at a family's home in Selma and wept. Distrust of Johnson among the movement's rank-and-file seemed to abate. On 6 August, after hard-fought battles on Capitol Hill, Johnson signed the historic Voting Rights Act, with King standing prominently at his side.

Yet even as the voting rights crusade prevailed with LBJ's support, events transpired that would soon lead Johnson's presidency to implode. One day after the bloody confrontation on the bridge at Selma, two battalions of the US Marine Corps landed on beaches near Da Nang, the first American combat troops sent to support South Vietnam (pl.34). By month's end, the number of troops had risen to 5,000; by the end of the year, there would be more than 180,000 US military personnel in Vietnam and the total American military death toll would exceed 1,800. Protests began as soon as the escalation started: in late March 1965, the first 'teach-in' featuring lectures and debates disputing the war took place at the University of Michigan; three weeks later, some 20,000 people gathered for an anti-war march, organized by SDS, in Washington DC; and in October, on the eve of large demonstrations in some 40 American cities, a religious pacifist named

David Miller became the first young man to burn his draft card. On 11 August, only five days after Johnson signed the Voting Rights Act, violent incidents between white police and local residents in the black Los Angeles neighbourhood of Watts, where relations between police

36 (left)
A couple watching film footage
of the Vietnam War on a television
in their living room, 1968,
photograph by Warren K. Leffler

37 (opposite)
A huge pall of smoke pours from
a burning building during race riots,
Detroit, 1967

and the community had long been tense, ignited five days of rioting that left 34 dead, a thousand injured, and $40 million in property damage.

The war did the most to wreck Johnson's presidency. From the start, Johnson later remarked, he had known that if he abandoned 'the woman I really loved – the Great Society' for 'that bitch of a war on the other side of the world' he would lose everything at home; but if he failed to prosecute the war, it would mark him as a coward and an appeaser. He had observed first-hand Senator Joseph McCarthy's Red Scare, intended to exploit the fear of communism and smear the Democratic Party's New Deal. Trapped by those cold-war orthodoxies left over from the late 1940s and early '50s, Johnson tried for a rapid and decisive victory, and when that failed he kept escalating the military commitment. He promised that, at last, there was 'light at the end of the tunnel', a phrase previously uttered by General Henri Navarre, the French commander who lost the battle of Dien Bien Phu in 1954 (during the First Indo-China War), and repeated by General William Westmoreland, the US commander in Vietnam, in November 1967. By the end of 1967, Johnson had more than doubled the number of American troops in Vietnam to 485,600, and nearly 20,000 had died. Privately, a number of Johnson's top advisers began telling him that the future looked bleak. 'There may be a limit beyond which many Americans and much of the world will not permit the United States to go,' Secretary of State Robert McNamara warned in a memorandum. 'The picture of the world's greatest superpower killing or seriously injuring 1,000 non-combatants a week, while trying to pound a tiny backward nation into submission on an issue whose merits are hotly disputed, is not a pretty one.' Yet even as his approval ratings plunged and he himself began to question the war's direction, Johnson would not back down.

Official statements calling the Vietnam intervention a limited 'police action' in response to Communist aggression met with public scepticism from the start. What became known as the 'credibility gap', a phrase popularized by the dissenting Senator William J. Fulbright, chairman of the Senate Foreign Relations Committee, widened as television news reports revealed the harsh realities on the ground (pl.36). When pictures began appearing of disfigured Vietnamese babies and children, their flesh melted by napalm bombs dropped by American B-52s, the gap became a chasm, and protest intensified. It would yawn following the surprise Tet Offensive by North Vietnamese and Viet Cong forces in January 1968, which exploded administration claims about slow but steady military progress.

Inevitably, the war diverted the White House and Congress from the Great Society. Almost all of Johnson's major social-reform legislation, from health care to immigration reform to education, was enacted in 1964 and 1965; thereafter, the war took top priority. The War on Poverty, meanwhile, according to the sociologist-turned-White House aide Daniel Patrick Moynihan, had been 'oversold and underfinanced to the point that its failure was almost a matter of design'. Moynihan exaggerated: in fact, thanks in part to Johnson's policies, the proportion of Americans living below the poverty line fell from 17 per cent in 1965 to 11 per cent in 1973, marking (apart from the recovery from the Great Depression during World War II) the sharpest drop in all of American history. Yet the distance between Johnson's grandiose vow to eliminate poverty and his administration's great but incomplete achievements fuelled resentment among both supposed beneficiaries who felt short-changed and tax-paying working-class whites who felt exploited. Even as the percentage of poor people declined, the numbers enrolled in the main federal welfare programme (Aid to Families with Dependent Children)

skyrocketed, accompanied by rising rates of teenage pregnancy, drug and alcohol addiction, and violent crime, which further inflamed white fear and anger. And as the war escalated and the 'the light at the end of the tunnel' failed to appear, bitterness and backlash overwhelmed the nation's politics.

Racial tensions worsened, especially in the nation's cities. The civil rights movement's great victories could not alleviate the hopelessness of urban ghetto life, sharpened by recurring violent incidents involving local police. After what were called 'the Watts Riots', in August 1965, clashes between armed white law-enforcement officers and poor black residents became endemic and provoked a series of successive explosions: 11 major riots in the summer of 1966 and 25 major riots a year later, including the decade's worst, in Detroit, which left 43 dead (pl.37). The liberal consensus on racial justice shattered: whereas in 1964 a majority of Northern whites supported Johnson's civil rights programme, by 1966 a majority believed the government was pushing too hard for racial integration. The political ground shifted in the 1966 elections, as Republicans made major inroads in the white South and the blue-collar North and picked up enough seats in the House to ruin Johnson's liberal working majority in Congress. Johnson was caught in a political vice, as the war in Vietnam and racial unrest fed

not only the rise of the Right but also frustration on the Left, generating radical rage.

The travails of the civil rights movement, and especially of Martin Luther King, Jr, traced the deepening crisis. After the Watts Riots, King decided to switch his focus from voting rights in the South to exposing the de facto segregation of schools, jobs and housing in the Northern cities. In 1966, the Baptist minister led his Southern Christian Leadership Conference (SCLC) into an ambitious open-housing campaign (to remove racial discrimination imposed by realtors and mortgage lenders and abetted by local legislators) in Chicago. But the campaign failed miserably, as angry working-class whites pelted demonstrators (including King himself) with rocks and bricks (pl.38). Then, less than a year later, seeing social and moral connections beyond the racial discord and urban violence, King disregarded the objections of other civil rights leaders and spoke out against the 'madness' of Johnson's war, calling the administration 'the greatest purveyor of violence in the world today', and declaring that 'the bombs that fall in Vietnam explode at home'. The rupture between King and the Johnson White House signalled the end of the historic alliance of protest and political process that had won the Voting Rights Act – and, with that, signalled the larger rupture between one phase of the '60s and another.

By the start of 1967, anti-war protests had evolved into a diverse political movement, strongest in colleges and universities but embracing Americans from every walk of life. Only a minority considered themselves militants of any kind. But as frustration grew, a few protest leaders became more aggressive: if marching alone had not halted the war, they reasoned, the movement would have to confront the warmongers directly. Draft card-burning and other acts of civil disobedience had already raised the stakes of anti-war activity (pl.35). Here and there, a few protesters brandished Viet Cong flags. Approaching the fall of 1967, one of the largest of the anti-war groups, the National Mobilization Committee Against the War ('the Mobe') announced in a new slogan a shift 'from protest to resistance'. A giant demonstration in Washington DC was planned for 21 October that would end with a mass march of 50,000 across the Potomac to the Pentagon, headquarters of the Department of Defense and America's war machine.

Brilliantly rendered by Norman Mailer in his 1968 book *The Armies of the Night*, the march on the Pentagon exhibited a certain frivolity as well as a new militancy. Co-ordinating the event were two veteran campaigners: Berkeley student organizer Jerry Rubin and his pal Abbie Hoffman, a civil rights activist. They had become enamoured of the counter-culture that had blossomed over the summer in San Francisco's Haight-Ashbury and the East Village in New York. With some media-savvy hippy hucksterism, Rubin and Hoffman sensed that the march could raise the movement's profile as well as its spirits, and their highly publicized effort to levitate the Pentagon building and exorcise its evil spirits through chants led by the poet Allen Ginsberg forged something of a fusion between hippy culture and the anti-war movement (pl.39). A few thousand more traditionally political demonstrators broke through lines of National Guardsmen and federal marshals and

actually reached the perimeter of the Pentagon building, where they faced armed soldiers, their generational peers in uniform, until at dusk US marshals dispersed them and arrested hundreds.

Mailer, who was jailed earlier in the day for an act of civil disobedience, at one point heard a distant peal of trumpets, which put him in mind of 'the cries of the Civil War' and 'the ghosts of old battles'. The historical echoes in Mailer's imagery come from deep within the American grain. But behind the militant cries at the Pentagon there were also varieties of revolutionary radicalism already declaring

40 (opposite)
Stokely Carmichael speaking
in London, July 1967

41 (following pages, left)
'What We Want: Black Panther
Party Platform' poster, 1966,
sketches by Akinsanya Kambon
V&A: E.301–2004

42 (following pages, right)
Assassination of Martin Luther
King, Jr, Memphis, 4 April 1968,
photograph by Joseph Louw

war on America itself. That radicalism had been developing for years on the campuses, most conspicuously inside Students for a Democratic Society, which had become the largest left-wing organization in the United States since the Great Depression.

Founded in 1962 as a successor to the old-line democratic socialist Student League for Industrial Democracy, SDS captured attention right away as the harbinger of a New Left, largely due to its founding manifesto. The 'Port Huron Statement' was written chiefly by Tom Hayden, a young graduate of the University of Michigan and veteran of the Southern civil rights struggle. Owing much to the spirit of the French existentialist writer Albert Camus, the statement propounded the creation of a 'radically new democratic political movement', based in colleges and universities and dedicated to the ethos of participatory democracy – a tempered utopian vision of a society in which individuals would have as large and direct a say as possible in the public decisions that governed their lives. Many of the group's members retained this core philosophy. But by the end of 1967 SDS had largely jettisoned its early existential radicalism in favour of trying to overthrow the American corporate and military governing elite, in an imagined grand alliance with the liberation movements of the Third World. The original animating utopian spirit had become associated with an idealization of the small-'c' communism of Cuba and North Vietnam (and, for some, Mao's China) as selfless and egalitarian, the highest stage of human fulfillment.

Always bound tightly to the civil rights struggle, SDS's history was inevitably entwined with that of the Student Non-Violent Co-ordinating Committee, which like SDS transformed itself in the mid-1960s. At its formation in 1960, SNCC (pronounced 'Snick') was a striking political innovation: an organization of and run by students, bent on using the strategy and tactics of non-violent resistance to force confrontations with local authorities in the South over Jim Crow segregation laws. In actions from the 'Freedom Rides' in 1961 to the 'Mississippi Freedom Summer' voting-rights drive of 1964 SNCC members acquired a unique aura of heroism. The group's ideal of a racially integrated, blessed community blended politics, ethics and personal morality every bit as powerfully as SDS's participatory democracy. Yet bitterness beset SNCC in the face of what its activists perceived as white-liberal treachery, notably in 1964, when Party officials, directed by President Johnson to offer a compromise, would not seat the entire integrated 'Mississippi Freedom' delegation at the Democratic National Convention. Black members also chafed at the news media's seeming preoccupation with the sacrifices of white participants and relative indifference to black organizers.

In June 1966, SNCC joined with several other civil rights organizations in a 'March Against Fear' through the Mississippi Delta to the State Capitol in Jackson. Martin Luther King, Jr, was figured to be the protest's pre-eminent spokesman, but along the route a SNCC organizer, Willie Ricks, fired up the crowd by shouting the simple slogan, 'Black Power!' The charismatic Stokely Carmichael, who three weeks earlier had won a disputed election as SNCC's chairman, picked up the refrain at a stop-off rally in Greenwood and made the most of it. 'What we are gonna start saying now is Black Power!' he exclaimed, and the crowd roared back, 'Black Power!', and suddenly the march belonged to Carmichael, not King (pl.40). The following December, under Carmichael's leadership, SNCC instructed white members to leave the organization.

If the phrase 'Black Power' struck many white listeners as terrifying, black audiences associated it with everything from pride in African American culture and history to a

What We Want

October 1966

Black Panther

Party Platform

1. We want freedom. We want power to determine the destiny of our Black community.

2. We want full employment for our people.

3. We want an end to the robbery by the CAPITALIST of our Black Community.

4. We want decent housing, fit for the shelter of human beings.

5. We want an education for our people that exposes the true nature of this decadent American society. We want education that teaches us our true history and role in the present day society.

6. We want all black men to be exempt from military service.

7. We want an immediate end to POLICE BRUTALITY and MURDER of black people.

8. We want freedom for all black men held in federal, state, county and city prisons and jails.

9. We want all black people when brought to trial to be tries in court by a jury of their peer group or people from their black communities, as defined by the Constitution of the United States.

10. We want land, bread, housing, education, clothing, justice and peace. And as our major political objective, a United Nations-supervised plebiscite to be held throughout the black colony in which only black colonial subjects will be allowed to participate, for the purpose of determining the will of black people as to their national destiny.

NEW HAVEN CHAPTER
BLACK PANTHER PARTY
P. O. BOX 7117
NEW HAVEN, CONN. 06519
(203) 562-7463

FREE HUEY

Minister of Defense,

Black Panther Party

NEW HAVEN CHAPTER
BLACK PANTHER PARTY
P. O. BOX 7117
NEW HAVEN, CONN.
562-7463

rallying cry encouraging black entrepreneurship. John Lewis, the SNCC chairman (and since 1987, US congressman) who was dislodged by Carmichael, was unimpressed, thinking it was 'just rhetoric', but also destructive. Carmichael himself seemed to have no fixed definition for the term, swerving from implicating Black Power in the worldwide struggle against Western imperialism to insisting it had to do simply with 'our blackness – nothing else'. But to some white New Leftists, especially the budding revolutionary factions in SDS, Black Power denoted the primacy of race in the structure of imperialist oppression at home and abroad, and of the absolute imperative of renouncing 'white-skin privilege'.

As SNCC became chiefly a platform for Carmichael and, later, his successor as chairman, H. Rap Brown, the Black Power ferment inspired the formation in October 1966 of the Black Panther Party for Self-Defense in Oakland, California (pl.41). The group was started by two young activists, Bobby Seale and Huey P. Newton. Heavily influenced by the writings of Malcolm X (a long-time minister of the Nation of Islam who had broken with the movement's leader, Elijah Muhammad, and been assassinated in February 1965 by Nation of Islam members), Seale and Newton came up with the idea of organizing resistance to police brutality, using violence if necessary as a step toward building a revolutionary political movement. Dressed in black leather jackets and black berets, and brandishing shotguns and rifles (as was then permitted by the California Penal Code), the Panthers cut a swaggering trail across the radical landscape, turning up armed at the State Capitol in Sacramento to protest against a bill that would have banned carrying unconcealed firearms, and organizing rallies with fearsome melodic chants: 'The revolution has come / Off the pig! / Time to pick up the gun / Off the pig!'

Newton, Seale and the party's eloquent new Minister of Information, convicted rapist Eldridge Cleaver (soon to publish a *New York Times* best-seller, *Soul on Ice*), awed New Left radicals, all the more so once the Panthers began throwing around snippets of Marxist–Leninist rhetoric and citing the theories of Algerian revolutionary Frantz Fanon as justification for violence. Unlike the Afrocentric nationalists in SNCC, the Panthers were open to working with white Americans so long as they remained in a supporting role. The Panthers' theatrical style and eagerness to take on the police thrilled some of their New Left admirers. But that militant style was more than black leather jackets; it led to repeated shoot-outs, not all of them initiated by racist cops. In October 1967, Newton was arrested and charged with murder, which many years later he would privately admit to having committed. Six months after Newton's arrest, a Panther ambush of police officers, led by Cleaver, resulted in the death of one young recruit and the arrest of a wounded Cleaver and other top Panthers.

Early in 1968, with a national election looming, it appeared as if, despite all the division and bitterness, protest and mainstream politics might once again be converging. Pushed by the anti-war movement, Senator Eugene McCarthy challenged President Johnson for the Democratic Party's presidential nomination, and on 12 March he stunned even his supporters by finishing a close second to Johnson in the New Hampshire primary. Four days later, Senator Robert F. Kennedy, brother of the murdered president, announced his candidacy. Two weeks after that, on 31 March, a beleaguered and exhausted LBJ told the country that he would not seek re-election – a previously unthinkable victory for the anti-war movement.

But then, before an astonished nation had time to catch its breath, all hell erupted. On 4 April, a white racist sniper assassinated Martin Luther King, Jr, in Memphis, and immediately rioting broke out in cities across the United States, most spectacularly in Washington DC – the greatest wave of violent unrest the country had experienced since the Civil War a hundred years before (pl.42). At the end of the month, the SDS chapter at Columbia, protesting against the action in Vietnam, but also the university's collusion in racism, seized administrative and classroom buildings; a week-long rebellion ended in a bloody crescendo when campus officials authorized New York City policemen to remove the protesters. The anti-war Eugene McCarthy and Robert Kennedy, sharp rivals now, kept winning primaries, with Kennedy gaining a lead in delegates. Then, on 4 June, immediately after he declared victory in California, Kennedy was assassinated. By midsummer, it was almost certain that the Democrats would nominate Vice President Hubert H. Humphrey, an old liberal hero now tainted by his fervent loyalty to Johnson's policies in Vietnam. Humphrey had not entered a single primary and would be imposed as the nominee of the Party Establishment. Protest was all that was left to the anti-war and civil rights movements, and thousands of demonstrators descended on Chicago in late August to confront the Democrats at their nominating convention, only to be set upon, beaten and jailed, in what

the US National Commission on the Causes and Prevention of Violence (appointed by President Johnson) later described as a 'police riot' (pl.43).

The fall election was a debacle for Humphrey. The Republican candidate, Richard M. Nixon, riding the wave of resentment that had revived his party, pledged to crack down on crime and restore 'law and order', while also peddling a non-existent secret plan to end the war in Vietnam. Humphrey refused to budge on favouring peace talks on Vietnam until it was too late; he was afraid of alienating Johnson, who was already engaged in negotiations – which Nixon's emissaries were busy sabotaging, for fear that a deal would derail the Republican campaign. Running on a third-party line, arch-segregationist and former Governor of Alabama George C. Wallace swept up the lower South but not enough of the Northern vote to endanger Nixon. One group on the Left, loosely organized under the umbrella of the Peace and Freedom Party (in some states called the Freedom and Peace Party), won a smattering of votes for the comedian-activist Dick Gregory. There were write-ins for Eldridge Cleaver, who three weeks after the election jumped bail on his murder charge and fled to exile in Cuba. (Radical third parties would continue springing up: in 1972, the Liberty Union Party formed in Vermont, led among others by a former civil rights activist, socialist Bernie Sanders, who was later elected to the Congress and campaigned as a 'movement' candidate for the Democratic presidential nomination in 2016.) Thanks to Wallace's presence, Nixon won the 1968 popular vote by a bare plurality of 0.7 per cent, but he crushed Humphrey in the Electoral College.

Nixon's victory, and his subsequent expansion of the war in Southeast Asia (even as he began a phased American withdrawal), hardly spelled the death of the anti-war movement. In October 1969, a new mainstream coalition, the Vietnam Moratorium Committee, led by liberal activists and advised by Democratic elders such as former Secretary of Defense Clark Clifford, co-ordinated a nationwide day of protest in which more than a million people, in hundreds of communities, participated. A month later, the largest anti-war demonstration the United States had seen drew half a million protesters to Washington DC. In April 1970, when President Nixon announced that he had ordered US ground troops into Cambodia, a national student strike involving hundreds of thousands hit some 700 campuses. Although mostly peaceful, some

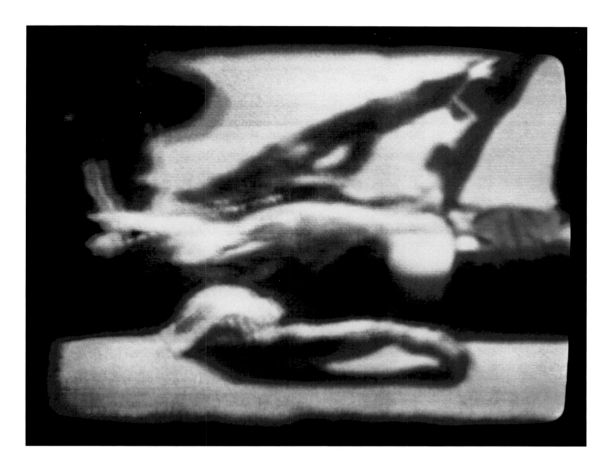

43 (opposite)
A police officer making threatening motions toward a pair of protesters in front of the Hilton Hotel during ongoing Democratic National Convention demonstrations, Chicago, 28 August 1968, photograph by Paul Sequeira

44 (right)
Kent State, 1970
Richard Hamilton
Screenprint from 13 stencils
67.3 x 87 cm (image);
73 x 102.2 cm (sheet)

of the protests turned violent: on 4 May, Ohio National Guardsmen shot dead four unarmed students at Kent State University (pl.44), and soon thereafter two more students died at Jackson State College, gunned down by Mississippi state police. A rattled Nixon backed off and by the end of June the American invasion force had left Cambodia. But the following spring, another group, Vietnam Veterans Against the War, led by John Kerry (later senator, Democratic presidential candidate and Secretary of State), dramatically brought a thousand anti-war veterans to camp on the Mall in Washington. In 1972, Senator George McGovern rallied diverse anti-war forces, including the dissident Democrats who had supported McCarthy and Kennedy four years earlier, and captured the Democratic presidential nomination, only to lose the election in a landslide victory for President Nixon.

Yet if the anti-war movement endured for the length of the war itself (which ended in 1975), the radical Leftists of SDS lost their collective mind. At the group's national convention in Chicago in 1969, the organization broke into warring factions, each one convinced it was the true vanguard of the coming revolution. The most militant faction called themselves the Weathermen (borrowed from Bob Dylan's lyric, 'You don't need a weatherman to know which way the wind blows') and set out to organize a guerrilla army that would help overthrow American imperialism. In the fall, after several days of 'kick-ass' violent demonstrations in Chicago – the main result of

which was to leave the city's chief attorney paralysed – the group's leaders went underground to begin a campaign of terrorist bombings that would last on and off for several years, would succeed in destroying some government property, but would get the most attention in February 1970 when an accidental explosion killed three members who were assembling bombs in a Greenwich Village townhouse.

Civil rights and Black Power activism suffered their own fates. With the Reverend King dead, the SCLC drifted under the comparatively lacklustre leadership of his right-hand man, Ralph Abernathy. SNCC fell apart after 1968, with some of its remaining leading lights joining the Black Panther Party; by 1970, Carmichael, who had changed his name to Kwame Touré, was living in self-imposed exile in Guinea. The Panthers, like SNCC, attracted the attention of the Federal Bureau of Investigation's notorious director J. Edgar Hoover, who called the group 'the greatest threat to the internal security of the country'. While the FBI and local police forces regarded them as alarming public enemies, they remained outlaw heroes to some white Leftists. But the Panthers suffered internal feuding, were implicated in protection rackets and numerous murders, and sputtered away under the increasingly erratic and volatile leadership of Huey P. Newton, who fled to Cuba, served time in prison, earned a doctorate from the University of California at Santa Cruz, and was murdered in 1989 as he left a crack cocaine house.

45 (below)
A march by the National
Organization for Women
(NOW), 8 May 1969

46 (right)
Karen DeCrow, the eastern
regional director of the National
Organization for Women (NOW)
with women's liberation posters,
21 August 1970

47 (opposite)
Young people celebrating outside
the boarded-up Stonewall Inn,
New York, 28 June 1969,
photograph by Fred W. McDarrah

    The movements that survived the revolutionary
late 1960s made enduring changes in American society.
A feminist reawakening – a 'second wave' – had begun
early in the decade, sparked by the publication of Betty
Friedan's *The Feminine Mystique* in 1963 and resulting in the
foundation three years later of the National Organization for
Women (NOW) (pls 45, 46). In an eight-point 'bill of rights'
issued in 1968, NOW demanded reforms on issues ranging
from sexual discrimination in employment and education to
securing women's health and reproductive rights, including
full access to contraception and abortion. Simultaneously,
feminist spirits stirred inside the New Left and the civil
rights movements, where radical young women were
growing restive under the sway of domineering men. These
women formed groups of their own, one of which, New York
Radical Women, came up with the idea of dramatizing their
breakthrough by disrupting and satirizing the Miss America
beauty pageant in Atlantic City. On 7 September 1968, 200
women gathered outside the city's convention hall to throw
a mini-pageant of their own, crowning a sheep and tossing

bras, girdles, and other 'beauty aids' into an oversized trash
can, while inside the hall stealthy protesters unfurled a giant
banner inscribed 'WOMEN'S LIBERATION'.

    Together, mainstream and radical feminists changed
laws as well as minds. They brought litigation that led to
Supreme Court rulings that the Constitution prohibited
differential treatment based on sex (*Reed v. Reed*, in 1971),
and overturned state laws prohibiting abortion (*Roe v.
Wade*, in 1973). But by pressing their concerns beyond purely
legal discriminations, the radical feminists also pushed
the boundaries of their struggle into unfamiliar terrain,
expressing deep moral outrage at conventions and practices
that went largely unnoticed, let alone unchallenged. Out
of the excitements and revelations of consciousness-
raising sessions came rudiments of the recognition that
the personal is the political, and that female subordination
inhered not simply in unfair laws and inadequate social
provision but in everyday life and perceptions – in the
very idea of women's beauty, in the unspoken rules of
housework and child-rearing, in the multitude of social
habits and standards and idioms that constructed
patriarchy. Here was a politics that spoke disconcertingly,
renaming the origins of spiritual malaise and reinventing
the quest for human liberation.

    The uprising of homosexuals that began with the
Stonewall Inn Rebellion in 1969 also had far-ranging effects

(pl.47). For four nights, Stonewall's male denizens crowded Greenwich Village's Christopher Street and faced down the police, at one point forming a Rockettes-style kickline that blended defiance with camp humor. ('We are the Stonewall girls / We wear our hair in curls / We wear no underwear / We show our pubic hair.') Politer assemblies of homosexual men and women had for years worked to ward off harassment and to guard civil rights, but out of Stonewall came a rip-roaring movement of prideful, openly gay men, soon joined by lesbians (many of them already galvanized by women's liberation) in a loose-knit Gay Liberation Front. Not unlike the radical feminists, the burgeoning gay rights movement sought to pull down ancient veils of presumption and shame; but their highest aim – above and beyond declaring who they were, and declaring that who they were was beautiful – was no more complicated than winning the right to love. By 1977, no fewer than 19 states had repealed their sodomy laws and 40 cities had approved measures that mandated gay rights. In 2015, the Supreme Court ruled in favour of an equal right to marriage.

The new environmental movement was less politically audacious, to the point of seeming uncontroversial, but it rapidly won a mass following and would provoke, in time, political and economic upheavals. The appearance of scientist Rachel Carson's polemic *Silent Spring* in 1962 had raised alarms about a poisoned natural environment, as did, four years later, *Science and Survival* by Barry Commoner, whom *TIME* magazine would describe as 'the Paul Revere of ecology', likening the biologist's clarion call to that of the American Revolutionary patriot. In January 1969, when a natural gas blow-out at an oilfield platform six miles off the coast of Santa Barbara, California, spewed 200,000 gallons of crude over a radius of 800 square miles, local protests erupted and national public opinion awakened. The president of the Union Oil Company, which was responsible for the spill, could not comprehend the outcry over 'the loss of a few birds' – but times had changed, and a new social movement rapidly took shape. 'Call it conservation, the environment, ecological balance or what you will', one *New York Times* editor declared, 'it is a cause more permanent, more far-reaching than any issue of the era – Vietnam and Black Power included.'

Later in 1969, the liberal senator Gaylord Nelson of Wisconsin, heeding the example of the early anti-war movement, proposed that a national teach-in on environmental issues be held the following spring. Not since the turn of the twentieth century had Americans joined in anything resembling an organized national conservation movement; the Progressives' undertakings had been conducted largely by wealthy, well-connected gentlemen like the first great pro-environment president, Theodore Roosevelt. Nelson's call initiated a '60s-style environmental crusade, which grew rapidly and led to the first Earth Day commemoration on 22 April 1970 – in which 20 million Americans, in colleges, primary and secondary schools, and hundreds of communities, paused to take part in tree-plantings and spring-time festivals, and to learn about and reflect on environmental reform (pl.48).

Designed purposefully as a non-political, non-confrontational occasion, Earth Day gathered support from political leaders of both parties, including officials inside the White House. Later in 1970 Nixon the pragmatist sought to co-opt its message, proposing the federal reorganization that gave birth to the Environmental Protection Agency. His administration saw the growing movement as, if nothing else, a welcome respite from anti-war demonstrations. But even on that first Earth Day of insistent good will, radical environmentalists in some cities picketed and booed administration spokesmen and corporate officials. By the mid-1970s, dissenting environmentalists were organizing protests, including civil disobedience, to try to shut down nuclear power plants. Established organizations such as the Sierra Club shifted emphasis from working on local issues to establishing a national political presence in Washington, alongside new groups including the Natural Resources Defense Council. When the environmental movement began turning its attention to the crisis of climate change in the 1990s, it provoked intense opposition from industries that decried its efforts as intrusive regulation that would interfere with the workings of the free market, and challenged the scientific findings.

'CHOPPING BLOCK'

Which sides, then, won? Which sides lost? And what exactly did they win or lose in the American frenzy of 1966–70? The results seem the clearest in politics and government, where conservatism has enjoyed a prolonged ascendancy. Between 1966 and 1970, the New Left along with the Black Power movement rose quickly and then crashed and burned, while American liberalism, as embodied in the Democratic Party, fragmented. The Vietnam War finally ended in 1975; Nixon's paranoia turned criminal and proved his undoing in the Watergate scandal in 1974, a year before the Vietnam War finally ended; but the greatest political benefits redounded to the right wing of the Republican Party, which had never trusted Nixon and which after his downfall rallied around Ronald Reagan. Not until Bill Clinton's breakthrough in 1992 did the Democrats begin seriously to update the egalitarian liberalism of the New Deal and Great Society, and begin the political task of rebuilding a winning national coalition. After two terms of Democratic government under Clinton, the Supreme Court's halting of repeated ballot recounts in the contested state of Florida in 2000 effectively selected George W. Bush as president by a five-to-four conservative majority. It thereby brought to power a combination of turbocharged Reaganism in domestic affairs and a hawkish neoconservatism in foreign policy that left the nation, eight years later, mired in war and plunged into the greatest financial disaster since the Great Depression. Bush's dramatic failures opened the way for the election of Senator Barack Obama of Illinois as the United States' first black president, a victory which many thought signalled the end of the contentious politics, especially over race and civil rights, that had originated in the unrest of the 1960s. But a resurgent, obstructionist and increasingly extreme Republican Congress – heirs to the radicalized Republican Party that arose between 1966 and 1970 – sought to destroy Obama personally and politically, just as they had with the impeachment of Clinton. They said Obama was not really an American, his birth certificate had been forged; and not a single Republican in the Congress voted for his economic recovery or health-care programmes.

The collapse of Great Society liberalism during the late 1960s and the long conservative aftermath have had another effect: they have led to the growth of vast new inequalities in American society. Beginning with the New Deal of the 1930s and mobilization for World War II, and lasting into the 1970s, the United States experienced the sharpest reduction in economic imbalance in its history. But the conservative era ushered in by Nixon's election in 1968 reversed that trend profoundly, in what the Nobel Prize-winning economist Paul Krugman has described as 'the great divergence'. After remaining fairly stable through most of the 1950s until the end of the 1970s, the share of total income going to the top 10 per cent of earners has increased dramatically since the mid-1980s, reaching 50.6 per cent in

2012, higher than any year on record since 1917. In 1982, the highest-earning 1 per cent of households received 10.8 per cent of all pre-tax income, while the bottom 90 per cent received 64.7 per cent. Three decades later, the top 1 per cent received 22.5 per cent of pre-tax income, while the bottom 90 per cent's share had fallen to 49.6 per cent. A rising plutocracy of the top 0.1 per cent, whose share of total household wealth, which had fallen to around 7 per cent in 1978, had grown to around 20 per cent thirty years later.

The civil rights movement never fully recovered from the divisions of 1966. In the aftermath, black nationalists were pitted against integrationist liberals. Conservative Republicans successfully portrayed what remained of the movement as just another fractious interest group out to secure special entitlements at the expense of hard-working white taxpayers. The precipitous decline in the poverty rate for black households from 1960 to 1970, steepest after 1965, began to level off thereafter; the rate fell again in the 1990s only to rise after 2000, although to nowhere near pre-'60s levels. Yet in 2011, 27.6 per cent of black households were in poverty, nearly triple the poverty rate for white Americans. The loss of urban manufacturing jobs has helped ensure that the ratio of black-to-white unemployment of roughly two-to-one has changed little: in 1963, the unemployment rate was 5 per cent for white and 10.9 per cent for black Americans, while in 2012 it was 6.6 to 12.6 per cent. Thanks to government commitment to reform and the enforcement of earlier court rulings, the proportion of black children in segregated (and thus unequal) schools fell dramatically to 62.9 percent in the early 1980s, but then the trend reversed, and slowly but steadily climbed to 74.1 per cent in 2010. Although overall high-school graduation rates, mostly stagnant after the mid-1970s, eventually showed signs of improvement, the figures for black Americans have consistently lagged well behind. Most strikingly, incarceration rates, especially for black men, skyrocketed more than three-fold between 1960 and 2010, to the point where the proportion of the black male population locked away in penal institutions was more than six times that of white men. The spate of well-publicized police shootings in 2014–15 that led to the rise of the loose-knit Black Lives Matter movement dramatized the gap in black and white perceptions of and experiences with law enforcement and the criminal justice system.

And still, many of the transformations of the 1960s, including those that arose from the feverish period between 1966 and 1970, have withstood the conservative reaction. Despite the Reaganite demonization of 'big government', the most imposing federal initiatives of the 1960s and 1970s – from Medicare, Medicaid and food stamps to the Environmental Protection Agency – have become firmly entrenched in American life. The temporary reversal under the Clinton administration of deepening broad-based inequality showed that the great divergence need not be inevitable. The major pieces of civil rights legislation from the 1960s, in time advanced by controversial but effective affirmative action efforts, created an African American middle class, in business and the professions, unlike any the nation had ever seen. Quite apart from Obama, the number of black public officials, appointed and elected, has risen strikingly. Thanks largely to the liberalization of immigration laws in the 1960s, an influx of newcomers from Central and South America, Africa, East and South Asia has transformed the nation's demography, and with it shaken the very idea of what it means to be an American.

The legacy of '60s cultural dissent has been profound, not least in feminism. Linking the personal and the political has transformed standards and prospects for women in everything from child-rearing to employment. Assumptions that certain kinds of work – from combat duty to firefighting – could only be performed by men have collapsed, and young women have come to believe that they should expect the same careers and salaries as men. Despite the rise of the right-to-life movement, courts and elected officials have not undone Roe v. Wade. In 1993, President Bill Clinton appointed the lawyer who wrote the plaintiff's brief in Reed v. Reed, Ruth Bader Ginsburg, to the Supreme Court. In mass-culture, portrayals of sexual preference as well as women's rights have become far more candid and tolerant. The gay rights movement, having pulled through the worst afflictions of the HIV/AIDS catastrophe of the 1980s, built considerable political clout while altering public attitudes, to the point where a conservative-dominated Supreme Court legitimized gay marriage.

The United States of the early twenty-first century would be almost unrecognizable to its former self of 50 years earlier. In 2015, the American pollster Stanley Greenberg summed up some of the most remarkable changes:

A majority of US households are headed by unmarried people, and, in cities, 40 per cent of households include only a single person. Church attendance is in decline, and non-religious seculars now outnumber mainline Protestants. Three-quarters of working-age women are in the labour force, and two-thirds of women are the breadwinners or co-breadwinners of their households. The proportion of racial minorities is approaching 40 per cent, but blowing up all projections are the 15 per cent of new marriages that are interracial. People are moving from the suburbs to the cities.

At about the same time as Greenberg published his findings, a Gallup poll reported that between 60 and 70 per cent of the country described gay and lesbian relations and having a baby out of wedlock, as well as divorce and having sex outside of marriage, as 'morally acceptable'. On

one social index after another, it would appear that the revolution of the 1960s has triumphed.

To be sure, these triumphs have not gone uncontested; indeed, the Republican Party has continually played upon the resentments that roiled the late '60s – resentments that, in the face of the trends Greenberg and others describe, have fostered an embittered politics of cultural despair. Successive conservative Republican leaders promised true believers, especially the evangelical Christian Right, a full-scale assault on abortion rights, affirmative action, the 'homosexual agenda', and everything else about modern life they charged was degenerate. Sometimes (as on abortion) they promised more than they ever intended to deliver; in any event, they promised far more than they won, and their supporters felt cheated. (Reagan, one right-wing activist remarked, paid lip service to the traditionalist crusade and 'offered us a bunch of political trinkets'.) Since the 1990s, an agitated and angry conservative electoral base has driven the Republican Party ever further to the Right. But after 2012, when even the right-wing Tea Party insurgency, heavily funded by Republican donors and channelled by Republican leaders, could not prevent Obama's re-election, the grassroots would no longer have anything to do with 'Establishment' Republicans, considered weaklings at best and, at worst, as pandering betrayers. In the second decade of the twenty-first century, much of the Right's emphasis has turned to rising immigration rates, including unauthorized immigration, particularly of Mexicans, even though by 2015 more Mexicans were leaving than entering the US. One such champion of the new nativism, Senator Ted Cruz of Texas, a Republican presidential candidate in 2016, claimed Reagan as his lodestar, even though Reagan was a prominent proponent of immigration and signed legislation both as Governor of California and as President allowing more Mexicans into the US. During the 2016 Republican primaries, the real-estate mogul Donald Trump touched a nerve and quickly rose to the top of the field when he angrily denounced undocumented Mexican immigrants as 'rapists' and 'murderers' and vowed to compel the Mexican government to build at its own expense an enormous wall at the US–Mexican border.

American liberals and Leftists have had great difficulty in reclaiming the initiative in politics and government, seized by conservatives in 1968. It has not been for lack of trying. In the 1990s, Bill Clinton tried to reinvent American liberalism in a conservative age. He had been involved in anti-Vietnam War protests, organized the anti-war McGovern presidential campaign in 1972 in Texas with the help of his then-girlfriend, the activist Hillary Rodham, and become the youngest Governor of Arkansas, guiding it to progressive policies after it had been the scene of momentous confrontations over civil rights. From their experiences with the dissenting movements of the 1960s and early 1970s, Bill and Hillary Clinton were determined to use practical politics in an attempt to realize those movements' ideals. But advancing social justice, they believed, would also require challenging what they beheld as outmoded Democratic orthodoxies on the use of American power abroad and the structure of the existing welfare state at home.

President Clinton soon found his first major initiative, on health-care reform, overwhelmed by corporate-funded propaganda and dissension in his own ranks, and thereafter he was forced to bob and weave to thwart the resurgent Right, advancing smaller-scale liberal programmes. Other Clinton efforts, above all over reforming the federal welfare system, offended leftists, who came to mistrust the president as a wolf in sheep's clothing. A slice of that mistrust was directed against the Democrat Al Gore in 2000 by supporters of third-party gadfly Ralph Nader, some of whom repeated Republican confabulations about Gore as 'an inveterate bribe taker' and worse. Nader, himself an important 1960s figure who had fought General Motors on car safety and won, had become a pioneer of the new consumer movement. Gore, too, was a product of the 1960s, both an anti-war activist and a Vietnam War veteran, who had emerged as a visionary on the environment and energy. Nader stood for the Green Party and wound up holding the thinnest of votes in Florida, in a contested result that split the Left and ultimately handed the presidency to the Republicans, even though Gore had won the popular vote by more than half a million.

After George W. Bush's disastrous presidency, a large share of the Left fancied that Barack Obama would be a 'movement president' in its own image. Obama was of the successor generation, but his anthropologist-activist mother, very much a figure of the 1960s, had raised him with progressive political values. In Chicago, Obama had been a community organizer, associated with the local Left in the Hyde Park district that encompasses the University of Chicago, and which he represented in the Illinois state senate. Obama expressly stated in his 2008 campaign that he would transcend the contentious politics of the 1960s that he felt had consumed American politics up to the present. It was time, he wrote, to get past 'the psychodrama of the baby boom generation – a tale rooted in old grudges and revenge plots hatched on a handful of college campuses long ago – played out on the national stage', and instead pursue 'a different kind of politics'. But when President Obama governed chiefly from the centre-left, and the Republican Party tried to destroy his administration, not sharing his naive belief in post-partisanship, Leftists were painfully disillusioned. That disillusionment carried over to the 2016 presidential primaries, when millions of younger voters rallied around the socialist Bernie Sanders and against Hillary Clinton, who ran as an 'effective' centre-left progressive.

Republicans, even as they lurched to the extreme right in order to catch up with their base, found their presidential expectations overthrown by the emergence of Donald Trump, and their larger political hopes damaged by the sudden death of the hard-line Supreme Court Justice Antonin Scalia in February 2016. (Were a Democratic president, either Obama or a possible Democratic successor, to nominate Scalia's replacement, the conservative majority on the Court, so crucial to the Republicans, would end.) Yet no matter whom they nominated for the presidency, and no matter whether they won or lost the general election, the Republicans had consolidated political power at the state and local level to go along with conservative majorities in the US Congress and (until Scalia's death) the Supreme Court. Republican control in the states, funded by a combine of right-wing billionaire donors including the Koch brothers, has altered national politics by forcing the gerrymandering that now virtually ensures GOP command over the House of Representatives through 2023. Republican domination at state level has had direct impacts in driving successful efforts to restrict voting rights for minorities, younger voters and other Democratic-leaning constituencies, gutting federal firearms legislation, depriving poor women of reproductive health care, and more, in large portions of the country where the backlash against that new America born in the '60s revolutions has been ferociously successful.

All of which might mean that it is too early to say who won or lost the revolutions of the 1960s. In many ways, those revolutions continue. From one perspective, it would appear that a paradoxical America has emerged over the last half century, at once politically conservative and culturally liberal, dysfunctional and frustrating. But from another, it would appear that we have seen something more like the rise of what Abraham Lincoln called, in very different but equally polarized circumstances, 'a house divided against itself'. Lincoln's house, divided over slavery, he believed could not stand – it would eventually become all one thing or all another, either free or slave. History proved him correct. So it may prove that the revolutionary '60s produced in America another house divided, one whose fate – as one thing or another – has yet to be decided 50 years later, but that sooner rather than later will face a reckoning. **SW**

This essay draws on the materials and insight in three indispensable books on the American 1960s: Paul Berman, *A Tale of Two Utopias: The Political Journey of the Generation of 1968* (New York: W.W. Norton, 1997); Todd Gitlin, *The Sixties: Years of Hope, Days of Rage* (New York: Bantam, 1987); and Maurice Isserman and Michael Kazin, *America Divided: The Civil War of the 1960s* (New York: Oxford University Press, 2000). On the 'great divergence,' see Paul Krugman, *The Conscience of a Liberal* (New York: W.W. Norton, 2007). The figures on changing demographics in the twenty-first century appear in Stanley Greenberg, 'Why 2016 Could Be Shattering for Republicans', *Washington Post*, 13 November 2015; see also Greenberg's *America Ascendant: A Revolutionary Nation's Path to Addressing Its Deepest Problems and Leading the 21st Century* (New York: Thomas Dunne Books, 2015).

50 (above)
CND March, Trafalgar Square,
London, Easter 1964,
photograph by
John 'Hoppy' Hopkins

51 (right)
CND March, 1966,
photograph by
John 'Hoppy' Hopkins

52 (opposite, top)
A protester being dragged away
by police during the Grosvenor
Square riots, London, 29 June 1966,
photograph by Clive Limpkin

53 (Opposite, bottom)
Harlem Peace March, 1967,
photograph by Builder Levy
V&A: E.286–2009

LIBERTAD PARA ANGELA DAVIS

oclae

$2.00

les Cockettes

9 (right)
Q. And babies? A. And babies'
poster, 1970, photograph
by Ron Haeberle, designed by
Artworkers Coalition
V&A: E.233–1985

50 (below left)
'War Is Hell!' poster, 1968,
issued by Student Mobilization
Committee to End the War
in Vietnam
V&A: E.309–2004

51 (below right)
'Stop Police Brutality and
Entrapment of Homosexuals' poster,
c.1970, designed by Tony DeRosa,
issued by Gay Liberation Front
Center for the Study of
Political Graphics, Los Angeles

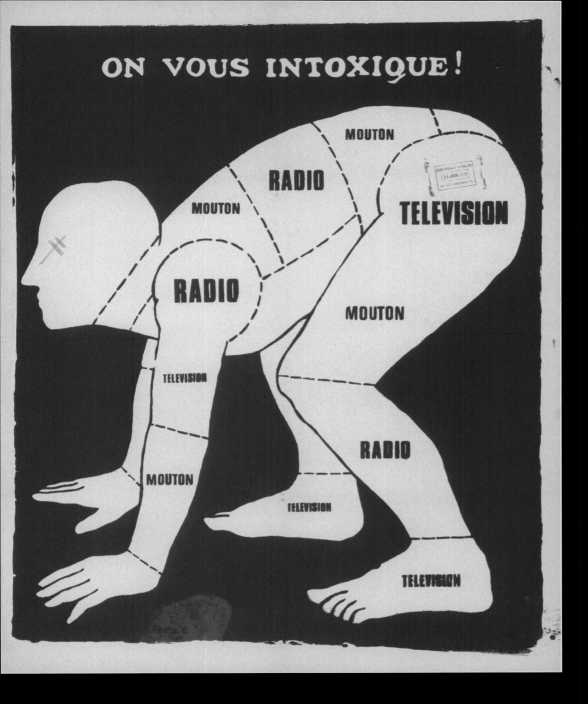

ON VOUS INTOXIQUE!

62 (above)
'*On vous intoxique!*' poster, 1968,
designed by Atelier populaire
V&A: E.1721–2004

63 (right)
De Gaulle/Hitler poster, 1968,
designed by Atelier populaire
V&A: E.1338–2004

64 (far right)
'*Armée ORTF Police*' poster, 1968,
designed by École des Beaux-Arts
V&A: E.1722–2004

Réformes ou Révolution ?

[dense multi-column French newspaper text, including sections:]

D'abord chasser de Gaulle

Au-delà du réformisme

Casser les classes

Le Mouvement

Des militants du Mouvement du 22 Mars.

Je jouis dans les pavés

Comité d'Information Révolutionnaire : J.-L. Brau — P. Loizeau — J.-J. Lebel — H. Hervé — Jean Franklin — G. Fabiani Gérant : F. Esvignaut Dépôt légal : 2º tri 1968.

BARRICADES

LE PAVÉ

TRACT
No 1
MAI 1968
Participation
aux frais
0,50 F
minimum

ROSA LUXEMBOURG.

[Les militants du Mouvement — TROTSKY]

GIRLS SAY YES

to boys who say NO

Proceeds from the sale of this poster go to The Draft Resistance.

56 (above)
Le Pavé pamphlet, 1968,
designed by Jean-Jacques Lebel
V&A: PROV.1634–2015

57 (right)
'GIRLS SAY "YES" to boys
who say "NO"' poster, 1968,
photograph by Jim Marshall
Oakland Museum of California

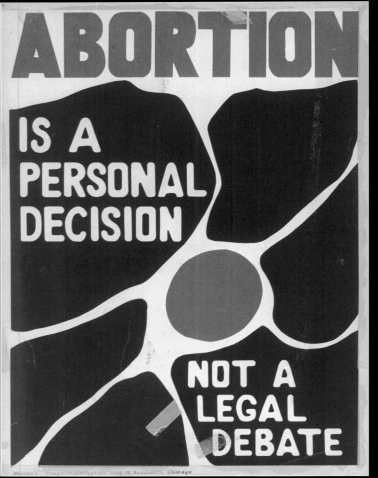

LET US DISCOVER THE LOVE IN EACH OTHER

68 (above)
'Abortion Is a Personal
Decision' poster, c.1970s,
designed by Women's
Graphics Collective
Center for the Study of
Political Graphics, Los Angeles

69 (right)
'Let Us Discover the Love
in Each Other' poster, 1970,
photograph by Dunstan Pereira,
published by Universal Poster Co.
Center for the Study of
Political Graphics, Los Angeles

70 (opposite)
'Poor People's Campaign' poster,
1968, designed by Kofi Bailey
V&A: PROV.1638–2015

POOR PEOPLE'S CAMPAIGN 1968

SCLC

SOUTHERN CHRISTIAN LEADERSHIP CONFERENCE
Martin Luther King Jr., President
334 Auburn Ave., N.W., Atlanta Ga., 30303
Telephone (404) 522-1420

DANGER
KEEP OUT
WATER
CONTAMINATED

EARTH DAY 22 APRIL

RAUSCHENBERG 70

Afro-American solidarity
with the oppressed
People of the world

SOLIDARITY WITH THE AFRICAN
AMERICAN PEOPLE   AVGVST 18, 1968
SOLIDARITE AVEC LE PEUPLE AFRO-AMERICAIN
LE 18 AOUT 1968
SOLIDARIDAD CON EL PUEBLO
AFRO-NORTEAMERICANO 18 DE AGOSTO, 1968

تضامن عالمي مع الشعب الافرو امريكي   ١٨ آب ١٩٦٨

71 (opposite)
'Earth Day 22 April 1970' poster,
1970, designed by Robert
Rauschenberg, published by
American Environment Foundation
V&A: E.3035–1991

72 (above)
'Afro-American Solidarity
with the Oppressed People
of the World' poster, 1969,
designed by Emory Douglas
V&A: E.756–2004

73 (right)
'Solidarity with the African
American People' poster, 1968,
designed by Lazaro Abreu,
illustration by Emory Douglas,
published by OSPAAAL (Organization
of Solidarity of the People of Asia,
Africa and Latin America)
V&A: E.798–2004

4 (below)
f i, 1969,
designed by Corita Kent
V&A: PROV.208–2016

5 (right)
Kathleen Cleaver with
shotgun in her doorway,
photographed by Alan Copeland
for the *Berkeley Barb*, 1968

6 (opposite)
'War Is Good Business' poster, 1969,
designed by Lambert Studios, Inc.
Center for the Study of
Political Graphics, Los Angeles

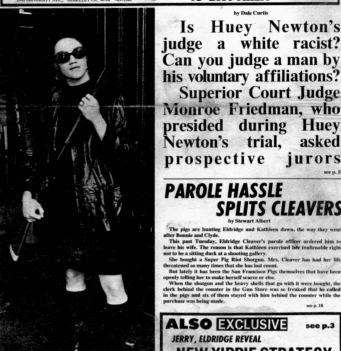

HUEY'S JUDGE-- EXCLUSIVE

RACIST?

story below

Berkeley Barb

VOL. 7 NO. 13 ISSUE 162 (PUB. FRIDAYS) SEPT. 20-26
2042 UNIVERSITY AVE., BERKELEY CA. 94704 849-1040

15¢ BAY AREA   20¢ ELSEWHERE

by Dale Curtis

Is Huey Newton's judge a white racist? Can you judge a man by his voluntary affiliations? Superior Court Judge Monroe Friedman, who presided during Huey Newton's trial, asked prospective jurors

see p. 5

PAROLE HASSLE SPLITS CLEAVERS

by Stewart Albert

The pigs are hunting Eldridge and Kathleen down, the way they went after Bonnie and Clyde.

This past Tuesday, Eldridge Cleaver's parole officer ordered him to leave his wife. The reason is that Kathleen exercised her inalienable right not to be a sitting duck at a shooting gallery.

She bought a Super Pig Riot Shotgun. Mrs. Cleaver has had her life threatened so many times that she has lost count.

But lately it has been the San Francisco Pigs themselves that have been openly telling her to make herself scarce or else.

When the shotgun and the heavy shells that go with it were bought, the clerk behind the counter in the Gun Store was so freaked that he called in the pigs and six of them stayed with him behind the counter while the purchase was being made.

see p. 18

ALSO EXCLUSIVE   see p.3

JERRY, ELDRIDGE REVEAL
NEW YIPPIE STRATEGY

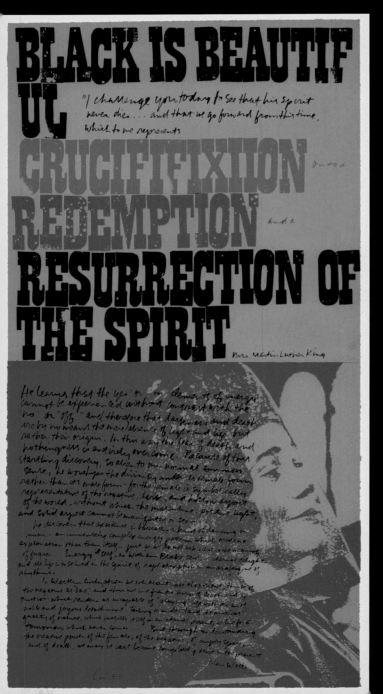

BLACK IS BEAUTIFUL

"I challenge you today to see that his spirit never dies... and that we go forward from this time, which to me represents

CRUCIFIFIXIION

On to a

REDEMPTION

and a

RESURRECTION OF THE SPIRIT

Mrs. Martin Luther King

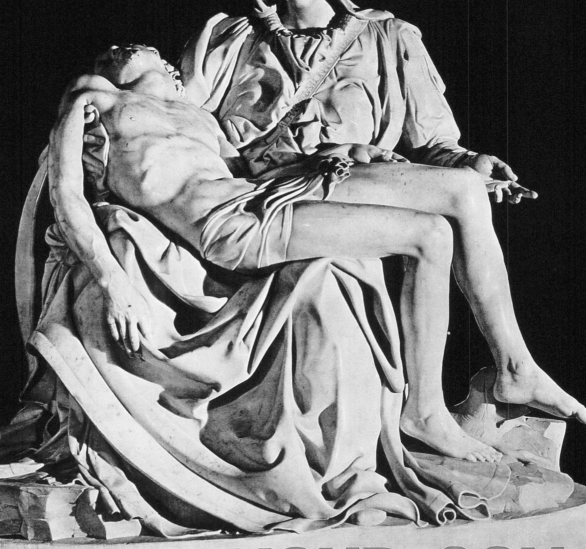

WAR IS GOOD BUSINESS

INVEST YOUR SON

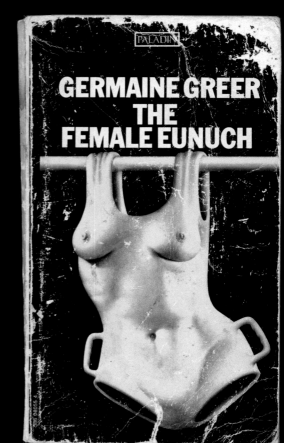

77 (above)
Women Strike for Equality
demonstration, New York,
26 August 1970, photograph
by Michael Abramson

78 (right)
The Female Eunuch by
Germaine Greer, 1970,
cover design by John Holmes

TOWN BLOODY HALL

'But *Town Bloody Hall* is not about the verdict. It is about the agony, the classical struggle; Germaine Greer and Norman Mailer are *both* Tiresias.' James Reich, 2012

On 30 April 1971, New York's Town Hall hosted one of the most remarkable events of the rapidly evolving women's movement. 'A Dialogue on Women's Liberation' took the form of a panel presentation and debate between renowned novelist Norman Mailer and four feminist luminaries: Germaine Greer, author of recently published *The Female Eunuch* (1970); Jacqueline Ceballos, President of the NY chapter of the National Organization of Women; literary critic Diana Trilling; and lesbian spokeswoman Jill Johnston. Documentary filmmaker D.A. Pennebaker captured the fiercely positioned discourse and interventions.

Greer delivers a considered speech on the male artist while Johnston's 'poetical' performance is interrupted by two women who eventually roll around with her on the stage groping her. At one point Mailer, perhaps an unlikely choice for a moderator despite his 'The Prisoner of Sex' having just been published in *Harper's*, shakes his fist at the hecklers in the audience, Susan Sontag and Betty Friedan among them. The chaos is conveyed by the rapid camera pans between the impassioned speakers, the boisterous Mailer and the combative audience. Little appears resolved but *Town Bloody Hall*, which remained unreleased until edited by Pennebaker's partner Chris Hegedus in 1979, remains a remarkable mix of drama, comedy and intellectual debate, capturing in its raw spontaneity the complexities of feminism wrestling to move forward into the 1970s.

79 (above)
Stills from *Town Bloody Hall*,
a film by Chris Hegedus and
D.A. Pennebaker, filmed 1971
and released 1979
Clockwise from top left:
Susan Sontag; Norman Mailer;
Germaine Greer and Mailer; Greer

80 (right)
'An Open Letter to the People of a Dying Planet' poster,
c.1970, Friends of the Earth
Center for the Study of
Political Graphics, Los Angeles

81 (below)
'Uneasy Riders ("We Blew It")'
poster, 1970, designed by
Celestial Arts, published by Orbit
Center for the Study of
Political Graphics, Los Angeles

An open letter to the people of a dying planet.

For years, experts have pleaded with you to conserve your resources.

Ecologists have warned that your fumes and bulldozers and wastes and chemicals have already tipped the balance of nature against you.

And still, the vast majority of you can't, or won't, comprehend.

Don't you realize that most of your food is hazardous to your health? That *you eat* the pesticides they spray on crops, *you eat* the drugs they feed your cattle, *you eat* the chemicals they use to preserve and flavor your food.

Don't you realize that most of your "disposables," such as plastic containers, aluminum cans and wax cartons, are just as dangerous as auto exhaust? (A city incinerator just changes them into poisonous smoke.)

Don't you realize that an entire ocean *can* be polluted? (Navigators actually include great seas of sewage in their charts.)

That nature actually *needs* the millions of animals you slaughter each year for clothing? (Remember, your sealskin coat was once a seal.)

That rampant and unlimited consumption eventually consumes *you?*

On April 22nd, thousands of students will be holding an environmental teach-in at their schools and colleges.

Their purpose is to discuss the ecological facts of death. And suggest alternatives.

Whether you're a student or not, you can still commemorate this day by taking a long look at what you're doing to destroy yourself. At what you wear, what you eat, what you waste and what you put up with.

Only your own living and buying habits will reclaim this planet.

Only your letters and votes will force politicians to place life over lobbies.

Only your buying power will convince industry that a dead planet is bad for business.

Set aside April 22nd as the day you start to save yourself.

There may be no time *but* the present.

Friends of the Earth
30 East 42nd Street
New York, N.Y. 10017

YOU SAY YOU WANT TO CHANGE YOUR HEAD?

THE COUNTER-CULTURE

BARRY MILES

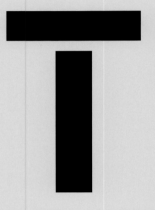he 'underground' was a catch-all sobriquet for a community of like-minded, anti-establishment, anti-war, pro-rock and roll individuals, most of whom had a common interest in recreational drugs. In the Bay Area there was greater interest in drugs, whereas LA was more into the music and dancing. In New York it was an older, more political crowd, and in London it was an uneasy coalition of hedonistic aristocratic black sheep and young people protesting against the entrenched class system and its values.

The American counter-culture can be seen as a reaction to the stultifying boredom of 1950s suburban living. White middle-class people went to church, satisfied that they were the moral guardians of the world in their fight against godless communism (pl.83). Post McCarthy, the US was still rigidly conformist in its morality and social norms, which included celebrating a consumer society that sincerely believed that 'what's good for General Motors is good for the country.'[1] By the turn of the decade, the civil rights movement was challenging endemic racism and political activists began to protest against US support for the brutal dictators in American client states. There was also growing anger over the escalating war in Vietnam: in 1965 the number of US troops there swelled from 23,300 to over 184,000 and that year 1,928 of them were killed. Many young people felt there was something fundamentally wrong with society.

The ideas of the beat generation writers helped fuel the inchoate response to Establishment thinking: Allen Ginsberg, William Burroughs and Gary Snyder emerged as mentors. The counter-culture was inspired by people as diverse as Herbert Marcuse, Timothy Leary, J.D. Salinger, R. Buckminster Fuller, Bob Dylan and the Beatles. They experimented with hallucinogenic drugs and together they evolved a new form of rock and roll. They questioned the sexual morality handed down by the church and state, and proposed many different models – extended sexual families, sex orgies, sex-therapy groups, tolerance and acceptance of homosexuality – but most of all a positive, joyful celebration of sexuality, instead of the uptight morality of their parents' generation. Singer Grace Slick wrote:

> We weren't saddled with the politically correct social/moral restrictions that would later predominate. … We were all friends, and one of the possible activities you could do with a friend was to have sex. We also had cures for all the sexually transmitted diseases of the time.[2]

This new value system was succinctly summed up by Ian Dury a decade later when he sang 'Sex and drugs and rock and roll are very good indeed'.[3]

British youths of the 1960s grew up surrounded by the effects of war in a way that Americans did not. The counter-culture was in part a reaction to a childhood climate of austerity, surrounded by bomb sites; a new, flamboyant personal style was a reaction to the cold, war-hardened, emotionally repressed male embodied by the returning soldier. Young men were almost purposefully effeminate in their satins and frills, in their revealed vulnerability and innocence, despite the Jagger-esque macho swagger, which was more flamenco dancer than apache and became the style of the underground. Jimi Hendrix would never have worn his decorated Spanish hat, crushed yellow velvet trousers, ostrich boa, ruffled silk paisley shirt, hand-painted jacket and cowboy boots had he still been living in New York.

In Britain it was only in the 1960s that most young people had any money. Full employment enabled the growth of British youth culture; young people began catering to their own interests and creating an alternative 'consumer society' based around clothes, music and drugs. The 1944 Education Act, which introduced universal free schooling, meant that most were better educated than their parents and had to look elsewhere for mentors. Increasingly, they turned to the United States, to their rock and roll heroes, to the beat generation writers, to avant-garde jazz and modern artists, and reinterpreted them in their native context.

The underground first emerged in Britain when elements of this new youth

culture were brought together with drug-taking art students and activists from the Campaign for Nuclear Disarmament (CND, founded in 1958). The Aldermaston-to-London CND march, held each Easter from 1959 to 1963, mobilized young people (pls 84, 85). For many it was the first time they had been to London or even left their small towns. They stayed in church halls and bowling alleys, slept under tables in pubs; they encountered like-minded peers from across the country, discussed political ideas, met loud-mouthed Scottish anarchists, Trotskyists and pacifist priests; they danced the Chelsea Hop to the Alberts and other traditional New Orleans-style bands; they met their first boyfriends and girlfriends – many relationships began 'on the march' – and lost their virginity; they tried marijuana for the first time. It was a four-day festival. They were different people when they returned home, bringing with them the burgeoning ideas of the counter-culture. But most of all it was the recreational use of drugs that

overwhelmingly set young people apart from their parents' generation, and from the authorities.

In the US the counter-culture was a broad church from its inception, spanning the political spectrum: from the all-American libertarianism of Ken Kesey and the Merry Pranksters to the left-leaning, anti-war pacifism of Allen Ginsberg, from the contemplative exclusivity of Timothy Leary's Millbrook commune to the competitive Acid Tests in San Francisco. Left and right wing came into open conflict on 16 October 1965, which could be a convenient day to mark the start of the US counter-culture: after an irreconcilable political argument, many of the participants attended the first of the big psychedelic dances that were to characterize the San Francisco scene.

That was the second day of the Berkeley Vietnam Day Committee's mass rallies, the first of the International Days of Protest organized by the New Left, or 'The Movement', at cities all across the country, and worldwide. Folk-singers

83 (previous page)
US patriots marching against
anti-Vietnam War demonstrations,
1970, photograph by Mary Ellen Mark
V&A: E.124–2003

84 (left)
CND March from Aldermaston to
London, early 1960s, photograph
by John 'Hoppy' Hopkins

85 (below left)
CND supporters from Aldermaston
join a Ban the Bomb march, 1963

86 (Below right)
The Jimi Hendrix Experience
(left to right: Mitch Mitchell,
Jimi Hendrix, Noel Redding), 1969

and anti-war activists including Lawrence Ferlinghetti and Allen Ginsberg addressed the crowd. In the afternoon, novelist and ex-wrestler Ken Kesey arrived with his major-domo Ken Babbs, an ex-marine who had flown helicopters in Vietnam, and his Merry Pranksters, who had painted their famous school bus bright red along with swastikas, American Eagles and other nationalist symbols. Kesey spoke out, telling the crowd of 15,000, 'You want to know how to stop the war? Just turn your backs on it, fuck it!' and walked off. Kesey was the promoter of the early Acid Tests that had made LSD so much more a part of San Francisco's underground scene than any other city's (pl.88). As Martin A. Lee described it, 'Kesey represented those elements of the hip scene that emphasized personal liberation without any strategic concern whatsoever; the task of remodeling themselves took precedence over changing institutions or government policy.'[4] The Pranksters meant it when they waved American flags.

On the evening of 16 October a different side of the counter-culture manifested itself in San Francisco. Luria Castell, Chet Helms and the original Family Dog group put on an event, named A Tribute to Dr Strange (after the comic-book character), at the Longshoremen's Hall (pl.87). An audience of several thousand people, including many from the Berkeley demonstration, wore what came to be seen as 'hippy' attire: vintage granny dresses, cowboy hats and boots, and American Indian-inspired beads and headbands, embossed leather accessories, embroidered jeans, fringes and feathers. There was no difference between how they looked and how the bands looked. It was one community, high on pot and dancing.

This discontinuity between the different branches of the US underground scene had manifested earlier, in 1964, when the Pranksters, driven by Neal Cassady, took their bus to New York to see the World's Fair. They decided to

visit Timothy Leary at his Castalia Foundation in Millbrook, upstate New York, housed in a 64-room mansion owned by the millionaire Billy Hitchcock. They arrived unexpectedly just as the residents were finishing a 72-hour high-dosage acid trip. Like Leary, most were professors, PhD holders or spiritual seekers of one form or another. The contrast could not have been greater, therefore, when, as they slowly came down from their trip and wrote up their notes, an enormous cloud of green smoke rolled up the driveway, out of which drove the psychedelic painted bus (pl.89), the Pranksters throwing smoke bombs from the roof, rock and roll blasting from their speakers and everyone shouting, waving flags and jumping around. Harvard psychologist Dr Richard Alpert (later Ram Dass) told Leary, 'I feel like we're a pastoral Indian village invaded by a whooping cowboy band of Wild West saloon carousers.'[5] Leary met Kesey briefly, then retired to his room, his contemplative trip ruined.[6] Kesey always said 'You are either on the bus or off the bus.' Leary was off the bus, though they later became allies, if not friends.

In Britain, you could date the emergence of the underground to 11 June 1965, the day of the International Poetry Incarnation at the Royal Albert Hall in London, when 7,000 people heard Allen Ginsberg, Lawrence Ferlinghetti, Gregory Corso, Adrian Mitchell and many others deliver an evening of poetry. The audience looked at each other and realized they were a community.

From that meeting underground papers were born, as were numerous art galleries, boutiques, friendships and relationships. The beat generation poets were a catalyst on both occasions (pl.90).

In both Britain and the US, the underground scene quickly grew big enough to develop its own alternative press; new schools of cartoon comic art, poster design and illustration; and, most of all, rock music. The press came first, and was responsible for spreading the ideas that made the counter-culture.

Art Kunkin's *Los Angeles Free Press* (*LAFP*) led the charge in the US in July 1964, published as a vehicle for his left-leaning and anti-Vietnam War news coverage, which was followed by Max Sherr's *Berkeley Barb* in August 1965, doing the same thing in the Bay Area (pl.91). New York's *East Village Other* (*EVO*) was started by Walter Bowart in October that year as an alternative to the (West) *Village Voice* when the *Voice* was on strike. *EVO* was highly graphic, utilizing Dada-esque collages and crazy headlines; also anti-war, it spoke openly about sex and was a strong supporter of Timothy Leary. Seventeen-year-old Harvey Ovshinsky started the *Fifth Estate* in Detroit in November 1965 after spending the summer working at the *LAFP*.

By 1966 the trickle of papers had become a flood: *The Illustrated Paper* in Mendocino, California; *The Rag* in Austin, Texas; *The San Diego Door*; *The Utah Free Press* from Salt Lake City. *The Oracle of the City of San Francisco* was devoted largely to essays on mind-expansion through drugs or spiritual means. Its use of rainbow-coloured inks to achieve a visual approximation of psychedelic vision was enormously influential and rainbow printing appeared everywhere from *EVO* to the *Barb*. By the end of the decade there were over 100 underground papers published worldwide.

In Britain, *International Times* (*IT*) launched in October 1966 with a party at London's Roundhouse, a disused railway engine repair shed. Pink Floyd and Soft Machine provided the music. *IT* (pl.92) was followed in 1967 by the London incarnation of *OZ* (pl.93), after which came *Friends* and *Ink*.

These papers were available through street-sellers, 'head shops', hippy boutiques and a new crop of independent bookshops. City Lights Bookstore was a landmark in San Francisco; there was Moe's in Berkeley; the Peace Eye, the Eighth Street Bookshop, St Marks Bookshop and East Side Books in New York. Indica Books and later Compendium appeared in London; and Shakespeare & Co., named after Sylvia Beach's famous bookshop, in Paris – to name only the major ones.

Underground comics were a direct reaction by a hip new generation of artists raised on the sanitized pap of their youth: *Batman*, *Superman*, *Archie*, *Veronica* and *Little Lulu*. A closely observed depiction of everyday hippy life and attitudes worthy of Gillray or Hogarth can be found in Robert Crumb's characters Mr Natural, Fritz the Cat (pl.94), Angelfood McSpade, the Snoid and Honey Bunch Kaminski, as well as his strips including 'Keep On Truckin', which appeared in *Snatch* and *Zap Comix*. S. Clay Wilson's Star-eyed Stella, Captain Pissgums and His Pervert Pirates, Ruby the

The International Times

October 14-27/1s.

EDITORIAL

YOU

EVERY day people pour into London to find out what is happening there. They have been told attractive stories — young, swinging, on the move, etc. — and they're keen for a taste. Frequently they are disappointed.

True, London is a comparatively free and happy city. But it isn't quite as switched-on as our ad-men make out. Things are happening all over the city, but there is a lack of togetherness: if you're on the jazz scene it's unlikely you'll be much in touch with what's going on in the art world, and vice versa. And, whatever scene you're on, with the possible exception of the pop music explosion, you're likely to discover that things aren't happening quite as they should.

Most of the "creative" people in the city— including everyone from paunchy, old artists to vague, smiling acid heads — seem agreed on the need for a change, a social change, a change in the **quality** of living. But no-one seems to be doing much about it.

A standard London process seems to be: things have to change . . . let's shake up this city . . . we'll start an avant garde theatre (or bookshop, or gallery, or political group, or newspaper, and so on) . . . but first we need bread . . . try the Arts Council . . . try and find a backer . . . set up a charity, maybe. A year later, if he's lucky, the change-maker has his particular Round House. Now he has to spend maybe another year in getting over all the legal hang-ups before he can use it.

CONTINUED ON PAGE 8. COLUMN 4

WHO US? WHAT US? WHY US?

Charles Marowitz on Vietnam at the Aldwych

THE real test of any play about Vietnam must be an ideological one. Before we ask how well it is done, we have to concern ourselves with where it stands, and what it sets out to say. The Royal Shakespeare Company's production of **US**, ideologically speaking, cancels itself out. It says—in word and effect—Vietnam is a nightmare of contradictions; we can never disentangle all its threads. It goes on to say—illogically—we must come to terms with its complications because the responsibility is ours, and in a contemporary power-struggle, there is no such thing as a non-combatant. If the double-entendre of the title means anything, it means the Vietnam War, which is to say organised and accidental mass murder, systematic torture, brazen deceit and chronic duplicity is **us**, rebounds on **us**, is answerable to **us**.

In short, the play tells us nothing that is not already being said day in and day out on news broadcasts, in films, TV and the press. It does not presume to press home a personal viewpoint, although even the fairest assemblage of facts cannot help but indict American Far East policy. It thunders its righteous indignation, but never wells up into a genuine protest because it takes refuge in the very disorder and contradiction it has been made to indict.

The evening is a long one. The first act lasts two hours and is crammed with sloppy, demonstrational acting and familiar extracts from Vietnam folklore, ancient and modern. The poverty of imagination and the gaucheness of execution in the play's first two hours is staggering when one considers (1) the director is Peter Brook; (2) rehearsals were in progress for over four months; (3) the company had the services of Jerry Grotowski from Poland and Joseph Chaikin from New York. Like the **Marat/Sade**, units of the play open and close like a series of fluttering umbrellas, but unlike the **Marat/Sade**, there is no style or thrust to any of these sections.

At times, the company looks like a ragged collection of ex-Unity Theatre regulars vainly trying to recapture the glory of the old Living Newspaper days; at other times, like summer-stock troupers trying to make zeal and sincerity substitutes for skill and expertise.

The first act ends with actors, their heads wrapped in supermarket bags, grunting and groaning in some kind of torturous symbol of the maimed and wounded, stumbling into the audience and flailing their way towards the exits. To call this pathetic audience intrusion a "happening" or anything like, only further debases a word which has already been raped into meaninglessness.

I assume the use of television monitors around the theatre was intended to provide other layers of meaning, but they blink and hum like unassimilated accoutrements and never re-enforce or counterpoint the main action to any good purpose.

* * *

The second act improves in one sense, because it stops trying so hard, but deteriorates in another, because the argument dwindles into a kind of romantic liberalism. Finally accepting the fact that it is not a revolutionary Happening but a rather old-fashioned dramatised documentary, it proceeds to concentrate on the spoken word, and on depicting social attitudes to the war.

The entire show is wedged into the framework of one of Adrian Mitchell's better poems about Vietnam, and to its credit, the production never sounds quite so natural and un-strained as when it stops circumlocuting imaginary theatrical heights, and returns to Mitchell's simple and direct verse-structure.

Glenda Jackson, wisely balancing casualness and fervour, gives a vivid rendition of the bourgeois argument against Vietnam sacrifice and then launches an unsparing attack on those of us who derive obscene satisfaction from the fact that human desecration is taking place thousands of miles away and

A scene from Royal Shakespeare Co. production of US. Photo:)Nina Raginsky.

CONT. BACK PAGE, COLUMN 1

92 (opposite)
International Times,
14–27 October
Editor: Tom McGrath
V&A: NAL

93 (below)
OZ no. 33, 1971
Editor: Richard Neville, cover
designed by Norman Lindsay
V&A: NAL

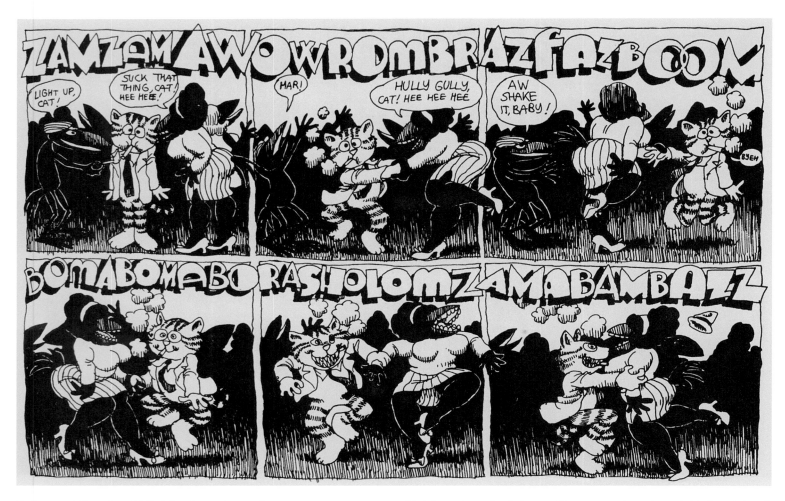

Dyke, and the Hog-Ridin' Fools motorcycle gang were an important influence on Crumb and, later, on Art Spiegelman. All three artists published work in the *East Village Other*. Trashman by Spain Rodriguez, also featured in *EVO*, was one of the few underground superheroes, matched only by Gilbert Sheldon's Wonder Wart-Hog, a parody of *Superman*. Sheldon's best-loved characters appeared in 'The Fabulous Furry Freak Brothers', which followed the lives of three stoned dopers and Fat Freddy's cat.

Whereas Harvey, National, Marvel and DC Comics had national distribution, the themes of sex, drug-taking and stoned humour in the publications of Kitchen Sink Press, Last Gasp, Rip Off Press, Print Mint and Apex Novelties meant that they were usually only available from local head shops. Even so, they sold in the tens of thousands, spreading counter-cultural ideas unexplored in the 'straight' press.

A new golden age of poster design originated with US artists such as Victor Moscoso, who introduced photo-collage into his psychedelic posters designed for the Family Dog and Matrix Club; comic-style work by Rick Griffin; Wes Wilson, who designed the blobby all-caps font common to many 1960s posters; Stanley Mouse and Alton Kelley, famous for their work with the Grateful Dead, including the 'skeleton and roses' poster. A separate British school was pioneered by Michael English and Nigel Waymouth, working as Hapshash and the Coloured Coat, responsible for the UFO

Club's series of rainbow-silkscreened posters (pl.95); Michael McInnerney; and Australian Martin Sharp, best known for his 'exploding' Jimi Hendrix poster.

Traditionally, posters set out their information in as clear a form possible; the so-called 'boxing poster' style. On psychedelic posters, however, ease of communication was sacrificed for a visual representation of the experience of the rock concert itself, with its meandering guitar solos and mind-blowing light-shows, as seen while on an acid trip. To know what was on the bill at a Family Dog concert, you had to be able to read melting, amoeba-like lettering, or dazzling op-art graphics, inspired by Aubrey Beardsley, Alphonse Mucha, Edmund Joseph Sullivan, Bridget Riley or Josef Albers.

The counter-culture transformed graphic design; not just in posters but in the casual layouts of the underground press – unjustified margins, collages – which were soon copied by the straight press, such as the (London) *Observer*. But nowhere was the effect on design more evident than in album sleeves, which the record companies wanted to use to attract buyers from the new underground scene. Robert Crumb's sleeve for Big Brother & the Holding Company's *Cheap Thrills* (1968) made both him and the band famous. Peter Blake and Jann Haworth's breakthrough collage design for *Sgt. Pepper's Lonely Hearts Club Band* (1967) by the Beatles became arguably the most famous and most

parodied sleeve of all time. EMI had never paid more than £50 for artwork before and demanded that the group pay its £1,800 cost if the album sold less than 100,000 copies. The Rolling Stones followed later the same year with *Their Satanic Majesties Request*, also photographed by Michael Cooper, this time in 3-D; another first. There were influential sleeves by psychedelic poster designers such as Stanley Mouse, who did the Grateful Dead's eponymous debut album (1967), and Michael McInnerney, who designed the sleeve for *Tommy* by the Who (1969). Andy Warhol's sleeve for the Velvet Underground's first album, *The Velvet Underground and Nico* (1967), with its peel-off banana-skin sticker, was revolutionary, as was its black-on-black follow up, *White Light/White Heat*, in 1968.

In New York the extremes of hot and cold were less conducive to hippie life than balmy California; and New York was a hard city then. Though New York was the home of the first head shop – the Psychedelicatessen on Avenue A at Tompkins Square – the true New York underground scene centred around Andy Warhol and his multimedia Exploding Plastic Inevitable, the Velvet Underground, the films and the whip dancing. The Warhol Factory people all wore black and their drug of choice was speed, and later heroin, not acid. The Velvets did not go down well in California (pl.96).

Bands were the counter-culture's greatest artistic contribution. During the 1960s they transformed rock and roll from a branch of the entertainment industry into an art form. Bob Dylan, the Velvet Underground, the Beatles and the Rolling Stones challenged popular music stereotypes with their arrangements and instrumentation, and introduced lyrics that dealt directly with the lives of their audiences. Housewives on tranquilizers: 'Mother's Little Helper' by the Rolling Stones; teenage angst: 'She's Leaving Home' by the Beatles; loneliness: 'Eleanor Rigby' by the Beatles; transvestism: 'Lola' by the Kinks; police brutality:

'For What It's Worth' by Stephen Stills; even personal grooming: 'Almost Cut My Hair' by David Crosby. Rock lyrics became the main way that the new ideas were spread. Every word on a new Dylan album was analysed in case he had slipped the secret of the universe in between verses; Beatles records were even played backwards by those looking for a secret message.

Musicians listened intently to each other's work, with certain records becoming tremendously influential. Dylan's 'Like a Rolling Stone', released in July 1965, was the first of these groundbreaking singles. Paul McCartney's reaction was typical: 'It seemed to go on and on forever. It was just beautiful ... He showed all of us that it was possible to go a little further';[7] whereas it made Frank Zappa want to quit the record business: 'If this wins and it does what it's supposed to do, I don't need to do anything else ... But it didn't do anything. It sold but nobody responded to it in the way that they should have.'[8] Another influential song was the Beach Boys' 'Good Vibrations' from October 1966, rumoured to have been constructed by Brian Wilson from 15 separate takes. This was the beginning of the studio being used as an instrument.

It was a widespread movement: Los Angeles provided the first counter-culture bands, with the Byrds, the Doors, Love, mid-period Beach Boys, Captain Beefheart, Iron Butterfly, Spirit, the United States of America, the West Coast Pop Art Experimental Band, and, most importantly, the Mothers of Invention, whose leader Zappa saw them as an agent of political change. In the sleeve notes to their first album, *Freak Out!*, released in 1966, he wrote:

Drop out of school before your mind rots from exposure to our mediocre educational system. Forget about the Senior Prom and go to the library and EDUCATE YOURSELF if you've got any guts. Some of you like PEP

RALLIES and plastic robots who tell you what to read. Forget I mentioned it. ... Rise for the flag salute.

The main San Francisco bands were Jefferson Airplane, the Grateful Dead, the Charlatans, Big Brother & the Holding Company with Janis Joplin on vocals, Country Joe & the Fish, Quicksilver Messenger Service and Moby Grape. They all played endless community benefits and were closer to their audience than rock groups in most cities. In San Francisco the bands epitomized the drug counter-culture. New York's bands were equally underground but less psychedelic: Pearls Before Swine, the Fugs, the Blues Magoos, the Blues Project and Vanilla Fudge. Texas supplied the 13th Floor Elevators and the Red Crayola; Michigan the Amboy Dukes. There was a major counter-cultural scene in Detroit centring around MC5 and their manager, John Sinclair, who was the founding member of the anti-racist, socialist, White Panther Party. His 10-year sentence for possession of marijuana in 1969 led to widespread protests that it was a politically inspired punishment. He was freed in December 1971.

Certain venues became associated with the movement, of which Bill Graham's Fillmore West in San Francisco (later followed by the Fillmore East in New York) was the biggest, featuring all the local bands – the Grateful Dead, Jefferson Airplane and Quicksilver Messenger Service – on a regular basis. The Family Dog's 'Tribal Stomps' at the Avalon Ballroom in San Francisco were more communal and more central to the movement, featuring the same bands, only as dances. The Whisky and the Troubadour in LA were more commercial and became the centre of the rock and roll groupie scene, initially seen as a positive proclamation of women's sexuality. These clubs were home to the Mothers of Invention, the Byrds, Love and the Doors, all part of the growing Laurel Canyon scene, memorialized by the singer-songwriter movement of the early 1970s.

The UFO Club, held in an Irish dancehall on London's Tottenham Court Road, was Britain's first underground club, held on Friday nights through until the buses started running again on Saturday mornings: 'the same length of time as an acid trip', as its proprietor, John Hopkins, once remarked. The club's house bands were Pink Floyd, Soft Machine and Arthur Brown. UFO became so popular that it was obliged to move to the much larger Roundhouse, in Camden Town. That venue became so closely identified with the counter-culture that during one drugs raid on a musician's house the police informed him, 'We intend to stamp out the Roundhouse and everything it stands for.'[9]

In Britain, virtually all the major bands were associated in some way with the counter-culture: Pink Floyd, Soft Machine, Cream, the Yardbirds, the Who (whose message to the older generation on their first single was 'Why don't you all f-f-f—fade away ... '[10]), the Pretty Things, Donovan, Procol Harum, the Incredible String Band, the Moody Blues and the Jimi Hendrix Experience. In London, the defining cultural event of the movement was the 14-Hour Technicolor Dream, an all-night benefit for the *International Times* held at Alexandra Palace on 29 April 1967, a mixed bill of 42 acts featuring poets, dance troupes, jugglers, dozens of rock musicians – Pete Townshend, Arthur Brown, Denny Laine, the Pretty Things, the Move – comedian Dick Gregory and Yoko Ono (pl.97). There was a helter-skelter and a fortune-telling tent. John Lennon, on a trip, had forgotten all about it and only realized when he saw it on the nine o'clock BBC evening news. He summoned his chauffeur and was driven in to London from his mansion in the stockbroker belt to attend. Pink Floyd, with lead guitarist Syd Barrett high on acid, played as dawn illuminated the huge rose window of the Great Hall at 5am, then everyone streamed outside to play in the park.

alexis korner
alex harvey
creation
charlie brown's
clowns
champion jack
dupree
denny laine
gary farr
graham bond
ginger johnson
jacob's ladder
construction co.
move
one one seven
pink floyd
poetry band
purple gang
pretty things
pete townshend
poison bellows
soft.machine
·sun trolley
social deviants
stalkers
the utterly incredibl¹
too long ago
to remember
sometimes shouting
at people
marc sullivan
martin doughty
maureen pape
john pape
mike stocks
noel murphy
dave russell
christopher logue
barry fantoni
ron geeson
john fahey
mike horowitz
alex trocchi
mike kenshall
yoko ono
binder edwards
& vaughan
26 kingly street
the flies
robert randell

international times
free speech benefit
alexandra palace N.22
8pm saturday
29 april » sun 30
tickets £1
in advance » only

indica better books colletts
dobells dave curtis 57 greek
st w.1 ger 1548 and main
it distributors
or your local agent
bus shuttle from wood green ⊖
highgate ⊖ 8:12pm

14
HOUR
TECHNICOLOR DREAM

TOM WILKES ©

JUNE 16·17·18

MONTEREY INTERNATIONAL POP FESTIVAL

TICKET OUTLETS: SAN FRANCISCO—DOWNTOWN CENTRE BOX OFFICE, 325 MASON ST./LOS ANGELES—ALL MUTUAL AGENCIES & WALLICH'S MUSIC CITY STORES • SPONSORED BY 'THE FOUNDATION', A NON-PROFIT ORGANIZATION.

Music was the main vehicle for the dissemination of counter-cultural ideas and it reached a considerably wider audience after the Monterey International Pop Festival, held 16–18 June 1967, just south of San Francisco, drawing A&R men from all the big record labels (pl.98). It was the scene of many firsts: the first time Janis Joplin sang outside the Bay Area; the Who's first West Coast appearance; the first predominantly white audience for Otis Redding and the American debut of the Jimi Hendrix Experience. Augustus Stanley Owsley III made a special batch of acid he called 'Monterey Purple'. Dennis Hopper wrote: 'The vibe was beautiful. The music was fantastic. To me, that was the purest, most beautiful moment of the whole '60s trip. It seemed like everything had come to that moment. And if that could have continued, it really *would* have been Camelot.'[11]

There were several other era-defining events in the US that year. One of the earliest was the Human Be-In, held in San Francisco's Golden Gate Park on the afternoon of 14 January 1967 (pl.99). Billed as 'A Gathering of the Tribes … a joyful Pow Wow and Peace Dance to be celebrated with leaders, guides and heroes of our generation,' these turned out to be Timothy Leary, Richard Alpert, Allen Ginsberg (and his on-off girlfriend Maretta Greer), Gary Snyder, Michael McClure and Lenore Kandel, aided and serenaded by Big Brother & the Holding Company, Quicksilver Messenger Service and the Grateful Dead. Crowds were fed by radical 'happening' organizers the Diggers, who persuaded local poultrymen to give them free turkeys and obtained fruit and vegetables from the market when it closed. 'Security' was provided by the Hell's Angels. The event was declared open by Snyder honking on a conch shell and closed by Ginsberg chanting a Hindu mantra. It was a prelude to San Francisco's 'Summer of Love'.

Woodstock remains the best-known of these gatherings, 'An Aquarian Exposition in White Lake, NY: 3 Days of Peace & Music' held two-and-a-half years later, on 15–18 August 1969. There, 32 acts performed to an audience of 400,000 people in upstate New York. Jimi Hendrix played 'The Star-Spangled Banner' at dawn, just as people were leaving. It was the last great expression of the 'Aquarian Age' of the movement and had no 'security' at all.

Despite the self-promotion of protest figures such as Abbie Hoffman and Jerry Rubin, the revolutionary rhetoric of the underground finally saw action not in New York but in Paris. In May 1968, a series of demonstrations by students at the Sorbonne led ultimately to a two-week general strike by 10 million workers and the occupation of universities and factories across France. Actions were characterized by their spontaneous, wildcat nature. Slogans including 'Be realistic: demand the impossible!' and 'Beneath the paving stones: the beach!' issued a clarion call for a better quality of life, a restructuring of society, self-management and the decentralization of power.

How magnificent it felt to take off our helmets and climb up to the roof of the Odéon in a city occupied by the children of revolution, exhausted after days and nights of street fighting and organizing, to watch the fury and smell the fire of our actions and listen to the cocktails and grenades explode on their targets and then crash, sleep and awaken kissing, sucking, fucking known or unknown comrades before going back to the other great dance in the streets. No more separations nor limits, total satisfaction of all our desires, utopia come true in real life.[12]

Jean-Jacques Lebel's description of the occupation of Paris's grand theatre captures the spirit of May 1968 when, for a few brief weeks, France once again celebrated the revolutionary spirit. The uprising is now considered to be a turning-point in the post-war history of France.

The American counter-culture was filled with strident alpha-males – Emmett Grogan, Abbie Hoffman, Jerry Rubin, Bill Graham, Timothy Leary, Richard Alpert, Allen Ginsberg, Gary Snyder, Neal Cassady, Ken Kesey, the list is enormous – whereas in Britain, where the scene was considerably smaller, organizers preferred a low profile. John Hopkins, who co-founded the *International Times* with the author of this essay, always handed over any project that he thought someone else could spend more time on or do better. Mick Farren, singer with the Social Deviants, emerged briefly as the leader of the British arm of the White Panthers and had a certain following. The best 'leader, guide and hero' in Britain was Caroline Coon, who, together with fellow artist Rufus Harris, started Release, a volunteer-run, free legal advice service for hippies who had been busted and needed help. It was to Release that George Harrison turned when

his house was raided vindictively by the drugs squad on Paul McCartney's wedding day.

San Francisco had its equivalent in HALO (Haight-Ashbury Legal Organization), which provided legal services for those up on drug-related charges; there was also the HIP Job Co-op with over 6,000 names on its part-time employment roster; Huckleberry's was a home for runaways and, importantly, there was the Free Clinic, providing an essential service in a country with no free health care. The Diggers, named after the seventeenth-century English communards, were started in San Francisco by Emmett Grogan. Working out of a storefront, they handed out food and offered shelter and transportation to hippies at no charge. Branches appeared in Los Angeles and Boston. A man called Galahad ran a notorious crash-pad in the Lower East Side in New York where he and his team worked hard at reuniting runaways with their parents (a major issue on the scene).

The connection to politics was often playful. Abbie Hoffman famously threw handfuls of dollar bills from the viewing balcony of the New York Stock Exchange in August

99 (opposite)
Timothy Leary and Allen
Ginsberg at the Human Be-In,
San Francisco, 14 January 1967,
photograph by Jim Marshall

1967 and watched while traders left their posts to scramble for the money. The Youth International Party (Yippie), co-founded by Hoffman in December that year, used street theatre to get across its anarchic point of view. In the 1968 presidential race ultimately won by Richard Nixon, Yippie ran a pig called 'Pigasus the Immortal' for president; Louis Abolafia, who came up with the slogan 'Make Love, Not War!', also ran, under the Nudist Party ticket as the naked candidate: 'What have I got to hide?'! In London, Amanda Feilding ran as the 'Trepanation for the National Health' candidate for Chelsea with the slogan 'Get ahead, get a hole!' and got 139 votes. She had a hole herself and claimed it made her permanently high, the operation memorably filmed in *Heartbeat in the Brain*.

As the counter-culture movement grew, opposition to its ideas mounted: in Britain from the entrenched Establishment, particularly from the police, and in the US as a result of street and university campus anti-Vietnam War demonstrations which led, by the end of the decade, to a societal divide in which it seemed as if all young people were the enemy. This culminated in the Kent State massacre, when on 4 May 1970 the Ohio National Guard fired 67 rounds at unarmed students demonstrating on campus against the US invasion of Cambodia. Four students were killed, two of whom were merely walking to class, and nine wounded. Over 450 colleges and schools were closed in protest at the murders, with over four million young people on student strike. Ten days later, two students were killed by police at Jackson State University in similar circumstances. Eventually the tide of public opinion turned and Henry Kissinger, who negotiated the US army's withdrawal, had to acknowledge the role of the peace movement in ending the Vietnam War.

The counter-culture produced a shopping mall full of ideas and philosophies, challenges and insights. Some of these offerings led to greater equality for all and greater respect for the planet, but at least one led to Charlie Manson. Its greatest legacy was a decade of exceptional musical experiment, but it also changed society for the better. The counter-culture fostered the gay liberation movement (Stonewall in 1969 released a tidal wave of activism); the ecology movement grew from the late-1960s commune movement and return to the land; 'widening the field of consciousness', as Allen Ginsberg put it, brought changes in attitude toward marijuana. It brought us rock festivals, New Age philosophies and religions, organic food, Burning Man and alternative information sources. The 1960s challenged puritan sexual attitudes and promoted free love. Female sexuality was celebrated, although the feminism that followed in the early 1970s was largely a reaction to the scene, which had retained the patriarchal attitudes of previous generations: the women cooked and cleaned while the men talked. As Robert Crumb described it: 'Free love meant free sex and food for men. Sure, women enjoyed it too, and had a lot of sex, but then they served men.'[13]

The legacy of the underground press lives on in WikiLeaks; there is now international concern about global warming; LGBT rights are being recognized; yoga and organic food have entered everyday life, and many members of those bands from the 1960s are still touring. But most critical of all, the counter-culture brought a healthy distrust of the Establishment that continues to this day. **BM**

100 (opposite)
Contact sheet for the cover of
Pink Floyd's *UmmaGumma*, 1969,
designed by Hipgnosis (Aubrey
Powell and Storm Thorgerson)

101 (below)
Tantric Lovers, pull-out poster
cover for *OZ* no.4, 1967, designed by
Hapshash and the Coloured Coat
(Michael English and Nigel Waymouth)
V&A: S.35–1978

102 (right)
Their Satanic Majesties Request,
lenticular transforming print for the
Rolling Stones album cover, 1967,
photograph by Michael Cooper
V&A: S.468–1984

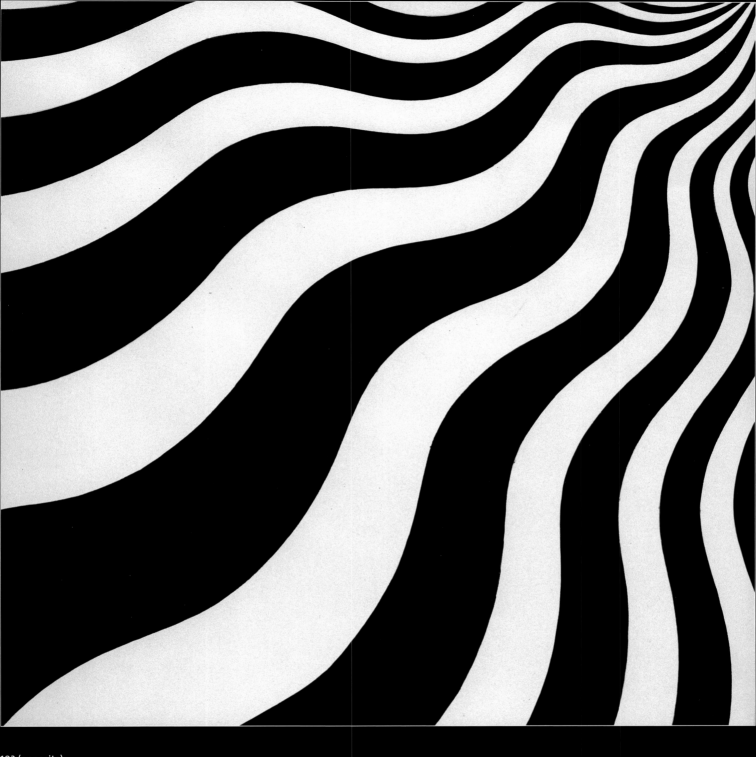

103 (opposite)
Bash Street School Magazine,
no. 1: 'New Tremors Are Running
Through the Atmosphere:
All We Need Is the Courage
to Face Them', 1969,
designed by Ron Hunt
V&A: PROV.9580–2016

104 (above)

105 (top left)
Play Power by Richard Neville, 1970,
cover design by Martin Sharp

106 (left and above)
Nasty Tales comic book,
cover and inside page, 1971
V&A, NAL

109 (opposite)
Headopoly game poster, 1970,
designed by Martin Sharp
V&A: PROV.1533–2015

110 (below)
Zodiac-Terré' poster, 1968,
designed by Nathan Terré
V&A: PROV.992–2014

111 (right)
The Politics of Experience,
1970, Jim Leon
pen and ink and watercolour
V&A: PROV.1809–2015

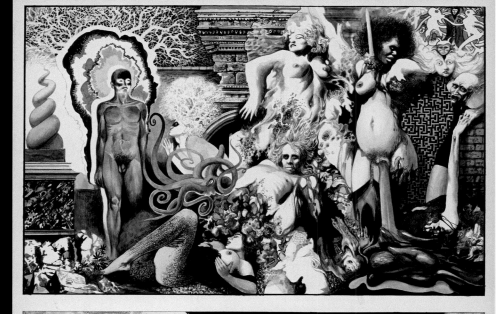

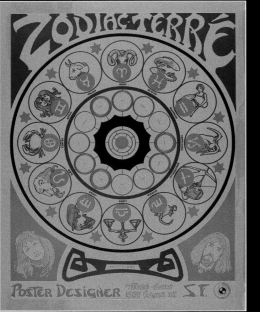

114 (above)
The Rolling Stones line up outside
the Tin Pan Alley Club in London,
1963: (left to right) Mick Jagger,
Keith Richards, Bill Wyman,
Brian Jones and Charlie Watts,
photograph by Terry O'Neill

115 (opposite)
Poster for two shows at
the Roundhouse UFO, 1967,
designed by Martin Sharp,
published by Osiris
V&A: E.1718–1991

116 (opposite)
Advertisement for Middle
Earth Clothing, 1967–70,
designed by Nathan Terré
V&A: PROV.994–2014

117 (above)
Lapel badges, 1960s
V&A, purchased through
the Julie and Robert
Breckman Print Fund

FRANK ZAPPA

118 (opposite)
'Zappa on the Toilet' poster,
1967, designed by Danny Harperin
for Osiris Visions, London,
photograph by Bobby Davidson

119 (above)
Poster for the Human Be-In,
1967, designed by Michael
Bowen, photograph by
Casey Sonnabend

©1967 EAST TOTEM WEST, 159 Throckmorton Ave., Mill Valley, California 94941   LISTEN SLEEP DREAM   Artist SÄTTY   Printed by Orbit Graphic Arts

120 (left)
'Listen Sleep Dream' poster
1967, designed by Sätty
(Wilfried Podriech)
V&A: E.3808–2004

121 (opposite)
'Legalise Cannabis:
The Putting Together
of the Heads' poster,
1967, designed by
Martin Sharp
V&A: E.8–1968

YOU SAY YOU'RE EXPERIENCED?

4

ALL TOGETHER NOW?

JON SAVAGE

t begins with a two-chord fanfare of unparalleled brutality: an aggressively sexual pelvic thrust. The riff comes in, underscored by massive drum beats: this is full-blown rock, the métier of the three-piece band that was just beginning to replace the line-up of the beat groups. With no rhythm guitar to flesh out the sound, both the guitar and the drums expand to fill all the space, while the bass holds everything down. It wasn't subtle, but in the second week of March 1967, 'Purple Haze' was the uncompromising sound of the future.

The second British single by the Jimi Hendrix Experience, 'Purple Haze' projected itself into something that hardly had a name yet. It wasn't just the single's deep sound — cut loud on the original 45 — and harsh tones, but the lyrics, which matched misery with mind-expansion: phrases like 'you got me blowin', blowin' my mind', 'is it tomorrow or just the end of time?' were augmented by strange, sped-up and compressed guitar tones. This was not just a record but a world-view.

It was at once threatening and exciting, angst-ridden and positive — an assault on the senses, an aural paradox. As such it was met with a certain amount of confusion. *Disc and Music Echo*'s Penny Valentine thought the record 'astounding, incredibly ugly but fascinating — rather like Hendrix himself'. The sight and sound of a black American decked out in Carnabetian gear seemingly beaming in from outer space led the British music press into all manner of contortions in that early spring: in one interview, Hendrix was accused of aping 'the Original Wild Man of Borneo'.

It was an inauspicious climate for the single's release: on 18 March 1967, Englebert Humperdinck's 'Release Me' was holding the Beatles' 'Penny Lane' off the top spot while the charts alternated between light pop and ballads: Vince Hill's 'Edelweiss' and two different versions of the nostalgic 'This Is My Song' — written by Charlie Chaplin in 1966 to evoke the spirit of the 1930s. By the time Hendrix's record reached the Top 10 in mid-April, it was vying with novelties like 'I Was Kaiser Bill's Batman' and 'Simon Smith and His Amazing Dancing Bear'.

With its ominous opening, spacey lyrics and otherworldly feel, 'Purple Haze' felt like a drug song, and was definitely interpreted as being part of that emergent culture. Even so, Hendrix was wary of talking about mood-altering substances to interviewers, preferring to couch his inspiration in terms of synaesthesia: in April 1967, he talked to *Disc and Music Echo* about wanting 'to get colour into music — I'd like to play a note and have it come out a colour'. To the *New Musical Express*, he revealed that the song was 'all about a dream that I had that I was walking under the sea'.

Dreams, colours: these were the early lyrical hallmarks of psychedelia, but to mention illegal drugs explicitly would have been commercial suicide. LSD or 'acid' had been outlawed in August 1966 and, by early 1967, its influence on pop was a hot issue. LSD-inspired records had been floating around for at least a year — ever since the Byrds' 'Eight Miles High', in hits like the Small Faces' 'My Mind's Eye', Donovan's 'Sunshine Superman' and the Beatles' 'Strawberry Fields Forever'. There had been high-profile busts, starting in June 1966 with pop-star Donovan's arrest for cannabis possession. But the public at large remained largely unaware of either the drug or its effect upon musicians.

By the end of 1966, the smart end of pop was defined by its use of LSD. The unitary nature of the British pop boom had fragmented into differing subcultures and tribes: the speeding soul-mad mods; the one-time Beatles fans, confused by their heroes; and the elite, who had begun to retreat into the world brilliantly depicted by Antonioni in the climactic party sequence of his film *Blow-Up*. This was

'But I don't want to go among mad
 people,' Alice remarked.
'Oh, you can't help that,' said the Cat.
'We're all mad here. I'm mad. You're mad.'
'How do you know I'm mad?' said Alice.
'You must be,' said the Cat,
'or you wouldn't have come here.'

Lewis Carroll, *Alice In Wonderland*, 1865

the world inhabited by the Beatles and the Rolling Stones: arty, drugged, opulent, closed off to the general public. There was, however, as the Stones' manager Andrew Loog Oldham recalled in his autobiography

a backlash coming. The Stones spending more time at home – framed by the perception of wealth with a non-stop life of chauffeurs, loafers, Rolls-Royces, Aston Martins, shopping, clubs, clothes, mates, hangers-on and dolly birds – was starting to get on the proverbial British tit, and it would only be a matter of time before the UK press would suss the mood of a nation and reflect it.

In January 1967, *The News of the World* began a three-part series on 'Pop Stars and Drugs: Facts that Will Shock You'. Prominently mentioned in the second part was Mick Jagger, admitting that he had taken LSD and the stimulant benzedrine. The only problem was that he hadn't: *The News of the World*'s reporter had mixed Jagger up with the far less discreet Brian Jones. Jagger threatened to sue and in order to shore up its story, the newspaper passed on a tip that illegal substances were to be consumed at Keith Richards' country home, Redlands, to the West Sussex Police. Redlands was raided on 12 February 1967, and Jagger, Richards and the gallerist Robert Fraser were arraigned on drugs charges (pls 122, 123).

That week, the Rolling Stones' latest record, 'Let's Spend the Night Together', reached its UK chart peak of number three. Thanks to Oldham's inspired positioning in the marketplace – the Stones as the anti-Beatles – the group had long courted controversy. From 1966, it had seemed as though they were upping the ante to the point of parody: from the blasphemy of the originally mooted title of *Aftermath – Could You Walk on the Water?* – to the drag photograph used on the sleeve of their single 'Have

You Seen Your Mother Baby, Standing In The Shadow', a comparative failure in the UK charts. Certainly, with its frankness about sex, 'Let's Spend the Night Together' was calculated to drive a wedge between the generations. 'Have the Stones Gone Gimmick Mad?' asked *Disc and Music Echo*, declaring that the record was 'certain to have headmistresses, archbishops, MPs, mothers' unions, Mrs. Mary Whitehouse and John Gordon raising a rumpus or at least locking up their daughters'. What the complainers missed was a sly reference to smoking marijuana in the first verse: 'Climb over here 'cause my mouth's getting dry / I'm high, but I try, try, try (oh my)'.

After that high-profile arrest, it was open season on drug use and pop music. In late March of 1967, a young group called the Smoke fell foul of *The News of the World*: with its lyric about eating sugar lumps (titrated LSD) 'My Friend Jack' was one of the very few songs to mention the drug itself. According to *Disc*, 'It cost EMI £750 and two months to re-record and change the lyrics four times before their doubts about its suitability were assuaged.' Even so, the record was banned by the BBC after the *NotW* exposé, one of several apparently dubious records – Pink Floyd's 'Arnold Layne' and the Small Faces' 'I Can't Make It' among them – that excited the censor that early spring.

Indeed, the presence of all those 'square' songs in the Top 10 spoke of a deep backlash against the perceived excesses of the pop modernists, from the Beatles and the Rolling Stones all the way down. 'Everybody is pretty fed up with the groups,' 'Edelweiss' singer Vince Hill told *Disc and Music Echo* mid-March. 'They've had a good run, but the novelty is wearing off. People want to hear a good, old-fashioned melody these days.' Experimentation, the shift from pop into the beginnings of rock – both played a part in this reaction, but it was drugs that excited the

most opprobrium. The following month, staff reporter Bob Farmer went on the attack:

> Not only are a fair proportion of pop stars taking drugs (naming names would lead to libel actions) but they are actually guilty of glorifying it, and what could be worse than a pop group singing the virtue of drugs to impressionable fans, whose only fault is wrongly believing what their idols tell them? *Disc* has decided that the drug menace and its infiltration of the pop scene needs public examination, to discover just how deep the drug roots go in pop, to detect how harmful drug-taking can be.

A week later, the paper reported that 'Beatles "drug" song is BANNED!', a reference to restrictions imposed by Los Angeles radio stations on 'A Day in the Life', weeks before its release. On 29 May, 10 days after the BBC had followed suit, Paul McCartney told the paper's Ray Coleman that 'Drugs must have been in their minds – not ours. And the point is, banning it doesn't help. It just draws attention to a subject when all the time their aim is to force attention away from it. … It's just beyond me what they mean.'

All of this was disingenuous. On 1 June 1967, the Beatles released their new album *Sgt. Pepper's Lonely Hearts Club Band*, which immediately went to the top of the LP charts: at number two was Jimi Hendrix's *Are You Experienced*. Just over two weeks later, in a prickly interview broadcast on the ITN news bulletin at 9pm, Paul McCartney admitted that he had taken LSD. The secret was out. The biggest group in the world were acid-heads, and the formerly most reasonable member was talking about the drug in positive terms on national television.

Two days later, the Beatles went back to work on their latest song, slated for inclusion in the world's first satellite TV link, *Our World*. On 25 June, their performance of 'All You Need Is Love' – videotaped in London's Abbey Road Studios – was watched by over 400 million people in 25 countries. Along with the Monterey International Pop Festival that same month, this event did more than anything to cement 1967 as the time that the drug culture emerged, to create the Summer of Love. By mid-July, the song was the top of both the American and the British charts, where it respectively replaced The Doors' 'Light My Fire' and Procol Harum's 'A Whiter Shade of Pale'. The genie was out of the bottle.

STONES: 'A STRONG, SWEET SMELL OF INCENSE'

Robert Fraser and Mick Jagger try to shield their faces from photographers on their way to court today.

Fans of the Rolling Stones at Chichester today before the hearing.

The agony of seeing your idols jailed ...

Story of girl in a fur-skin rug

BY A SPECIAL CORRESPONDENT
Chichester, Sussex, Wednesday

ONE of the party guests at Rolling Stone Keith Richard's house, when it was raided by police one night last February was a young woman wearing only a fur-skin rug, the West Sussex Quarter Sessions jury heard today.

Mr Malcolm Morris, QC, prosecuting, said there was a strong, sweet smell in the house. He suggested that it was incense, being burned to hide the smell of cannabis resin, traces of which were found in ash deposits.

Detective Inspector Lynch, Scotland Yard's Drug Squad, said Mr Morris, would tell the court what effect cannabis resin (Indian hemp) had on people.

"It produces an effect of tranquility and happiness and tends to dispel inhibitions," said Mr Morris.

"All she wore"

"It seems to have had exactly that effect upon one of the guests. This was the young lady who was sitting on the sofa.

"All that she was wearing was a light-coloured fur-skin rug which, from time to time, she let fall, disclosing her nude body.

"How people behave in their own houses is usually no concern of anybody else. The only significance of that young lady is that when the police arrived in force she remained unperturbed and apparently enjoying the situation.

"Indeed, although she was taken upstairs to be searched and into a bedroom where her clothes were, she returned downstairs afterwards where, apart from Mr Richard and five guests there was a large number of plain-clothes policemen, still only wearing that fur rug."

No alcohol

There were no glasses containing alcohol in the drawing-room, said Mr Morris.

He admitted that the reason why Richard was not surprised at the young lady's behaviour was because he knew cannabis resin was being smoked on the premises.

Richard, aged 23, of Redlands Lane, West Wittering, Sussex, is accused under his full name, Keith Richards, that, as the occupier of "Redlands," Redlands Lane, West Wittering, he permitted the premises to be used for the smoking of cannabis resin on February 12 this year. He was pleading not guilty.

The group's lead singer Mick Jagger, and London art gallery director, Robert Hugh Fraser, appeared on different charges yesterday relating to the same date and were remanded in custody for sentence at the end of the hearing.

Jagger, aged 23, was found guilty of being in possession of four tablets containing amphetamine sulphate and methylamphetamine hydrochloride on February 12. He had denied the charge. He spent last night in Lewes prison.

Fraser had pleaded guilty to being in possession of 24 heroin tablets.

Jagger and Fraser were in handcuffs when they arrived at the court from jail in a police van.

Black suit

Remanded on bail yesterday.

KEITH RICHARD—he wore a black four-button Regency style suit, trimmed with black braid. With it he had a white high-necked shirt.

WHITE TABLETS

On the case against Fraser, Mr McCowan said a police officer found a dark coloured jacket behind the drawing room door. From inside the right-hand pocket he took out eight green capsules and handed them to a detective constable.

Jagger, wearing a yellow frilly shirt and black tie with a light green jacket, mopped his brow after hearing his sentence and was led away into the cells holding his head and whistling softly.

Jagger, 23, had earlier been found guilty of possessing Italian pep pills.

In pipe

Also on the table was a briar pipe-bowl. This was taken away and on analysis its contents were found to contain traces of cannabis resin.

The constable was not satisfied and searched him. The constable took from a pocket a tin containing pieces of a brown substance and a decorated wooden pipe.

Shown the briar pipe found in the house, Mr Richard said it originally came from Los Angeles, where it was given to him by an American road manager.

There was also an envelope containing herbal cannabis—unprocessed hemp—and a substantial ball of brown substance which, when analysed, turned out to be 132 grains of cannabis resin.

Detective Inspector John Lynch, of the Drug Squad at New Scotland Yard, said it was normal practice to pass sticks or incense to be burned to nullify the smell of cannabis resin.

Det Sgt Cudmore said a well-known national newspaper gave him the information which led to the visit to Richard's house.

Sgt Cudmore also named Mr X as David Henry Schneidermann, alias Britton, a Canadian who left the country two days after the raid.

Jagger was wearing a green jacket, white shirt and dark grey floral tie. Richard a navy-blue jacket and pink tie, and Fraser a light grey suit.

At this stage Mr Havers, helped by his junior, produced a large fawn and white fur rug with orange lining, holding it up between them. Mr Havers said: "It is an enormous thing. It is a bed cover."

(Proceeding)

WOODEN PIPE

Plastic
Phial
Italian writing

The phial containing the tablets had Italian writing on it.

From Milan

ROLLING STONE Mick Jagger—on right in picture—and Mayfair art gallery director Robert Fraser were handcuffed yesterday during journeys between Lewes Prison and the Chichester court.

A Home Office spokesman explained last night that the two men travelled with other prisoners to the court and all were handcuffed for security reasons. Although they made the return journey on their own, Jagger and Fraser were still handcuffed because prison officers had not received further instructions.

THE RATHER grim scenes of Mick Jagger and Robert Fraser appearing handcuffed at the Chichester court this morning are surely an unnecessary humiliation. Are the two really considered dangerous criminals liable to make trouble unless they are manacled?

The Governor of Lewes prison and the police, who are jointly responsible for security arrangements in the movement of prisoners, apparently think so. The Home Office explanation is that when a number of prisoners who are security risks are being moved together it is "desirable for them all to be handcuffed." To the public, however, it must seem in this case an act of unnecessary harshness.

Robert Fraser's gallery is currently in enough to draw Lady Jane Ormsby-Go... (left), seen chatting with Michael Rainey, owner of a Chelsea men's shop he calls Hung on You.

...and gay." Says Robert Fraser, owner of London's most pioneering art gallery: "Right now, London has something that New York used to have: everybody wants to be there. There's no

Incense found

Mr McCowan said that when he officers arrived at Richard's house they noticed a very strong, sweet and unusual smell.

Police found sticks of incense and a tin which appeared to contain incense

Rolling Stone Brian remanded

Keith Richard ... after being remanded on bail

In London today ... Brian Jones.

Brian Jones, 25-year-old Rolling Stones guitarist, and Prince Stanislas Klossowski de Rola were remanded on £250 bail at West London today on a drugs charge.

The two, who wore "mod" gear and arrived in a Rolls Royce, were accused of unauthorised possession of cannabis resin (Indian hemp).

Prince Stanislas is known to his friends as "Stash." His father is a director of the Villa de Medici in Rome and he played several small roles in Hollywood before joining the pop world.

The two, who live in Courtfield Road, South Kensington, were remanded for three weeks. Fuller report—PAGE 17.

Jones appeared in court, wearing a blue lounge suit, a white shirt with lace cuffs and a large blue and white polka-dot tie. Prince Stanislas wore a brown fur-type coat over a blue suit.

When the two men left the court after the two-minute hearing, a crowd of about 60 people was waiting, many of them young girls, some of whom screamed: "They're gorgeous."

They drove away in a silver Rolls Royce.

with lace cuffs... dot tie, Prince Stanislas wore a brown fur-type coat over a blue suit.

NEWS SUMMARY

Jones (of the Stones) on drug charge

One of the Rolling Stones pop group, (Lewis) Brian Jones (25), was charged in Kensington last night with unlawful possession of a dangerous drug—cannabis resin. He is to appear in West London court to-day.

Charged with him—and also to be in court to-day: Stanislas Klossowski de Rowla, Baron de Witeville (24), Swiss born entertainer. Both were bailed.

The charges followed a Yard drug squad raid yesterday.

2 Stones for trial

Mick Jagger (23), lead singer of the Rolling Stones, Stones' guitarist Keith Richard (23) and art gallery director Robert Hugh Fraser (29),

Stones: switch on way to court

Evening Standard Reporter

CHICHESTER, Wednesday.—Police were on duty ready to stop any fan access when the Rolling Stones Mick Jagger and Keith Richard appeared on drug summonses at Chichester today.

They were accused together with West End art gallery director Robert Hugh Fraser, of Mount Street, Mayfair, of offences under the Dangerous Drugs Act alleged to have occurred at Richard's home at West Wittering.

After lunch, Mr Jagger had changed his bright green jacket to one of charcoal grey and Mr Richard had changed out of a jacket with black, white and white stripes into green.

Overnight at Redlands, West Wittering, Richard's country home, a few miles from Chichester. They left for the court in a Daimler but changed to another car on the way to a Minor 1000.

It drove into car park by mist... yards along the through blue gate immediately shut guard inside.

MICK JAGGER

KEITH RICHARD

KEITH RICHARD

Richard Hamilton and the gallery's undaunted secretary

MICK JAGGER

Keith Richards, more soberly dressed in pale-pink T-shirt and jeans, rushed to the court with it in his blue Bentley just before the court adjourned.

KEITH RICHARD
"Party guests"

A crowd of about 50 waited at the rear exit of the court in the hope of seeing Jagger —dressed in an eggshell-green jacket with dark green trousers—leave.

They rushed forward as a blue police van drove out, but it was a false alarm. Only policemen were inside.

Keith Richard.

ROBERT FRASER
Runs a gallery

Lord Parker said that Fraser, the son of a merchant banker, was educated at a famous public school and had served in two renowned regiments.

"Those privileges, if anything, raise greater responsibilities and would tempt the court to give more rather than less by way of sentence than to a person whom I will deem the man in the street."

ROBERT FRASER

SPECIAL JASMINE

Jagger, pale and trembling slightly, wore tight trousers, a yellow flounced shirt with a large green tie. On his trouser-belt was a button badge: "Mick is sex."

Granting Mr Jagger an appeal certificate, Judge Block told Mr Havers: "I wish you the best of luck."

MICK JAGGER, in frilly orange shirt and embroidered tie, celebrating his freedom in a Fleet Street public-house last night. At his elbow—a glass of vodka and lime.

'TABLETS WERE FOUND IN A GREEN JACKET'

Richards's Regency-style suit with black choker collar contrasted with the blue denims he wore in the Scrubs.

My clothes were taken away and I was dressed in blue prison uniform, but you don't care what you look like in a place like that."

Green capsules

like a James Cagney film except everything went black.

JAGGER APPEAL
"Wish you luck"

When the case against Jagger ended Mr Michael Havers, QC, defending, intimated there would be an appeal on a point of law.

Judge Block, who tried the case agreed, adding: "I wish you luck."

JAGGER, 23, wore a pale green double-breasted jacket with white buttons, olive green trousers a floral shirt and green and black striped tie. He sat in the dock beside Richard, who pleads not guilty.

Richard, with hair down the back of his neck like Jagger, wore a navy blue frock coat, black military-style trousers, a lace collar and maroon and black shoes.

Marianne Faithfull, Mick Jagger's girl friend, lunched today at the same hotel in Chichester as Keith Richards.

Meal in a cell for Mick Jagger

HOTELIER Arthur Collings carries meals to prison cell yesterday for Mick Jagger and Robert Fraser.

ROLLING STONE Mick Jagger is driven to jail in a police van last night after being found guilty on a drug charge.

With him he took three books—one about art, another about "The Tibetan Book of the Dead," 43 tipped cigarettes, a bar of chocolate and a jigsaw puzzle.

A suitcase full of clothing was brought for him.

Moroccan cooking

Describing the day's events before the raid Richard said that they had been to the beach and on a mystery tour. In the evening a Moroccan servant at one of the guests cooked a Moroccan dish, highly spiced, for a buffet dinner.

Afterwards they switched on the television without the sound and played records. Asked about using incense, Richard said he had used it for some time. "I picked it up from fans who used to send me joss sticks." It was not done to cover up the smell of hemp.

below the court, where they waited all day.

For Jagger there was prawn cocktail, roast duck and mint sauce, fresh strawberries and cream, and two half-bottles of Beaujolais.

Fraser had beef madras, fresh salmon salad and strawberries and cream.

REDLANDS, THE HOUSE IN WHICH POLICE SAID THEY FOUND DRUGS

Tudor-style farmhouse in West Wittering.

Redlands is a beautiful old thatched farmhouse partly surrounded by a moat. It is in a secluded position at the end of a lane in West Wittering, Sussex, and is owned by Keith Richards of the Rolling Stones.

Proper course

The Editor of the News of the World was made aware of the information. He decided that since there was no doubt of the informant's sincerity,

A third man, Robert Hugh Fraser, aged 29, art gallery ... Fraser runs a fashionable gallery in Mount street Mayfair, London.

He specialises in "pop" paintings and sculptures.

...on Robert Hugh Fraser, aged 39, London art gallery director, for possessing 24

Mr Fraser runs an avant-garde gallery where works by contemporary and pop-type artists are often on view.

ROBERT HUGH FRASER

Art man's sentence to stand

REGINA v. FRASER

Before the LORD CHIEF JUSTICE, LORD JUSTICE WINN and MR JUSTICE CUSACK

MOD-STYLE SUIT AND STRIPED SHIRT

Keith Richard stood in the dock wearing a four-button Mod-style black suit and a Regency-striped, high-necked shirt.

A green jacket

"Name blackened"

ROBERT FRASER IN HIS GALLERY

Fraser (29), of Mount Street, Mayfair.

Pop idol Mick Jagger of the Rolling Stones went to court today in a lime green jacket, dark green trousers, a green and black tie and a floral-pattern white shirt to answer drug accusations.

lilac green jacket with white buttons, a fancy floral shirt, loud black-and-green striped tie, olive-green pin-stripe trousers.

The Swinging City

Robert Fraser Gallery 69 Duke street, grosVENor Square, lonDon w1.

GREEN JACKET
CHANGE OVER

Jagger wore a double-breasted green jacket, cream silk shirt and fancy grey tie in court and Richard had a black coat and orange tie.

After lunch Jagger appeared wearing each other's jackets.

MICK JAGGER, lead singer in the Rolling Stones pop group, arrived at a court yesterday in a blue Bentley. He left last night in a grey van—bound with other men on remand to spend a night in Lewes Jail, Sussex.

MICK JAGGER
Eggshell-green jacket

Mr Jagger appeared dazed after the judge had passed sentence.

About 20 minutes after the sentences had been passed a blue Bentley with darkened windows drove out of the back entrance of the court and sped off in the direction of West Wittering. It returned about 20 minutes later and drove straight into the rear entrance again.

Miss Marianne Faithfull, the singer, got out and went up the steps into the court building. She was crying.

The main group of the party had arrived at Redlands at 11 and 12 midnight on the same night, followed by the married couple. "Everyone was a little hungry so I cooked some eggs and bacon.

Richards said some of the guests might have been drinking Coca-Cola but not alcohol. There was a smell of incense pervading the house because he had dropped it in the grate.

This aroma was mixed with that of the highly-spiced Moroccan meal guests had eaten.

KEITH RICHARD
Screaming girls

Marianne Faithfull, 20-year-old pop singer and girl friend of Mick Jagger—she is seen here signing autographs in Chichess today was hoping to visit Jagger in the Sussex cells this evening.

Earlier, Marianne had failed to see Jagger but sent in a draughts board and 60 cigarettes.

She wore a two-tone brown trouser suit and a green scarf and had large cuff links in her shirt.

Jagger and Fraser had lunch sent into the cells from a local hotel.

I sit here everyday
Looking at the sky
Ever wondering why
I dream my dreams away
And I'm living for today
In my minds eye

The Small Faces, 'My Mind's Eye',
Decca single, December 1966

122 (previous pages, left)
Swingeing London 67 (a), 1968/69
Richard Hamilton
oil on canvas and screenprint
67 x 85 cm

123 (previous pages, right)
Swingeing London 67 – poster, 1968
Richard Hamilton
photo-offset lithograph
69 x 47 cm (image);
70.5 x 50.0 cm (sheet)

124 (opposite)
Syd Barrett pretending to drop LSD,
California, November 1967,
photograph by Baron Wolman

The pill, the sugar cube or the drink is consumed. There is a deepening sense of anticipation. How strong is the dose? When will it come on? Where will it take me? This anxiety fuses with the onset of the drug to stimulate a metallic taste in the mouth. The concentration is suddenly drawn out of time, fixed to a particular object. Suddenly the world has changed. The drug has taken full effect: it's as if everything is seen from a great distance, yet individual elements are picked out to an infinite degree of detail. There is a bombardment of sensory stimuli, so constant and vivid as to be overwhelming. Time disappears under this chemical barrage.

LSD – lysergic acid diethylamide – is a very strong and unregulated drug. In the duration of its effects – usually about eight hours – and intensity, but also in the time it takes to work its way through the system and the need for assimilation, indeed recuperation, after the experience, it creates a rupture in everyday life. Few people can afford a couple of days or more out of the quotidian. When it began to spread into pop/youth culture, from mid-1965, it had a dissolving impact on existing values that was only equalled in America by the escalation of the Vietnam War and in the UK (geographically closer to cold war flashpoints) by the still-powerful fear of nuclear annihilation.

Indeed, early LSD records were troubled and confrontational. Recorded in April 1966, the Beatles' 'Tomorrow Never Knows' was an all-out assault on linear time: a sound picture, based on one chord, that matched the limits of studio technology with a tamboura drone, looped overdubs capturing the zaps and zings of LSD's perceptual overload. Suggesting the eternal present to be found in the study of Near Eastern religions, or at least 'The Psychedelic Experience', lyrics wound around themselves like the serpent uroboros: 'lay down all thoughts, surrender to the void'.

LSD opened a window into another world, but it was so strong that it easily derailed the fragile and the unwary. This is the contradiction that 'Tomorrow Never Knows' and other early LSD records like the Dovers' 'The Third Eye' and the Byrds' 'Eight Miles High' encode. Lyrically and vocally they attempt to recapture a moment of visionary transcendence. The rational mind seeks to define the experience in positive, if awestruck, terms. But if the words speak of eternity, the chaotic intensity of the performances tells you that the whole experience is all too much. You're left with a disturbed aftertaste, a growl of chemical electricity or an acid disharmony that is anything but resolved or peaceful.

The history of how LSD spread from a chemical accident to cold war psy-ops, from carefully monitored psychological studies to the chaos of mid-1960s pop culture, is well known. Although most of the activity was concentrated in the United States, it's worth noting that the British Defence Science and Technology Laboratory at Porton Down ran tests on army and navy personnel during 1953 to discover its potential as a 'truth drug'. Due to its strength and the volatility, the results were often disastrous.

In Los Angeles, psychiatrists including Dr Sidney Cohen began to conduct traditionally regulated, clinical LSD therapy in the mid-1950s, while the first programme in Britain was run by the psychiatrist Dr Ronnie Sandison of Powick Hospital, near Worcester. After visiting Sandoz laboratories in Basel, Sandison began using LSD on a number of patients who had 'very difficult psychiatric problems', with a 70 per cent cure rate. After he published his results in 1954, *The News Chronicle* reported his success with the headline 'Science Has Alice-in-Wonderland Drug'.

Thoughtful commentators immediately realized the power of psychedelic drugs. After his experiences with mescaline, Aldous Huxley wrote in 1954's *The Doors of*

143

Perception that it brought on 'the understanding ... that Love is the One'. But he also noted how it overrode the gatekeeping function of the brain. Everyday consciousness depends on the sheer immensity and rapidity of impressions being carefully filtered: if they are not, the sheer weight of incoming data results in overload and worse. Huxley suddenly had 'an inkling of what it must feel like to be mad. Schizophrenia has its heavens as well as its hells and purgatories'. Huxley graduated to LSD.

LSD was kept firmly in the clinical firmament until the early 1960s, when it was introduced into US youth culture by two principal circuit-breakers: Timothy Leary, a Harvard Professor who had developed a messiah complex after taking the drug, and Ken Kesey, a best-selling novelist who used LSD to explore his theories about chaos, chance and the nature of madness. While Leary insisted on set and setting, gathering followers at his Millbrook estate, and yoked the acid experience to a certain religiosity, Kesey took the full-on madness of LSD on the road in the summer of 1964 with his group the Merry Pranksters.

Acid began to filter into existing youthtopias: teen zones based on clubs, consumption and congregation. On the West Coast, the Merry Pranksters held nine Acid Tests – public parties centred around taking LSD – in the first three months of 1966. Five were held around Los Angeles, in Northridge, Hollywood and, bizarrely, the riot-torn district of Watts; and three in San Francisco, where there had long been a burgeoning bohemian, politicized scene centred around the University of California in Berkeley and the hardcore beats had moved into the Haight-Ashbury district. As ever in that period, the Beatles showed the way. Sometime *Rolling Stone* staffer Charles Perry described the ubiquity of the Beatles as 'the soundtrack of Haight-Ashbury, Berkeley and the rest of the circuit. You could party hop all night and hear nothing but *Rubber Soul*'. The Psychedelic Shop opened on Haight Street,

stocking anything and everything an acid-head might find interesting or necessary. Later that month, the Merry Pranksters joined local activist Stewart Brand (founder of the *Whole Earth Catalog*) in hosting the Trips Festival: over three nights, more than 6,000 people attended. At the same time, the Sunset Strip club scene was beginning to gain national news attention.

In the UK, the drug had begun to filter through into the underground scene as early as 1961, but it wasn't until the activities of two proselytizers in autumn 1965 that it really began to spread. Poet and filmmaker John Esam, then living at 101 Cromwell Road in London, not too far away from the BEA Air Terminal, was its first major conduit: among his visitors was Donovan, who wrote about this 'LSD Ashram' in the song 'Sunny South Kensington', as well as talking about the 'sugar cube' in 'Hey Gyp (Dig the Slowness)'. A gathering of the tribes took place in June 1965, with the International Poetry Incarnation at the Royal Albert Hall – an event organized by John 'Hoppy' Hopkins, Marcus Field and Michael Horovitz, which included readings by Esam, Lawrence Ferlinghetti, Adrian Mitchell, Allen Ginsberg, William Burroughs and Harry Fainlight, who stumbled through his poetic account of a bad LSD trip, 'The Spider'.

The second was Michael Hollingshead, an adventurer and early LSD adept who arrived back in the UK in October 1965 – after a long association with Timothy Leary, whom he had turned on to LSD – with instructions to set up a British equivalent of Millbrook. Armed with enough LSD 'for 5,000 sessions', Hollingshead found a flat at Pont Street in Chelsea and, together with the Lloyd's underwriter Desmond O'Brien, founded the World Psychedelic Centre. Although it started off with high-minded principles – attracting such notables as Alex Trocchi, Roman Polanski and R.D. Laing – it quickly descended into chaos: drug busts and tabloid exposés, most notably in the *People* and *The News of the World* ('Menace of the Vision of Hell').

125 (opposite)
The Psychedelic Eye mosaic, 1966,
John Herrick, after a design
by John Lennon
The mosaic (1.55 x 4.65 m)
consists of *c.*14,000 tiles,
each 1.9 cm square.

126 (left)
The Exploding Plastic Inevitable
featuring the Velvet Underground,
Los Angeles, 1966, photograph
by Steve Schapiro

By March 1966, the LSD experience was the subject of scare stories in both the British and American media. 'LSD has been taken up by a large, underground cult,' opined *LIFE*. 'Starting in artistic, bohemian and intellectual circles, the cult has now become a dangerous fad on the college campus. At least one million doses of LSD ... will be taken in the US this year.' As in the UK, this was seen as a plot to inundate the country with an odourless, undetectable substance that threatened to dissolve all known values. It was like the plot of a paranoid 1950s science fiction movie: a laboratory experiment gone disastrously wrong. LSD sent existing concerns about illegal drug use and youth lifestyles – primarily focused on amphetamines, marijuana and hair-length at this stage – spiralling off into the stratosphere. This wasn't mere teen obnoxiousness but the advance guard of a full-blown youth revolution: the youthful/artistic desire to create one's own world was heightened by LSD. No drug, before or since, had driven such a wedge between those who had or who had not (over 99 per cent of all adults) taken the test.

The simple fact was that, after taking acid, nothing was the same. It was that fundamental. 'I saw everything there is to see,' stated an American student in an experiment recorded by John Cashman in his book *The LSD Story*. 'It was ecstasy and it was horrible and I saw it all and understood it all.' A Stones intimate in 1967, Stash Klossowki de Rola later told the author Paul Buck that 'psychedelics made everything seem multidimensional, and revealed consensus reality as threadbare. After it, the game of life had changed.'

The overwhelming concentration on the present moment that was a hallmark of the LSD experience fed into wider trends: 1966 was the year of the total environment, and the United States led the way. Whether it be the hostile provocations of Andy Warhol's Exploding Plastic Inevitable (pl.126) or the consumerist Cheetah discotheque – a vast space dominated by 3,000 multicoloured lightbulbs and huge aluminium sheets – or the light shows developed in the Avalon and Fillmore ballrooms in San Francisco, it all came down to one overwhelming obsession: the everlasting NOW.

The manifestations of the new youth culture were like catnip to the established news media. They gave great copy, they offered the opportunity for shocked moralizing with attention-grabbing photos, they played on adults' fears of a generation that was slipping out of their control, they gave reporters and editors an agenda: the banning of this powerful and subversive substance – which duly occurred in both Britain and the United States during 1966. LSD tapped into a zeitgeist because it initiated new ways of perception just when the full effect of what Marshall McLuhan called the 'Information Age' was becoming apparent.

LSD was a product of its time. Its impact on youth culture in the 1960s was two-fold. It became a pop style, reaching its full flowering at the end of 1966 and during 1967, and for two years thereafter the object of commercial exploitation in tandem with a deeper stylistic exploration. The drug also became a crucial agent in the counter-culture that would aim to sidestep, if not subvert, materialistic capitalism. In both roles LSD would have a huge impact on the decades that followed: one as a kind of experimental, generous touchstone, the other as a source of recalibration and regeneration that still reverberates today.

WHITE RABBIT

Happiness is hard to find
We just want peace to blow our minds

Tomorrow, 'Revolution', Parlophone single,
September 1967

The British psychedelic style was first set, as in so many other things, by the Beatles. Between April and June 1966 they recorded 16 songs for their next album and a stand-alone single. Both *Revolver* and 'Paperback Writer' / 'Rain' showed the benefits of a nearly three-month break that the group had taken at the beginning of the year, which had allowed them time to experiment with avant-garde techniques, mood-altering drugs, and the thought, verbalized by John Lennon to the *Evening Standard*'s Maureen Cleave, that there might be life beyond the Beatles: 'You see, there's something else I'm going to do, something I must do ... All I know is, this isn't it for me.'

Following on from the tonal experiments of *Rubber Soul*, *Revolver* was smoother but even more immersed in alternative perceptions. With the full resources of Abbey Road and a more relaxed working schedule, the group explored Indian modalities – most obviously the sitar on 'Love You To', but also the harshly horizontal harmonies on 'Paperback Writer' and the guitar solo of 'Taxman' – backwards tapes ('Rain', 'I'm Only Sleeping'), soul music ('Got to Get You Into My Life'), lush West Coast harmonies ('Here, There and Everywhere') and Bernard Herrman style strings ('Eleanor Rigby').

Two John Lennon songs set the psychedelic mood. 'Tomorrow Never Knows' is justly famous as a mass-market avant-garde artefact that fused radical technology – in particular the use of tape loops, backwards tapes and Leslie speakers – with the most explicit evocation yet in popular culture of mystical transcendence. Here form reflected the circularity of the lyrics – taken from the introduction to the LSD guidebook, Timothy Leary and Ralph Metzner's *The Psychedelic Experience* – which closed with 'the end of the beginning', the perennial present caught as if in a Möbius loop. 'She Said She Said' was the last song to be recorded for the album. Lennon's inspiration came from his second LSD trip, which occurred in Los Angeles during the Beatles' 1965 US tour. Staying in the Hollywood Hills, he had become irritated by Peter Fonda's insistence on recalling a near-death experience. He set this depiction of psychedelic unease to a storming, albeit skewed rocker that elicited a strong group performance, particularly from Ringo Starr, but the song's most direct moment came in the middle break, when Lennon intoned, in a childlike voice, 'when I was a boy, everything was right, everything was right'.

London had its own small psychedelic scene, fuelled by the activities of the London Free School and given shape by the new magazine *International Times*, launched in October 1966 with a rave at the Roundhouse. Two months later, John Hopkins and Joe Boyd opened a new club in the centre of London, called UFO. Around 400 people turned up and Pink Floyd, Britain's leading psychedelic group, improvised at length: their manager Peter Jenner membered that 'what had been the guitar break was becoming long waffly solos, so it seemed like the average song was about ten minutes long.'

With the time lag between media coverage and record company schedules, almost no music from the San Francisco scene had filtered over to the UK. Pink Floyd, for instance, were influenced by free jazz and records from Los Angeles and New York. 'We never heard any West Coast music,' Jenner recalled, 'until "White Rabbit", we never heard it. Love and the Fugs, they were it. I don't know how it came about, but a Velvet Underground cassette was passed around amongst us.' Unlike the Bay Area groups, many British musicians had come out of the R&B/soul boom, which gave a tougher underpinning to their future experiments. Having assumed managerial responsibilities for the then-leading UK psychedelic group, Jenner steered them to writing their own material: 'the really successful bands wrote their own songs. Buddy Holly, Beatles, Stones.

147

Everly Brothers. You don't need another band playing "Dust My Broom" and "Louie Louie". When I first saw them, the Floyd were doing that, and then they were doing these things of Syd's in the middle. I think nearly all the songs that Syd is recognized for were written in 1966.'

Without the Vietnam War as a generational focus – the Labour Prime Minister, Harold Wilson, had refused President Johnson's request to send UK troops to Vietnam – British acid culture developed along its own lines. The return to childhood was a dominant theme, amplified by the near-simultaneous studio recording of the Beatles' 'Strawberry Fields Forever' and the BBC showing of Jonathan Miller's *Alice in Wonderland* in December 1966. Soundtracked by Ravi Shankar, this extraordinary adaptation was saturated in perceptual textures and presented the numinous, spirit-ridden English countryside as a key LSD location.

Both sides of the Beatles' February 1967 single, 'Penny Lane' / 'Strawberry Fields', defined British musical psychedelia in the short term. On the A-side was a piccolo trumpet; the flip's headlong dive into the subconscious – the murk and muck of childhood memories, soundtracked by swooping strings and an Indian harp called the swarmandal – resolving into a long and chaotic outro dominated by Ringo

Starr's clattering drum parts, repeated harsh guitar notes and crazily looping mellotron melodies. While 'Penny Lane' was a song about memory framed by its author's customary optimism, everything about 'Strawberry Fields Forever' was shrouded in confusion. Lennon's LSD explorations had been framed by then-fashionable ideas about psychological reprogramming: the characteristic features of the psychedelic experience, Leary had written, 'are the transcendence of verbal concepts, of space-time dimensions, and of the ego or identity'. By late 1966 this was beginning to lead Lennon down into uncharted waters.

Despite a singles chart stuffed full of ballads and novelties, psychedelic hits came thick and fast in the spring: the Move's opportunistic but highly effective 'I Can Hear the Grass Grow', Pink Floyd's 'Arnold Layne', Traffic's 'Paper Sun'. On 10 June, Procol Harum went to number one with their first single, 'A Whiter Shade of Pale': a canny mixture of the piano/organ patch used by Bob Dylan and the Band with a funereal, if not Gothic, pace. The song mesmerized the British public (including the Beatles), who sent it to the top spot for six weeks. 'A Whiter Shade of Pale' was replaced at number one by 'All You Need Is Love' in late July.

That same week, Pink Floyd's second single, 'See Emily Play', spent its third week in the Top 10. This was another founding British LSD document, with abstruse lyrics about games for May and losing your mind. Dominated by Rick Wright's soaring organ, the song could have come straight out of *Alice in Wonderland* – an uncanny evocation of British childhood mixed with a native paganism that included, like many of Syd Barrett's songs from this time, a disturbing undertow. Peter Jenner remembers:

He was very into Lewis Carroll, Hillaire Belloc, A.A. Milne, all these traditional English children's stories, often quite weird and bleak, and there's a strong element in there. Even perhaps Beatrix Potter. Yes, it's a reversion to childhood. Those were the good days, and now it's a bit more complicated somehow. There's a lot of that in Syd's writing. And a lot of tragedy, in terms of parents being killed in the war, and things like that.

Largely stimulated by *Sgt. Pepper*'s convincing use of the long-playing format, 1967 was the first year that the album outsold the 45 single. By early September the first Pink Floyd LP had reached the UK Top 10, settling in among the usual 'Best Of's – that hardy perennial *The Sound of Music*, for example – but also *Sgt. Pepper* and *Are You Experienced* (both massive sellers that summer). *Piper at the Gates of Dawn* defined the new era with extended space explorations, long jams, bizarre chants and idiosyncratic songs about garden gnomes, the I Ching, domestic cats and children's literature. It was Syd Barrett's zenith.

Released on 22 September, Tomorrow's 'Revolution' encapsulated British psychedelia. Beginning with a minatory introduction which presented the title as a riddle, it exploded into the chorus: 'have your own little revolution now!' Being Britain, this was not the total overthrow being

rehearsed in the US but something rather more small-scale and domestic: 'Flower children spreading love – that's a start / You can tell those with a heart / Sunrise – it's so nice / Open eyes – see it twice'. In these terms, 'revolution' meant smoking a joint and avoiding the police. By late September, the singles Top 10 was full of this change in the weather: there were records that enshrined the return to fairy tale with children's voices (Keith West's 'An Excerpt From a Teenage Opera', Traffic's 'Hole in My Shoe'), that talked about the elements in mystical terms (the Move's 'Flowers in the Rain', the Small Faces' 'Itchycoo Park'), and two exploitation tunes that referenced the new pop capital (Scott McKenzie's 'San Francisco' and the Flower Pot Men's cheesy 'Let's Go to San Francisco').

LSD had long been seen as a white thing, but even Motown was going psych: at number five on 30 September were Diana Ross and the Supremes, with 'Reflections' – a moody, introverted song with swirling electronic oscillations and perceptual lyrics ('trapped in a world that's a distorted reality'). At the same time, Otis Redding recorded '(Sittin' on) The Dock of the Bay', his gentle reflection of the San Franciscan sound he had encountered at Monterey: although it would not be released until early 1968, it captured the mood of that summer and acted as afterglow as well as tribute.

As the autumn progressed, however, the high summer of exploration began to morph into grandiose travelogues like the Herd's 'From the Underworld' or Simon Dupree and the Big Sound's 'Kites' – exotica dressed up as mind expansion. Certainly, there was a rash of songs that sought to return to an idyllic, children's picture book state: Tomorrow's 'Auntie Mary's Dress Shop', the Blossom Toes' 'I'll Be Late for Tea', Kaleidoscope's 'Mr Small the Watch Repairer Man'. The whole trend was satirized by the Bonzo Dog Doo Dah Band with their 'Equestrian Statue',

while the rejected third Pink Floyd single, 'Scream Thy Last Scream', took some of these Toytown elements – children's laughter, surreal lyrics and crowd noise sound effects – into something infinitely darker and more disturbing.

The UK's Christmas number one in 1967 was the Beatles' deceptively simple 'Hello, Goodbye', accompanied by the *Magical Mystery Tour* EP and television film – a classic example of acid reflux. At the same time, many landmark British albums were released: Traffic's *Dear Mr Fantasy*, the Who's *The Who Sell Out*, the Rolling Stones' *Their Satanic Majesties Request*, Cream's *Disraeli Gears* and *Axis Bold As Love* by the Jimi Hendrix Experience. At the sharp end of pop, the album was king: as time unfolded in the mind, so the two- to three-minute single was too short to reflect the new demands of possibility and ambition.

Even so, by the end of 1967, the overt signifiers of psychedelia had already become a cliché and were on their way to becoming a memory. All those lyrics about colours and dreams and minds, those Bach-like organ fugues, the mellotrons, the phasing, the sitars, the Toytown imperative – they would persist into 1968 like an overly rich dinner on the point of being rejected for plainer fare.

The golden age of '60s British pop was over. The freewheeling anarchy and endless airtime of the pirate radio stations (which had sprung up in 1964 and 1965) was finally curtailed in the middle of August 1967 when the

Marine Offences Bill became law. Despite employing several pirate DJs, the BBC's new youth station, Radio 1, was no substitute. The charts became increasingly formulaic and mainstream: the oddities and mavericks that had come through the pirates' random programming had disappeared, and the big guns held their fire for long-players. Groups including Cream began to uphold their reluctance to release singles as a virtue.

The influence of LSD was not over, of course. The first few months of 1968 saw sterling psych-exploitation hits like Status Quo's 'Pictures of Matchstick Men' and fine LPs by the Nice, Tomorrow, and the Zombies (*Odessey and Oracle*). However, without the same grounding in mythos and youth culture as its US variant, British psychedelic music as a style was more vulnerable to rapid turnover and quick obsolescence. There was a move toward rootsier styles: a very brief rock and roll revival, the return to pure blues epitomized by groups like Fleetwood Mac, the start of the heavy rock pioneered by Cream and Jimi Hendrix. Acid style deliquesced into a more general atmosphere of exploration, inventiveness and indulgence that would inform the rock music of the next few years. By the end of that year, the original psychonauts were hitting the limits of LSD. It was in the nature of acid that more meant less: continued use of the drug produced not an even more enlightened state of satori but psychic overload, if not worse – the sense of being permanently adrift, of not being able to find any way home.

Two double albums released at the end of 1968 showed this simultaneous ambition and exhaustion. Jimi Hendrix's *Electric Ladyland* showcased a dazzling variety of improvisational jams, pop songs, blues tropes and, in '1983: A Merman I Should Turn to Be', the ultimate acid statement, a 13-minute travelogue that ended on an unknown and deserted shore. At the same time, Hendrix was tinkering with a new song called 'Roomful of Mirrors'

— a statement of dislocation that he would rerecord over the next two years, never finishing it to his satisfaction. *The Beatles* (also known as the *White Album*) offered an even more dazzling kaleidoscope of styles and moods. Side four remains the group's ultimate statement: a tour-de-force that moves through two different evocations of 'Revolution', some *amuse bouches* ('Honey Pie', 'Savoy Truffle') and Lennon's last psychedelic song, 'Cry Baby Cry', the sinister reworking of a childhood fairy tale. A long piece of *musique concrète*, 'Revolution 9' was simultaneously disturbing, futuristic and nostalgic: it resembled a radio scan from the recesses of memory.

A wider cultural shift had taken place. For 1968 was the year when the student radicalism that had been simmering in the US since mid-decade and in the UK since late 1966 exploded into direct action, if not mass protest. Purchasing power had become conflated with political power: infuriated by the endless churn of the Vietnam War and the slow rate of change in Western society, and encouraged by the various liberation movements, the young sought not to change their clothes, but to transform society itself. In that, they both took from and greatly augmented the already existing counter-culture.

I'm interested in the whole idea of an alternative society growing out of what's happened in the last few years. Not a specific hippy thing or even drugs thing, but just a general re-evaluation of things that a lot of people are getting into, which is beginning to threaten a lot of barriers that old-style society has put up. I think it will be the ending of one society and the starting of another rather than just changing of the old society into the new one.

Mick Jagger, interviewed by Miles, *International Times* no. 31, 17 May 1968

The British underground started small: from the International Poetry Incarnation through Steve Stollman's 'Spontaneous Underground' nights at the Marquee in London to the distribution of the Global Moon edition of *The Long Hair Times* at the annual CND march in Easter 1966. Over the previous eight years, CND had provided a nationwide framework for youth dissidence but, by the mid-'60s, its influence was waning: Vietnam was the organizing issue and the beatnik lifestyle associated with the movement was changing under the impact of hallucinogens. On the cover of John Hopkins and Barry Miles's new paper *International Times* was the legend 'LSD 25'. The new approach was about changing the frame of reference, as John Hopkins, distributing underground newspapers, remembered:

> There's a photo somewhere of Harry Fainlight holding up a placard, and it's got a question mark on it. The exchange of ideas about ideas, that you could think differently but still inhabit the same territory. CND was the main substrate on which this stuff started to grow. That was where a great deal of energy was concentrated.

The impulse – derived from the period's radical politics, the infrastructure already created by CND, and the blurring effect of LSD (pl.131) – that a youth group should engage with its wider community, was also a facet of the London underground as it developed during summer 1966.

Breaking down the barriers between disciplines, roles, races and individuals was an explicit part of the London Free School's utopian mission. In tandem with Rhuane Laslett – a notable community figure who had established a 24-hour legal advice service for local residents – its young activists helped to set up the Notting Hill Fayre in September 1966. This was the beginning of the Notting Hill Carnival – a major music and community event in London and Afro-Caribbean life that continues today. Although the London Free School didn't last long, its mixture of idealism and pragmatism would be the model for many grassroots organizations over the next few years. Ideas about alternative communities also began to filter over with the greater exposure given to the San Francisco scene from 1968 onwards, with the UK release of records by Jefferson Airplane, Moby Grape and the Grateful Dead, the UK availability of *Rolling Stone* magazine, and articles about Haight-Ashbury in *OZ* and *International Times* (for instance, John Wilcock's article about the Human Be-In in *IT* no. 8, 13 February 1967; and the Diggers in *OZ* no. 8, February 1968).

Notting Hill Gate and the surrounding area of North Kensington was the counter-cultural epicentre. Founded in summer 1967 by Caroline Coon, Release – on Princedale Road, nearby to *OZ*'s offices in Palace Gardens – aimed to supply a 24-hour 'underground welfare service'. Coon designed the first 'know your rights' card in the world, the release bust card. Release gave assistance to the increasing numbers of young people in trouble with drugs and the law, as well as agitating for greater information on the subject and a change in the law.

The area was frequently covered in the underground press: *IT* no. 23 had a feature by Courtney Tulloch about the Afro-Caribbean community; Michael X was interviewed in *OZ* no. 7, while *IT* no. 30 was a themed issue about the 'three villages' of north-west London – Notting Dale, Westbourne Park and Portobello – with a map and details about community concerns from the construction of the Westway to the provision of children's adventure playgrounds and the importance of the London Free School in kickstarting the new era.

As the commercial hook of the new culture, music percolated through counter-cultural magazines, including

both *OZ* and *International Times* (pl.132). *IT* had regular coverage from the off, getting scoops with Miles's interview with Paul McCartney in no. 6 and George Harrison in no. 13. By issue no. 27, it was featuring more music coverage – a pop supplement no less – and a regular column by John Peel, the DJ most closely involved with the underground. *OZ* regularly featured large adverts from record companies and it began a music review section in issue no. 14.

The Beatles themselves were infected by the communal impulse of the time. In his *IT* column for issue 28 (8–21 March 1968), Miles wrote about the growing pains of their Apple company: 'the concept as outlined by Paul is to establish an "Underground" company above ground as big as Shell/BP or ICI but there is no profit motive as the Beatles profits go first to the combined staff and then are given away to the "needy".' Describing the Beatles as 'workers seizing control of the means of production', Miles described the idea as a 'large company structure not geared to exploitation of men and making profit but to exploitation of ideas and sharing profits.'

This powerful idea of an alternative community fed wider into pop during 1968 and 1969. After parting company with Pink Floyd in 1968, Peter Jenner and Andrew King continued Blackhill Enterprises as a vehicle through which to manage Syd Barrett and later, the Edgar Broughton Band, the ultimate street hippy group. Starting in the summer of 1968,

they organized a series of free concerts in Hyde Park: the first few featured popular underground acts of the day Pink Floyd, Tyrannosaurus Rex, Jethro Tull, Roy Harper, Traffic, Fairport Convention, and Family, and were fairly low-key.

The two that they organized in June and July 1969, however, were massive affairs. The first starred Blind Faith, the supergroup formed by Eric Clapton and Ginger Baker from Cream, Stevie Winwood from Traffic and Ric Grech from Family: they were supported by Edgar Broughton and Donovan. The second was headlined by the Rolling Stones in an infamous appearance, their first full show in the UK since 1966, and the debut of new guitarist Mick Taylor only days after the death of Brian Jones. The concert was attended by a crowd estimated at between 250,000 and 500,000 people.

The turn of the decade was a time of 'free' interventions. The squat at 144 Piccadilly – a deserted five-floor mansion on Hyde Park Corner, in the very centre of London – attracted national attention in September 1969: it was set up by the London Street Commune, who aimed, as the Diggers had in San Francisco, to give shelter and succour to the young hippies sleeping rough in their city. It reached capacity after a free show in Hyde Park by Quintessence, the Deviants and the Edgar Broughton Band on 20 September – the day before the police moved in with some considerable force.

131 (previous pages)
LSD meets CND, London,
1960s, photograph by
John 'Hoppy' Hopkins

132 (opposite)
*Summer Sadness for John
Hopkins, International Times*
no. 14.5, 9 June 1967,
designed by Michael English
V&A: E.1748–1991

The counter-culture attracted intense police attention and judicial hostility from its very beginnings. In March 1967, *IT* was raided by the police, on the grounds of obscenity: 8,000 copies were seized, along with all the magazine's files, in an attempt to close it down. On 1 June, John Hopkins was jailed for six months for the offence of allowing cannabis to be smoked in his flat. After the infamous trial of Mick Jagger and Keith Richards – an international cause célèbre in summer 1967 – the harassment of *IT* and *OZ*, as well as the arrests of major pop stars – including John Lennon, Brian Jones and George Harrison – became routine.

The only conclusion that can be drawn is that various sections of the Establishment – the newspapers, lawyers, the police – and some of the general public saw the counter-culture as a profound threat to the fabric of society. To some extent, this was to confuse rhetoric with action, and in general the British counter-culture was less strident and less obviously revolutionary than its American counterpart. In 1970, however, this would change with the start of the Angry Brigade's bombing campaign, which brought home-grown terrorism to the UK and shifted the counter-culture into a new, even more polarized phase.

In August 1970, the third Isle of Wight Festival – the biggest pop gathering ever held in the UK, with 600,000 attending – was declared a 'free festival' after agitation by various anarchist groups, who tore down the fences surrounding the site: as Richard Neville wrote in *Friends* magazine (an outcrop of the UK edition of *Rolling Stone*), 'Smashing the fences is a logical philosophical progression of underground lifestyle and it also represents a maturing of a collective insight.' He observed the contradiction in the fact that 'for the last decade, rock music, through its lyrics style and energy has symbolized and promoted personal anarchy' but is 'marketed by an entrenched profiteering establishment.'

By that time, as Neville observed, there was a severe disjunction between the psychedelic superstars and the values that they had appeared to embody. Much of this had been the product of a particular moment – the positive burst of energy that had radiated during 1967 – but counter-cultural values would prove surprisingly durable. Just as the first wave of performers who had come to prominence at Monterey began to falter, the networks of magazines, head shops, small magazines, communes and community projects were stronger than ever in the UK.

The music industry had moved on from psychedelia, but the changes the counter-culture had wrought had changed it for ever. The moment was marked in 1970 by the commercial success of the *Woodstock* movie and soundtrack LP. That was, in some ways, business as usual: capitalism in hippy drag, a mass-marketing of the counter-culture. But there was a reaction to such gargantuan events. Local was better, smaller was beautiful: September 1970 saw the first ever festival at Worthy Farm, an small, idyllic event attended by 1,500, that showcased Marc Bolan, Terry Reid and Quintessence at the same time as it celebrated a deep English mysticism – Albion Dreaming indeed (pl.133).

In 1971, the Underground Press Syndicate published a list of 271 registered publications in the US, Europe and the UK, with a potential readership of millions. In England, members included *OZ*, *IT*, *Red Mole*, *Friends* in London; *Zigzag* in Buckinghamshire; *Grass Eye* and *Mole Express* in Manchester; *Ops Veda* in Sheffield. While not comprehensive, it illustrated the spread of the ideas that had begun with a few people five or so years before: the structures initiated and developed during those years would continue to affect British pop and youth culture during the next decade.

The International Times No.14·5
FRIDAY 9 JUNE

SUPPLEMENT~
SUMMER SADNESS FOR JOHN HOPKINS news ⟩

We only wanna break
the chain of society
Put the people back on
the road to reality
We only wanna turn
the whole world on

Family, 'How-Hi-The-Li',
Family Entertainment,
March 1969

LSD was one of six major transformational agents in 1960s culture, the others being the mass media; the Vietnam War; the spread of popular culture, informed by commerce and demographics; the fear of mutually assured nuclear destruction; and the example set by the civil rights movement. Although taken by a comparatively small number of people, LSD's effects were broadcast internationally through the media and by successful pop musicians. It inspired the cultural leaders of a generation – born between the early to mid-1940s – to change both themselves and society, with unpredictable but lasting results.

LSD blurred more than just the senses, more than individual consciousness: in its overwhelming nature, it undermined the very fabric of society. It seemed to suggest connections, not differences, at the same time as it forcibly emphasized that everyday reality was just a construct, that only a small fraction of the senses were ever used, that indeed there could be more to life. Its more

thoughtful adepts sought to set up alternative systems that could translate that overwhelming sense of newness and possibility into real, on-the-ground change.

The communal imperative lasted in popular culture well into the late decade and continued to have practical applications well into the 1970s: it is hard, for instance, to imagine the success of punk's DIY movement without this previous groundwork. The insistence on local activity and strong, grassroots connections gained extra impetus after the 1973 OPEC strike and the publication of the British economist E.F. Schumacher's *Small Is Beautiful,* with its warnings about unsustainability and ecological degradation. In that, many late-1960s ideas seem not time-locked or nostalgic, but still latent and powerful, waiting to be activated by a new generation. **JS**

136 (above)
Dandelion, 1969, artwork by
John Hurford for a record centre
label for Dandelion Records
(John Peel's record company)
V&A: E.380–2010

137 (left)
Letterpress-printed tickets for
the Isle of Wight Festivals, 1969,
designed by Dave Roe

138 (top)
The 'Big Five' San Francisco
poster artists (left to right:
Alton Kelley, Victor Moscoso,
Rick Griffin, Wes Wilson,
Stanley Mouse), 1967,
photograph by Bob Seidemann

139 (above)
Poster for The Family Dog presents:
Big Brother & the Holding Company,
the Oxford Circle, Bo Diddley plus
Sons of Adam, 1966, designed by
Alton Kelley and Stanley Mouse
V&A: E.48–1999

140 (opposite)
'Jimi Hendrix' poster,
1967, designed by
Larry Smart
V&A: E.6–1968

141 (right)
Jacket belonging
to Jimi Hendrix,
1967, designed by
Dandie Fashions

PROCOL HARUM
POCO · MUNGO JERRY

LIGHTS BY DR ZARKOV
OCTOBER 29·30·31 NOVEMBER 1
FILLMORE WEST

SINGER

OCTOBER 28   SPECIAL WEDNESDAY SHOW   PRICE $3.00
AN EVENING WITH **SMALL FACES** WITH **ROD STEWART**

© BILL GRAHAM 1970 # 254   TICKETS   TEA LAUTREC LITHO · SAN FRANCISCO
ALL MACY'S TICKET OUTLETS · SAN FRANCISCO · FOX PLAZA BOX OFFICE NINTH & MARKET · CITY LIGHTS BOOKSTORE 261 COLUMBUS AVE
THE TOWN SQUIRE 1318 POLK · OUTSIDE IN 2544 MISSION   BERKELEY · DISCOUNT RECORDS · SHAKESPEARE & CO.   SAUSALITO · THE
TIDES   REDWOOD CITY · REDWOOD HOUSE OF MUSIC   SAN MATEO · TOWN & COUNTRY RECORDS   SAN JOSE · DISCOUNT RECORDS
MENLO PARK · DISCOUNT RECORDS   SAN RAFAEL · RECORD KING

142 (opposite)
Poster for Bill Graham presents:
Procol Harum, Poco, Mungo Jerry,
1970, *d*esigned by David Singer
V&A: E.484–2004

143 (below)
'Job' poster, 1898, designed
by Alphonse Mucha
V&A: E.260–1921

144 (right)
Poster for The Family Dog presents:
Jim Kwesin Jug Band, Electric Train,
Big Brother & the Holding Company,
1966, designed by Alton Kelley
A 1960s take on Alphonse Mucha.
V&A: E.58–1999

145 (above)
Poster for The Family Dog
presents: Grateful Dead and
Oxford Circle, 1966, designed by
Stanley Mouse and Alton Kelley
V&A: E.62–1999

146 (right)
'Skull and Roses' poster for the
Family Dog presents: Grateful Dead
and Oxford Circle, 1966, designed
by Alton Kelley and Stanley Mouse,
later used on the Grateful Dead's
eponymous 1971 album cover
V&A: E.55–1999

147 (opposite)
Poster for The Family Dog presents:
Quicksilver Messenger Service,
Sons of Champlin and Taj Mahal &
The Blueflames at The Avalon
Ballroom, 1967, designed by Rick
Griffin for Family Dog Productions
V&A: E.396–2004

The Family Dog

AVALON BALLROOM · FRI·SAT·SUN·OCTOBER·27·28·29 · DANCE·CONCERT·LIGHTS·IBIS

YOU SAY EVERYTHING SOUNDS THE SAME?

THE FILLMORE, THE GRANDE AND THE SUNSET STRIP

THE EVOLUTION OF A MUSICAL REVOLUTION

HOWARD KRAMER

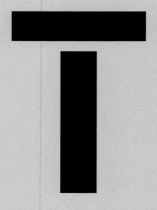

The recipe is similar no matter where or when it occurs. Take a group of artists looking for a place to express themselves, an under-utilized piece of real estate or two, an enterprising business catalyst, a media outlet and a general population that looks at the proceedings and offers ridicule. Occasionally, overzealous authorities make attempts to derail events and invariably cause them to thrive. It has been repeated again and again, in art, music, politics, literature, fashion: as identity asserts itself and evolves in the hands of youth, change is born. The process is not formulaic, despite this somewhat minimal explanation. Each event is a result of its time and place: regionalism abounds. The character of each locale is an active agent.

The 1960s, particularly the portion of that decade explored in this book, was a truly worldwide event. No less a figurehead of that time than Bob Dylan once remarked, unromantically, that the 1950s didn't really end until 1965. And when the 1950s ended, and the commonly accepted myth of the 1960s began, it manifested itself in a cellular, organic manner. The broad strokes that tried to paint it all hippy-dippy or as belonging to a bunch of seething radicals missed the point that the movements grew at different speeds in different places. When reflecting on the music of the era, the soundtrack is too often reduced to a small playlist and an even more brief list of names conveniently lumped together. Vibrant scenes sprouted all across the US, each with its own flavour. The wake of the Beatles, the evergreen influence of folk music, the rise of soul, a new California ideal and innumerable other factors fed the growth. Many of these styles popped up in San Francisco, which has a legitimate claim to being the centre of the psychedelic musical universe, but that's just one point on the curve. It's also a good place to start.

San Francisco's reputation as a safe harbour for individualism is the key reason why it has been a great incubator for change and progress. A relatively small city by American standards – just 49 square miles and a population of 740,000 in 1960 – its size has meant that rich and poor, black, white and Asian communities all maintain close proximity. Being a port, it's intrinsically full of transients. Some are knowingly passing through, while many never leave after experiencing 'the City'. It's a destination and a destiny all at once.

The North Beach neighbourhood was traditionally an Italian immigrant conclave. Among the apartment buildings, restaurants, bars and nightclubs that dot the area, nestled in a retail slot just south of Broadway on Columbus Avenue, stands City Lights Bookstore (pl.149). Founded in 1953 by Peter D. Martin and poet Lawrence Ferlinghetti, it was more than a place to buy books. Martin's vision was to create an outlet for new and adventurous writers from the Bay Area. This sympathetic little store became a second home to the beats, a wave of new, restless and daring writers. The group, which included Jack Kerouac, William S. Burroughs and Allen Ginsberg, among others, represented a revolution in thought. In their hands language and subject matter were made elastic. In post-war America, where much of the population craved a quiet normalcy, these writers saw a different country, one that wrestled with its very soul. At a time when many people still read books as a primary activity for entertainment and information, their words gave voice to the outlier and the misfit.

Ken Kesey, a student of the beat style, captured the nation's imagination with his debut novel *One Flew Over the Cuckoo's Nest*, published in 1962. He and his associates,

148 (below)
The Warlocks (later the Grateful Dead),
1965, photograph by Paul Ryan

who went by the name the Merry Pranksters, advocated exploring human experience through the use of LSD. The drug was not yet classified as illegal at the time, a loophole that provided the opportunity to rally like-minded individuals. Kesey himself was a bold and sometimes intimidating figure. While he counted Neal Cassady and Allen Ginsberg among his compatriots, he also hung out with members of the Hell's Angels motorcycle club, an unlikely pairing to say the least. Among the group orbiting the Pranksters was a band that often played five sets a night at crappy little go-go bars on the peninsula south of San Francisco. The drummer and keyboard player were rhythm-and-blues fans; the bassist was a modern classical composition student at Mills College with almost no interest in rock and roll. One guitarist wasn't out of his teens and had no business being in any of the joints they played and the other was a nine-fingered folkie to whom people seemed to gravitate. They were called the Warlocks (pl.148), and they provided the soundtrack to the first Acid Test, which took place near Santa Cruz in August of 1965.

Up in the City, the Family Dog, a group of like-minded arts-centric individuals, had their own scene going (pl.151). Chet Helms, who had arrived from Texas in '62, was its co-founder and de facto leader. The collective sought to present music made by its members and by other individuals and musical stylists they liked. The first event they produced took place in October 1965 and was entitled A Tribute to Dr Strange. It featured performances from Jefferson Airplane, the Charlatans, the Marbles and the Great Society. Jefferson Airplane was the house band at the Matrix, a club in the Cow Hollow neighbourhood owned by Marty Balin, one of the band's singers. This was their first gig on another stage. The Great Society was playing only their second-ever show, with a line-up that featured three members of the Slick Family: husband and wife Jerry

and Grace, and Jerry's brother Darby. The Charlatans had spent the previous summer in Virginia City, Nevada, as the house band at the Red Dog Saloon (pl.152). In between performing for the tourists, scouring stores for vintage cowboy gear and Victorian clothes, firing guns in the desert and consuming copious amounts of LSD, the Charlatans had formed into a tight little band. Naming the event after a character from Marvel Comics sent out a message like a dog-whistle and those who responded found themselves in Longshoreman's Hall surrounded by people who appeared to be just like them.

The next Family Dog dance/concert took place the following week. A Tribute to Sparkle Plenty, a nod to a character in the long-running Dick Tracy newspaper cartoon series, captured an even larger group of self-identifying freaks. Suddenly it wasn't just a few people randomly scattered across the area, it was an actual community. As Paul Kantner wrote in his foreword to Jack McDonough's 1985 book *San Francisco Rock: The Illustrated History of San Francisco Rock Music*:

There was an interweaving of the rock and roll world and the political world, the world of labor unions and the armed forces and kids and hippies and yippies and weathermen and democrats, mods and rockers, policemen worlds and the drug world, artists, craftsmen, Sierra Clubs and Hell's Angels, women's movements and Black Panthers, gurus, Jesus freaks, punks, lawyers, doctors, and Indians – you get the picture, I hope. I certainly didn't then.

Bill Graham, a former actor, was managing the San Francisco Mime Troupe, an experimental street theatre group that was perpetually in need of funds. Their performances, which often featured pointed social commentary, attracted the ire of the Parks Commission, who had them arrested on grounds of obscenity. Graham produced a series of benefit concerts, featuring some of San Francisco's new bands, to fund the Mime Troupe's legal defence. With razor-sharp business acumen, Graham saw in the Family Dog's activities an opportunity and a model: he knew that a commercial approach to presenting music in San Francisco might have a substantial financial yield if the benefit shows were any indication. By the third Mime Troupe Appeal in January 1966, Graham was in motion. He moved on from the Mime Troupe and signed

a lease with the Fillmore Auditorium, a ballroom in a historically black part of town. The original plan was to split the venue with the Family Dog; each would present events on alternating weekends. By April 1966, the Family Dog had set up shop at the Avalon Ballroom on Sutter Street, at Van Ness Avenue, and Graham had the Fillmore to himself. Ralph J. Gleason explained in his 1969 book, *The Jefferson Airplane and the San Francisco Sounds*:

> The reason the ballroom scene could flourish in San Francisco was that urban renewal had not taken hold. San Francisco was still lingering on the edge of the nineteenth century and the city was full of old buildings, the kind that can't be built today for any kind of money, and the Fillmore Auditorium was one such building – the Avalon, California Hall and the Carousel (on Market Street since the Thirties and now the Fillmore West) were others.

It was the beginning of the rock and roll concert business, as we now know it. It should be noted that the Warlocks played at the final Mime Troupe show, but under their new name: the Grateful Dead.

The genesis of the Grateful Dead is not too dissimilar from that of many other Bay Area bands. Many key

personnel, including Paul Kantner, Jorma Kaukonen, Peter Albin, Jerry Garcia and David Freiberg, came out of the folk scene that encircled the region. Both Garcia and Kaukonen, then also known as Jerry, offered guitar and banjo lessons out of the Offstage Folk Music Center in San Jose prior to the formation of their best-known groups. Rock and roll, though, was the universal language of this particular generation. It bound them together. The weekly dance/concerts brought many budding musicians together as audience members first, and bands seemed to sprout from those events. One year after the Tribute to Dr Strange show Quicksilver Messenger Service, Big Brother & the Holding Company, Sons of Champlin, and Country Joe & the Fish were all playing regularly. Weekend after weekend they performed alternately at the Fillmore and the Avalon with occasional forays into the East Bay, Marin County and the high school circuit.

Indicative of the times is the willingness of the entire musical community to perform at benefit concerts of all sorts. Artistic activism reflected a growing sense of political

153 (opposite)
Poster for Bill Graham presents:
Jefferson Airplane, Grateful
Dead, Fillmore Auditorium,
1966, designed by Wes Wilson

154 (following pages, left)
'Zig-Zag Man' poster for the
Family Dog presents: Big
Brother & the Holding Company,
Quicksilver Messenger Service,
1966, designed by Stanley
Mouse and Alton Kelley
V&A: E.413–2004

155 (following pages, right)
Poster for Bill Graham
presents: the Grateful Dead,
Junior Wells, Chicago Blues
Band and the Doors, 1966,
designed by Wes Wilson
V&A: S.700–2010

awareness. The war in Vietnam was a personal issue for American youth. Young men between the ages of 18 and 25 were still subject to compulsory conscription, in place since World War II. An annual lottery determined the draft order based on date of birth, spurring anxiety among families nationwide. The fear of death was as valid a catalyst as any for the growing youth movement. Despite constant exposure to this risk, the scene continued to blossom in San Francisco.

An integral part of the San Francisco music scene was the method of its advertising. The earliest shows of 1965 were publicized with handbills and posters featuring charmingly amateurish art and graphics. In early 1966, Chet Helms recruited San Francisco State University drop-out Wes Wilson, who was working at a local printing press, to design artwork for the Family Dog events. It is not an overstatement to say that Wilson single-handedly invented the psychedelic poster. In 1966 alone, he produced almost every announcement for Bill Graham Presents and half of those for the Family Dog. Wilson's keen eye for contrasting colour, amorphous shapes and hand-lettering blazed a trail for an entire movement. Soon the Bay Area was papered with cutting-edge works from Stanley Mouse, Alton Kelley, Victor Moscoso, Bonnie MacLean, Lee Conklin and Rick Griffin – in stores, on utility poles and in mailboxes – and those images quickly made their way to other cities. Its common designation as 'underground' art diminishes the fact that this was a revolution in illustration and graphic design. In some ways, the aesthetic created by this group of artists became nearly as important as the music.

Getting the word out to the audience also involved radio. Even a show as esoteric as the Dr Strange event featured an emcee from Top 40 broadcaster KYA. One of that station's best-known personalities was a Philadelphia transplant who would change broadcasting in America. Tom Donahue was a big man with a big personality. He came to San Francisco in 1961 and became an integral part of the scene. His label Autumn Records released titles from Bobby Freeman, the Beau Brummels and the Great Society; his house producer was none other than Sly Stone, then a DJ on KSOL. Donahue grew to loathe Top 40 radio and assured his permanent departure from it with an article entitled 'A Rotting Corpse Stinking Up the Airwaves', which he wrote for the second issue of *Rolling Stone* magazine in November 1967. Earlier that year he had struck a deal with struggling FM station KMPX to take over the programming. At the time AM radio was king and FM was a distant cousin that stayed alive only because the broadcasters who owned rights to the frequencies had to put something on the air, usually classical music or 'ethnic' content. Donahue and fellow DJ Larry Miller began with diverse music programming running from 8pm through the night. As their audience and revenue grew, they replaced the foreign-language programmes with more free-form broadcasts. Within a year, Donahue and management had come to loggerheads and he and the staff went out on strike. It was an event that mobilized the entire music community. In May 1968, KSAN went on the air, turning a frequency used by a classical station over to the former KMPX staff, and a San Francisco institution was born. Pete Townshend in 1996 recalled the Who's earliest visits to San Francisco and said 'KSAN was such a great station to get stoned and listen to. ... They used to play all kinds of different stuff. I remember string quartets, I remember jazz, I remember whatever were the hit records of the day. And I kinda miss that.'

For all San Francisco had going for it, it was still a provincial city. The scene had an early mainstream media champion in Ralph J. Gleason, music critic for the *San Francisco Chronicle*, who saw the musical and cultural explosion happening before him as a legitimate

BILL GRAHAM PRESENTS IN SAN FRANCISCO

JEFFERSON AIRPLANE GRATEFUL DEAD

FRI 12 AUG.

SAT 13 AUG.

FILLMORE AUDITORIUM

TICKETS   "GRATEFUL DEAD" Photo by Herb Greene

SAN FRANCISCO: City Lights Bookstore; The Psychedelic Shop; Bally Lo (Union Square); The Town Squire (1318 Polk); Mnasidika (1510 Haight) BERKELEY: Campus Records; Discount Records; Shakespeare & Co.   MILL VALLEY: The Mod Hatter   SAUSALITO: The Tides Bookstore; Rexall Pharmacy.

ZIG - ZAG

June 24

June 25

BIG BROTHER & HOLDING THE COMPANY QUICK SILVER MESSENGER SERVICE

SAN FRANCISCO
9 PM

AVALON ballroom sutter at van ness

lights by BILLHAM

14(3) ©Family Dog '66

TICKETS

156 (left)
Janis Joplin performs
with Big Brother &
the Holding Company
at Monterey, 1967

157 (opposite)
The Beach Boys,
19 November 1964

movement. Still, there was no entertainment industry infrastructure there. This allowed the musicians to grow on their own, untethered by the machinations of the music business, which was centred in New York and Los Angeles – and that mattered. Word of what was happening in San Francisco travelled down the coast. Southern California bands like Love, the Grass Roots, and the Byrds became regular visitors. The Grateful Dead spent time in Los Angeles trying to expand their audience. The event that brought both scenes together became a pivotal moment.

The Monterey International Pop Festival wasn't the first modern rock and roll festival – that had occurred in Marin County two weeks earlier – but it was the most important. Produced by a group of LA-based professionals including Lou Adler, John Phillips of the Mamas and the Papas, former Beatles/then Byrds publicist Derek Taylor, promoter Benny Shapiro and manager Alan Pariser, the three-day event in mid-June 1967 was held at the familiar site of the Monterey Jazz Festival. The bill was a mix of known hit-makers and newer talents. Of the latter, many came from San Francisco and most of those had only recently released their debut recordings. In this charged atmosphere performers from all over minted reputations,

notably the Jimi Hendrix Experience and the Who. Big Brother & the Holding Company were so well received on the first day of the festival that they played a second set on the closing day to secure inclusion in the film of the event (pl.156).

A few of the Los Angeles artists featured at Monterey were well established. Many of those performers who made it to LA went there expressly to be noticed, to be discovered and to find success. Record labels including Epic, Capitol, ABC-Dunhill, Warner Bros and Atlantic were either based there or maintained a significant presence. The talent pool was deep and had been for a long time.

Central Avenue in Los Angeles during the 1940s was, arguably, as important to blues and jazz as Beale Street in Memphis or East 52nd Street in New York. It was a hotbed of nightclubs, mostly catering to a black clientele, and teeming with talent. Many black Americans had headed west during World War II to find work in the munitions and aircraft industries of southern California, and Central Avenue rose to meet their demand for entertainment. This district was where such talents as Charles Brown, Dexter Gordon, Lowell Fulson and Ray Charles came to prominence. But while these players helped shape rock and roll, few of them participated in the movement.

In its early years, rock and roll was mostly a Southern invention: a significant proportion of the artists came from and recorded in the American South (Elvis Presley, Carl Perkins, Little Richard, Fats Domino). Gene Vincent, a Virginia native, was a rare exception, cutting many of his sides at Capitol Studios in Hollywood. Eddie Cochran, Ricky Nelson and Ritchie Valens all lived and recorded in Los Angeles. It was the arrival of the Beach Boys in 1961 that popularized the mythology of southern California (pl.157). Their odes to surfing life had an appeal that captured the imaginations of kids from the plains of Nebraska to the market towns of England. A vision of sun-drenched beaches, sports cars, drive-ins and 'two girls for every boy', their clean-cut California was a dreamlike destination, rather than the endpoint of a journey as described by Chuck Berry in his 1965 take on 'The Promised Land'. Surfing had come to the US in the 1920s as part of a Hawaiian pop-culture explosion that also included grass skirts, ukuleles and music characterized by lots of slack-key guitar. After World War II, a surfer counter-culture emerged. It shared much of the post-war disillusionment of the beat generation in San Francisco, but its dedication to physical activity and being outdoors was incongruous with the lifestyle the beats embraced. As the baby boomers embraced surfing in the 1960s, the culture came to reflect the new teen lifestyle invented by that generation. The Beach Boys, Jan & Dean, the Ventures and many others illustrated the picture to the world.

If the southern California days were meant for the beach, nights were made for the Sunset Strip. A stretch of clubs, bars and restaurants, along with an assortment of retail stores, the Strip runs through West Hollywood, winding its way west along Sunset Boulevard and terminating at the Beverly Hills city line. The area came alive at night with scores of young people either cruising up and down the streets in cars or walking along from venue to venue. By late 1965, it was home to numerous bands, most notably the Byrds, the Standells and the Seeds. The latter two were straight-up rock and roll bands, their purpose to get people moving on the dance floor. The influence of the Rolling Stones, the Animals and the Yardbirds loomed large in the image and sound of these groups. It was riff-heavy, grimy rock and roll, the type found all across the US as the British Invasion inspired kids to pick up instruments. While San Francisco was growing its own scene of innovative new bands, the East Bay also had its share of these combos, as did most cities across the US.

PINNACLE CONCERTS SAT FEB 10
JIMI HENDRIX
& THE SOFT MACHINE WITH
THE ELECTRIC FLAG
AND BLUE CHEER
SHRINE AUDITORIUM 8:30 PM
RESERVED SEATS NOW AVAILABLE AT ALL
WALLICH'S MUSIC CITY STORES AND ALL MUTUAL AGENCIES
VISUALS BY THOMAS EDISON LIGHTS & ACME CINEMA

The Byrds were cut from a different cloth (pl.159). In many ways they had more in common with the San Francisco bands: virtually all of them had played in folk groups of some repute. As its members migrated to Los Angeles and found each other, they made a conscious effort to become a successful rock and roll band. The sound they developed – ringing guitars, lush harmonies, solid songwriting and inspired interpretations of Bob Dylan compositions – assured their place as a leading US band. Chris Hillman of the Byrds, interviewed by Barney Hoskyns for *Waiting for the Sun*, his 2009 history of the Los Angeles music scene, said, 'The point about the Byrds and the [Buffalo] Springfield is that we weren't garage bands. We came out of folk music so the major focus was on the song – if you were going to get up in front of an audience with just an acoustic guitar, the material had better be good.' The Byrds began with two formidable songwriters, Jim McGuinn and Gene Clark. David Crosby would blossom soon after. Buffalo Springfield boasted Neil Young and Stephen Stills, two incendiary talents that could barely fit within the confines of one band. It was clear to most of

the people frequenting the Strip that these two groups were something special.

The ongoing popularity of the Strip led to an inevitable confrontation. In November 1966, local businesses and residents lobbied the city to pass a 10pm curfew intended to curb the underage crowds, ease traffic and reduce noise. A rally of young people outside the Pandora's Box nightclub was met by a contingent of police and many of those gathered were arrested. Television and media coverage amplified the event, giving the area an even higher profile and a notorious reputation. Their use of weighted terms like 'riot' can be attributed to the exploitative nature of newspapers at that time and the media's still deeply entrenched conservatism. The protest of 12 November didn't approach the scale of the rioting that would be seen on the streets of Newark, Detroit and Baltimore the following year, but it sold papers (pl.161). Witnessing and participating in the events of the day were many of the musicians who lived nearby and worked the clubs. Stephen Stills' version of those events, the song 'For What It's Worth', placed Buffalo Springfield on the national charts:

158 (previous pages, left)
Poster for Jimi Hendrix & the
Soft Machine, with Electric Flag
and Blue Cheer, at the Shrine
Auditorium, Los Angeles, 1968,
designed by John Van Hamersveld

159 (previous pages, right)
The Byrds performing
'Turn Turn Turn' on *The Ed Sullivan
Show*, New York, 1965

160 (below)
Buffalo Springfield (left to right:
Richie Furay, Stephen Stills,
Bruce Palmer, Neil Young, and
in front Dewey Martin), Malibu,
30 October 1967

161 (below right)
Teenagers protesting the curfew
on the Sunset Strip, 1966,
photograph by Julian Wasser

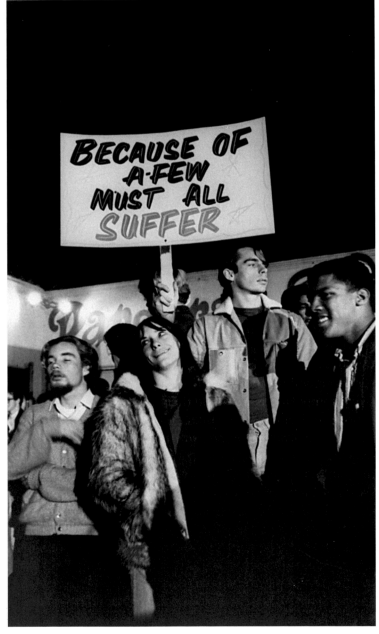

There's battle lines being drawn
Nobody's right if everybody's wrong
Young people speaking their minds
Getting so much resistance from behind.
It's time we stop, hey, what's that sound
Everybody look what's going down

The 'riots' also opened up the LA scene to a new level
of Hollywood exploitation. Inasmuch as movies helped
kick-start teen culture and rock and roll (*The Wild Ones*
and *Blackboard Jungle*) the two mediums hadn't quite
worked toward the advancement of either. *Riot on
Sunset Strip*, released in 1967, followed the formula for
teen sensationalism that made American International
Pictures a successful studio. It didn't really matter that
the Standells and the Chocolate Watch Band appeared
in the film. Credibility wasn't being garnered. It just

162 (right)
Grande Ballroom,
Detroit, late 1940s

seemed to further the brand of mass-market hippy culture – at least the Los Angeles version.

The exploitation didn't stop there. If San Francisco had a dearth of music-business types, Los Angeles more than compensated. Just as Raymond Chandler's novels of the 1930s and '40s portrayed, dubious characters came to the land of sunshine to make a fortune no matter the cost or manner; the entertainment business had always attracted hustlers and the youth-culture explosion of the 1960s was no exception. Names need not be named but rare is the artist from that scene who didn't get burned in some way. And in all fairness, mismanagement was not the exclusive domain of the LA bands. Many of their San Francisco brethren had terribly poor business direction as well.

Which brings us back to Monterey Pop. That festival and subsequent documentary film heralded the end of the era to some. It was no longer an underground scene. Outside forces, the mass media and the record industry in particular, moved in. The Summer of Love was in full bloom. Within just five weeks, the Beatles released *Sgt. Pepper's Lonely Hearts Club Band*, the Monterey International Pop Festival occurred and *TIME* magazine ran a cover story entitled 'The Hippies: Philosophy of a Subculture'. As more and more young people flocked to the Haight in San Francisco and the Strip in Los Angeles, the very elements that had made it special became lost in the tide. The image of a young person hitch-hiking from some Midwestern farming town to the West Coast swiftly progressed into cliché. San Francisco had a hard time taking in all the new arrivals. What had once been a scene was now a movement. Those who'd been there for a while resented sharing the secret charm of their town, no longer a secret.

The movement may have become national but the intense media glare that Los Angeles, San Francisco and even London received was never cast in the same way

upon other cities. Detroit, Michigan, experienced its own youthquake and musical revolution. Its claim to fame was the automobile industry, but the city produced an astounding number of accomplished musicians. A partial roll call of Detroit jazz players includes Milt Jackson, the Jones Brothers (Elvin, Thad and Hank), Dinah Washington, Ron Carter and Kenny Burrell. It was where John Lee Hooker made his first recordings and became a blues sensation; the city gave the world rhythm and blues legends Hank Ballard and Little Willie John. And certainly no discussion of Detroit can be had without the inclusion of Berry Gordy Jr's empire, Motown. Gordy mined a seam of talent unlike any before or since. From the session players to the songwriters, the vocal groups to the dance instructors, the Motown Record Corporation, founded in 1959, was a pop music behemoth Detroit born and bred – but with worldwide appeal. It was, as touted, the 'Sound of Young America'.

In 1965, Motown was the only competition to the Beatles' world dominance. The rest of the music scene in Detroit resembled so many others around the country: scrappy little bands playing covers gigs at school dances and in church basements. A former University of Michigan student named Ed Andrews, who was better known by the nickname 'Punch', opened a teen club called the Hideout to present local bands. The idea quickly caught on. Andrews and his partner Dave Leone opened a series of them in the Detroit area and created a thriving circuit. One of Andrews' earliest successes was a band from Ann Arbor, the Bob Seger System. As of this writing, they continue to work together as manager and artist.

In the fall of 1966 Russ Gibb, a radio DJ and teen-club promoter from Detroit, went to San Francisco to attend a friend's wedding. While there, he went to the Fillmore for a show starring the Byrds. Impressed with the venue, crowd and vibe of the room, he sought out Bill Graham, who

UNCLE RUSS TRAVEL AGENCY

PRESENTS A DANCE! CONCERT IN THE SAN FRANCISCO STYLE

THE FAMOUS MC-5 AVANT-ROCK

AND THE CHOSEN FEW

SEE THE COSMIC LIGHT BEAMS

SEE THE MAGIC THEATRE

DETROIT'S FIRST PARTICIPATORY ZOO DANCE

AT THE GRAN-DE BALLROOM

GRAND RIVER 1 BLOCK SOUTH OF JOY RD.

FRI-SAT. OCTOBER 7-8

9PM TILL 2AM SEAGULLS ADMITTED FREE

Fourth edition · Art © Gary Grimshaw 1966, 2013

Gary Grimshaw

163 (opposite)
Poster for Uncle Russ Travel Agency
presents: MC5 and the Chosen Few at
the Grande Ballroom, Detroit, 1966,
designed by Gary Grimshaw

164 (below)
MC5 performing at Mount
Clemens, Michigan, 1969,
photograph by Leni Sinclair

165 (bottom)
Iggy Pop of the Stooges at Crosley
Field, Cincinnati, Ohio, 23 June 1970,
photograph by Tom Copi

166 (following pages, left)
The Who onstage at the
Grande Ballroom, Detroit, 1968,
photograph by Tom Weschler

167 (following pages, right)
Firefighters kneel amid rubble
in the street and spray water
from a hose into a burning
building during riots; a line
of armed soldiers guards the
intersection just beyond
them, Detroit, late July 1967,
photograph by Declan Haun

graciously answered Gibb's questions. On 7 October 1966, the Uncle Russ Travel Agency, his new company, presented its first show at the Grande (pronounced 'gran-dee') Ballroom on Detroit's west side. Like San Francisco, Detroit had a number of ballrooms remaining from the Big Band era of the 1930s and '40s that were long past their prime and available for rent. Even as Uncle Russ presented concerts, portions of the Grande were leased out by a furniture store to warehouse mattresses (pl.162).

Gibb made the most of recreating the San Francisco experience. The poster for the first weekend show billed the event as 'a dance/concert in the San Francisco style' and 'Detroit's First Participatory Zoo Dance' (pl.163). Local artist Gary Grimshaw created the poster design, in the freehand lettering style that Wes Wilson had pioneered. Along with 'cosmic light beams' and 'the Magic Theatre', two bands performed: the Wha? (not the Chosen Few) and MC5.

Motor City 5 came from the working-class suburbs of an area known as Downriver. Their early recordings for the A-Square label reveal them to have been edgier than most garage bands. They had two of the hottest guitarists in Fred Smith and Wayne Kramer, and their lead singer, Rob Tyner, was a gap-toothed banshee with a massive Afro-style haircut (pl.164). The band understood the meaning of creating a show and found inspiration in the Rolling Stones and James Brown. Their showmanship raised the bar for other bands in the area and put pressure on touring acts, particularly if the MC5 were opening (pl.166).

Their manager was as untraditional a business type as could be imagined. John Sinclair came from Flint, a city about an hour north of Detroit best known for one of the American labour movement's greatest victories, when the United Auto Workers staged a sit-down strike against General Motors in 1936–7. A college dropout, a writer, a poet and a jazz aficionado with a true beatnik heart, Sinclair was

a charismatic guy who walked it like he talked it. He thought the MC5 were a powerful band that could give powerful voice to the causes he championed – the advancement of civil rights and ending the Vietnam War. They also liked to have a good time and regularly availed themselves of psychedelic drugs and marijuana. The authorities in Detroit didn't take kindly to Sinclair, the 5 or any of their associates, and systematically harassed them.

The Grande became a beacon in Detroit just as the Fillmore had in San Francisco. The MC5 was practically the house band, appearing almost every weekend. The multi-band bills featured mostly rock and roll acts such as the Scott Richard Case and Southbound Freeway, but also blue-eyed soul merchants the Rationals. By the fall of 1967, 'Uncle Russ Presents' was the name at the top of each poster, and both national and international talent like Cream and the Grateful Dead began appearing at the Grande. It garnered a reputation among performers as one of the best places to play, despite also being a tough room. You had to bring your best or the audience would let you know in no uncertain

terms. Oddly, some of the best-known and most enduring Detroit rock and roll artists, like Mitch Ryder and Bob Seger, never appeared at the Grande during this time.

The riots on the Sunset Strip were nothing compared to the riots that took place in Detroit in July 1967. Simmering resentment of hardline tactics from the mostly white police force exploded when police raided an illegal after-hours establishment owned and patronized by the black community. Over the next five days, dozens died and hundreds were injured as citizens and the authorities faced each other in armed struggle. Flames engulfed neighbourhoods and the National Guard was called in to impose order. When the smoke and dust cleared, Detroit was forever changed (pl.167). Many young people saw the brutality of the police and military as a true attack on freedom and liberty. Taking inspiration from the Black Panther Party in Oakland, California, in 1968 John Sinclair formed the far-Left White Panther Party. In addition to fully supporting the Black Panther Party's 'Ten-point Program', the White Panthers' platform advocated 'total assault on

the culture by any means necessary including rock and roll, dope and fucking in the streets'. If John Sinclair and the MC5 were harassed before, now they were full-on targets.

When the Psychedelic Stooges made their Grande debut opening for jazz-rockers Blood, Sweat & Tears in March 1968, they followed in the spirit of full-on musical assault advocated by the MC5. Instantly polarizing, you either loved the Stooges or hated them (pl.165). Hard rock bands like the Iron Butterfly or Blue Cheer relied on volume and catchy riffs, but next to the sheer primitive grind of the Stooges, other bands seemed puny. When Elektra Records talent scout Danny Fields came to Detroit to check out the MC5, he signed not only them but also the Stooges. It was an inspired move.

Almost all of the primary participants in the 1960s cultural transformation felt that they could make a difference. Change was forged out of the belief that this was their time. And, in their time, they reset the landscapes of their own communities. What began as isolated and remote groups became interconnected through shared beliefs. What they didn't realize is that the changes they instigated

would fully come to fruition only years and decades later, or that the music would endure and continue to find new audiences, influencing younger musicians far from where it had been created. Though they didn't change the world in an instant, the musicians, writers and true believers who made and lived the art, who marched on the marches and created the method and means to ensure that their voices were heard, inspired many who watched from the sidelines. That next wave infused their own scenes – in art, music, cinema, poetry, prose, fashion, politics – with the energy and commitment they had witnessed in the 1960s. And that's what happened in London and New York in the mid-1970s with punk rock. And again, after a period of time, in Queens, Compton, Houston and Atlanta with hip-hop.

The power and identity of youth is defined more by its music than by any other single characteristic. It is the secret code and unifying language that transcends all borders. In the age of instant worldwide communication, today each revolution has the potential to spread wider and faster than ever before. **HK**

WOODSTOCK
MUSIC & ART FAIR

presents

AN
AQUARIAN
EXPOSITION

in

WHITE LAKE, N.Y.*

3 DAYS of PEACE & MUSIC

Skolnick

WITH

FRI., AUG. 15
Joan Baez
Arlo Guthrie
Tim Hardin
Richie Havens
Incredible String Band
Ravi Shankar
Sly And The Family Stone
Bert Sommer
Sweetwater

SAT., AUG. 16
Canned Heat
Creedence Clearwater
Grateful Dead
Keef Hartley
Janis Joplin
Jefferson Airplane
Mountain
Quill
Santana
The Who

SUN., AUG. 17
The Band
Jeff Beck Group
Blood, Sweat and Tears
Joe Cocker
Crosby, Stills and Nash
Jimi Hendrix
Iron Butterfly
Ten Years After
Johnny Winter

ART SHOW
Paintings and sculptures on trees, on grass, surrounded by the Hudson valley, will be displayed. Would be artists, ghetto artists, and accomplished artists will be glad to discuss their work, or the unspoiled splendor of the surroundings, or anything else that might be on your mind. If you're an artist, and you want to display, write for information.

CRAFTS BAZAAR
If you like creative knickknacks and old junk you'll love roaming around our bazaar. You'll see imaginative leather, ceramic, bead, and silver creations, as well as Zodiac Charts, camp clothes, and worn out shoes.

If you like playing with beads, or improvising on a guitar, or writing poetry, or molding clay, stop by one of our work shops and see what you can give and take.

FOOD
There will be cokes and hotdogs and dozens of curious food and fruit combinations to experiment with.

**HUNDREDS OF ACRES
TO ROAM ON**
Walk around for three days without seeing a skyscraper or a traffic light. Fly a kite, sun yourself. Cook your own food and breathe unspoiled air. Camp out: water and restrooms will be supplied. Tents and camping equipment will be available at the Camp Store.

MUSIC STARTS AT 4:00 P.M. ON FRIDAY, AND AT 1:00 P.M. ON SATURDAY AND SUNDAY.

It'll run for 12 continuous hours, except for a few short breaks to allow the performers to catch their breath.

AUGUST 15, 16, 17.

One day $7.00 Two days $13.00 Three days $18.00

For tickets and information write to:
**WOODSTOCK MUSIC
BOX 996, RADIO CITY STATION
NEW YORK 10019**

✳ check papers and radio for additional acts.
All programs subject to change without notice

*White Lake, Town of Bethel, Sullivan County, N.Y.

170 (top)
Panorama of festival stage and audience, with members of Joe Cocker's Grease Band setting up for their performance, 17 August 1969, photograph by Elliott Landy

171 (above) and 172 (right)
The crowd at Woodstock, 1969, photographs by Baron Wolman, Ralph Ackerman

173 (opposite top)
Carlos Santana (right) and bassist David Brown perform with the other members of Santana at Woodstock, 16 August 1969, photograph by Tucker Ransom

174 (opposite bottom)
Sly Stone performs at Woodstock, 17 August 1969

175 (opposite)
Kaftan worn by Grace Slick
at the Monterey International
Pop Festival, 1967
V&A: PROV.9056–2016

176 (below)
Roger Daltrey
at Woodstock, 1969

177 (right)
Roger Daltrey's Woodstock
costume, 1969
V&A: S.204&A–1978

YOU
SAY
YES?

YOU SAY YOU WANT A REVOLUTION?

LOOKING AT THE BEATLES

VICTORIA BROACKES

Composer Aaron Copland, whose own work achieved a new, modern, distinctively American style – incorporating jazz into classical symphonies – declared that 'If you want to know about the Sixties, play the music of the Beatles.'[1] But the importance and symbolism of the band extends beyond the music they created: the Beatles' success and their status as public and media figures allowed them not just to experience but to shape the times in a way that few others could. Tracing the evolution of their lives and careers paints a picture of the wide-ranging social changes that took place in Britain and the US in the 1960s. This chapter looks at the Beatles' story in the second half of that revolutionary decade, through music, costume, photography and lyrics.

The Beatles' fame gave them access to a huge range of influential musicians and inventive styles, which they pursued both as a band and as individuals. From pop contemporaries like Bob Dylan and Brian Wilson of the Beach Boys to Ravi Shankar and the Eastern sitar tradition, to avant-garde classical and electronic composers including John Cage, Delia Derbyshire[2] and Luciano Beriano, their musical tastes crossed genres without limit. Similarly, their talents, personal connections and diverse interests were far-reaching, spreading into the arts and the wider counter-culture.

There were other successful bands, but perhaps what set the Beatles apart was their decision, in 1966, to work only in the studio and to cease touring. George Martin, the Beatles' producer, had left EMI to set up his own company but still often worked out of Abbey Road Studios. This freed the Beatles from the scheduling constraints imposed by a commercial record company, allowing them with Martin to take the time to pursue new ideas both outside and inside the studio, in creative exploration and innovation, and to push the Abbey Road studio technology to its limits. 'Musically', writes Scott Plagenhoef, 'the Beatles began to craft dense, experimental works; lyrically, they matched that ambition, maturing pop from the stuff of teen dreams to a more serious pursuit that actively reflected and shaped the times in which its creators lived.'[3]

RUBBER SOUL

With 1965's *Rubber Soul*, the Beatles' sixth album, there had come a notable shift in style and focus. What had changed definitively was the realization that 'they didn't have to segregate their professional work from their inner lives', a melding of art and life in which 'they consciously experimented in much of the *Rubber Soul* material'.[4] A large part of this experimentation for the band, and most likely their followers and the wider constituency, was down to drugs: marijuana, but also LSD, recently experienced by three of the Beatles in Los Angeles.[5] (Also credited to that visit is George Harrison's growing interest in the music of Indian sitar-player Ravi Shankar.) Recorded in October 1965, the album followed a spring and summer of charts on both sides of the Atlantic full of lyrically and musically groundbreaking singles, such as Dylan's 'Subterranean Homesick Blues' in March and the Yardbirds' June release 'For Your Love', with the Who's 'My Generation' imminent. The Summer of Love was still 18 months away and the word 'hippy' was not yet in use, but nonetheless pop music was beginning to connect on a deeper social and political level. The counter-culture in Britain had already begun to coalesce at the International Poetry Incarnation at the Royal Albert Hall on 11 June 1965; in the United States, October 1965 saw the first International Day of Protest organized at Berkeley. The day following the Poetry Incarnation, the Palace announced that the Beatles would receive MBEs, causing some other award-holders to send theirs back. (John Lennon would later return his in protest at British and American military policy.)

For the as yet apolitical Beatles, protest songs were not in their sights. Paul McCartney informed the *New Musical Express* in October 1965 that he and Lennon had found a different direction: 'We've written some funny songs – songs with jokes in. We think that comedy numbers are the next thing after protest songs.'[6] The first of these jokes was perhaps the album title itself – *Rubber Soul*, a play on words with shoe soles, was Paul McCartney's response to the term 'plastic soul', coined to describe the output of white musicians playing 'black' soul music (pointedly aimed at the Rolling Stones).

While this might seem an ill-fitting response to the rising tide of challenging world affairs, in fact humour and performance techniques were absolutely in the vanguard, encapsulating the zeitgeist of 1960s political activism. Innovative strategies of social action enlisted absurdity and theatricality in pursuit of their aims, out of frustration with traditional forms of democratic protest and in recognition of the power and reach of performance. The Beatles, though not overtly political, were at the forefront of the counter-cultural transformation that was already beginning to take place in London and parts of the US, and as their life and work became integrated, so this burgeoning revolution is clearly visible in their work.

The album cover of *Rubber Soul* presents a photograph of the band by Robert Freeman, with the title overlaid in one corner, both image and lettering distorted. The name of the band does not appear – by this time everyone knew who they were – a confidence borne out when the album entered the charts on 3 December straight at number one, displaced briefly for a week by *The Sound of Music* soundtrack before regaining top slot for a further eight weeks. It stayed in the UK charts for an astonishing 43 weeks; released in the US in January, it spent six weeks at number one in a chart run of 51 weeks. It has been suggested that the warping of the cover portrait mirrors the visual distortions of drug use, reflecting the band's recent forays into psychotropics.[7] In the same way, the typography, designed by Charles Front, anticipates Wes Wilson's psychedelic bubble lettering that burst onto the West Coast scene the following year – a style that quickly became an international counter-cultural phenomenon on both sides of the Atlantic.[8] As important as the album cover image, it suggests the creativity and freedom – visual and otherwise – that were to come, both for the band and for society in general, and positions the Beatles at the cutting edge of events that were changing the world, and the design world, around them. Indeed, Ken Kesey's Acid Tests would be brought to a wider public in the Trips Festival, co-organized with Stewart Brand, in January 1966, the month of *Rubber Soul*'s US release. Alongside acid, *Rubber Soul* marks their increasing fascination – George Harrison's particularly – with spirituality and Eastern religion, introduced to them by Bahamian dignitaries in February 1965 while they were there filming *Help!*[9] But it was with *Revolver* that these changes really took hold.

REVOLVER

In April 1966 *TIME* magazine's cover dubbed London 'The Swinging City', reflecting its dramatic rise to the centre of world attention. A huge upheaval was taking place across British social and artistic values, and the Beatles were at the forefront, entering the studio to start recording *Revolver* that month. Drugs were an important agent: taking LSD was seen as a way of opening the 'doors of perception' to an entirely new way of seeing, a spiritual and self-liberating quest for enlightenment. John Lennon

was using LSD regularly by the beginning of 1966, and Paul McCartney admitted to the press in 1967 to having taken it four times. (Its use was criminalized only in 1966.[10]) The effect of taking acid was to create a fundamental shift not only in what you saw when under the influence, but also in your opinions of existing value systems when you were not. The use of psychotropic drugs during the 1960s was as important in its effects on the creative psyche as Freud's theories of dreams and the unconscious had been to the

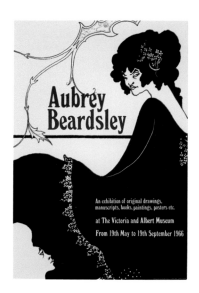

Surrealists, and it formed the basis for a wave of new experimentation in music, art, film and literature as well as breaking down the barriers between these genres.

Revolver was released in August 1966. Music journalist Nicholas Schaffner, writing about the band's 'psychedelic' period, proposed: 'That adjective implies not only the influence of certain mind-altering chemicals, but also the freewheeling spectrum of wide-ranging colours that their new music seemed to evoke.'[11] This experiential approach is demonstrated most clearly in the track 'Tomorrow Never Knows' (whose original title 'The Void' was abandoned as too obvious a drug reference), John Lennon's response to his third trip, taken in January 1966. Many of the lyrics derive directly from Timothy Leary's instructional text *The Psychedelic Experience*, including the opening 'Turn off your mind, relax and float downstream.'[12] Lennon is said to have tape-recorded excerpts from the book and played them back as the acid took effect. The song is one of the most influential records the Beatles ever made, introducing LSD and Leary's psychedelic revolution to millions of young people across the Western world (pls 181, 183).

Revolver's album cover art is significant: it was a complete departure from the conventional personality portrait, highlighting the Beatles' interest in graphic arts. Lennon asked the German artist Klaus Voormann, whom they knew from their early days in Hamburg, to design the sleeve. Voormann was inspired by the Victorian

illustrator Aubrey Beardsley and his stylish, monochrome line drawings, creating a cover that combines this style with photomontage, each member of the band appearing several times. Again the Beatles were tapping into the zeitgeist: in May 1966 the V&A had opened a landmark Beardsley exhibition (pl.182), which heralded a huge revival in popularity of his designs (Alphonse Mucha, whose Art Nouveau style inspired another strain of psychedelic art, had also been popular at the museum in 1963). George Melly, writing about the exhibition in the counter-culture issue of the *Observer* of the following year, described his surprise at 'find[ing] it packed with people' and feeling that he 'had stumbled for the first time into the presence of the emerging underground'.[13] *Revolver* was the first Beatles record to win a Grammy Award for Best Album Cover, confirming the importance of the cover art and not just the content. The credits also list the lead singer on each song, reflecting the growing individuality of the four band members.

Revolver also signalled a change in the Beatles' music. The band were eagerly exploring new ground, moving away still further from the conventional love song. This confidence created the self-assuredness of *Revolver* – created over a whopping 300 studio hours – and would allow them to redefine the genre of pop music. This album was the first signal that 'they were no longer mere anomalies within the world of pop, no longer potential fads; they were avatars for a transformative cultural movement.'[14] Their potential was fully realized in the album that followed.

① Turn off your mind, relax and float downstream
it's not dying, it's not dying.   (oterer no. dying
And all the colours of the earth you'll hear
it's not thinking, it's not thinking
Yet you may see the meaning within
Itself being. it's all being

② Love is all and love is everyone
that is learning
Though ignorance or beauty don't mourn the dead
it is believing, it is believing.
here is the all and love is everyone
it is everiving it is younger
Put down all thoughts, await shining void
is it gleaming of dying?

Turn off your mind, relax and float downstream
And listen to the colours of the earth seen
Yet you may see the meaning of within
Through ignorance or faith don't mourn the dead
here is the all, and love is everyone
Put down all thoughts await for shining void
is it gleaming

Turn off your mind, relax, and float downstream
                                    it's not dying.
Put down all thought, await, the shining void
                                    it is gleaning?
That you may see the meaning of within
                                    it is being.
That love is all and love is everyone
                                    it is learning.
That ignorance of faith body mourn the dead
                                    it is believing
                                    it's not dying
But listen to the colours of the dream
That being   it is living.
OR play the game existence to the end
                        of the beginning the beginning

SGT. PEPPER

The Beatles' *Sgt. Pepper's Lonely Hearts Club Band* is one of the most celebrated and analysed albums of all time. In the words of Allen Ginsberg, the Beatles 'had, and conveyed, a realization that the world and human consciousness had to change'.[15] The record's reception must have been all the more exciting following prior speculation in the press that the band might be running out of new ideas: 10 months was the longest fans had ever had to wait for a new Beatles album (although the pre-release earlier in the year of the astonishing double A-sided single 'Strawberry Fields Forever' / 'Penny Lane', originally destined for *Sgt. Pepper*, must have partially dispelled those fears). Ian MacDonald recounts that the LP's release was

a major cultural event ... Paul Kantner of ... Jefferson Airplane remembers how the Byrds' David Crosby brought a tape of *Sgt. Pepper* to their Seattle hotel and played it all night in the lobby with a hundred

LUCY IN THE SKY WITH DIAMONDS

~~ORGAN~~

① Picture yourself in a boat on a river
   with tangerine trees and marmalade skies   [drums f.]

ORGAN
TAMBURA   Somebody calls you, you answer quite slowly.
   a girl with kaleidoscope eyes.

          Cellophane flowers of yellow and green

Guitar   towering over your head
dropping look for the girl with the sun in ~~your~~ her eyes
bass   and she's gone.

Piano.   Lucy in the sky with diamonds.

② Follow her down to a bridge by a fountain
   where rocking horse people eat marshmallow pies
   Everyone smiles as you drift past the flowers
   that grow so incredibly high

          Newspaper taxis appear on the shore
          waiting to take you away
          Climb in the back with your head in the clouds
                                    and you're gone

          Lucy in the sky with diamonds.

③ Picture yourself on a train in a station
   with plasticine porters with looking glass ties
   suddenly someone is there at the turnstile
   the girl with kaleidoscope eyes.
          Lucy in the sky with diamonds

young fans listening quietly on the stairs, as if rapt by a spiritual experience.[16]

Elsewhere in the US normal radio play ceased and only tracks from *Sgt. Pepper* were played. Back in the UK, in *The Times*, Kenneth Tynan called it 'a decisive moment in the history of Western Civilization'.[17]

The group enlisted Pop artists Peter Blake and Jann Haworth to work on the cover, having been introduced by famous art dealer Robert Fraser, who had a gallery in Duke Street, Grosvenor Square. The impetus for the album's concept came from Paul McCartney: it was his idea to create a fictitious Edwardian-era military band, and he produced an initial ink drawing of the cover.[18] Blake and Haworth's design incorporated 88 figures, including the band members, into a visual collage – the Beatles, replete in acid-bright frogging and epaulettes (a contemporary fashion for spoof military wear), (pls 193, 195) stood among mostly life-sized cut-outs of notables from Lewis Carroll to Oscar Wilde, Edgar Allan Poe and Bette Davis (pls 186, 187). The band's thick moustaches and longer hair are a marker of the new hippy style. A photograph by Michael Cooper of the massed ranks produced the final image.

The adopted group persona gave the Beatles further freedom to experiment musically, and also visually. In the album's overture, McCartney sets the scene: 'May I introduce to you … Sgt. Pepper's Lonely Hearts Club Band'; the cover brings to life their new identity, forcing the audience to reconsider who they believe the band to be. Individual pop stars and artists had used stage names to project performance personalities, but the Beatles' sustained continuation of a collective imaginary identity through the album was a radical act. The creative benefit was to allow the group to break their own mould. Its influence and extension can be seen in the 'concept album' work of many pop performers since, notably David Bowie's *The Rise and Fall of Ziggy Stardust and The Spiders from Mars*, released five years later, in 1972.

Blake and Haworth's design was the most expensive Beatles album cover yet, costing over 35 times the standard rate.[19] *Sgt. Pepper* had a significant influence on record sleeve design, achieving new heights for this artform for not just the Beatles but pop music as a whole. Recording also took even longer than previous albums; but because studio time was not deducted from the band's royalties, they could afford to take their time.[20] *Sgt. Pepper* was paradigmatic in its use of available recording technology, pushing it to its limits as part of the creative process. Both the album and its artwork included a huge variety of styles and references to wide-ranging cultural influences.

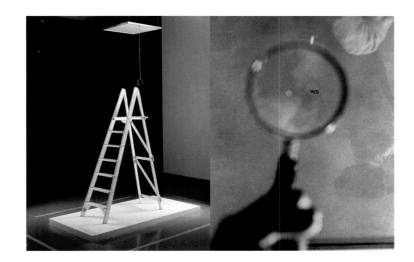

Lennon and McCartney's adoption around this time of counter-cultural ideas in music and art, of randomness and fragmentation, connect directly to their associations, interests and lifestyles in late 1966. Lennon had recently and fatefully met artist Yoko Ono at Indica, in Mason's Yard, which, alongside Fraser's Duke Street space, also in St James's, was the central hipster art gallery of the time. Ono was a leading light of the New York-based International Fluxus movement, which focused on creative process over finished artefact, and the disruption of bourgeois life (pl.188). Its members were greatly influenced by John Cage, whose compositions fascinated McCartney. The Indica Gallery, co-owned by Barry Miles, Peter Asher and John Dunbar, was at the heart of the tight-knit circle of the counter-culture and epitomized the closeness of its interrelationships: Dunbar was married to singer Marianne Faithfull; Paul McCartney's girlfriend at the time was Peter Asher's sister, the actor Jane Asher; and Miles's *International Times* was run from the Indica bookshop when it moved to Southampton Row.

These connections are perhaps most clearly identified in 'A Day in the Life', the last track on *Sgt. Pepper*, but the first they worked on. The song takes as its subject the death of socialite Tara Browne in a car crash.[21] McCartney had suffered a motorbike crash when riding with Browne just a month before. Alongside the news of the tragedy itself the lyrics address media alienation: the contrasting absurdity of the second news story, about the number of holes (4,000) in Blackburn, Lancashire (in the roads), perfectly manifests this feeling. The final message – that, as MacDonald puts it, 'life is a dream and we have the power, as dreamers, to make it beautiful'[22] – is a foreshadowing of the poetic wall slogan of the Paris demonstrators in May 1968, 'Beneath the paving stones: the beach!'; encouraging listeners to look beyond the 'society of the spectacle' toward poetic consciousness is the refrain 'I'd love to turn you on'.

With this album, the Beatles acted on their desire for records to be no longer simply a vehicle for music, but each to be an object in its own right, and in doing so created a string of firsts which went on to be adopted as the norm.[23] It was the first album with a decorated inner sleeve, not just a white paper envelope – this was conceptualized by The Fool, a Dutch design collective who would work on the Beatles' ill-fated Apple boutique a year later. *Sgt. Pepper* was also the first album to contain an additional artwork, in the form of a cardboard sheet of cut-out 'memorabilia' (of military accoutrements) and collaged photographs. The centrefold photograph of the Beatles looking straight at the viewer (pl.195) was designed to be infused with love, as McCartney explained:

One of the things we were very much into in those days was eye messages ... So with Michael Cooper's inside photo, we all said, 'Now look into this camera and really say I love you! Really try and feel love; really give love through this! It'll come out; it'll show; it's an attitude.[24]

189 (right)
David Frost, George Harrison
and John Lennon discussing
transcendental meditation
on *The Frost Programme*,
29 September 1967

190 (below)
George Harrison's
purple jacket worn on
The Frost Programme

The first album to employ an overarching visual and musical concept, it was also the first to have the song lyrics printed in full on the back of the cover.

Public reaction to the album's release was also unprecedented: it sold 250,000 copies in its first week and 2.5 million in the first three months – not just to young people, but to fans of all ages. *Sgt. Pepper* immediately took the number one slot and stayed there for 27 weeks, charting for a total of 148. One immediate accolade that highlights the competitive camaraderie existing between musicians generally, as well as the communality of the small world of the pop counter-culture at the time, came three days after the record's release, when Jimi Hendrix covered the opening track in a concert at the Saville Theatre in London (owned by the Beatles' manager, Brian Epstein) – playing it back to Paul and George, who were in the audience.[25]

The powerful beam of love staring out from the central gatefold photograph extended its reach just three weeks following the album's release, when the Beatles took part in the world's first public satellite television broadcast, *Our World*. Their performance of 'All You Need Is Love' – videotaped in London's Abbey Road Studios – was watched by over 400 million people in 24 countries and perfectly captures a '60s moment when one of the dominant themes of political activism was the invocation of love and peace. The 'Love' jacket worn by John Lennon was designed for him by The Fool (pl.194).

Within three months of *Sgt. Pepper*'s release, Brian Epstein –

the Beatles' business manager, confidant and friend – was found dead in his bedroom. The shock had a profound effect on the band, who later saw his loss as the beginning of the end of the group. News of his death reached them while they were attending a meditation conference with their guru Maharishi Mahesh Yogi in Bangor, Wales. Their developing interest in Eastern spirituality and culture had been reflected, since *Rubber Soul*, in songs and that used Indian instruments and described their experiences of the subcontinent.[26] George Harrison was by then an accomplished sitar player and proponent of the Indian sound (pl.192).

Epstein's commercial instincts had not been unimpeachable, but what followed was a series of idealistically noble but commercially disastrous ventures. The Apple boutique on Baker Street opened in December 1967, designed and stocked by The Fool, and lasted fewer than eight months, but the manner in which it lived and died were also very much in keeping with the communal impulses of the times, with a profit-share for staff. (The principles of Apple Corps, founded in January 1968, ran along similar lines.[27]) Its final hours were almost a 'happening', in which the entire contents were given away to the public. Fittingly, the spectacular mural painted by the design collective on the building's exterior fell foul of planning regulations and was white-washed – elegantly mirroring the transition from the psychedelia of *Sgt. Pepper* to the minimalism of the *White Album*.

191 (top)
George Harrison in the
'Blue Jay Way' sequence
from the *Magical Mystery
Tour* film, 1967

192 (bottom)
George Harrison with
Ravi Shankar and sitar,
Los Angeles, 3 August 1967

193 (opposite)
George Harrison's
Sgt. Pepper suit,
1967, designed by
M. Berman Ltd

194 (right)
'Love' brocade frock
coat worn by John
Lennon on the 'All You
Need Is Love' broadcast,
1967, designed by
The Fool (Marijke Koger,
Simon Posthuma
and Josje Leeger)

195 (following pages)
Sgt. Pepper centrefold
image, 1967, photograph
by Michael Cooper

WHITE ALBUM

Continuing their trailblazing cover collaborations, their next album, *The Beatles*, was so distinctive-looking as to be one of the first to be known by its design rather than its title. The *White Album* was designed by Richard Hamilton at the request of Paul McCartney. Hamilton was a painter and collage artist, known as the 'father of Pop Art', whose work during the 1950s directly inspired Peter Blake, *Sgt. Pepper*'s co-designer. Hamilton chose to design something in stark contrast to the previous album, saying that it was his habit always to look for the opposite, for something completely different. For *The Beatles* he delivered a plain white cover.

Hamilton thought the album cover should be treated like a very small edition of poems, with just a serial number printed on the front. But he recognized that 'it still had to be an artistic event'[28] and created a poster of collaged photographs from personal, unpublished material provided by the Beatles, as well as four individual photographs of the band members, to go inside the album sleeve (pl.204).

196 (opposite)
The Beatles album cover,
1968, designed by
Richard Hamilton

197 (left)
John and Yoko 'Bed-In',
Presidential Suite of the
Hilton Hotel, Amsterdam,
25 March 1969

The embossed lettering of 'The Beatles' was a concession to marketing the album. Not only did Hamilton's cover signal a complete stylistic break from its colourful predecessor, it was also distinct from the rest of the contemporary album market, which had been heavily influenced by *Sgt. Pepper*. At a time when everyone else seemed to be following the Beatles' example of the previous year, with acid-inflected psychedelia, 'the biggest group in the history of popular music were being as minimal and unpsychedelic as you could imagine.'[29] The *White Album*, with 'no design, no photos [and] no illustration',[30] was an inspired riposte to expectations. Once again the Beatles underlined their position as trendsetters, as leaders not followers.

Just as *Sgt. Pepper*'s imaginative, maximalist colour-burst cover reflected its eclectic score, so too the *White Album*'s design, in its minimalist denial of specific, descriptive figuration, could be seen to convey an unwillingness to be pinned to a single style. The album is a collection of songs in a vast range of musical styles, often attributed to the group's broadening preoccupations and gradual separation from each other. Its original working title, *A Doll's House*, was abandoned after the band Family released an album called *Music in a Doll's House* in July 1968. Ian MacDonald laments the loss of this 'apt title', one which perfectly describes the album's 'musical attic of odds and ends, some charming, others sinister ... all absorbed in the interior worlds of their authors. There is a secret unease in this music, betraying the turmoil beneath the group's business-as-usual façade.'[31]

The song 'Revolution 1' – which gives title to this book and exhibition – was first recorded on the evening of 30 May 1968, the same day around 400,000 protesters led by the Confédération Générale du Travail (CGT, a national trade union) marched through Paris, chanting '*Adieu, de Gaulle!*' British students were declaring solidarity and a state of anarchy, two days into an occupation and protest at Hornsey College of Art, which would spread to art schools around England. Earlier in the year, the start of the Tet Offensive by North Vietnamese and Viet Cong forces had prompted thousands of anti-war protesters to march on the US embassy in Grosvenor Square in London; civil rights activist Martin Luther King, Jr had been assassinated on 4 April. Student demonstrations and uprisings had begun in France, Poland, West Germany, Czechoslovakia and at universities in the United States. At a time of unprecedented political activism, and struggle against poverty, war and prejudice, John Lennon was vilified for his continued doctrine of peace and love. Responding to an attack on 'Revolution 1' in the journal *Black Dwarf* in January 1969, however, he declared himself against both Establishment and New Left:

> I'll tell you what's wrong with the world: people. So do you want to destroy them? Until you/we change our heads, there's no chance. Tell me of one successful revolution. Who fucked up communism, Christianity, capitalism, Buddhism, etc.? Sick heads, and nothing else.[32]

His ambivalent attitude comes through loud and clear in lyrics such as 'You can count me out ... in'. This was the first recording affected by the presence in the studio of Yoko Ono, and if Paul McCartney had until this stage been the most receptive and exposed to avant-garde influence and exploration, this marks the point from which Lennon was quick to come to the fore, taking the political reins (pl.197).

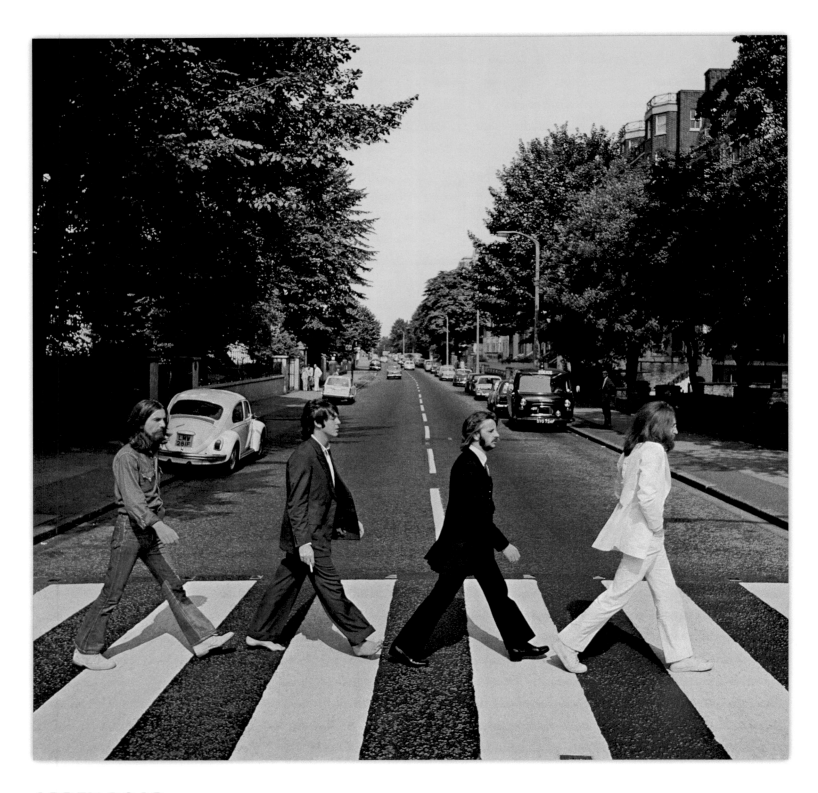

ABBEY ROAD

For their penultimate release, in September 1969, the Beatles chose a title that pays tribute to the legendary studio at Abbey Road in St John's Wood, north London, where they had spent so much time with producer George Martin, particularly since 1966 following the end of touring. This time it was John Lennon who appointed the artist who would create the cover. But as with *Sgt. Pepper* and *The Beatles/White Album*, McCartney was behind its initial design: he gave the photographer Iain MacMillan a sketch

showing how the picture should look. Unlike the extensive research and conceptualizing that went into to the cover of *Sgt. Pepper*, simple production and practicality lay behind the *Abbey Road* image, a photograph taken in a lunchbreak outside the studio. MacMillan added his own sketch to McCartney's to confirm the layout, after which the photo shoot took only ten minutes and six frames to complete, with the fifth chosen for the cover as it was the only one with the band members' legs in perfect formation. There

are no written clues, either to the album's title or the name of the band. Though the cover is in some ways visually unremarkable, it is one of the most popular and recognizable of all the Beatles' portraits or covers.

The first song on the album, 'Come Together' was written by Lennon during his and Yoko's Montreal 'Bed-In'. The couple held two week-long Bed-Ins for Peace, one at the Hilton Hotel in Amsterdam and one at the Queen Elizabeth Hotel in Montreal, intended to be non-violent protests against wars, an experimental new way to promote peace. Timothy Leary had asked Lennon to write a campaign song for his race against Ronald Reagan for the governorship of California in 1969; the title was Leary's slogan. The campaign was derailed by Leary's arrest for possession of marijuana; but coming at the end of the decade, the song encapsulates a generational shift from ethical debate toward drug-inspired individual relativism. The lyrics manifest Lennon's exasperated rejection of dogma from all sides, most prominently in the line 'one thing I can tell you is you got to be free'.

The mythology let loose as a result of the huge fame of the Beatles and their music led certain fans to obsess over hidden details and meanings in every area of their output. Perhaps most sinister of all it included murderous Charles Manson's obsession with the *White Album* and perceived hidden messages in the song 'Helter Skelter', but the cover of *Abbey Road* also enjoys a certain notoriety. It served to fuel a bizarre rumour that began circulating in 1969 that Paul McCartney had died in a car crash and was replaced in the band by an imposter. Advocates of this theory believe that the band felt guilty about Paul's death and placed hidden clues on the album cover for their fans, so that this 'simple image of the group on the zebra crossing acquired a mystical significance among the more gullible fans', not to mention the traffic havoc created by fans recreating its famous pose.[33]

198 (opposite)
Abbey Road album cover, 1969, photograph by Iain Macmillan

199 (above)
At the shoot for the *Abbey Road* album cover, 1969, photograph by Linda McCartney

LET IT BE

Almost all the songs on *Let It Be* had been recorded before work began on *Abbey Road*. The album went through many changes before finally being released. Originally, the band wanted to record the album live, perceiving their recent albums to have been over-produced, but its initial planned release in mid-1969 was postponed when 'Wall of Sound' producer Phil Spector was enlisted. The atmosphere in the studio was uncomfortably tense, caused in part by Yoko Ono's presence, constant feuding among the band, and their growing disillusionment with the album. The record was finally released as *Let It Be* in May 1970, one month after the Beatles had broken up. The album cover, four individual portraits, shows their distinct separation, each photograph styled like an LP cover for a solo artist, which by then Lennon, McCartney, Harrison and Starr were.

The idealism of the late 1960s left significant traces in the years following: from civil rights to multiculturalism,

from the permissive society to feminism and gay liberation, from environmentalism to communality. But as Ian MacDonald puts it, 'The true revolution of the Sixties — more powerful and decisive for Western society than any of its external by-products — was an inner one of feeling and assumption: a revolution in the head.'[34] It is in this arena, in the minds of ordinary people, beyond politics, that a permanent and radical shift took place. The Beatles and their music served as a cynosure and symbol, often intertwining with change, as the band and their listeners dared to dream of a better world.

When the Beatles broke up in 1970, their demise paralleled that of many of the revolutionary movements of the time, which petered out and fragmented because of internal tensions and differing ideas of how to proceed. The combined forces that seemed to bring things to a grinding halt — consumerism, naivety and individualistic materialism — were equally part of their story. The 'revolution' of utopianism and the hippies fell into decline; the anti-war and anti-Establishment groups became radicalized, moving away from the peaceniks into organizations such as the Baader Meinhof Group and the Red Brigade. The Beatles and the counter-culture had reached a shared peak in 1967, but what they had achieved in just a few years effectively forged a new world order. **VB**

200 (opposite)
Let It Be album cover, 1970, photograph by Ethan Russell

201 (above)
Illustration by Alan Aldridge for 'Revolution' from *The Beatles Illustrated Lyrics*, 1969

202 (opposite)
John Lennon's 'Imagine'
jacket, 1973, designed
by Renoma

203 (right)
John Lennon's *Abbey Road*
suit, 1969, designed by
Ted Lapidus

204 (opposite)
The Beatles, 1968
Richard Hamilton
photo-offset lithograph
86.5 x 58 cm (sheet)

205 (above)
Wonderwall film poster, 1968,
Apple Corps (Film producer)
V&A: E.276–2002
Purchased through the
Julie and Robert Breckman

206 (right)
Dress, 1967,
designed by Marijke
Koger of The Fool
V&A: T.314–2009

207 (opposite)
'A Is for Apple' poster,
1960s, designed by
Marijke Koger of The Fool
V&A: E.277–2002
Purchased through
the Julie and Robert
Breckman Print Fund

YOU SAY YOU WANT SHORTER SKIRTS?

7

BRITISH FASHION 1966—70

'A STATE OF ANARCHY'

JENNY LISTER

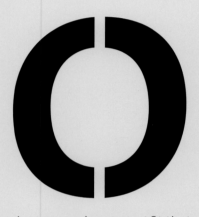

On 15 November 1966 Mary Quant received her OBE medal from the Queen, presented in recognition of her contribution to British fashion. At Buckingham Palace with her business partners Archie McNair and Alexander Plunket Greene (also her husband), Quant arrived coatless, in a monochrome outfit that made little concession to the grandeur and formality of the occasion, conspicuous among other female visitors in their below-the-knee tailored suits and dark overcoats (pl.208). Photographs of the designer, leggy and youthful in her cream jersey minidress, were printed in newspapers the next day, promoting her distinctive head-to-toe look. This was completed with nude lipstick, tightly fitting gloves with a circular cut-out (which neatly echoed the circular zip-pulls on her dress), a woollen beret, opaque tights and low-heeled shoes, all Quant-designed and manufactured by other companies under licence. These styles found popularity throughout North America, Western Europe, Australia and New Zealand. Captured that day, Mary Quant's 'complete look', including her Vidal Sassoon haircut and the miniskirt itself, inescapably associated with her name, has come to represent the 1960s and all its revolutions, in society, music and clothing. Her husband's double-breasted suit with contrasting buttons, incidentally, demonstrates the slightly more flamboyant styles newly available to men, while Archie McNair is conservatively dressed, as befitted his role as a lawyer and the business genius underpinning the success of the Mary Quant brand.

Mary Quant was one of several design and retail pioneers including John Stephen and Biba's Barbara Hulanicki who had helped to transform the King's Road, Carnaby Street and Kensington's Abingdon Road, previously quiet and unexceptional parts of London, into visitor attractions, now permanently set in global consciousness as 'London: The Swinging City' by TIME.[1] For the first time, the world of fashion focused on street style, on London's young ready-to-wear designers and their boutiques rather than the great Paris couture houses. By 1966 the leg-revealing miniskirt was ubiquitous – a fashion that embodied the restless, anti-establishment spirit of the educated and increasingly affluent creative circles of London from the mid-1950s: 'painters, photographers, architects, writers, socialites, actors, con-men and superior tarts. There were racing drivers, gamblers, TV producers and advertising men'.[2] Worn by young 'mods', and improvised by teenagers who rolled over the waistbands of their school skirts, the mini was picked up by designers including André Courrèges in Paris and Quant, who took it to new extremes in London, culminating in her mini-smocks worn with tiny shorts in 1967. John Bates, costume designer for Diana Rigg in the television series The Avengers, eliminated the skirt altogether for Emma Peel's leather catsuit, in 1965; other versions of this action-ready style followed, for instance for Marianne Faithfull in the 1968 film Girl on a Motorcycle. Journalists with a sharp eye for such new trends, such as the Daily Mirror's Felicity Green, helped to bring such developments to public attention with newspaper headlines as early as 1964.[3] As Quant recognized, the young, thin, rule-breaking 'Chelsea Girl' had become a global phenomenon: 'Chelsea ceased to be a small part of London; it became international, its name interpreted as a way of living and a way of dressing far more than a geographical area.'[4] The women who lived and shopped for clothes in

There is a state of anarchy in fashion
– a 'why not?' that has toppled all the
unwritten rules that used to inhibit
the choice of clothes ... The questioning
and rejecting is going on in more
significant areas than fashion, but it is
in dress that it shows most.

Brigid Keenan, 'Fashion Is Dead, Long Live Clothes',
Nova magazine, September 1968

'60s Chelsea were recalled vividly by publisher Alexandra Pringle, looking back on her childhood:

> Local residents stared and pointed as young women catwalked up and down the King's Road ... They wore big floppy hats, skinny ribbed sweaters, key-hole dresses, wide hipster belts, and, I believed, paper knickers. They had white lipsticked lips and thick black eyeliner, hair cut at alarming angles, op-art earrings and ankle-length white boots. They wore citron coloured trouser suits and skirts that seemed daily shorter ... They had confidence and, it seemed, no parents.[5]

The power of growing print media ensured that nascent trends reached the expanding youth market. Many new fashion-focused magazines were launched, such as *Nova* (1965) and *Petticoat* (1966), joining established women's titles including *Vogue* and *Queen*, which underwent revamps of both staff and sections, tuning into the new climate while still catering for the older, middle-class reader. At *The Sunday Times* and *Observer*, the introduction of colour supplements (in 1962 and 1964) also brought a regular fashion fix to middle-class homes throughout the UK. Fashion editors such as Ernestine Carter, a formidable American who headed *The Sunday Times* style pages, were instrumental in promoting young designers, including Mary Quant and Jean Muir (who made her a supple suede dress in a vibrant shade of purple) in 1966.

A vital youth-culture mix was transmitted to living rooms each week by television music programmes. *Ready Steady Go!* was presented by Cathy McGowan, an early Biba devotee, whose long, straight hair, heavy fringe, eye make-up and nonchalant attitude were copied by her many fans. The commercial potential of her accessible style was exploited by the development of Cathy McGowan

branded make-up in 1965 and lines of clothing available at British Home Stores. Such ventures were often short-lived, but other celebrities including singer Sandie Shaw and model Twiggy gave their name to fashion ranges in the later 1960s (pls 210–12). 'Twiggy Dresses' was among the most successful, launched in 1967 in collaboration with two graduate designers from the Royal College of Art. Twiggy insisted on approving each dress as one that she would happily wear herself, and the strong branding of her distinctive image (each dress came with a portrait hanger),

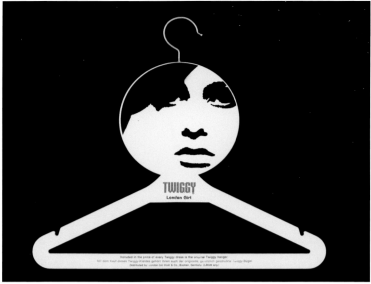

helped the brand to last for three years, although the manufacturers behind the label were unable to keep up with demand in the longer term. The following decade, Twiggy recalled the clothes favourably in her autobiography: 'I still think it was a very good, young collection of clothes – catsuits, print shifts gathered under the bust, Bermuda-length jumpsuits, shirt dresses with long pointed collars, jersey culotte dresses, a pinstripe gangster-style trouser suit – and all for between six and twelve guineas.'[6] Such examples show the power of celebrity to promote commercial fashion, ever-pervasive in the twenty-first century with global, 24-hour fashion and celebrity media inextricably entwined.

While some of London's young designers and their boutiques were amateurish (at least to begin with) and short-lived, much of the commercial success of Quant's vision, and that of those who followed in her footsteps, was supported by an existing infrastructure in British wholesale fashion manufacturing, and promotional backing provided by the London Model House Group. The predecessor of the British Fashion Council, the Group arranged a biannual London Fashion Week from 1958, as well as exhibition tours to Europe and America. Menswear entrepreneur John Stephen and others who answered the demand for young, mod fashion in Carnaby Street from the late 1950s were also capitalizing on the flexible skills of tailors in London's rag trade, based in Soho (pl.209). 'In those days the whole of Soho was manufacturing clothing. You could have anything made in the tiny workrooms in those dingy streets. You could also find anything you wanted – trimmings, linings, materials, buttons, embroidery', Bill Franks, John Stephen's business partner, recalled.[7] Like Quant, Stephen was ahead of his time, anticipating what people wanted before they knew they wanted it. At the height of his success he owned 15 shops along Carnaby Street, named variously as His, Mod Male, Domino Male and Male W.1. and his designs were

sold in 40 department stores in the United States. Musician George Melly described the appeal of Carnaby Street in 1972:

Stephen's clothes were and remained well-made. His imitators realized this to be unnecessary. It didn't matter how quickly everything fell to bits. The clothes weren't meant to last, but to dazzle. Their shops, blaring pop music and vying with each other for the campest window and decor, spread the length of Carnaby Street and its environs.[8]

While Carnaby Street's reputation for stylish, well-priced menswear grew, the King's Road became known for unusual but more exclusive styles from new names such as Kiki Byrne and John Michael.[9] Additional groundwork for the flourishing of British fashion during the 1960s was laid down in British art schools, and particularly by the diploma course in fashion design at London's RCA, led by Janey Ironside from 1956. Her students, often from regional art schools, were 'fed on couture',[10] given a range of experiences in the industry and taught by notable external tutors; early graduates who went on to international success include Gerald McCann and Gina Fratini.

Marion Foale and Sally Tuffin completed the three-year RCA course in 1962 and set up their own business, initially selling to department store Woolland's innovative boutique 21 Shop in Knightsbridge. By 1966 the duo were established in their eponymous shop in Marlborough Court just off Carnaby Street (a location chosen because of its chance proximity to their friend the milliner James Wedge and the low rent: 'a no-man's land ... there was a dairy, a saddlemaker ... very run down).[11] They had taken part in the celebrated 'Youthquake' trip to New York to promote British fashion; Susannah York wore Foale & Tuffin in the film *Kaleidoscope* (1966); boutiques including Wedge's

208 (previous pages)
Mary Quant receiving her
OBE, November 1966

209 (opposite left)
Carnaby Street, London,
1966, photograph by
Jean-Philippe Charbonnier

210 (opposite right)
Twiggy coathanger

211 (left)
Twiggy, 1967, photograph
by Ronald Traeger
V&A: E.72–1996

212 (below)
Fashion design for an outfit
to be worn by Twiggy in *Vogue*,
1969, designed by Bill Gibb
V&A: E.122–1978

213 (left)
'Double D' dress, 1966,
designed by Foale & Tuffin
V&A: T.29–2010

214 (opposite)
Jenny Boyd modelling
'Double D' dress, 1966,
photograph by Sidney Pizan

215 (following pages, left)
Ritva knitwear, *Nova* magazine,
November 1967, photograph
by Clive Arrowsmith

216 (following pages, right)
Film still showing the
fashion shoot from *Blow-Up*
(1966), directed by
Michelangelo Antonioni

Countdown and Top Gear on the King's Road sold their work. British *Vogue* often featured their designs in its 'Young Idea' section, edited by the influential Marit Allen, who brought together the key photographers, models, designers and even musicians to collaborate on her pages. In this productive creative environment, the worlds of work and pleasure blurred and these groups socialized together – often in clubs such as the Ad Lib and Scotch of St James. A liberating pop sense of fun and irreverence characterized Foale & Tuffin's designs – as seen in the 'Double D' dress with its pocket design inspired by a brand of beer (pls 213, 214). The rigorous technical training the women had received was evident in their beautifully made dresses in high-quality fabrics, often from Liberty, and the groundbreaking tailored trouser suits they introduced in 1965. Foale & Tuffin dresses, however, remained expensive: the designers did not follow Quant and develop a cheaper wholesale range in the UK.

Ritva and Mike Ross were part of the vibrant, transatlantic art, fashion and music scene of the 1960s and '70s, and they produced some of the most innovative knitwear of the period. Ritva came to London from Helsinki in the 1950s, wanting to be 'free, and unrestricted'; she gravitated to the King's Road area 'like other eccentrics'. She worked as a model, and particularly remembers the 1966 prêt-à-porter shows in Paris, where she overheard her French counterparts laughing at the ultra-short skirts of '*les Anglaises*'.[12] Ritva started her eponymous company with Mike Ross that year, wholesaling to boutiques such as Annacat on the Brompton Road, Browns on South Molton Street and Countdown on the King's Road, and later from their own boutique on Hollywood Road. Made by outworkers across London, her body-hugging garments included minidresses, skirts and even jumpsuits, and used both a variety of stitches (including crochet) and different yarns (wool, silk, acrylic), in a range of colours imported from

France. The sinuous knitted trouser suit illustrated in *Nova* in November 1967 has a strong graphic appeal, typical of the confrontational treatment of fashion and women's issues in the magazine (pl.215). In Ritva's hands, the fuddy-duddy image of knitwear was transformed: it became a vehicle for strong colour and rebellion against pre-existing uniforms. From 1969, label 'The Ritva Man' did the same for men's knitwear.[13] Unisex fashions in sweaters and T-shirts (another global phenomenon to emerge from the period) developed in tandem with the increasing presence of mass-produced denim jeans in the later '60s, which could be customized 'to express individualism, independence and even revolution'.[14]

As the diverse range of outfits worn in the fashion shoot scene in *Blow-Up* (1966) suggests (pl.216), while experimentation with new silhouettes and materials such as modern acrylics, plastics and disposable paper minidresses (pls 217, 218) looked ahead to the future, at the same time a wider counter-cultural reaction was growing, in which softer, retrospective styles and ethnic dress would come to dominate fashion. British *Vogue*'s January 1966 edition featured four pages showing Jane Ormsby Gore, the editor of the 'Shop Hound' section, wearing a selection from her eclectic wardrobe including a Victorian lace dress, a Turkish embroidered coat, a jacket by Paul Poiret found in the Portobello Road and an Edwardian motoring hat owned by her grandmother. This was the future of fashion. Ormsby

Gore was one of the first of London's young, unconventional aristocrats to become known for appropriating family jewellery and textile heirlooms, and wearing these with second-hand couture — an early intimation of boho, festival or 'hippy chic'. She combined these elements with treasures brought back from travels in North Africa, new clothes from boutiques including Biba, and miniskirts and jeans. Looking back on this period, in 2006, Ormsby Gore remembered the pleasure of creating her own style:

> I loved that sort of thing ... suddenly to have flashy jewels which you wear with your jeans, which now everybody wears all the time ... from the Biba tailored look to the ethnic look with all those wonderful embroidered Indian and Palestinian dresses. I started wearing all of them when I was pregnant ... it was very chic compared to the the mainstream hippy Afghan coat look, the let it all hang out look ... it wasn't messy.[15]

Ormsby Gore was married to Michael Rainey, owner of the exclusive menswear boutique Hung on You, which sold customized vintage clothing and colourful, historically inspired shirts and suits 'the colour of Smarties', initially in Cale Street and, from 1966, around the corner at 430 King's Road (pl.219).[16] For three years, from 1965 until 1968, Hung on You sold prohibitively expensive clothes to

221 (right)
Christopher Gibbs and
owner Michael Rainey at
Hung on You, King's Road,
London, 1966, photograph
by Colin Jones

Rainey's friends, other dedicated dandies and the new rock aristocracy including Mick Jagger and members of Pink Floyd. The suede jerkin loosely based on Native American clothing, as worn by interior designer David Mlinaric in 1967, reflects the esoteric thinking behind the store, as Ormsby Gore explained: 'we were seeking the Holy Grail and were always very high-minded and spiritual, those leather jerkins were all to do with rising spirit' (pl.232).[17] Once the King's Road became commercial, the Raineys moved out: 'we noticed other changes; people were on heroin or cocaine and we saw the pattern of our new order starting to fall apart. Youth was suddenly making a dash for the dosh. We were back where we came in. For us the period was over.'[18] The boutique at 430 King's Road continued to be one of the most cutting-edge in London: it was taken over by Tommy Roberts and Trevor Miles of Mr Freedom, and subsequently by Malcolm McClaren, who began trading from the site as Let it Rock from 1971.

A few yards further down the King's Road, at number 488, was Granny Takes a Trip – another shop to provide the possibility of personal reinvention and an alternative lifestyle through its clothes, and catering (without competing) for a similar clientele (pl.220). Opened in December 1965 by designer Nigel Waymouth, his girlfriend Sheila Cohen and John Pearse (a mod and Savile Row-trained tailor), Granny Takes a Trip sold Victorian and Art Deco dresses, customized second-hand clothes and high-quality, flamboyant menswear, including velvet trousers, floral shirts and languid jackets in William Morris furnishing fabrics, made using Savile Row's outworkers. The beaded dress worn by Veruschka in the poster for *Blow-Up* is one of many now-iconic garments sold by the store.[19] Granny's is also thought to have been the source of the Beatles' Afghan coats; John Lennon was photographed wearing his at the press launch of the *Sgt. Pepper* album in 1967.[20] Originally an inherently exclusive counter-fashion, the first of these sheepskin coats were elaborately embroidered, rare examples from the Ghazni province in Afghanistan. Later versions could be both useful and spectacular (David Bowie wore one to his wedding in 1970, pl.222), but the market quickly became flooded with inferior, often unpleasant-smelling imitations widely available from boutiques such as I Was Lord Kitchener's Valet of Carnaby Street.

Toward the end of 1967, Mary Quant was interviewed for a *Guardian* column called 'The Permissive Society'. Here Quant expressed her approval of the changes in attitudes that had happened since the 1950s, and particularly the American conscientious objectors to the Vietnamese War, although, a mod at heart, she felt ambivalent about counter-cultural hippy and vintage styles, seen on both sides of the Atlantic. Quant explained:

We are less permissive to authority. The Beautiful
People are non-violent anarchists, constructive
anarchists. They are a real breakthrough. But I have
been worrying about the way they dress. It can't be
called fashion, because it's old clothes, and it's always
depressing to wear clothes of the past.[21]

The same year, Quant designed a matching jacket and skirt
for her 'Ginger Group' wholesale line, sold in boutiques

and department stores throughout the UK. Made out of a
monochrome printed fabric ('Marigold', designed by William
Morris in 1875 and revived for interiors by Sanderson), the
suit extends an idea from menswear, specifically mens'
jackets made from floral upholstery fabric by Granny Takes
a Trip, and it acknowledges the growing appetite for pattern
and nostalgia among her customers (pl.233). The simple
summer suit demonstrates fashion's ambivalence that year,
even in the mainstream, unifying modernity and Victoriana.

The move toward fancy dress or 'costume' in the
fashions of 1967 can be seen at its most extreme in the
designs of The Fool, a design collective from Amsterdam
– Simon Posthuma, Marijke Koger and Josje Leeger. Marit
Allen's editorial in *Vogue* described their clothes as 'a
magician's impression of texture and colour – a touch
of velvet, glimpse of satin, a smash of red, clash of blue,
whispering voiles and brocades helter skelter everywhere,
boleros, headdresses, trousers and capes'.[22] The Fool
fashion was available at the Apple boutique, financed
by the Beatles, at 94 Baker Street. A huge psychedelic
three-storey mural made the building an instant tourist
attraction; designs by The Fool could also be seen marking
out John Lennon's Rolls-Royce as a psychedelic 'gipsy
caravan'. The clothes were extraordinarily expensive, being
usually one-off and custom-made, frequently decorated
with appliquéd felt flowers or beading. No detail was
compromised to save cost, down to the woven silk labels
inside each garment. The textiles were specially designed
too, and often linked directly with The Fool's psychedelic
murals and posters. Despite the Beatles connection, the
sightseers failed to spend their money at the shop and it
closed down within seven months, reportedly at a loss of
£100,000. By this time the band was also supporting Apple
Tailoring at 161 King's Road, which was managed by John
Crittle of Dandie Fashions. The Beatles went on to give their

custom to Tommy Nutter of Savile Row, whose business was backed by the pop singer Cilla Black.

Meanwhile, competitively priced versions of the more avant-garde fashions of London could always be bought on Carnaby Street. Lord John was a boutique set up in 1963 by three brothers, Harold, David and Warren Gold, who enjoyed great success, perhaps in part because of the inevitable but mistaken association of their brand with John Stephen, 'the King of Carnaby Street'. Lord John clothes responded quickly to new styles and the Gold brothers' empire expanded to a chain of over 30 shops by the early 1970s. A 'Nehru' style jacket made of a synthetic woven floral brocade exemplifies the Carnaby Street take on the 'Peacock Revolution' styles worn by fashionable young men in the late 1960s.[23]

The revolution in menswear was also visible in the traditional world of Savile Row bespoke tailoring. A new group of entrepreneurs, often from aristocratic backgrounds, spotted the shift in taste and rejected traditional careers in the City, instead opening shops in the area around Piccadilly and Jermyn Street, long famous for dressing the British gentleman. Blades, established in 1962 by Old Etonian Rupert Lycett Green and Charley Hornby, with expert cutter Eric Joy, built a reputation for comfortable, lean tailoring, using interesting fabrics. The shop presented the first ready-to-wear menswear fashion show in 1967. Jackets were cut with narrow sleeves and high armholes, trousers fitted neatly; Lycett Green recalled that they 'wanted to make men's clothes sexy. We aimed to sell men's clothes that women would like and find sexy. Men like clothes to attract women.'[24] The jacquard-woven silk used in 1968 for one of Lycett Green's own suits, now in the V&A collection, was a salvaged length from a run of only 100 yards, made in France in 1953 (pl.223).

One of the most original characters in the story of the Peacock Revival in menswear is Mr (Michael) Fish, who had no formal training but gravitated to the prestigious companies of Jermyn Street, transforming Turnbull & Asser into the most exciting shirt-makers in London; he is also thought to be the originator of the 'kipper tie'. His shop opened in Clifford Street in 1967, stocked with a range of unusual shirts with Byronesque ruffles or roll-neck collars. Mr Fish attracted a wealthy and international following, including David Mlinaric, the original owner of the V&A's much admired striped velvet suit (pl.224). Fish's flamboyant style was translated into notorious men's dresses for Mick Jagger and David Bowie (worn at the Hyde Park concert in 1969, and for the original UK album cover for *The Man Who Sold the World*, 1971). The V&A collection includes a semi-transparent ikat-printed silk example of his provocative kaftans, worn by men and women alike.[25]

The appreciation of unusual fabrics that characterized the eclecticism and flowing loose lines of the hippy look was stimulated by the couture designs of Thea Porter. Her shop in Greek Street, Soho, attracted similarly glamourous customers, including Faye Dunaway, Barbara Streisand and Talitha Getty, as well as members of Pink Floyd and other British rock royalty. Her business opened in 1966, about the same time that wealthy, adventurous members of London's in-crowd began to travel to Morocco and Tunisia, bringing back indigenous textiles and clothing. Porter began by decorating her clients' houses, later gaining an international reputation for her signature outfits based on authentic traditional dress from North Africa; she combined knowledge acquired in Damascus and Beirut, where she had spent parts of her early life, with an appreciation of early twentieth-century European designers Poiret and Fortuny, who had in turn been inspired by older ideas of the exotic and 'Arabian Nights'. Porter's luxurious, voluminous abayas (often mislabelled as kaftans) were also purchased by wealthy clients in the Middle East. Some abayas combined

239

240

224 (opposite)
Man's suit, 1968,
designed by Mr Fish
V&A: T.310&A–1979

225 (right)
Talitha and Paul Getty, Jr
in Morocco, British *Vogue*,
January 1970, photograph
by Patrick Lichfield

oversized printed silks with textiles from the region, and were embellished with beads and braid (pl.231). The French couture response to this look is defined by images of Talitha Getty in Morocco, wearing Yves St Laurent (pl.225). For many the appropriation of traditional costume and generic 'peasant' styles of dress was purely an expression of personal identity or sympathy with counter-culture values, without a thought of wider implications. But these developments in fashion strengthened Britain's trade links with Asia and North Africa through clothing imports, and stimulated the production of imitations in local rag trades, as David Gilbert and Sonia Ashmore have suggested.[26]

Commercial fashion also took inspiration from historic Western dress, whether found in family dressing-up boxes or bought from the more focused dealers to be found in Chelsea Antiques Market, the antecedents of the now lucrative and international second-hand or 'vintage' market. Drawing on 1930s couture, and recognized at the time as the work of a world-class talent, Ossie Clark's designs remain highly collectable, both by museums and those who wear vintage today. His sinuous, sexy chiffon dresses (and transparent shirts for men), were the result of his innate originality and exacting technical knowledge, paired with Celia Birtwell's exuberant floral prints. After graduating from the RCA in 1965, Clark sold his designs in Alice Pollock's boutique Quorum of Radnor Walk, the generational equivalent of Quant's Bazaar a decade earlier. Clark quickly became a celebrity in his own right and was known for his 'rock and roll' lifestyle, but a lack of business sense resulted in a sad decline during the 1970s. Norman Parkinson's photographs of his star-printed dress modelled by Ingrid Boulting at Lacock Abbey, the birthplace of photography, capture the tail end of the 1960s spirit, a blend of romantic innocence and idealism, before the heavy clomp of glam rock and platform shoes arrived (pl.226). This elegiac tone in

Ossie Clark's distinctive aesthetic has been seen as marking 'a change of spirit in the British fashion scene – one where the playful, bright naivety of the generation of Quant was replaced by a darker edge and distinctive subversive intent'.[27] A similar feeling was present in the clothes available at Biba, and shown in the pages of its mail-order catalogues.

Initially working as a fashion illustrator, and after a *Daily Mirror* mail-order experiment, Barbara Hulanicki opened her first Biba store in an old chemist's shop on Abingdon Road, a quiet cul-de-sac off Kensington High Street, in 1964. Expanding to larger stores in 1966 and 1969, her last, most ambitious enterprise was to take over Derry & Toms department store around the corner in 1973. All the Biba stores recreated the original's nostalgic, decadent atmosphere, complementing the romantic, sensual appeal of her clothing with loud music, stylish staff, dimly lit period interiors and chaotic changing rooms. The clothes were sometimes utterly black, in itself a style statement at a time when, in conventional day dress, black still meant mourning, but often coloured and patterned with 'granny prints', 'though only in sludgy tones, plums, earthy browns, dusty blues, never anything bright', as Jenny Diski has described.[28] They were good value, so young working women could shop for 'feather boas, wild hats, floaty garments for drifting around in at home or at parties, slick mini-dresses to snap about the streets in', alongside models, singers and actors.[29] The brand, like others including Mary Quant's, represented a 'lifestyle' approach that defined the direction of British retail in the 1970s and afterwards. Hulanicki has described the legacy of Biba as

not that particular look, that particular style, but rather what it stood for. Style can be a way of life, of self-expression, that is available to everyone. We started with our customers, with their needs and desires, and created a framework for them to discover themselves. We never told them what to do or wear, or how to live. We simply gave them an alternative to the mainstream and invited them in to play.[30]

The vivid and sometimes strange new images of women in the pages of late-1960s magazines – whether wearing baby-doll dresses, tailored business suits, kaftans or Art Deco evening gowns – reflected revolutionary developments in contemporary life. Clothes demonstrated the breaking down of traditional Western gender stereotypes in patriarchal society, while, arguably, shopping and consumerism replaced motherhood as the goal of the 'single girl'. Despite the complex and sometimes contradictory relationship between fashion and feminism, the discovery of fashion's democratic, liberating, storytelling potential for the individual (of all genders) is an enduring inheritance of these years. The heavy price – the massive environmental and humanitarian impact of the global fashion industry – has since become widely apparent.

Today, we unthinkingly experience daily reminders of the innovations in dress and maintaining appearances from half a century ago, both practical and psychological – from washing machines to jeans or miniskirts worn with tights, to cheap and adventurous cosmetics and, in democratic societies, relaxed dress codes and increased options in creating personal identities. Having flourished in London's shopping districts, street style is accepted as a dominant influence, constantly promoted by bloggers and fashion forecasters. Fashion in the 1960s pioneered instant, affordable design, which is now delivered with minimal effort to the consumer by the Internet. Mary Quant and other independent boutique owners and design students of the '60s led the way in establishing London as the centre of forward-thinking fashion; the city went on to produce radical designers such as Vivienne Westwood and Alexander McQueen, although the property boom has shifted the focus of new talent to the east, from Chelsea to Hoxton and Shoreditch. Clothing is no longer manufactured on a large scale in the UK, but students from across the world choose to study at the prestigious fashion design courses at British universities.[31]

When considering the impact of the fashion revolution that emanated from 1960s London, it is impossible to avoid its inherent ambiguity – simultaneously superficial and yet inescapably political. In twenty-first-century developed societies, where democratic values and high living standards are reflected in our unprecedented freedom and scope for creativity, wit and irony in dress, there is perhaps less potential than 50 years ago to shock with clothing or to use it as an obvious means of displaying and decoding a person's politics, occupation and socio-economic status. Paradoxically, now that fashion is more available, it is less meaningful. Back in the 1960s, for some, clothes became almost existentially important. In the words of Marc Bolan of T. Rex, they represented 'wisdom and knowledge and getting satisfaction as a human being'. In those days, 'if you designed a new suit or a pair of light green shoes with buckles all over them, it was like you conceived it and saved up for it – which might take you three months – and then you got the shoes, and those shoes were, for three months, the only thing that made you go ... a pair of shoes was like meeting God – it was a very strong buzz.'[32] **JL**

244

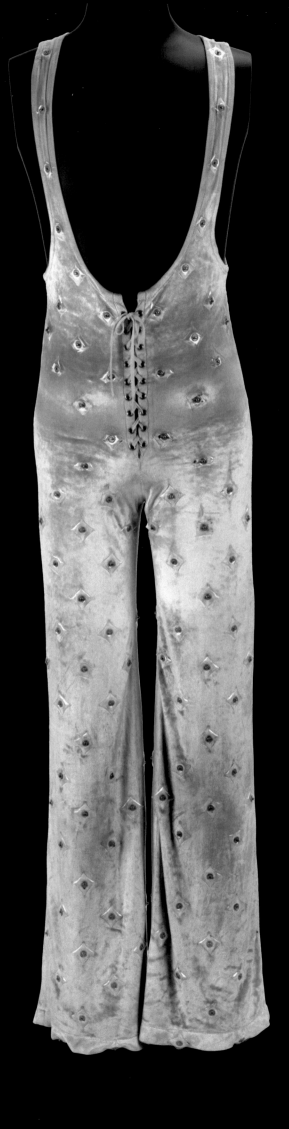

227 (opposite)
The Souper Dress, c.1967,
produced by Campbell's
Soup Inc. using artwork
by Andy Warhol
V&A: T.66–2016

228 (left)
Mick Jagger costume,
1972, designed by
Ossie Clark
V&A: S.1066–1983

245

229 (opposite)
British model Jean Shrimpton
walking barefoot on the
King's Road in Chelsea,
London, 1963, photograph
by Terry O'Neill
V&A: E.314–2011

230 (right)
Buy Granny Takes a Trip
and Join the Brain Drain!'
poster, 1968, designed by
Hapshash and the Coloured
Coat (Michael English
and Nigel Waymouth)
V&A: S.48–1978

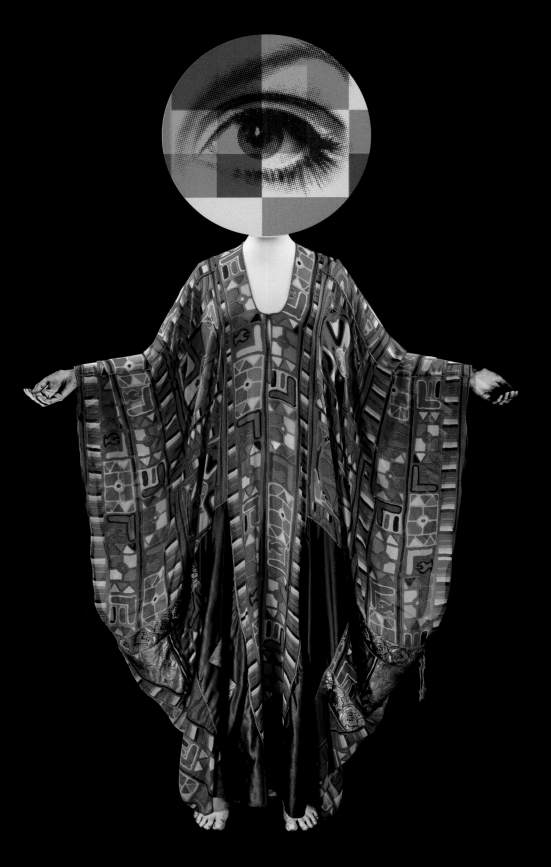

231 (below)
Abaya, 1968, designed
by Thea Porter
V&A: T.221–1992

232 (right)
Jerkin, 1967, designed by
Mirandi Babitz and Clem
Floyd for Hung on You
V&A: T.313–1979

233 (below)
Matching jacket and skirt in
William Morris 'Marigold' printed
cotton furnishing fabric, 1967,
designed by Mary Quant
V&A: T.8:1 to 2–2014

234 (right)
Dress worn by Sandie
Shaw at the Royal
Variety Performance,
13 November 1967
V&A: S.983–1982

YOU
SAY YOU
WANT IT
CHEAPER?

THE CHROME-PLATED MARSHMALLOW

THE 1960S CONSUMER REVOLUTION AND ITS DISCONTENTS

ALISON J. CLARKE

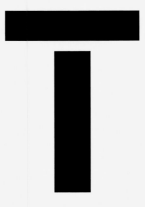

The revolutionary hubris of the 1960s was accompanied by a cacophony of popular consumer culture heralding a seismic shift in the world of 'things'. Where objects once anchored and reproduced pre-existing norms and social structures, in the 1960s consumption emerged as a newly transient, expressive phenomenon unhinged from the strictures of tradition and convention. Plastic inflatables, portable media technologies, the foibles of an accelerated fashion culture applied indiscriminately to once-utilitarian products; the decade witnessed a revolution in things as much as in political ideals. In Europe, this shift was accompanied by a growing disquiet over the vulgarizing effect of an imported, *Americanized* version of consumer capitalism.

The Independent Group (a network of artists, designers and architects) had, in 1950s Britain, famously embraced the blossoming of commercial culture, defining the concept of 'pop' by celebrating the products of a burgeoning consumer culture – in defiance of rationalist modernist taste. Beyond the art world, however, there remained a deep intellectual unease over the shift from home-grown manufacturing to a full-blown consumer-led society.[1] British design critic Reyner Banham sought to quash this anxiety by advocating a wholesale shift in societal values to match the ephemerality of the new pop era:

> We are still making do with Plato because in aesthetics ... we still have not formulated intellectual attitudes for living in a throwaway economy. We eagerly consume noisy ephemeridae, here with a bang today, gone without a whimper tomorrow –

movies, beach-wear, pulp magazines, this morning's headlines and tomorrow's TV programmes – yet we insist on aesthetic and moral standards hitched to permanency, durability and perennity.[2]

By the 1960s, antipathy toward the perceived corrosive effect of consumerism peaked among the European cultural elite, from filmmakers to novelists. Anthony Burgess's controversial 1962 novel *A Clockwork Orange* (translated to film by the iconic director Stanley Kubrick in 1971) depicts a violent dystopia, a not-too-distant future in which new media has spawned a sinister brand of youth culture. Kubrick's interpretation proffers a future of relentless hyper-visual, multimedia, saturated surround, which seamlessly melds the inanity of American commercial culture with European 'high art'. The narrative's chief protagonist, Alex, turns his back on the garish conformity of his parents' petit-bourgeois apartment in favour of gang ultra-violence and socializing in the pop-opulence of the psychedelic-drug-dispensing Korova Milk Bar, a dystopic inversion of a benign post-war teetotal institution, replete with Allen Jones-style fetishized sculptures depicting naked women as submissive, objectified plastic furniture (pl.235).

Kubrick's masterpiece *2001: A Space Odyssey* (1968) articulates design in a markedly prescient and technologically prophetic rendering of the future, whereas in *A Clockwork Orange* he uses design (from Brutalist exteriors to iconic 1960s pop design in the form of Ettore Sottsass's *Valentine* typewriter) to unsettle and disturb. Alex's family home, with its clichéd corner cocktail bar and three-piece suite, is a sardonic, psychedelic version of British working-class taste as described by Richard Hoggart in his groundbreaking cultural study *The Uses of Literacy* (1957): the otherwise conventional middle-aged mother serving afternoon tea wearing incongruous red,

When human wants do not exist, we invent them: 14-carat golf tees, mink-covered toilet seats, electric carving knives and electronic nail polish dryers are fostered and sold to an unsuspecting public who consent to this perversion of design and taste.

Victor Papanek, 'Pop Culture', 1963

shiny plastic go-go boots. Scenes of violence and sexual brutality are played out in a setting of super-hip interiors familiar from the pages of glossy contemporary colour-supplements. Here 1960s modern art and design operate as signifiers of amoral dysfunction rather than social progressiveness, rendering a chilling, alienated vision of a society in which the trusted mechanisms of taste and social propriety have descended into sweeping cultural relativism. *A Clockwork Orange* encapsulates a decade-long ambivalence toward the perilous combination of popular consumer and emerging youth culture.

In 1968, the year of the Paris student riots, a revolutionary book titled *The System of Objects* offered a theoretical interpretation of society's newly insatiable appetite for consumption. Penned by the Marxist French philosopher and sociologist Jean Baudrillard, it described how late-capitalist consumer culture had stripped meaning from 'concrete symbols' through a hyper-abstraction of signs and signifiers, and the dislocation of 'things' from any pretence of utilitarian value. Previous generations had read 'stuff' as a blueprint of social structure, in which the 'arrangement of furniture', Baudrillard declared, might stand as 'a faithful image of the familial and social structures' of a period: bourgeois interiors emphasizing 'unifunctionality, immovability, imposing presence and hierarchical labelling'.[3] The emergence of a mediated 'system of objects', in which 'real' stuff was rendered redundant, created a qualitatively different, dislocated relationship between people and 'things' in the new information-led, technological society.[4] The myth of consuming as a satiable phenomenon 'tied to the realm of needs', Baudrillard concluded, had finally been eliminated.[5]

Techno-erotic fantasies popularized in films such as *Barbarella* (1968); lush, shag-pile interiors of Verner Panton psychedelic party-dens; the youthful funkiness of

Aarnio Eero's *Globe* chair — all evolved as a shorthand to describe the loosening-up of lifestyle that accompanied the revolutionary spirit of the 1960s. Yet it was the discontents of consumer culture as much as the celebrants of its playful, disposable and visual exuberance who would define the 1960s, transforming material life and politics into the twenty-first century.

Set against the enormity of the Vietnam War, the civil rights movement and the assassinations of President John F. Kennedy and Martin Luther King, Jr, the shallowness of a youth culture defined by the material trappings of individual lifestyle choice was thrown into sharp relief. Design activists, Leftist intellectuals, feminists, sociologists and anti-corporate consumer-rights campaigners carved out areas of cultural critique aimed at exposing the selfishness inherent in a market economy fuelled by the naive idealism of counter-culture movements. They challenged the pursuit of the false gods and fetishes of pop culture, and the erosion of social conscience and cohesion by a ceaseless novelty-driven hedonism. Ultimately, in the global interconnectedness of the twenty-first century these once-discrete strands of protest and lifestyle would emerge as one: political engagement reduced to online petition campaigns where a simple click registers opposition to anything from authoritarian regimes to the naming of zoo animals.

Some contemporary critics argued that the decade's relentless lust for the latest (from experiential music to psychedelic graphics) was a fruitlessly tragic pursuit, while others saw the founding of a cultural revolution.[6] By the late 1960s, the lone voices and marginal groupings of dissent had concretized as a distinct critical body, a popular environmental and ecological movement spawning diverse counter-cultural responses, from the publication of the *Whole Earth Catalog* in the United

States to the establishment of the Centre for Alternative Technology in Britain. The dematerialization of static things into images, signs and ephemera transformed design from a practice of styling into one of mediation, experimentalism and consciousness-raising. In the late 1960s, the material and media experiments avant-garde modernist designers had entertained in the first half of the twentieth century emerged as a form of 'hippy modernism' steering technology away from corporations and the military–industrial complex toward a utopic vision of progressiveness as social good. According to design historian Andrew Blauvelt, 'caught between the proverbial rock of technocratic progress and a hard place of impending social disaster' alternative forms of consumption (experiential, networked and collectivized) blended a 'fascination with new media, materials, and technologies – taped music, synthesized sounds, feedback and distortion, light effects, slide projectors, portable video cameras, television, plastics ... and computers'.[7]

The turn away from conventional commodity culture can be traced through the legendary *Whole Earth Catalog* (1968–72), the pages of which achieved the confluence of counter-culture initiatives and emerging cybernetic technologies that would arise as a mode of 'digital utopianism'.[8] Instigated in California by Stewart Brand, the *Whole Earth Catalog* featured products that challenged the mainstream Western market-driven economy, advocating instead a cloud identification manual or instructions for a self-build Buckminster Fuller geodesic dome as part of a broader quest for the authenticity of a pre-pop, anti-consumption design ethic.

The late-1960s and early-'70s boom in experiential design and media – with an emphasis on the individual psyche, alternative environmental politics and cyber-networked culture – generated the 'outside-the-box' creative entrepreneurialism defining present-day Silicon Valley culture. As Fred Turner argues in *From Counterculture to Cyberculture*: 'Bay Area computer programmers had imbibed the countercultural ideas of decentralization, personalization, along with a keen sense of information's transformative potential, and had built those into a new kind of machine.'[9] But the roots of the simultaneous revolutions in information and material culture, which the decade's media guru Marshall McLuhan described in 1964 as a world 'not of wheels but of circuits, not of fragments but of integral patterns', lay in earlier debates regarding the role of designers poised at the helm of a 'neophiliac' revolution.[10]

235 (opposite)
Film still from *A Clockwork Orange*
(1971), directed by Stanley Kubrick
The Korova Milk Bar, furnished with
life-size plastic depictions of women
in contorted submissive poses
(overtly referencing controversial
'anti-feminist' sculptures of British
Pop artist Allen Jones) conjured up
a dystopic vision of 1960s youth-
oriented consumer subculture.

FROM THE NEOPHILIACS TO THE WASTE-MAKERS

Significantly, antipathy toward consumption, and US corporate power, predates late-1960s youth culture. At the very start of the decade, design's integral relation to the mechanisms of consumer-culture desire was laid bare with the publication in the United States of two highly significant, but entirely contradictory, exposés on its inner workings: *The Waste Makers* (pl.236) by social critic Vance Packard and *The Strategy of Desire* (both 1960) by marketing aficionado Ernest Dichter, a Viennese émigré. Dichter's treatise offered a corrective retort to Packard's 1957 condemnation of the advertising industry in the best-selling *The Hidden Persuaders*. Together these works highlighted the paradoxes inherent in burgeoning materialism, outlining the dichotomy of a debate that would ensue over the coming decade among marketing pundits and European intellectuals. *The Waste Makers* proved to be an enormously popular critique of US industry's conspiracy of artificial, planned style obsolescence. Lifting the lid on the murky worlds of marketing psychology and industrial design, it gave readers an insight into their cynical methods, from the application of useless product features and technological gimmickry to boosting sales through stoking an ever-rapid turnover in product styles.[11] A typical chapter, 'How to Outmode a $4,000 Vehicle in Two Years', traces the Machiavellian strategies of consumer-consciousness manipulation, through which perpetual 'dynamic obsolescence' had transformed once-durable products into sham props decorated with ephemeral fashion details. Even the most basic of consumer appliances was subjected to this regime of bogus styling: 'I counted 35 buttons and dials on one Hotpoint gas stove ... certain of the dials had no connection underneath the cover. They were dummies', laments Packard. Worse still, the emergence of a 'Kleenex culture'

of disposable design, concocted through the machinations of marketing psychologists, had undermined an American character born of the Puritan ethos of thrift and rationality. Packard indicts one figure in particular as the culprit responsible for this unprecedented shift to consumptive hedonism: Ernest Dichter, the so-called 'Freud of Madison Avenue'. Dichter, president of the Institute for Motivational Research, was openly accused of steering a generation of Americans toward a 'new mood of self-indulgence' replacing old-fashioned tastes with 'whims and desires'.[12]

Dichter's *The Strategy of Desire* was published in the same year as *The Waste Makers*, in open defiance of Vance Packard and similarly moralizing critics. His treatise champions the application of psychoanalytical theory to the study of consumer motivation, arguing against his detractors by declaring the divide between rational and emotive consumer behaviour to be entirely erroneous. In a chapter provocatively titled 'THE SOUL OF THINGS', featuring the evocative headings 'THE SOUL OF METALS', 'THE EMOTIONAL FACETS OF GLASS' and 'TEXTILES — THE FABRIC OF LIFE', Dichter parodies his opponents' overly-simplistic approach: '"Our life is becoming too soft. We are too much interested in material things." So goes the lament. Few who seek easy applause with such statements have bothered to tell us what they really mean by material or spiritual values.'[13]

Far from being objects of delusion, Dichter argues, everyday products – from food mixers to vacuum cleaners – are objects of 'psycho-economic' value. 'Objects have a soul', he declares, '[p]eople on the one hand, and products, goods, and commodities on the other, entertain a dynamic relationship of constant interaction'.[14] In direct contradiction to Packard's approach, which viewed the 1960s boom in

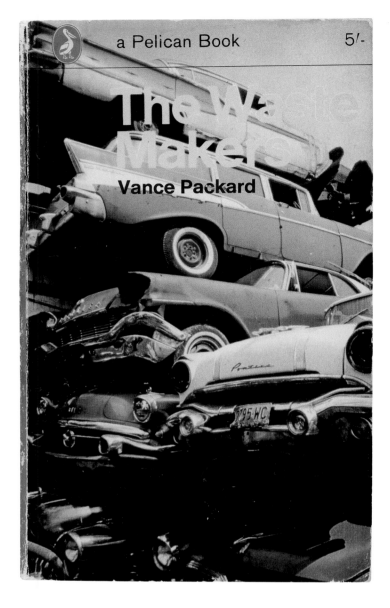

236 (left)
The Waste Makers by
Vance Packard, 1960
This best-selling critique
of the rise of disposable
consumer culture highlighted
the societal consequences
of a throwaway culture
driven by the 'built-in'
obsolescence of goods.

237 (opposite)
SDO, journal cover
Pan-Scandinavian Design
Student Organization, 1968,
designed by Timo Aarniala

city of tomorrow, dubbed 'Cornucopia City', will ban the repair of any appliance over two years old; its supermarts feature conveniently located receptacles 'where the people can dispose of the old-fashioned products they bought on a previous shopping trip'.[18] Over the next decade, Packard predicts, consumers will be encouraged to 'tingle at the possibility of using voice writers, wall-sized television screens, and motorcars that glide along highways under remote control'.[19]

This 1960s rhetoric of a 'liberated' future defined by disposability, advanced telecommunications, mobile living and multimedia environments was far from confined to social criticism or the realms of science fiction. In 1967 Walter Cronkite (America's leading news journalist) headed CBS's series *The 21st Century*; the episode 'At Home, 2001', sees Cronkite, anachronistically dressed in a conservative 1950s suit, taking viewers through a vision of portable inflatable furniture, throwaway dishes, networked home computers and centralized home entertainment systems.[20] A 25-minute documentary featuring interviews with architects and designers, including arch-modernist Philip Johnson, the programme echoed the 'future-filled' 1967 Montreal Expo *Man and His World*, famously epitomized by the spectacular Montreal Biosphere designed for the US pavilion by maverick architect and technologist R. Buckminster Fuller.

On one hand, then, there was a popular mainstream appetite for a consumption-led future, exploding with devices and technologies that blew conventional rituals and social relations out of the water, promising the next generation a revolution in lifestyle. On the other hand, a deep mistrust in the implications of this revolution gave voice to a growing counter-discourse questioning the benefits of a culture defined by youthful excess.

consumerism as indicative of a growing alienation within modern life, *The Strategy of Desire* posits the exact opposite: objects offered 'a new and revolutionary way of discovering the soul of man'.[15]

The hedonistic consumption of the 1960s, condensed into the opposing perspectives of Packard and Dichter, differed markedly from the 1950s model of consumption as an expression of US democracy. According to Fred Turner, the 1950s consumer 'enjoyed a freedom to choose not only from an array of expressive styles or a slate of political leaders, but from a range of consumer goods'.[16] By the 1960s, the pervading notion of consumer culture's inherent tie to ideal democracy, popularized by David Potter's *People of Plenty: Economic Abundance and the American Character* (1954), gave way to an emphasis on individual satiation and the emergence of youth counter-cultures focused on lifestyle, the politics of consciousness and 'getting loose'.[17]

In one of the most prescient passages of *The Waste Makers,* Packard envisages a design culture driven by product designers reinvented as futurologists. The

&/sdo

Skandinaviska Desingstuderandenas Organisation
Scandinavian Desingstudents Organization

Fmk 3.00 (sis. lvv)
Skr 4.00 (inkl. oms)
Dkr 5.00 (inkl. oms)
Nkr 5.00 (inkl. oms)

2 68

238 (left)
Tin Can Radio (Radio Receiver Design for the Third World), *c.*1962, designed by Victor J. Papanek and George Seegers

239 (opposite)
Off-road vehicle for 'third world terrain', designed by student team under direction of Victor J. Papanek at School of Design, North Carolina State College, 1964

If Dichter had appeared in Packard's eyes to be dabbling in dark arts born of his Viennese heritage, summoning forth a new generation of hapless consumer victims through his application of psychoanalysis, it would be a fellow Viennese émigré (of the next generation), Victor Papanek, who led the battle against '"toys for adults", killing machines with gleaming tailfins, and "sexed up" shrouds for typewriters'.[21] Exposing the 'modern Mad Ave myths', Papanek began his crusade as a little-known designer and budding design theorist, who in 1963 launched an educational television series titled *Design Dimensions*, which dealt with 'man's relationship to things'.[22] Papanek's mission was to expose the absurdities of a newly fledged popular consumer culture driven by 'corrupt marketers' and Svengali-like figures: 'In this age of squeeze-bottle martini, the stereophonic babysitter and the change-a-plate divorce, what could be legitimate areas of design for the industrial designers? It is design for money instead of design for many.'[23] Although Papanek's polemic of design for a 'real' rather than profit-driven society seemed to fit neatly into the genre of American social criticism dominated by Packard, and later elaborated in Ralph Nader's exposé of the US motor industry in *Unsafe at Any Speed* (1965), in fact it owed as much to an émigré social discourse honed by the Frankfurt School of sociology. An influential post-war essay, 'Borax, or the Chromium-Plated Calf' written by Edgar

Kaufmann, Jr, head of Industrial Design at the Museum of Modern Art, New York, and published in the *Architectural Review* in 1948, had castigated commerce's trivializing impact on industrial design. Papanek would go on to recast the 1950s modernist 'Good Design' ethos championed by Kaufmann at MoMA in the framework of a socially responsible design agenda.

'The Chrome-Plated Marshmallow', the fourth of Papanek's design-analysis shows, openly alluded to Kaufmann's work. But the series as a whole drew on the emergence of an immersive, subjective, 1960s non-fiction writing style honed by the so-called 'new journalism' of figures such as Tom Wolfe. Wolfe's well-known collection of essays *The Kandy-Kolored Tangerine-Flake Streamline Baby* (1965) takes its title from his study of custom-car drag racing, preserve of the working-class white male, which had originally appeared in *Esquire* magazine in 1963.[24] Countering the elitism inherent within early-twentieth-century Frankfurt School critiques of working-class culture – exemplified by Adorno and Horkheimer's influential 1944 essay 'The Culture Industry: Enlightenment as Mass Deception'[25] – Wolfe represents the connections between social class and mass culture from a non-judgmental perspective, affording 'outsider' culture an equal status to that of any high-brow cultural practice. In contrast to the anxiety invoked in the work of

Baudrillard or Packard, Wolfe celebrates 'pop' consumer culture as a radical force for societal change.

Victor Papanek would go on to become the era's most influential critic of design in consumer culture, with the publication of his *Design for the Real World* (1971), which melds hardcore polemic with a Wolfe-style immersive rhetoric that appealed directly to a youth culture hungry for change. Under the heading 'Do-It-Yourself Murder', Papanek accuses designers of peddling dangerous goods, many of which even maim and kill. 'Members of the profession have lost integrity and responsibility and become purveyors of trivia', he warns, continuing, '[yet] the health and energy requirements of the world's people ... lie well within the scope of long-range design planning'.[26]

In 1968, under the slogan 'Actions Speak Louder', Papanek was invited by Finnish student activists and the members of the Pan-Scandinavian Design Students Organization (pl.237) to lead a transnational, interdisciplinary design team devising an environmental installation for children affected by cerebral palsy. The *CP-1 Cube*, a portable installation generated through ethnographic observation of the 'user group', which included clinicians, psychologists and children, stood as a prototype for the potential of social design operating beyond the market. As an enormously popular design figure in Scandinavia, Papanek introduced eager

design activists to his earliest experiments in socially responsible design pedagogy: a three-wheeled off-road vehicle for 'third world terrain' (pl.239) and a radio made from a recycled tin can (pl.238), powered by dung, which was offered to UNESCO as a prototype for use in communities disempowered through lack of access to broadcast media.[27]

Industrial Design magazine, the mouthpiece of the US design establishment, ran an article in which Papanek hailed the 'grass-roots' anti-consumer-culture approach to design as a force for social inclusion, alluding to the moral bankruptcy of American design culture and its cliquey conventions. 'Too many martinis, slight morning hangovers, overheated hotel rooms ... boring dry-as-dust speeches ... all of these combined with a degree of back-slapping bonhomie, spell "design conference".'[28] This was a thinly veiled dig at America's high-profile International Design Conference in Aspen (IDCA), attended by the corporate hotshots of design and 'peddlers' of consumer culture. Papanek's adoption of Finnish design activism, which operated in a socialist welfare-driven model, provocatively called into question profit-based capitalist consumer culture more generally.[29] By the end of the 1960s, an alternative design culture led by figures such as Papanek addressed design for 'the greater number' appealing to social conscience rather than profit.

THE GREATER NUMBER: TOWARD DESIGN FOR THE REAL WORLD

The Milan Triennial, in Italy, one of the design profession's most prestigious events, might have been expected in 1968 to showcase the bounty of a booming industry buoyed by the rise of disposable income and heady explosion of styles competing for the attention of a new consumer generation. *La XIV Triennale di Milano*, organized by the cutting-edge urban architect Giancarlo De Carlo, sat instead in tatters. Stormed by an angry student activist mob and occupied by a political protest on its opening day (pl.240), the exhibition witnessed ugly scenes in the ensuing police intervention. Its executive committee was already cowed by a growing political antipathy toward design as the major conduit of elitist consumer capitalism; De Carlo had been astutely chosen to steer the event toward the theme of design's responsibility in the community under the title *Triennale del Grande Numero* ('the greater number'). The doomed 1968 exposition had sought to unite artists, designers, planners and architects through installations exploring issues of urban demographics, the politics of natural resources and environmentalism.[30]

From the Paris riots to the ransacking of the 14th Milan Triennial in May 1968, dissent toward consumer culture and the perceived erosion of authentic labour politics lay at the core of protest. In the 1967 cult book *Traité de savoir-vivre à l'usage des jeunes generations* (literally 'A Treatise on Living for the Younger Generations', although the later English translation was published as *The Revolution of Everyday Life*), a must-read staple of the 1960s student bookshelf, philosopher and Situationist Raoul Vaneigem decried the death of the working class and the rise of the consumer, whose only power resided in the act of shopping. 'Purchasing power is a license to purchase power,' Vaneigem proselytized. 'The old proletariat sold its labour in order to subsist' whereas 'the new proletarian' was now reduced to trading his or hers 'in order to consume'.[31]

An ersatz manifesto for activism, *The Revolution of Everyday Life* would reach anglophone youth several years after it had kindled the May 1968 Paris student uprisings. But along with fellow Situationist Guy Debord's *The Society of the Spectacle*, published in English in 1970 (originally, *La Société du spectacle*, 1967), it helped concretize and popularize a neo-Marxist critique of commodity fetishism, inspiring a rejection of consumer culture. Like Baudrillard, Vaneigem and Debord identified a momentous shift from an era of authentic social life to a contemporary state in which the commodity had colonized every aspect of daily life, leaving in its wake a generation of depoliticized dupes wallowing in 'false consciousness'. Philosophers such as Wolfgang Haug – in his widely read polemic *Critique of Commodity Aesthetics* (1986), originally published in German as *Kritik der Warenästhetik* (1971) – castigated designers as the 'hand-maidens' of consumer capitalism, working in collusion with advertisers.[32]

Far from being confined to the coffee-house banter of Left-leaning intellectuals, the influence of anti-consumerist philosophers and activists spread to mainstream discourse and eventually to the upper echelons of the design establishment. In the same year that Jean Baudrillard debunked the model of consumption as a needs-based phenomenon in his newly honed critical theory titled *The Consumer Society* (1970), the conservative IDCA invited him to attend their conference as one of a collection of scholars dubbed the 'French Group', sponsored by an IBM International Fellowship. The Aspen convention, widely renowned as the US corporate design scene's hottest and most glamorous ticket, was a peculiarly incongruous setting

for radical French thinkers. Displaying exactly the kind of smug 'bonhomie' at which Papanek had sneered in his 1968 article for *Industrial Design* magazine, the conference kicked off with cocktails served against the spectacular backdrop of sunset amidst a mountain range. Charles and Ray Eames, Herbert Miller, George Nelson and their ilk mingled, confident in their position as the 'old guard' of design, content with purveying corporatized 'good' design to an eager consumer public. Like the organizers of Italy's doomed Milan Triennial two years previously, wary of a potential student uprising, the IDCA's executive committee had been especially attentive to the interests of 'youth', embracing the theme 'Environment by Design'.[33]

Architect Jean Aubert, along with Baudrillard a member of the Paris-based UTOPIE radical design collective, was one of the French Group.[34] Together, Aubert and Baudrillard oversaw the eponymous journal *Utopie: L'Architecture comme problème théorique* (Utopia: Architecture as a Theoretical Problem). Their high international profile as anti-establishment

designers within the European vanguard chimed with the committee's desire to appease potential student activism. Aubert was an advocate of and innovator in inflatables, a form that acted as a type of 'design-meme' of the late 1960s. Pneumatic blow-up structures garnered mainstream and avant-garde popularity alike.[35] According to architectural historian Esther Choi, they occupied a unique position within the material culture of design in neutralizing 'discrepancies between high and low, military and recreation, unique and disposable, professional and amateur' through their mobility, buoyancy and ephemerality.[36] Thus undermining formalist and bourgeois models of design, inflatables symbolized the era's irrepressible youthfulness and stood as a materialization of the 1960s cultural revolution (pl.242).

When the avant-garde architectural and environmental design group Ant Farm arrived at Aspen in 1970, defacing the institute's founding modernist design by defiantly erecting a vinyl inflatable 'atop the sacrosanct landscape designed by Bauhaus luminary Herbert Bayer',

241 (left)
CalArts students' performance, *c*.1969, part of the radical pedagogy of the new institute

242 (below)
The Khanh family in Pneumatic Apartment, Paris, 1968, designed by Quasar Khanh (born Nguyen Manh Khanh), 1968
Blow-up structures were a 'design-meme' of the 1960s empasizing the buoyancy, mobility and ephemerality of contemporary consumer culture.

243 (right)
Special Edition of Aspen Times, IDCA, 1971, designed by Sheila Levrant de Bretteville

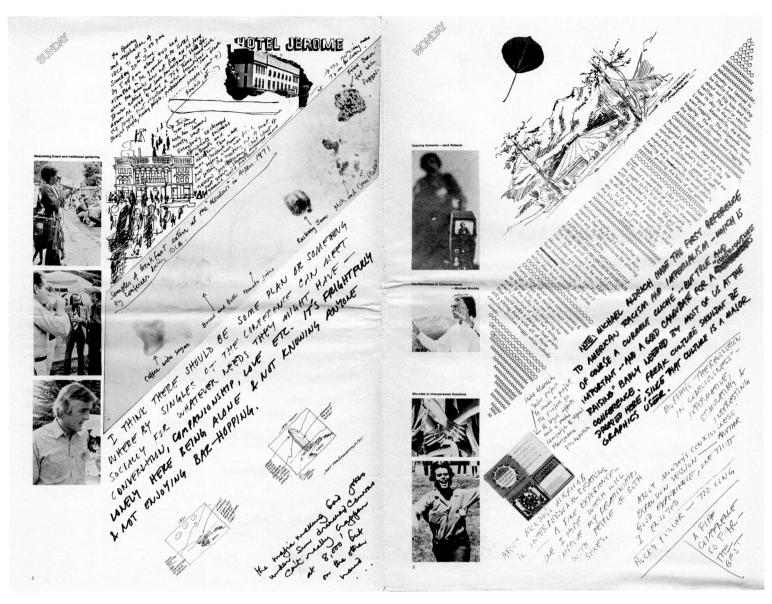

it quickly became evident that the Aspen conference would result (as Reyner Banham would later put it) in 'a guaranteed communications failure'. The 'inflatable' gesture would be one of many provocations aimed at the increasingly defensive Aspen organizers who, after denying the activists access to main conference events, left 'the Ant Farm contingent lurk[ing] at the margins of the event as self-proclaimed "rabble-rousers"'.[37]

Echoing the outcome of the 1968 Milan Triennial, IDCA 1970 descended into an acrimonious confrontation involving several groups: design outsiders and student activists, counter-culture and environmental groups, who together ridiculed the ingenuousness of the corporate organizers' attempt to address the political and social implications of design in society. A watershed in design culture, the resignation of the IDCA committee's luminaries led to direction of the conference being handed over, in 1971, to the newly formed California Institute of Arts (CalArts), which rather aptly named the follow-up event *Paradox*. *Design Journal* described the 'paradox' theme as being 'left deliberately vague, but discussion ... likely to centre around social problems of the day, in particular communications, consciousness, sexual politics and the third world'.[38]

The transferral of conference power from an arch-conservative, white-male-dominated Aspen committee to the radical, ultra-progressive CalArts faculty revealed the extent of youth's revolutionary influence on design. Students at CalArts were engaged in a new genre of critical study (pl.241). Watching Michelangelo Antonioni's post-industrial apocalyptic film *Red Desert* (1964), and reading environmental treatises such as Rachel Carson's *Silent Spring* (1962), the focus was on the social and transformative possibilities of design: design for the elderly, the poor, the sick, the disadvantaged. *Paradox* at IDCA in 1971 showcased a new generation of luminaries, harnessing the revolutionary and utopian counter-culture of the late 1960s, extending a global vision of design for societal purpose. The presence of zeitgeist figures including writer Tom Wolfe

244 (below)
'taste and style just aren't
enough' three-dimensional
poster, 1970, designed by
Sheila Levrant de Bretteville

If the designer is to make
a deliberate contribution to society,
he must be able to integrate
all he can learn about
behavior and resources,
ecology and human needs;

taste and style just aren't enough.

For information regarding admission,
graduate & undergraduate study, and financial
write:

School of Design

California Institute of the Arts
2404 West 7th Street
Los Angeles, California 90057

opening fall 1970

signalled the interdisciplinary and broader cultural aspirations of the new Aspen agenda.

Graphic designer Sheila Levrant de Bretteville, who had spent the previous year in Milan mixing with Giancarlo De Carlo (the overtly Left-leaning architect who had overseen the doomed Milan exposition of 1968), proved instrumental in visualizing and communicating the participatory, interactive, non-hierarchical agenda of the radical conference format.[39] Her graphic designs for

the CalArts prospectus and those for the 1971 *Paradox* newspaper, though vastly different in style, summoned forth design as a conduit of radical social change (pls 243, 244). Her 'Special Edition' of the *Aspen Times* was formulated through the recording and collation of participants' handwritten, subjective experiences, thus subverting the usual top-down authorship of designer and organizing committee.[40] Most significantly, de Bretteville founded the first women's design course, which (along with the Feminist Art Program run by Judy Chicago and Miriam Schapiro) generated the renowned *Womanhouse* project in 1972. This feminist intervention/exhibition included sardonic inversions of the gender politics around consumerism, including Camille Grey's *Lipstick Bathroom*, which featured lipstick-daubed walls, an installation of hundreds of red-variation lipsticks and a fur-lined bath (pl.245).[41] Despite being a self-professed guru of design for 'the greater number', Victor Papanek openly opposed de Bretteville's women's design programmes as a move toward 'ghettoization'.[42]

Indeed, some critical voices recognized that far from being geared toward 'the greater number' the anti-consumption debate had been hijacked by a privileged few. In one exceptionally prescient article, published in 1970 in the New Left US cultural magazine *Ramparts*, women's liberation activist Ellen Willis observed that 'If white radicals are serious about revolution, they are going to have to discard a lot of bullshit ideology created by and for educated white middle-class males. A good example of what has to go is the popular theory of consumerism.'[43] Blowing apart the revolutionary romance surrounding counter-culture and design activism, Ellis went on to debunk the great patriarchal lineage that constituted anti-consumer critique from Packard to Papanek, casting it as an alternative form of oppression: 'consumerism theory

245 (below)
Lipstick Bathroom by
Camille Grey, 1972,
part of *Womanhouse*
feminist intervention

has, in recent years, taken on the invulnerability of religious dogma', she protested, whose 'basic function is to defend the interests of its adherents – in this case the class, sexual and racial privileges of Movement people.'[44]

By the early 1970s, the discourse around consumer culture had evolved far beyond the dichotomous dialogue – pro (Ernest Dichter) versus anti (Vance Packard) – that had defined the early 1960s. Issues of gender, ethnicity and social class, inspired by broader social movements of gay,

women's and workers' rights, threw into sharp relief the crude stereotypes of the 'consumption debate' in which women and the working classes were cast as 'incapable of spending money rationally' – an analogous racial stereotype, according to Willis, being 'the black with his Cadillac and magenta shirts'.[45]

The criticism of anti-consumerism as a 'bullshit ideology created by and for educated white middle-class males' might legitimately be applied to the majority of counter movements celebrated in art and design history of this period. One typical example is the radical Italian *Global Tools* initiative (1973–5), in which leading (male) architects and designers formerly engaged in conventional design turned to anthropology, hand-crafts, and anti-design as an antidote to the alienation of post-industrial commodity capitalism.[46] The participation of women in these 'heroic' movements and events is typically confined to their roles as models or muses, background supporters looking on from the periphery, as the 'other'.

Despite the limitations during the 1960s and early '70s of design's emancipatory breadth, a revolution in the politics of consumption would forge a new, liberating anthropology of design that evolved around user-participation. Underpinned by Marshall McLuhan's theories of contemporary media saturation, a new generation of conceptual practitioners identified design's potency as a mediator of information and interactivity poised to revolutionize emerging communication technologies and transform social worlds.

246 (below)
Section of 'Big Character
Poster No. 1: Work Chart for
Designers', [1969] 1973,
designed by Victor Papanek,
Victor J. Papanek Foundation

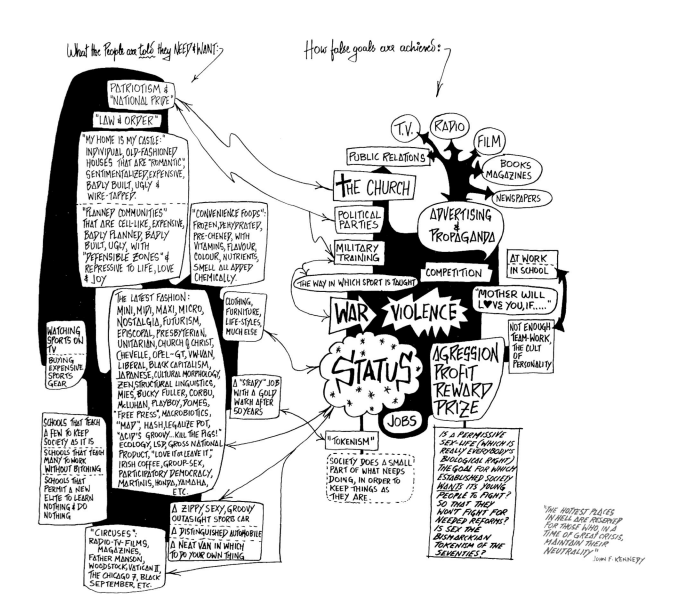

247 (below)
'The Minimal Design Team',
from 'Big Character Poster
No. 1: Work Chart for Designers',
[1969] 1973, designed by
Victor Papanek, Victor J.
Papanek Foundation

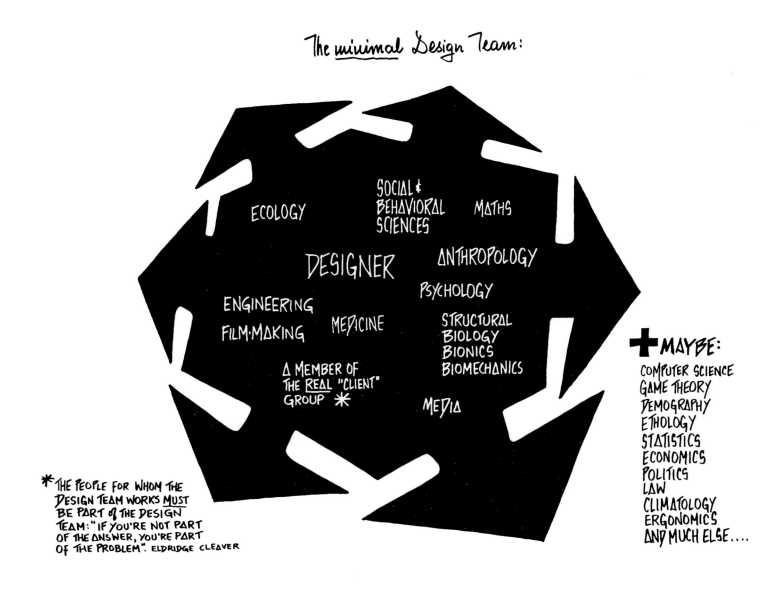

The minimal Design Team:

ECOLOGY
SOCIAL & BEHAVIORAL SCIENCES
MATHS
DESIGNER
ANTHROPOLOGY
PSYCHOLOGY
ENGINEERING
FILM·MAKING
MEDICINE
STRUCTURAL BIOLOGY BIONICS BIOMECHANICS
A MEMBER OF THE REAL "CLIENT" GROUP ✳
MEDIA

✚ MAYBE:
COMPUTER SCIENCE
GAME THEORY
DEMOGRAPHY
ETHOLOGY
STATISTICS
ECONOMICS
POLITICS
LAW
CLIMATOLOGY
ERGONOMICS
AND MUCH ELSE....

✳ THE PEOPLE FOR WHOM THE DESIGN TEAM WORKS MUST BE PART OF THE DESIGN TEAM: "IF YOU'RE NOT PART OF THE ANSWER, YOU'RE PART OF THE PROBLEM". ELDRIDGE CLEAVER

248 (left)
Electronic Tomato, 1969,
designed by Archigram
(Warren Chalk and David Greene)
Collage with newsprint, ink,
tape and felt-tip pen

249 (below left)
Info Gonks, 1966, designed
by Archigram (Peter Cook)
Collage with newsprint,
tracing paper and ink drawing

250 (below)
*Design for the Real World:
Human Ecology and Social
Change* by Victor Papanek,
1971, cover design by Helen
Kirkpatrick, photograph by
George Oddner

CONCLUSIONS: TOWARD A CRITICAL DESIGN

Toying with the ambivalence toward consumer society, some conceptual designs in particular resound as uncanny precursors to contemporary technologies. *Info Gonks* (1968) by radical London-based collective Archigram, described retrospectively as a 'speculative design maquette for educational television glasses and headgear', predates twenty-first-century Google Glass technology by several decades (pl.249).[47] Similarly, the collective's *Electronic Tomato* (1969), a 'speculative proposal for a mobile sensory stimulation device', pre-empted the normalization of domestic surveillance devices and the extension of the body through digital technologies (pl.248): 'Direct your business operations, do the shopping, hunt or fish, or just enjoy electronic instantmatic voyeurism from the comfort of your own home.'[48] Archigram, renowned for embracing the rhetoric of consumer culture as a liberating force, evocatively described the *Electronic Tomato* as 'a groove gizmo that connects to every nerve end to give you the wildest buzz'.[49] Predictably, despite their visionary detail, illustrations for both of the visionary designs used passive female models as their consumer–muses.

In 1971, Victor Papanek, in his best-selling book *Design for the Real World*, produced an illustration of the networked power relations of design, culminating in a diagram of the 'minimal design team', presaging the user-integrated and co-design models utilized by leading design creatives today (pls 246, 247, 250). Design's salience now resided beyond the form, its societal value far exceeding that of the simple bare-faced Western commodity, decorated by the product stylist's hand to maximum seductive affect.[50] A new brand of design had emerged – part futurology, part anthropology – mixing social observation, user participation and innovation in a way that would frame the dematerialized consumption of the twenty-first century and its 'Internet of Things'.[51]

As such the legacy of the 1960s consumer revolution and its discontents resides in the plethora of start-ups, critical and speculative design labs, design anthropologists and ethnographers that have emerged to envisage design within a contemporary neoliberal, global economic climate fraught with new environmental and geopolitical complexity.[52] And what of the revolutionary spirit that saw international design expositions ransacked by protesters, and walls of suburban bathrooms daubed in scarlet lipstick? Its inheritance is most obvious today in anti-corporate campaigns directed at gargantuan corporations such as Google or movements against social inequality such as Occupy. Suspicions regarding the role of designers in brokering the less humane aspects of technological progress, as well as manipulating unwitting citizens in directions most advantageous to corporations, are certainly mounting.[53] But it is the role of designers as futurologists, foretold so succinctly in Vance Packard's *The Waste Makers* (1960), which chimes so poignantly with the anxieties of twenty-first-century culture. As technologies emerge ever more clearly as extensions of ourselves, our futures precariously intertwined, these designer–futurologist hybrids wield a magnitude of power that would have made 1960s anti-consumerists quake. **AC**

269

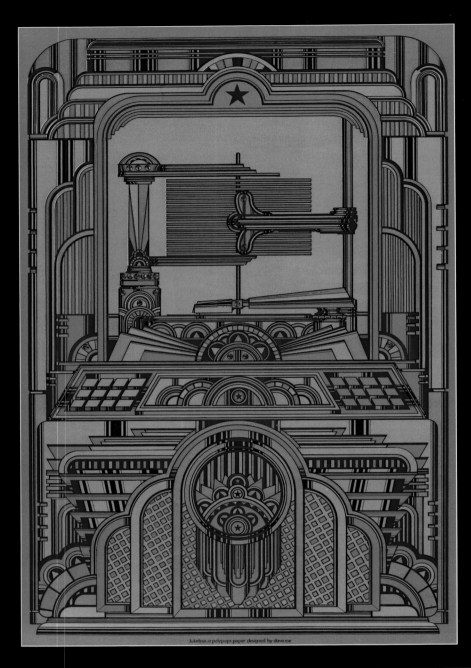

Jukebox, a polypops paper designed by dave roe

251 (left and opposite)
Jukebox and *Pinball*,
Polypops wrapping paper
series, 1968, designed by
David Fairbrother-Roe
V&A: PROV.1527–2015

252 (below)
Design for a living area
by Ralph Adron and
Max Clendinning, 1968
V&A: E.825–1979

Pinball. a polypops paper designed by dave roe

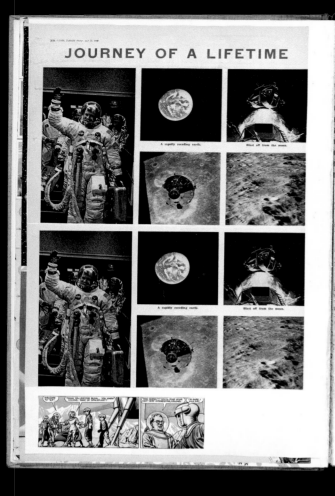

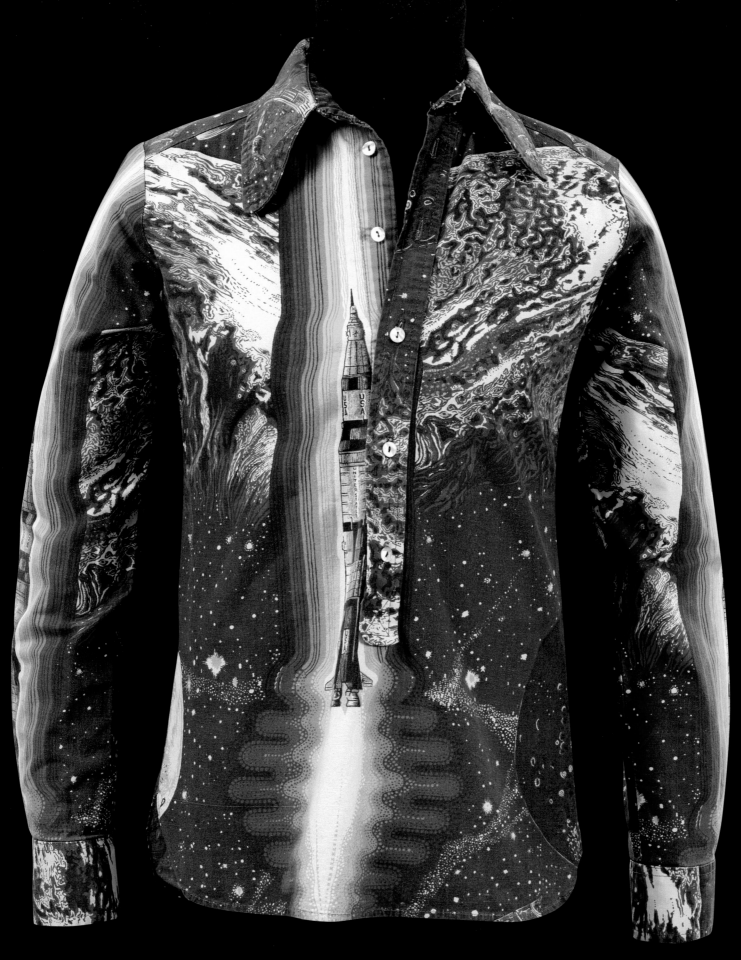

253 (opposite)
Eddie Squires scrapbook
V&A: E.1050–2000

254 (above)
'Lunar Rocket' printed cotton
shirt, 1969, designed by Eddie Squires
V&A: PROV.1918–2015

255 (opposite)
Space Race
Alan Aldridge, 1967

256 (below)
William (Bill) Anders'
spacesuit is checked
before the Apollo 8
mission, 1968

257 (right)
Moon Landing
Wolf Vostell, 1969
Deutsches Historisches
Museum, Berlin

YOU
SAY YOU
UNDERSTAND
WHOLE
SYSTEMS?

9

'WE ARE AS GODS...'
COMPUTERS AND AMERICA'S NEW COMMUNALISM, 1965–75

FRED TURNER

I n the spring of 1965, a handful of artists wandered out on to the high plains of Colorado and bought a small patch of grassland. To the local ranchers they must have looked like hobos: long-haired, short on cash, they scavenged lumber-mill cast-offs and old telephone poles and hammered them into the dirt to frame up their first shelters. They slapped mud onto chicken-wire to make walls. Pretty soon they were wielding axes down at the local junk-yards, chopping the roofs off old cars. When they got back to their land, they cut these sheets of metal into precisely angled panels and tacked them together into wondrously higgledy-piggledy, particoloured versions of geodesic domes. Within a year, they had turned a dusty patch of scrubland into a launch pad for the largest wave of commune-building in American history, Drop City (pl.258).

To many at the time, Drop City and the back-to-the-land movement it helped inspire signalled a generational abandonment of mainstream society. Between 1965 and 1975, tens of thousands of mostly young, mostly white, mostly middle-class Americans gave up their jobs, walked away from university campuses and headed out into the comparatively impoverished rural wilds. By the early 1970s, three-quarters of a million people were living in more than 10,000 communes — some in cities, but many scattered across the countryside.[1] Young communards grew their own food, they built their own houses, and, one after another, they tried to build communities that might model a more hand-hewn future. At the peak of what pundits were learning to call 'The American Century', these back-to-the-landers seemed to have rejected all that the United States stood for.

Fifty years later, we know better. Far from having forsaken society, the communes of the 1960s embraced some of its deepest values. In heading out to the wilds, the back-to-the-landers were acting out the ancient American dream of seeking the frontier. And though they seemed to have turned their backs on the country's military–industrial complex and its consumer culture, they actually organized themselves according to principles derived from both. For all their efforts to shuck the trappings of civilization, the dreams of the rural communards of the 1960s belonged as much to the frontiers of contemporary American engineering as they did to the geographical frontiers of the past — so much so in fact that, over time, they helped pave the way for a revolution that had already begun in the heart of the Establishment: the rise of networked computing.

THE NEW COMMUNALISTS AND THE NEW LEFT

To see how, we need to return to the San Francisco Bay Area of the early 1960s. When we think of the counter-culture today, we tend to think of it as a single social movement. But the cultural upheavals of the 1960s featured at least two distinct camps: the New Left, and a second group that I'll call the 'New Communalists'. Each had its own understanding of the best way to improve society.

From its earliest days, the New Left was primarily a political movement. Rooted in the civil rights struggles of the 1950s and responding to the failure of the 'Old Left' of the 1930s, the New Left sought to change American politics by *doing* politics. Its members formed organizations, drew up manifestos, chose leaders and marched. In 1962, for instance, 59 student radicals gathered in Port Huron, Michigan, and drafted the founding document for a new student organization, Students for a Democratic Society (SDS). Like many in the early nuclear era, they were seized with a terrible urgency. 'Our work is guided by the sense that we may be the last generation in the experiment with living,' they wrote. To these students, the atom bomb served as a grotesque reminder that American society as a whole was sick – sick with racism, with rampant alienation, with extreme inequality. To save it, they called for the creation of 'mechanisms of voluntary association ... through which political information can be imparted and political participation encouraged.'[2] Like their predecessors in the 1950s civil rights movement, they hoped to drive political change in a way that preserved and even foregrounded their individual humanity.

The Port Huron students' vision animated the 1964 Free Speech Movement in Berkeley and nearly a decade of marches against the Vietnam War. But theirs was not the only form of protest. In the late 1950s and early 1960s, a diverse array of poets, musicians and performance artists began gathering in New York City and San Francisco. To this community, organized party politics was beside the point at best. For figures such as musician John Cage or poet Gerd Stern, and for the New Communalists who followed their lead, it was party politics itself that had led the United States to the edge of nuclear Armageddon. And the problem wasn't just bad leaders; it was the hierarchical nature of bureaucratic governance.

In 1967, an underground Chicago newspaper called the *Seed* published a poem that neatly captures the emerging communalist consensus:

> Beware of leaders, heroes, organizers.
> Watch that stuff. Beware of structure freaks.
> They do not understand.
> We know the system doesn't work because we're living
> in its ruins. We know that leaders don't work out
> because they have all led us only to the present,
> the good leaders equally with the bad ... What the
> system calls organization – linear organization – is a
> systematic cage, arbitrarily limiting the possible. It's
> never worked before. It always produced the present.[3]

For those who were about to head back to the land, it was not politics but consciousness that held the key to a healthy society. In his best-selling 1969 book *The Making of a Counter Culture*, historian Theodore Roszak explained that a new mindset was emerging among America's disaffected young. Their parents had been plagued by the 'scientific world view, with its entrenched commitment to an egocentric and cerebral mode of consciousness': as a result, they had broken faith with each other and with the natural world. Those

in power had become psychologically fractured, politically divided, unable to pull back from the brink of nuclear war or to recognize their common humanity. According to Roszak and the New Communalists, all that was about to change:

> This is the primary project of our counter-culture: to proclaim a new heaven and a new earth so vast, so marvellous that the inordinate claims of technical expertise must of necessity withdraw in the presence of such splendour to subordinate and marginal status in the lives of men. To create and broadcast such a consciousness of life entails nothing less than the willingness to open ourselves to the visionary imagination on its own terms.[4]

At first glance, such millenarian vision quests might seem entirely antagonistic to the worlds of science and engineering. But the truth is a little more slippery. In his 1970 book *The Greening of America*, a book as influential at the time as Roszak's, Yale law professor Charles A. Reich made the distinction clear. The industrial era had brought us to a robotic state of mind, he argued. Industrial man was a man suitable for operating machines and working within organizations. He is a man who permits himself to be dominated by technique ... an artificially streamlined man, from whom irrationality, unpredictability, and complexity have been removed as far as possible. He is oversimplified in the service of reason; he tries to control himself by reason, and the result is not man but a smoothed-down man.[5]

Yet, Reich argued, the same technocracy that had produced such machine-like people had also opened the door to a visionary alternative. The consciousness then emerging among the young was a

> product of two interacting forces: the promise of life that is made to young Americans by all of our affluence, technology, liberation, and ideals, and the threat to that promise posed by everything from neon ugliness and boring jobs to the Vietnam War and the shadow of nuclear holocaust. Neither the promise nor the threat is the cause by itself; but the two together have done it.[6]

TECHNOLOGIES OF CONSCIOUSNESS

The Greening of America captured a deep ambivalence inherent in the mindset of the New Communalists. Though they abhorred mainstream culture and the technologies of mass destruction, they were part of the first generation to be able to roam a nationwide highway system in cheap, high-quality cars. They were the first to enjoy the birth-control pill, LSD and electric guitars. Even as they turned away from industrial bureaucracy and its military analogue, the New Communalists refused to give up small-scale consumer goods. On the contrary, they reimagined them as tools with which to transform their consciousness and with it, the world.

There was perhaps no one at the time who saw this more clearly than Stewart Brand (pl.260). In the early 1960s, the young Brand was stationed at Fort Dix, New Jersey, wrapping up a brief stint in the US Army after graduating from Stanford University. He found his way into the downtown New York art scene and Gerd Stern's multimedia performance troupe USCO (for 'The Us Company'). Like the artists who would soon found Drop City, the members of

USCO hoped to return to a tribal, collaborative mode of art-making. They lived and worked communally, organizing themselves according to a mix of ideas drawn from Eastern mysticism and the ecological 'systems thinking' that dominated American military and industrial research centres at the time (pl.259). And much as the pioneers out at Drop City repurposed the tops of cars to make futuristic domes, the performers of USCO turned stereo speakers and flashing lights into tools for the transformation of consciousness (pl.263). In 1965, for instance, they travelled to San Francisco and built a multimedia environment they called 'We R All One'. There they surrounded visitors with slide projections, whisked sounds from speaker to speaker around the room, and spun strobe lights across the bodies of dancers, all to create a completely immersive and disorienting sensory tumult (pl.261). At the end of the event, they dimmed the lights. For the next 10 minutes, the speakers emitted a steady chanting of 'Om'. As Stern put it, the show was designed to move the audience from 'overload to spiritual meditation'.[7]

As he worked with USCO, Brand immersed himself in the emerging New Communalist ethos. In the fall of 1968, he built that ethos into what became the flagship publication of the New Communalist movement, the *Whole Earth Catalog*, which came out twice a year until 1972.

Brand had been living in the San Francisco Bay Area for several years by that time. He had discovered LSD, taken up with Ken Kesey's infamous psychedelic performance troupe the Merry Pranksters and, in early 1966, helped stage the Trips Festival, a three-night celebration of the communitarian power of music, art and, though it was by then illegal, LSD. Brand marvelled as the psychedelic counter-culture blossomed around him in San Francisco: the long hair and communalism that characterized USCO had become ubiquitous; so too had its faith in the transformative power of drugs and of consciousness-expanding multimedia art. In 1967, tens of thousands had gathered in Golden Gate Park for what they called a 'Human Be-In,' (pl.264) where they listened to Timothy Leary exhort them to 'Turn on! Tune in! Drop out!' and danced to Jefferson Airplane and to Janis Joplin's Big Brother & the Holding Company. Within months, hundreds of runaways had descended on San Francisco, looking for a way into the scene, and busloads of tourists roamed the Victorian streets of the Haight-Ashbury neighbourhood, spotting hippies.

For many of the early counter-cultural residents of the Haight, it was all too much. They began to leave the city and to buy plots of land in the countryside where they could live communally without intrusion. Brand wanted to help and so in the spring of 1968 he and his then-wife Lois set out for New Mexico and Colorado in a beat-up Dodge pickup truck, carrying a mimeographed list of about 120 items they imagined the commune-dwellers might need, and samples of many. In a month they sold about $200 worth of goods. By the time they returned to San Francisco, they had reimagined their business: from then on, they no longer sold direct. Rather, starting with the first issue of the *Whole Earth Catalog* that fall, they offered the New Communalists 'access to tools'. Brand explained their aim on the inside cover of the first edition:

> We are as gods and might as well get used to it. So far, remotely done power and glory – as via government, big business, formal education, church – has succeeded to the point where gross obscure actual gains. In response to this dilemma and to these gains a realm of intimate, personal power is developing – power of the individual to conduct his own education, find his own inspiration, shape his own environment, and share his adventure with whoever is interested. Tools that aid this process are sought and promoted by the WHOLE EARTH CATALOG.[8]

What kind of tools did Brand have in mind? For the cover of the first edition (pl.267), Brand selected a photograph of Earth taken from space by a 1967 NASA expedition (pl.265). Much as NASA's camera had given us a new understanding of our collective interdependence on planet Earth, Brand implied that the array of tools in the pages to follow would give readers a new consciousness of their place in the world. The tools he chose made the point as well. A reasonable observer might think that a generation heading out into the countryside would want access to tools for digging and construction, machinery such as tractors and water pumps, most of all. Yet in its first edition, the catalogue offered pointers to only three mechanical devices out of its 133 items. More than half of its 'tools' were books. Its first section, for instance, entitled 'Understanding Whole Systems', featured an atlas of the galaxies only pages away from a book that depicted the human form as a landscape in its own right. Further on was a guide outlining how to subscribe to *Scientific American* and *New Scientist* magazines. The *Whole Earth Catalog* even offered access to Hewlett Packard's most powerful tabletop calculator at the time, the 9100A.

What possible use could people who had taken up hand tools have for something like the 9100A? None at all, if we imagine the calculator's utility to reside only in its

ability to add and subtract very large numbers. But in the *Whole Earth Catalog*, tools existed not so much to help users accomplish some task in the world as to help them recognize that the world itself was an information system. With that understanding in mind, the New Communalists believed they could finally build a society based not on political negotiation so much as a shared exchange of energies across invisible circuits. To sceptics, such circuits might have seemed like mystical nonsense. But to the New Communalists, a calculator that could manipulate unseen patterns of information and electricity made them real.

To hammer home the point, Brand celebrated the writings of two leading technocrats: R. Buckminster Fuller (pl.266) and Norbert Wiener. 'The insights of Buckminster Fuller are what initiated the catalog,' Brand told his readers, and the architect–designer's books filled its first pages.[9] Buckminster Fuller claimed to have discovered previously unknown geometric patterns and principles of tension in nature, and to have designed geodesic domes and other forms in keeping with them. The young communards interpreted his work as a call for every right-thinking citizen to take the products of mass industry (such as car roofs) and repurpose them in such a way as to better align their own individual lives with the forces of nature.[10] Norbert Wiener was a mathematician, a military researcher during World

War II, and a professor at MIT. He was one of the founders of cybernetics, a discipline that imagined the world as a series of information systems and computers as the tools most fit to model and manage those systems. 'Society, from organism to community to civilization to universe, is the domain of cybernetics,' wrote Brand. 'Norbert Wiener has the story, and to some extent, is the story.'[11]

To young men and women seeking a way to escape hierarchical forms of organization, the geometry of geodesics and the information theories of cybernetics offered powerful models. Never mind that geodesic domes had been the preferred housing for military radar domes since the 1950s, or that cybernetics had been the lingua franca of the military–industrial establishment for 20 years. The New Communalists were quite happy to turn the technologies of mainstream America into tools for personal transformation. They had left conventional politics behind. In its place, they had set about turning the products of American heavy industry into a new kind of psychological infrastructure. At Drop City, for instance, the geodesic domes were meant to sustain an open, interlinked social practice. One of the co-founders of Drop City, who went by the name Peter Rabbit, put it this way: 'There is no political structure at Drop City. Things work out; the cosmic forces mesh with people in strange

complex intuitive interaction ... When things are done the slow intuitive way the tribe makes sense.'[12]

To people like Peter Rabbit, the *Whole Earth Catalog* offered another example of the ways that the systems of mainstream American culture could be realigned to support New Communalism. On one hand, the *Whole Earth* was a catalogue. As such, it represented one of the most common genres of American consumer culture – something the communards claimed to be fleeing. On the other, it didn't actually sell anything. Rather, it listed ways for readers to find something themselves. In that sense, it was a stand-alone information machine, one that empowered its users one at a time. Moreover, Brand soon began soliciting recommendations for new tools from commune-dwellers across the United States, paying $10 for each one he printed. The catalogue quickly became not only a guide to new tools, but an information *system*; one in which readers provided links to new tools, to new information and to one another. In its pages readers could find a map of an emerging commune network and a way to enter it. They could see the members of that network as people in the world and as bits of information in the pages of the catalogue at the same time. They could even begin to imagine the entire globe as Norbert Wiener had some time ago: as a pattern of information made material.

WHOLE EARTH CATALOG

access to tools

Fall 1968

$5

Ordering from the CATALOG

The CATALOG functions primarily as a pointer rather than a seller and prefers to be absent from most of the transactions it encourages.

Address order to the supplier given with the item unless you know of a better one (if you do, let us know); if the price is not listed postpaid find out the postage or express cost from the supplier's location to yours (consult post office or express agency for rates); add state tax if transaction is within your state; and send check or money order with your order.

If the supplier gives you poor service, let us know. That information can be added to his review.

Blank order envelopes are provided at the back of the CATALOG for your convenience and so that suppliers have some idea of the CATALOG's effect on their business — if strong enough it may result in price or service advantages to CATALOG users. Don't use the envelopes if you don't want to.

With some indicated items, books mostly, the CATALOG also will ship. There is no price difference with the service; the CATALOG gets the markup instead of the other guy, is all. For west coast orders it may mean faster service.

Generally, the closer the supplier is to you, the quicker and cheaper the shipping will be. If the item you're getting is at all delicate (Don Buchla tells us), or if you are in a hurry, air express is the best deal. REA mangles.

Anything overseas, by air.

Subscribing to the CATALOG

$8.00 per year. This includes Fall and Spring issues of the CATALOG and four Supplements. Subscription forms are on page 63. Memorize your zip code.

Suggesting

The validity of the information in the CATALOG is only as good as the transmitted experience of users. For any item, we have to

* Learn about it.
* Get thorough information on it, and
* Stay current with its changes and with the improvements of its competitors.

FROM YOUR EXPERIENCE
HOW WOULD YOU ALTER
per catalog   THIS CATALOG
per category   THESE ITEMS
per item   THIS REVIEW

Reviewing

The CATALOG pays its reviewers $10 an item for: getting familiar with the item, its usefulness, and its competition; evaluating the item; selecting samples of graphics or text (with page references) for the review; and writing a 200 – 300 word review here.

Both reviewers and first suggestors of items are credited in the CATALOG.

We invite reviews that improve on present reviews or accompany suggestions for new items. On acceptance for publication reviewers will be paid $10 per accepted review. Unused reviews will not be returned. Polish of submitted material is irrelevant unless it is meant to be camera-ready.

New items that have had some favorable comment, and that we want reviews for, will be listed in the Supplement.

Corresponding

If the content of the WHOLE EARTH CATALOG is mostly products, the content of the Difficult But Possible Supplement is mostly processes.

Commentary from CATALOG users that is of general interest — and not a specific review — will be in the Supplement. Critical comments, new design processes, no-cash techniques, news of specific enterprises, useful fantasies, design student work, time and trouble shortcuts, new uses for common or exotic materials, other mains for the CATALOG to consider, etc., etc. —all welcome. The Supplement could wind up being more useful than the CATALOG.

Advertising

Suppliers, manufacturers, creators of listed items are eligible to advertise in the CATALOG. They may advertise only an item listed or their own catalog. All ads are placed at the back of the Supplement.

Rates:

| full page $200 | $75 |
| | $25 $10 $5 |

Selling

The CATALOG and Supplement are available for resale at 50% discount – minimum order 5. Single copy list price of the CATALOG is $5 ; the Supplement , $2 .

Donating

Portola Institute, Inc. is a tax-exempt, non-profit corporation. Donations to Portola or the CATALOG may be deducted.

Retaining subscriptions to the CATALOG are $25 for one year ($17 tax deductible). Sustaining subscriptions are $100+ per year ($90+ tax deductible). Names of retaining and sustaining subscribers will be given in the CATALOG.

CATALOG policy with suppliers and users

The CATALOG is under no obligation to suppliers. Users are under no obligation to the CATALOG.

Suppliers (manufacturers, creators, etc.) may not buy their way into the CATALOG. Free Samples or other blandishments are cheerfully accepted by CATALOG researchers; response not predictable. No payment for listing is asked or accepted. We owe accurate information exchange to suppliers, but not favors.

Our obligation is to CATALOG users and to ourselves to be good tools for one another.

This Issue of the CATALOG, the first, is heavy on books because they are easy to start with (low cost, simple to get and evaluate). As more CATALOG users report in and we develop better facilities to try stuff out, later issues should contain more information on materials.

This issue of the CATALOG was prepared by:

Stewart Brand
Sandra Tcherepnin
Joe Bonner

with   Steve Baer
Jane Burton   Steve Durkee
James Fadiman   Ralph Metzner
Richard Raymond   Gurney Norman
Larry McCombs   Robert Albrecht

We are grateful to Ortega Park Teachers Laboratory for temporary use of their mountain idyll for production space.

The WHOLE EARTH CATALOG and Difficult But Possible Supplement to the WHOLE EARTH CATALOG is published at Portola Institute, 558 Santa Cruz, Menlo Park, California 94026 on the following schedule:

CATALOG	November
Supplement	January
Supplement	March
CATALOG	May
Supplement	July
Supplement	September

Preparation of the CATALOG was done on an IBM Selectric Composer and a Polaroid MP-3 camera with instant half-tone system. Nowell Publications, Menlo Park, printed the contents, and East Wind Printers, San Francisco, printed the cover.

Subscription rate: one year — $8. Application to mail at second class postage rates is pending at Menlo Park, California.

Buckminster Fuller

The insights of Buckminster Fuller are what initiated this catalog.

Ideas and Integrities
Buckminster Fuller
1963; 318 pp.
$10.00
from:
Prentice-Hall, Inc.
Englewood Cliffs
New Jersey 07631
or
WHOLE EARTH CATALOG

Nine Chains to the Moon
Buckminster Fuller
1938,1963; 375 pp.
$2.45 postpaid

No More Secondhand God
Buckminster Fuller
1963; 163 pp.
$2.25 postpaid

both from:
Southern Illinois University Press
600 West Grand
Clarksdale, Illinois 62903
or
WHOLE EARTH CATALOG

WGSD Document 1

WGSD Document 2

The World From Above

Close-up glamor shots of the Earth. Mystery shots (What is that ? What's our altitude above it, 10 feet or 10,000 ?) (Fold out captions tell all.) Good traffic flow pattern shots: surface anatomy of civilization. Not a bad compendium; it'd do until they reprint E.A. Gutkind's Our World From the Air.

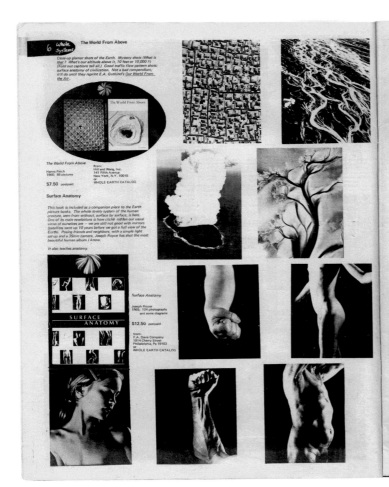

The World From Above
Hanns Reich
1966; 88 pictures
$7.50 postpaid
from:
Hill and Wang, Inc.
141 Fifth Avenue
New York, N.Y. 10010
or
WHOLE EARTH CATALOG

Surface Anatomy

This book is included as a companion piece to the Earth picture books. The whole lovely system of the human creature, seen from without, surface by surface, is here. One of its main revelations is how cliché-ridden our usual views of ourselves are – we are still not good with mirrors (satellites were up 10 years before we got a full view of the Earth). Posing friends and neighbors, with a single light set up and a 35mm camera, Joseph Royce has shot the most beautiful human album I know.

It also teaches anatomy.

Surface Anatomy
Joseph Royce
124 photographs
and some diagrams
$12.50 postpaid
from:
F.A. Davis Company
1914 Cherry Street
Philadelphia, Pa 19103
or
WHOLE EARTH CATALOG

Geology Illustrated

A artist of aerial photography, Shelton uses some 400 of his finest photos to illuminate a discussion of the whole-earth system. Not a traditional textbook, but a fascinating exploration of the problems posed by asking "How did that come about?" Worth buying for the photos and book design alone, but you'll probably find yourself becoming interested in geology regardless of your original intention.
[Reviewed by Larry McCombs]

As a means of communicating geological concepts, the pictures are fully as important as the words that accompany them. On most pages the photographs represent the facts, and words supply the interpretation. Many of the illustrations will, therefore, repay a little of the kind of attention that should be lavished on the real picture in the field. In keeping with this, almost no identifying marks have been placed on the photographs and very few on the drawings. The text (which almost invariably concerns an illustration on the same or a facing page) aims at an expanded legend for the picture, if, while reading it, it is necessary to look more than once to identify some feature with certainty, this is no more than Nature asks of those who contemplate her unlabelled cliffs and hills.

Geology Illustrated
John S. Shelton
1966; 434 pp.
$10.00 postpaid
from:
W. H. Freeman & Company
660 Market Street
San Francisco, Ca 94104
or
WHOLE EARTH CATALOG

Sensitive Chaos

Schwenk directs an insitute in the Black Forest devoted to the study of the movements of water and air. Within the last few centuries, he says we have "lost touch with the spiritual nature of water." As a result, we have attempted to control the fluids in ways contrary to their nature, and the results are evident in the problems of pollution, damage to the ecosystem, and even drying up of natural water sources. Schwenk attempts to penetrate beyond the mere observable phenomena to an ability to "read" the true spiritual nature of flowing substances.

I found the book to be a peculiarly fascinating mixture of overgeneralization, simplification, undifferentiated fact and theory, and shrewd observation and insight. If you regard analogy as the weakest form of argument, this book is definitely not for you. On the other hand, Schwenk's juxtaposition of similar forms in different flowing media may spark some exciting bioclarities, if you are open to them. The section of 88 pages of black and white photos at the back of the book could stand alone as a beautiful art collection.
[Reviewed by Larry McCombs]

Sensitive Chaos
Theodor Schwenk
1965; 144 pp. 88 plates
$12.00 (Air postpaid)
from:
Rudolf Steiner Press
35 Park Road
London NW1
England
or
$8.70 postpaid
from:
WHOLE EARTH CATALOG

COUNTER-CULTURAL COMPUTING

The *Catalog* soon reached far beyond the commune scene. By 1972 when it officially ceased publication, it had grown from 61 to nearly 450 pages. It had sold more than a million copies; it had even won the National Book Award. And it had become a beacon to a new generation of computer-builders. As Steve Jobs told the graduating class at Stanford University in 2005, 'The *Whole Earth Catalog* ... was one of the bibles of my generation. ... It was sort of like Google in paperback form, 35 years before Google came along: it was idealistic, and overflowing with neat tools and great notions.'[13] Jobs had grown up in Los Altos, California, near the Stanford University campus in Palo Alto and just a few miles down the road from the *Whole Earth Catalog*'s Menlo Park offices. When he and his friend Steve Wozniak began tinkering with computers, they were only two of dozens of programmers and technologists whose world intersected that of the catalogue.

Conventional histories of the cold war often suggest that the military–industrial complex and the counter-culture had nothing to do with each other. But on the San Francisco peninsula in the late 1960s, they were thoroughly entwined. Geography made the encounter easy: working just 40 miles south of the city, in a region speckled with communal houses and counter-cultural bookstores, the engineers of what would soon be called 'Silicon Valley' could hardly have missed the long-hairs in their midst. Yet the deep ties that emerged also owed something to the very specific logic of New Communalism. In Berkeley, on the other side of San Francisco Bay, the New Left marchers of the Free Speech Movement had hung computer punch cards from their necks (pl.269). The cards had been punched through to read 'FSM', for Free Speech Movement, and 'STRIKE'. For these protesters, and for many anti-war activists in the years that followed, computers were the paradigmatic tools of the cold-war state, the very emblems of the hyper-rationalized bureaucracies that had brought the world to the edge of Armageddon. But among New Communalists like Brand, cybernetics and information theory were seen as models of an alternative to bureaucracy. 'If we could but see and manage flows of energy and information among ourselves', thought many communards, 'we could build a levelled, egalitarian society that would render militarized hierarchies obsolete.' To the extent that computers could aid in that project, they too could qualify as tools for counter-cultural transformation.

Between 1968 and 1972, two groups of computer scientists clustered near Stanford embraced both the communalism and the tool-oriented recipes for social change promoted in the *Whole Earth Catalog*. The first group comprised engineers associated with Douglas Engelbart's Augmentation Research Center (ARC) at the Stanford Research Institute and, later, Xerox's Palo Alto Research Center (PARC). Engelbart had invented the computer mouse several years earlier; between 1966 and 1968, he and his ARC group focused on integrating the mouse, the standard QWERTY typewriter keyboard and the CRT (cathode-ray tube) monitors that would shortly become the standard for desktop computers into what they called the 'oN-Line System' (NLS). Before the Internet existed, and at a time when most people thought of computers as stand-alone mainframe behemoths, NLS allowed users to work on documents from multiple sites at the same time, to jump from point to point within texts and to connect texts through hyperlinks. More importantly, from Engelbart's point of view, it enabled users to work – and live – in an egalitarian relationship with one another.

As they used the system, Engelbart believed they would not only amplify their individual skills, but develop a shared mindset. The computer environment would support that work and evolve alongside the group. Like the domes of Drop City, the linked computer system would become an infrastructure for the transformation of consciousness, and through it, social structure.

Such a vision was deeply consonant with both the cybernetics-driven world of military–industrial research in which Engelbart had worked since the mid-1950s and the communalist social sphere in which he had begun to travel. At the same time that he was developing NLS, Engelbart found his way to LSD and, through Bill English, ARC's chief engineer and the builder of the first mouse, to Stewart Brand. Steve Durkee, a former member of USCO and since 1967 the leader of a commune called the Lama Foundation, visited Engelbart's lab at Brand's invitation. Engelbart and English later travelled to the Libre commune in New Mexico, where they met Steve Baer, a designer of geodesic domes. In 1968, when Engelbart staged the first-ever public demonstration of a computer with the mouse–keyboard–screen interface we now take for granted, he hired Stewart Brand to film the occasion (pl.268).[14]

Both Brand and the *Whole Earth Catalog* would go on to have an extraordinary impact on San Francisco Bay Area computer science. Together they helped reframe the computer as a personal technology and as an information tool like the catalogue itself (pl.270). They also showed that computer scientists could adopt the same collaborative, anti-hierarchical modes of organization that characterized the counter-culture – they need not work solely for large military–industrial contractors but could work for themselves. In 1972, for instance, Lois Brand joined Bob Albrecht, a former engineer for Control Data Corporation and Honeywell, to help start a bi-monthly newsletter, the *People's Computer Company*, around the corner from the *Whole Earth Catalog*'s offices, which would later spawn a store called the People's Computer Center. Both the publication and the store aimed to show that anyone could learn to program, that small computers

had arrived, and that these machines could inspire hubs of local, anti-hierarchical collaboration.

By the early 1970s, the vision of peer-to-peer information-sharing that drove the *People's Computer Company* had become commonplace not only among New Communalists, but among members of the New Left as well. In 1971, for instance, a programmer, former Free Speech marcher and persistent anti-war activist named Lee Felsenstein joined Resource One, a group of technologists who had left the University of California at Berkeley to protest against the invasion of Cambodia. Together they worked to build computer terminals at a Berkeley record store, a San Francisco library and several other locations. They called their project 'Community Memory'. Though what they created was principally a shared digital bulletin-board, they saw their work as part of a much larger counter-cultural project.

In a 1975 issue of the *People's Computer Company*, Efrem Lipkin, one of Community Memory's leaders, explained that 'People must gain a sense of understanding of and control over the system as a tool. ... [Computer] intelligence should be directed toward instructing [the user], demystifying and exposing its own nature, and ultimately giving him active control.'[15] As Felsenstein would later argue, this vision echoed the calls for self-reliance that animated the *Whole Earth Catalog*. For mainstream Americans in the late 1960s, he recalled, technology was a 'secular religion'. Stewart Brand had 'set up an alternate temple of the same religion, of the church of technology, telling people in technological society that people needed to learn to use tools'. As Felsenstein put it, the *Catalog* taught its readers that 'you don't have to leave industrial society, but you don't have to accept the way it is.'[16]

270 (opposite)
Apple 1 Computer, designed by
Apple (Steve Wozniak, Steve
Jobs and Ron Wayne), c.1976

THE NEW COMMUNALISM TODAY

In 1975, Lee Felsenstein became a co-founder of the Homebrew Computer Club. It was there that Steve Jobs would begin his life's work of proclaiming that the computers made by Apple were more than machines: that they were tools of counter-cultural change. And he would hardly be alone.

Over the last 40 years, marketers of everything from cell phones to social media have declared that digital technologies have turned our culture upside down, freed us to be ever more ourselves, and allowed us to know one another as never before. Their claims have deep roots in the commune movement of the 1960s. And that fact should give us pause. By the mid-1970s, almost all of the communes that had flowered in the late 1960s had withered and died. Those that survived often had authoritarian leadership or a strong religious mission. The technology-enabled politics of consciousness turned out to be a terrible way to govern: quite simply, it offered no practical way to talk about the distribution of resources or the management of power. Moreover, when they abandoned the traditional institutions of democratic governance, many communes ended up amplifying patterns of prejudice that had long haunted American culture. Before they collapsed, many had replicated the racism and sexism of mainstream society. For all the rhetoric of 'free love' and universal acceptance, the back-to-the-land communes of the 1960s far too often became just as white and just as traditional in their gender roles as any red-lined suburb.

Today, we are again awash in claims that if we only choose the right technology, we can build a new, more egalitarian society. The language of consciousness has faded from view, but communal hopes for a social world built on sharing rather than contractual exchange still animate the promises of technology firms. In a famous advertisement directed by Ridley Scott, Apple Computer claimed that their Macintosh machines would free users from the totalitarianism of Big Brother and would be the reason 'why 1984 won't be like *1984*'. Today, companies including Uber and Airbnb promise that they are helping workers and customers escape the bureaucratic clutches of the taxi and hotel industries for a new mode of collaboration, the 'sharing economy'. Across the United States and Europe, technology firms clamour to go unregulated on the grounds that they – not governments – are the true engines of benevolent social change.

Beneath all of these claims lies the cybernetic faith that the world is a system of information patterns and, with it, the counter-cultural dream of linking our individual patterns together in a communal utopia. When they first appeared, these twin streams of idealism offered a social vision so powerful that it lured tens of thousands of young Americans into the rural wilds. To the children of the Eisenhower era, the *Whole Earth Catalog* must indeed have appeared as wondrous as Google does to us. But the *Catalog* didn't monitor our information searches, as Google does. Nor did it collaborate with America's National Security Agency, as Google has. This is perhaps the deepest irony behind the lingering influence of the 1960s communes and their view of technology. The dream of using information technologies to create a global community of consciousness is in fact being realized – but by the very military–industrial complex so many young Americans once hoped to undermine. **FT**

271 (above)
Grain of Sand, 1963–5
Mati Klarwein

272 (above)
Poster for The Doors/Peanut Butter
Conspiracy at The Kaleidoscope Rose,
1967, designed by Victor Moscoso

TIMBRES expo67© STAMPS

EXPOSITION
UNIVERSELLE ET
INTERNATIONALE
DE 1967
MONTRÉAL, CANADA,
28 AVRIL —
27 OCTOBRE, 1967

expo67

TERRE
DES
HOMMES

© Copyright 1965 par Compagnie Canadienne de l'Exposition Universelle de 1967. Litho au Canada sur papier fabriqué au Canada.

🇺🇸 UNITED STATES

A huge bubble-dome—187 feet high and 250 feet across—encloses the pavilion. The geodesic dome is constructed of a light-weight metal frame covered with plastic and glass sheets. Inside the dome exhibit platforms at various levels are connected by escalators.
Location: Ile Sainte-Hélène across the LeMoyne Channel from the pavilion of the U.S.S.R.
Exhibits: The underlying theme of the pavilion is "Creative America" with supporting exhibits to illustrate notable American accomplishments in the arts, space and technology. Scale models of equipment to be used in the United States Apollo flight to the moon in 1970 will be displayed against simulated lunar conditions. Current trends in evidence in American painting and sculpture will be exhibited in an art gallery. New computer technology and break-throughs in the fields of communications and transportation will be shown in a display of objects chosen on the basis of technical excellence. An exhibit of artifacts and authentic documents will illustrate the American heritage. "Creative America" in action will be shown in a 20-minute film and a variety of live entertainment will be offered in the Special Events theatre.

🇨🇦 CANADA

The central and most prominent feature of the pavilion is a great inverted pyramid called Katimavik, 108 feet high with sides of 192 feet, resting on four V-shaped columns. White diamond shaped roofs distinguish the surrounding exhibition buildings with a more rectangular structure housing an arts centre. Landscaped terraces are stepped down to plazas, surrounding canals, a lagoon and the river.
Location: Ile Notre-Dame.
Exhibits: On the four inside walls of the huge inverted pyramid, the Katimavik (an Eskimo word for "meeting place") are display representations of time, navigation, nature and man which can be viewed from a promenade running around the rim of the Katimavik. At the base, exhibits and a rotating film theatre will tell the story of Canada's social and political growth. Under pyramidic roofs clustered around the Katimavik are displays dealing with aspects of Canadian life: cultural adaptation, ethnic diversity, urban growth and work patterns. Standing in the centre of the exhibit is the stylized maple tree. The People of Canada, with its leaves formed of hundreds of photographs of Canadians. The Children's Creative Centre in the pavilion is a combined play area for children and workshop for teachers with a one-way glass observation corridor. The art gallery will display about 50 paintings by Canadian artists as well as exhibits of architectural drawings, graphic design, and fine photography; and outside it, works by fifteen Canadian sculptors will be set in a sculpture court. A wide variety of the performing arts in Canada will be presented in a bandshell and theatre with a daily performance by Les Feux Follets—a folk dance troupe. A library contains over 3,000 volumes in English, French and many of the languages of Canadians of other ethnic origins. In a lagoon, every hour on the half hour, a two-headed monster, called Uki, will rise breathing fire and smoke.

l'expo67 instruit

TERRE DES HOMMES

"Etre un homme,
c'est sentir, en posant sa pierre, que l'on contribue
à construire le monde"

expo67 edu-kit

MAN AND HIS WORLD

"To be a man
is to feel that through one's own contribution
one helps to build the world"

274 (opposite)
Living on the Earth by Alicia Bay
Laurel, 1970 (this edition 1971)

JOHN 'HOPPY' HOPKINS (1937–2015)

277 (above)
Ringo Starr

278 (left)
Poster for the International
Poetry Congress, 1965

279 (opposite)
Naked Ginsberg, 1965

These pages acknowledge the immense contribution of the late John 'Hoppy' Hopkins to London's counter-culture. 'Hoppy' was recognized affectionately across the underground scene both for his role in organizing some of its key events and in documenting its various personalities. Along with poet Michael Horovitz, he helped convene the 1965 International Poetry Incarnation at the Royal Albert Hall, an event now regarded as a milestone in the formation of London's counter-culture. In 1966, he co-founded the *International Times* newspaper with Barry Miles, in which he espoused recreational drug-taking, sexual liberation and political protest against the Establishment. The publication's launch party at the Roundhouse featured music by Pink Floyd, who soon after would play at the short-lived but now-legendary music venue established by Hoppy and record producer Joe Boyd: the UFO Club. As a photographer, he documented everything from CND marches to happenings. Arrested for cannabis possession in 1967, Hoppy served six months in prison. After his release, he remained a member of *IT*'s editorial board although his focus shifted to community-based education initiatives and video projects at the 'Fantasy Factory' ranging from work with UNESCO to the Arts Council. Hoppy's legacy lives on in the more liberated London of today and in his photographs, which provide a unique record of the characters and places during the city's social evolution in the 1960s.

EPILOGUE

MICHAEL SANDEL ON WHERE WE GO FROM HERE

There are some things money can't buy, but these days, not many. Today, almost everything is up for sale. Here are a few examples:

- A prison cell upgrade: $82 per night. In Santa Ana, California, and some other cities, nonviolent offenders can pay for better accommodations – a clean, quiet jail cell, away from the cells for nonpaying prisoners.

- Access to the car pool lane while driving solo: $8 during rush hour. Minneapolis and other cities are trying to ease traffic congestion by letting solo drivers pay to drive in car pool lanes, at rates that vary according to traffic.

- The services of an Indian surrogate mother to carry a pregnancy: $6,250. Western couples seeking surrogates increasingly outsource the job to India, where the practice is legal and the price is less than one-third the going rate in the United States.

- The right to immigrate to the United States: $500,000. Foreigners who invest $500,000 and create at least ten jobs in an area of high unemployment are eligible for a green card that entitles them to permanent residency.

- The right to shoot an endangered black rhino: $150,000. South Africa has begun letting ranchers sell hunters the right to kill a limited number of rhinos, to give the ranchers an incentive to raise and protect the endangered species.

- The cell phone number of your doctor: $1,500 and up per year. A growing number of 'concierge' doctors offer cell phone access and same-day appointments for patients willing to pay annual fees ranging from $1,500 to $25,000.

- The right to emit a metric ton of carbon into the atmosphere: €13 (about $18). The European Union runs a carbon emissions market that enables companies to buy and sell the right to pollute.

- Admission of your child to a prestigious university: ? Although the price is not posted, officials from some top universities told *The Wall Street Journal* that they accept some less-than-stellar students whose parents are wealthy and likely to make substantial financial contributions.

Not everyone can afford to buy these things. But today there are lots of new ways to make money. If you need to earn some extra cash, here are some novel possibilities:

- Rent out space on your forehead (or elsewhere on your body) to display commercial advertising: $777. Air New Zealand hired thirty people to shave their heads and wear temporary tattoos with the slogan 'Need a change? Head down to New Zealand.'

- Serve as a human guinea pig in a drug safety trial for a pharmaceutical company: $7,500. The pay can be higher or lower, depending on the invasiveness of the procedure used to test the drug's effect, and the discomfort involved.

- Fight in Somalia or Afghanistan for a private military company: $250 per month to $1,000 per day. The pay varies according to qualifications, experience and nationality.

- Stand in line overnight on Capitol Hill to hold a place for a lobbyist who wants to attend a congressional hearing: $15–$20 per hour. The lobbyists pay line-standing companies, who hire homeless people and others to queue up.

- If you are a second grader in an underachieving Dallas school, read a book: $2. To encourage reading, the schools pay kids for each book they read.

- If you are obese, lose fourteen pounds in four months: $378. Companies and health insurers offer financial incentives for weight loss and other kinds of healthy behavior.

- Buy the life insurance policy of an ailing or elderly person, pay the annual premiums while the person is alive, and then collect the death benefit when he or she dies: potentially, millions (depending on the policy). This form of betting on the lives of strangers has become a $30 billion industry. The sooner the stranger dies, the more the investor makes.

We live at a time when almost everything can be bought and sold. Over the past three decades, markets — and market values — have come to govern our lives as never before. We did not arrive at this condition through any deliberate choice. It is almost as if it came upon us.

As the cold war ended, markets and market thinking enjoyed unrivaled prestige, understandably so. No other mechanism for organizing the production and distribution of goods had proved as successful at generating affluence and prosperity. And yet, even as growing numbers of countries around the world embraced market mechanisms in the operation of their economies, something else was happening. Market values were coming to play a greater and greater role in social life. Economics was becoming an imperial domain. Today, the logic of buying and selling no longer applies to material goods alone but increasingly governs the whole of life. It is time to ask whether we want to live this way.

NOTES

NOTE: Where dates are uncertain or there is contradictory evidence the most likely has been chosen.

A TALE OF TWO CITIES: LONDON, SAN FRANCISCO AND THE TRANSATLANTIC BRIDGE (pp. 18–52)

1   *A Tale of Two Cities* is claimed as the best-selling novel of all time. Charles Dickens's description of the impact of the 1789 French Revolution on Paris and London is a reminder that the huge upheavals that periodically sweep through life – 1848, 1870, 1917 … the 1960s – eventually blow out, settle down and set the foundations of the next revolution.

2   Alan George Heywood Melly (1926–2007) was an English jazz and blues singer, critic, writer and lecturer. From 1965 to 1974 he was a film and television critic for the *Observer*. His *Revolt into Style: The Pop Arts in Britain* (1970) provides an interesting analysis of the role of pop music in creating the generation gap. He was a defendant for *OZ* magazine during the famous 1971 trial.

3   For more gritty comparators, see *I'll Never Forget What's 'Isname* (1967) *and Cool It Carol!* (1970). The latter directed by Peter Walker in the twilight of Swinging London was described as a 'glossy and entertaining morality tale' – with film stills alluding to the Profumo affair. Cult film review website *Cinedelica* noted, 'compared to a movie like *Smashing Time*, *Cool It Carol!* is probably the more realistic portrayal of the swinging London dream. But we're still in the land of the exploitation flick, so don't expect Ken Loach-like realism.' In considering attitudes to sex in films in the UK during the period it is worth remembering that the highest-grossing British movie of 1974 was *Confessions of a Window Cleaner* – an approach that, along with the Carry On films (*Carry on Camping* in 1969, … *Loving* in 1970, … *Girls* in 1973 – the first of these banned in Ireland) harked back to the traditions of music hall and bawdy seaside postcards rather than unbridled eroticism.

4   Then slated for demolition but saved after a Grade I listing in November 1967.

5   Actually Lismore Street, in Gospel Oak (an area of Camden), where demolition to make way for the Lismore Circus Estate had been put on hold while filming took place. The replacement flats are claimed to be the longest continuous blocks of public housing in Europe.

6   The rivalry between 'Green Berets' and 'California Dreamin'' by the Mamas and the Papas was so fierce that the two records tied for the number one record of 1966.

7   The official title is *Quotations from Chairman Mao Tse-tung*. It was first published in 1964 with a definitive edition in 1965 including 427 quotations.

8   See their film, *Dig*, which includes shots of the exhibition. The flat was later demolished to make way for the West Cross Route roundabout; the site of the excavation is now covered by the Roseford Court tower block. Participant Gustav Metzger organized the Destruction in Art Symposium (DIAS) later that year, 9–11 September 1966, bringing together a diverse group of international artists, poets and scientists, including representatives of the counter-cultural underground. It attracted international attention from both the media and art communities.

9   As Home Secretary, Roy Jenkins aimed to create 'a civilized society' in the UK, with measures including the abolition of capital punishment, legalization of abortion, decriminalization of homosexuality, relaxing of divorce law, suspension of birching and end of theatre censorship. On 23 May 1966 Jenkins delivered a speech on race relations, asking: 'Where in the world is there a university which could preserve its fame, or a cultural centre which could keep its eminence, or a metropolis which could hold its drawing power, if it were to turn inwards and serve only its own hinterland and its own racial group?'

10 Deirdre McSharry's headline in the *Daily Express*. Twiggy, *Twiggy on Twiggy* (London 1976), pp.42–3.

11 The film went on to become an Oscar-nominated cult classic – highlighting the superficiality of the new world of fashion, models and parties, with their enjoyment-now-and-hell-to-the-future attitude. At the time of filming, Vanessa Redgrave was simultaneously starring in *The Prime of Miss Jean Brodie* at Wyndham's Theatre (opened 5 May) and filming *Red and Blue* (1967).

12 Westway is the longest elevated motorway in Europe, stretching for 3.5 kilometres. However, spiralling costs and community opposition led to cancellation of the rest of the 'London Motorway Box' in 1973, leaving the Westway as a fragmentary monument to a 1960s vision of car-topia.

13 It was not until 1973 that a woman could have a Barclaycard in her own right.

14 During the prolonged ending, during which the actors stood in silence among the audience, critic Kenneth Tynan (then the National Theatre's literary manager) shouted out 'Are we keeping you waiting, or are you keeping *us*?'

15 The launch was described by Daevid Allen of Soft Machine as 'one of the two most revolutionary events in the history of English alternative music and thinking'. The *IT* event was important because it marked the first recognition of a rapidly spreading socio-cultural revolution.

16 John met Yoko on 6 November, the day her show was hung. The private view was on the 7th and the show opened to the public on the 8th.

17 Written by Jeremy Sandford, the BBC 1 television programme was seen by 12 million viewers, then a quarter of the viewing population. It was repeated on 11 January 1967 but then not shown again until 1976. In 2005 it was listed by industry magazine *Broadcast* as the most influential UK television programme of all time; in 1966 it led to a Parliamentary debate and the foundation of homelessness charity Shelter.

18 The union hall of San Francisco's longshoremen, an impressive concrete-span, modernist hexagon erected in 1959, is still in use. Its construction, one block back from the Embarcadero waterfront, is testimony to the power of the city's dockside workers before the impact of mechanization/containerization in the 1960s. Prior to the first Acid Test at Soquel on 27 November 1965, the hall had played host to Jefferson Airplane on 16 October and the Lovin' Spoonful on 24 October. Dancing had been strictly controlled in San Francisco but the layout of the hall made it easy for a mass audience to flout the city regulations. The fact that many Longshoremen were Hell's Angels helped smooth the organization of events.

19 In practice, this ruling brought censorship of literature, plays and adult film to an end in much of the US and a general liberalization of official attitudes. At that time, to be declared obscene a work of literature had to be proven by censors to: 1) appeal to prurient interest, 2) be patently offensive, and 3) have no redeeming social value. The book in question in this case was *Fanny Hill* (or *Memoirs of a Woman of Pleasure*, 1749) by John Cleland; the Supreme Court held in *Memoirs v. Massachusetts* that, while it might fit the first two criteria (it appealed to prurient interest and was patently offensive), it could not be proven that *Fanny Hill* had no redeeming social value. These judgements were part of the Warren Court period (1953–69) when the Chief Justice was the progressive Earl Warren, previously the Republican Governor of California (1942–53) and Republican candidate for vice president in 1948.

20 In the 1960s minorities made up about seven per cent of San Francisco's police force and about two per cent of officers. The equivalent percentages in Oakland were much lower.

21 On Thursday 21 April the *San Francisco Chronicle* published support for Bill Graham's application for a dance licence at the Fillmore; it was granted as a result. In mid-July, Graham secured a three-year lease on the venue, which set him on the road to becoming America's leading rock promoter. See *Bill Graham and the Rock & Roll Revolution* (Skirball Cultural Center, Los Angeles, 7 May – 11 October 2015); his book with Robert Greenfield, *Bill Graham Presents: My Life Inside Rock and Out* (New York: Doubleday, 1993); and John Glatt, *Live at the Fillmore East & West: Getting Backstage and Personal with Rock's Greatest Legends* (Guildford: Lyons Press, 2015). After his death in a helicopter crash on 25 October 1991, his company Bill Graham Presents (BGP) passed through a number of owners, which eventually led to the creation of Live Nation, the world's largest concert production/promotion company. The original master leaseholder in 1966 was the famous African American promoter George Sullivan, 'The Mayor of Fillmore', well regarded in the ethnically mixed neighbourhood. He was found shot dead on 2 August that year, just off Market Street. His murder remains a mystery, see G. Carr, 'Who Shot the Mayor of Fillmore?', *The New Fillmore*, 4 September 2014, which includes some fascinating photographs of African American life in San Francisco. Available at: http://newfillmore.com/2014/09/04/who-shot-the-mayor-of-fillmore/

22 See B.W. Joseph, 'My Mind Split Open: Andy Warhol's Exploding Plastic Inevitable', *Grey Room* 8 (Summer 2002): 80–102. See also Ronald Nameth's 12-minute film *Andy Warhol's Exploding Plastic Inevitable* (1967) available from Electronic Arts Intermix (EAI).

23 The exact date of the riot remains unknown due to the destruction of relevant police records. Cross-dressing had been criminalized in San Francisco in 1863, so police could use the presence of transgender people in a bar as a pretext for making a raid and closing the premises. See the documentary *Screaming Queens: The Riot at Compton's Cafeteria* (2005 Distributor: Frameline). The film's promotional material states, 'Perhaps the most intriguing commentary is Sgt. Elliot Blackstone, who helps explain the conflict between the San Francisco Police Department and the city's transgender community and how the San Francisco Police Department's policies changed to reflect greater acceptance in the years following the 1966 riot. This documentary also explores the connection between transgender activism and the larger social upheavals affecting the United States in the 1960s, such as the civil rights and sexual liberation movements, the youth counter-culture, urban renewal, and Great Society antipoverty programs.' See also collections at the GLBT History Museum, San Francisco.

24 Candlestick Park Baseball Stadium. This would be the Beatles' last live concert as a touring band.

25 In total 12 issues were published through to February 1968. In mid-1966, the Underground Press Syndicate was established to connect local underground publications across the US. From five original members it grew to over 200, see Thorne Dreyer and Victoria Smith, 'The Movement and the New Media', *The Rag* (March 1969). Membership granted cost-free copying of articles, which allowed ideas and news to spread extremely quickly. By the late 1960s women's issues were becoming increasingly important, see generally Ken Wachsberger (ed.) *Voices from the Underground: A Directory of Resources and Sources on the Vietnam Era Underground Press* (Tempe, AZ: Mica, 1993).

26 See 'Hunters Point – Cops shot into Community Centre sheltering two hundred Children, *The Movement* 2 no. 9 (October 1966): 1

27 Peggy Caserta was a notable bisexual and partner of Janis Joplin, see Peggy Caserta with Dan Knapp, *Going Down with Janis* (New York: Dell, 1973), a period piece in its own right.

28 See the Digger Archive, at www.Diggers.org.

29 See Joshua Bloom and Waldo E. Martin, *Black Against Empire: The History and Politics of the Black Panther Party* (Berkeley: University of California Press, 2013) for the founding and early years of the Black Panthers.

30 As a result he did not box from 1967 to 1971, when the Supreme Court overturned his conviction by 8–0, and thus Ali lost the best years of his career.

31 Jim Haynes recalled in October 1969, as the Lab closed, 'People flowed through – young, old, fashionable, unfashionable, beautiful, bored, ugly, sad, aggressive, friendly ... They asked, "What's the product? What's its name?" The real answer was Humanity: you can't weigh it, you can't market it, you can't label it, and you can't destroy it'. Quoted in Barry Miles, *London Calling: A Countercultural History of London Since 1945* (London: Atlantic, 2010), p. 240.

32 Members of the Merchant Navy and those serving in the British Armed Forces have been allowed to be open about their sexuality only since 2000, following a ruling by the European Court of Human Rights. Homosexuality was decriminalized in Scotland by the Criminal Justice (Scotland) Act 1980 and in Northern Ireland by the Homosexual Offences (Northern Ireland) Order 1982.

33 On Saturday 1 July the BBC had made the first colour broadcast on television – Wimbledon tennis on BBC 2.

34 Prime Minister Harold Wilson famously said in a ministerial broadcast: 'From now the pound abroad is worth 14 per cent or so less in terms of other currencies. It does not mean, of course, that the pound here in Britain, in your pocket or purse or in your bank, has been devalued.'

35 Having devoted his life to spiritual study in his native India, A.C. Bhaktivedanta Swami Prabhupada (1896–1997) decided to go to America in 1965, at the age of 69, to spread the message of Chaitanya Mahaprabhu, a sixteenth-century Bengali spiritual teacher. He sailed on the freighter *Jaladuta*, with only a suitcase, an umbrella, a supply of dry cereal, about eight dollars of Indian currency, and a few books. The first temple he founded in the US was at 26 Second Avenue, New York. His arrival coincided with growing interest in Eastern religions and mysticism. San Francisco, with its long-established Asian population, had hosted a centre for Zen Buddhism since the 1930s.

36 Scott H. Bennett, *Radical Pacifism: The War Resisters League and Gandhian Nonviolence in America, 1915–1963* (Syracuse University Press, 2003), p. 240

37 The festival was held at the 4,000-seat Sidney B. Cushing Memorial Amphitheatre high on the south face of Mount Tamalpais, on the north side of the Golden Gate. At least 35,000 people were bused up on 'Trans-Love Bus Lines' to the first major event of the Summer of Love and what was, in effect, the world's first rock festival. Profits from a $2 admission fee went to the Hunters Point Child Care Center, a popular cause given the events of the previous September.

38 The song was produced by John Phillips and Lou Adler, who used it over the next month to promote the Monterey International Pop Festival held in June. The song has been called 'the unofficial anthem of the counter-culture movement of the 1960s'. See Scott McKenzie obituary, *Daily Telegraph*, 20 August 2012, available at http://www. telegraph.co.uk/culture/music/music-news/9487213/Scott-McKenzie-1960s-counter-culture-singer-dies-at-73.html

39 In 1967, 16 US states still had laws banning mixed-race marriages. Chief Justice Earl Warren's opinion for the unanimous court held that: 'Marriage is one of the "basic civil rights of man," fundamental to our very existence and survival ... To deny this fundamental freedom on so unsupportable a basis as the racial classifications embodied in these statutes, classifications so directly subversive of the principle of equality at the heart of the Fourteenth Amendment, is surely to deprive all the State's citizens of liberty without due process of law. The Fourteenth Amendment requires that the freedom of choice to marry not be restricted by invidious racial discrimination. Under our Constitution, the freedom to marry, or not marry, a person of another race resides with the individual and cannot be infringed by the State.' See https://www.law.cornell.edu/supremecourt/text/388/1. Alabama only adapted its laws to match this decision in 2000. In June 2007, on the 40th anniversary of the decision, Mildred Loving said: 'I believe all Americans, no matter their race, no matter their sex, no matter their sexual orientation, should have that same freedom to marry ... I am still not a political person, but I am proud that Richard's and my name is on a court case that can help reinforce the love, the commitment, the fairness and the family that so many people, black or white, young or old, gay or straight, seek in life. I support the freedom to marry for all. That's what *Loving*, and loving, are all about.'

40 Monterey International Pop Festival – three day concert event held from 16 to 18 June 1967 at the Monterey County Fairgrounds. See http://montereyinternationalpopfestival.com/festival/

41 Joan Baez served 10 days at the Santa Rita Rehabilitation Center. There were linked protests in many other cities.

42 Transcription available at http://kingencyclopedia.stanford.edu/encyclopedia/ documentsentry/ive_been_to_the_mountaintop/

43 http://www.rollingstone.com/music/lists/500-greatest-albums-of-all-time-20120531/the-jimi-hendrix-experience-electric-ladyland-20120524

44 See Robert Poole, *How Man First Saw the Earth* (New Haven, CT; London: Yale University Press, 2008).

45 The film was based on the 1963 book by Nell Dunn.

46 There would be further trouble at a demonstration in October.

47 The explosion caused a wave of public opposition to high-rise housing. Further such projects were abandoned and new buildings legislation introduced, marking the beginning of the end of comprehensive slum redevelopment and, from the early 1970s, sparking a growing interest in restoration rather than demolition of run-down neighbourhoods. Ronan Point was eventually demolished in 1986.

48 The Hayward Gallery was opened on Tuesday 9 July. With the Tate and the Whitechapel London now had four publicly funded art galleries – along with the Royal Academy. The Hayward's first exhibition was a major retrospective of the paintings of Matisse.

49 It eventually became *Time Out*. Also in 1968 John 'Hoppy' Hopkins founded BIT, a spin-off from *International Times*, which provided listings and local information in person and by telephone. The *BIT Guide* passed on travellers' tips from those who had already been on the road.

50 Powers of theatre censorship belonging to the office of the Lord Chamberlain, in place since 1737, were abolished on 26 September by the Theatres Act 1968.

51 It was during the debate on the Act that MP Enoch Powell made his famous 'Rivers of Blood' speech in Birmingham on Saturday 20 April. The ensuing furore led to Powell's dismissal from his shadow Cabinet position by Edward Heath, Leader of the Opposition, and walkouts by London dockers.

52 Following the death of their manager Brian Epstein on 27 August 1967, the Beatles sped up development of a new company, Apple Corps, which would handle their various business interests. Their plan was to have five divisions: records, electronics, film, publishing and retailing. This included the famous Apple Boutique at 94 Baker Street, which was designed (along with a lot of the clothes) by the Dutch design collective The Fool. It opened on 7 December 1967, with Lennon and Harrison attending, and closed a little over seven months later, on 31 July 1968. It was never profitable – partly due to extensive shoplifting.

53 On 31 March President Johnson had said he would not run for re-election, leaving an opening for Senator Robert F. Kennedy. His death left the Democrats in disarray and ultimately gave Nixon a narrow victory later in the year.

54 In May 1970, the California Appellate Court reversed the conviction and ordered a new trial. After two subsequent trials ended in hung juries, the district attorney said he would not pursue a fourth trial.

55 The film starred Jack Nicholson, who had written the screenplay for *The Trip* (1967), exploring the use of LSD, and who then found fame in *Easy Rider* (1969).

56 On Wednesday 21 June, Douglas Englebart at the 'Research Center for Augmenting Human Intellect' at Stanford Research Institute (SRI) had filed a patent for the 'mouse'. The December event, now known as the 'Mother of All Demos', is recognized as a key event in the history of computing. The live demonstration unveiled a hardware and software system called the oN-Line System (NLS) that included almost all the elements of modern personal computing: windows, hypertext, graphics, efficient navigation and command input, video conferencing, the mouse, word processing, dynamic file linking, revision control and a collaborative real-time editor. The demo was filmed by Stewart Brand, editor of the *Whole Earth Catalog*.

57 The single was released on Friday 11 July although it had been written in January following the publication of the Apollo 8 'Earthrise' photograph. It reached number five, giving Bowie his first UK hit. On Saturday 16 August Bowie organized the Beckenham Free festival in south-east London to coincide with Woodstock Festival in the US.

58 The event was planned over three days but ran into a fourth, on the Monday.

59 Paul McCartney had married Linda Eastman on 12 March 1969. On 30 January the Beatles had staged their last public performance on the roof of Apple Corps at 3 Saville Row, recorded for the documentary film *Let It Be*. John Lennon's parting shot as the police stopped the performance was 'I hope we passed the audition'.

60 Concorde's maiden flight was on 2 March, in France. The first scheduled supersonic passenger flights started on 21 January 1976 on the London–Bahrain and Paris–Rio (via Dakar) routes. Concorde was initially banned in the US because of protest against the sonic booms. After the ban was lifted scheduled service from London to New York began on 22 November 1977.

61 The Who had released *Tommy*, their 'rock-opera' album, on 23 May. David Bowie sat in the front row and then went backstage to give Pete Townshend an advance copy of his new single 'Space Oddity' – which had been played over the PA system at Hyde Park.

62 This was the only concert Dylan played between 1966 and 1973. The extraordinary story of how he was attracted to the festival is told in Ray and Caroline Foulk, *Stealing Dylan from Woodstock: When the World Came to the Isle of Wight* (London: Medina, 2015).

63 Poetry was a key component of the counter-culture. Indeed, the International Poetry Incarnation, which attracted 7,000 to the Royal Albert Hall in London on 11 June 1965, is often taken as the start of the counter-culture in the UK. Peter Whitehead filmed the event and released it as *Wholly Communion* (1965). Performers included Ginsberg, Corso, Ferlinghetti, Fainlight, Horovitz, Trocchi, Logue, Voznesensky, Mitchell and Jandl.

64 On 30 September 1968, Diana Ross and the Supremes had released 'Love Child', which became a number one hit in the US. Motown had generally avoided 'message' records but this song raised the issue of unplanned pregnancy and babies doomed to grow up in a ghetto environment. To match the mood of Black Struggle, the group appeared on *The Ed Sullivan Show* in street clothes – Diana in a sweatshirt emblazoned 'Love Child', cut-off jeans and Afro hair – in contrast to their usual elaborate sequinned outfits.

65 The park led to increasingly violent conflict between the protesters and the University of California, Berkeley. California Governor Ronald Reagan had called the campus 'a haven for communist sympathizers, protesters, and sex deviants', as quoted in Christopher Carter, *Rhetorical Exposures* (Tuscaloosa: University of Alabama Press, 2015), p. 85. Eventually, he called in the National Guard to clear the area. On 15 May buckshot and teargas were fired at protesters and student James Rector was killed.

66 Walkouts and strikes preceded a splintering at the *Berkeley Barb*. Ultimately *Berkeley Tribe* was taken over by a feminist faction. Underground newspapers saw many fights over sex advertising revenue, which was usually a key part of overall financing.

67 Charles Manson was eventually convicted of the murders. He had moved to LA in 1967 and attracted a following of dropouts – 'the Family' – establishing a pseudo-religious commune at two ranches near Death Valley. Manson expounded a theory of race war in US cities and claimed this was predicted by the Beatles in messages encoded in the song 'Helter Skelter' on the *White Album*. In August 1969 Manson ordered members of the Family to carry out specific murders with slogans to encourage racial conflict. The trial was a bizarre media event, with Manson saying 'the music is telling the youth to rise up against the establishment.' He was sentenced to death in 1971, but this was commuted to life imprisonment in 1972. Manson is currently incarcerated in Corcoran State Prison, California.

Native American protesters stayed for 19 months, leaving on 11 June 1971.

…e performance by the Rolling Stones at the concert …hown in *Gimme Shelter* (1970) a documentary film …cted by Albert and David Maysles and Charlotte …in. The murder of 18-year-old Meredith Hunter, who …ulled out a gun, became a symbol of the decline of …idealism at the end of the 1960s. *Rolling Stone* in its …ary 1970 edition said, 'Altamont was the product of …al egotism, hype, ineptitude, money manipulation, …se, a fundamental lack of concern for humanity'.

…tment of Defense Program. The first …n on the ARPANET (Advanced Research Projects …ork, the precursor of the Internet) was the …LA to SRI on 29 October 1969. By 1972 the …ected 37 computers across the US.

…credited, including Thelma Schoonmaker, …ho was also one of the cameramen), …igh. Schoonmaker was nominated for …for Film Editing and Dan Wallin and L.A. …ated for Best Sound.

72 The couple on the cover, Bobbi Kelly and Nick Ercoline, married in 1971 and are still together – 'Woodstock was a sign of the times, so many things were churning around in our world at that time: civil rights, the Vietnam War, women's rights. It was our generation.' (*Sydney Morning Herald*, 16 August 2009, available at http://www.smh.com.au/national/the-love-and-peace-live-on-after-40-years-20090815-elpt.html.) '[Jim] "Corky" [Corcoran] is lying on the ground to the right of us. He'd just returned from Vietnam. To me there's something particularly symbolic about that: a festival dedicated to peace with a Vietnam marine on the cover of its album. We remain good friends.' *Guardian*, 7 August 2015, available at https://www.theguardian.com/artanddesign/2015/aug/07/thats-me-in-the-picture-woodstock-bobbi-ercoline.

73 Figures from http://www.earthday.org/about/the-history-of-earth-day. In 1969, at a UNESCO Conference in San Francisco, peace activist John McConnell proposed a day to honour the Earth and the concept of peace, to be celebrated on 21 March, the first day of spring in the northern hemisphere. This was sanctioned in a Proclamation written by McConnell and signed by the UN Secretary General. A separate Earth Day was founded by United States Senator Gaylord Nelson as a day of environmental activism and was first held on 22 April 1970.

74 Quoted in Judith Weintraub, 'Germaine Greer – Opinions That May Shock the Faithful', *New York Times*, 22 March 1971.

75 In April 1966, on Boeing's 50th Anniversary, Pan Am had ordered 25 of these aircraft. Celebrating the signing of the contract, Juan Trippe, the Head of Pan Am, said the plane would be '... a great weapon for peace, competing with intercontinental missiles for mankind's destiny'. (Quoted in Graham Simmons, *The Airbus 380: A History*, Barnsley: Pen and Sword, 2014, p. 31.) Heathrow Airport was booming: Terminal 1 opened in April 1969. Passenger numbers rose from 5 million in 1970 to 27 million by the end of the decade.

76 Margaret Harrison founded the London Women's Liberation Art Group in 1970. In 1971 her exhibition was closed by the police for its 'pornographic' depiction of men, including one of Hugh Hefner as a Bunny Girl. The UK Gay Liberation Front held its first meeting at the London School of Economics on 13 October 1970.

77 This issue, including Rupert Bear in compromising positions, led to the famous *OZ* obscenity trial in 1971, see Geoffrey Robertson, *The Justice Game* (London: Chatto & Windus,1998). It was guest-edited by a talented young group of teenagers who went on to forge successful careers, including: Charles Shaar Murray, writer for *NME*; Peter Popham, foreign correspondent for *The Independent*; Deyan Sudjic, founder of *Blueprint*, editor of *Architectural Digest* and now director of the New Design Museum; Colin Thomas, photographer; and Trudi Braun, who became a senior editor at *Harper's*.

78 It transferred to the West End and ran through to 1980, in 3,918 performances.

79 In J.G. Ballard's novel *Concrete Island* (1974), his version of the Robinson Crusoe character is marooned on an imaginary motorway intersection on the Westway.

80 The audience was estimated at 600,000, on an island with a population below 100,000. This was the last of three consecutive festivals. As a result of the Isle of Wight Act 1971 and three subsequent renewals, gatherings of more than 5,000 people were effectively banned for 32 years. The event was filmed by Murray Lerner but for financial reasons the material was only released in 1997 as *Message to Love*. Three weeks later, on Saturday 19 September 1970, the Piltdown Festival was held at Worthy Farm, Glastonbury – the first incarnation of what would become the UK's longest-running annual festival – a small crowd of 1,500 paid a £1 entry fee which included free milk from the farm. Jimi Hendrix had died the previous day.

81 There had been earlier protests in the US, notably at the Miss America Pageant in Atlantic City on 7 September 1968, coverage of which included the *New York Post* headline 'The Bra Burners' (12 September 1968). Bra-burning connected the feminist protest and anti-war protesters who burned their draft cards. A local paper had reported that 'the bras, girdles, falsies, curlers, and copies of popular women's magazines burned in the "Freedom Trash Can"', though protesters maintain categorically that no bras were burned. The phrase nonetheless became an international trope and was then linked with 'liberated' women who chose to go braless.

82 The event says much about attitudes in the UK in 1970, when Miss World was the most popular programme on television, attracting 24 million viewers. It was already a highly controversial year for competition: South Africa had been allowed two entrants, one black, one white. On the day, the Angry Brigade exploded a bomb under a BBC outside broadcast van in an attempt to prevent transmission. Jennifer Hosten (Miss Grenada) was the first black woman to win Miss World; second place went to the black contestant from South Africa (Miss Africa South); the white representative (Miss South Africa) was fifth. The Prime Minister of Grenada was on the judging panel! Numerous complaints about the result were sent to the press, and accusations of racism were made by all sides, leading the organizing director to resign – all of which helped raise awareness of the Women's Liberation protest.

83 Neil Young composed the song 'Ohio' as a protest anthem in response ('Tin soldiers and Nixon coming / We're finally on our own / This summer I hear the drumming/ Four dead in Ohio'), having seen the photographs in *Life* magazine. He said the event was 'probably the biggest lesson ever learned at an American place of learning'. The song was recorded in Studio 3 at the Record Plant, Los Angeles, on 21 May and rush-released by Atlantic as a single, backed with Stephen Stills' 'Find the Cost of Freedom'. It reached number 14 on the US *Billboard* Hot 100. Crosby, Stills & Nash had 'Teach your Children' in the charts at the same time. The song is ranked 395th in *Rolling Stone*'s Greatest Songs of All Time (2004).

84 'The Mobilization brought over one hundred thousand people to rally in Washington on only ten days' notice, although plans for civil disobedience – around a White House shielded by sixty buses – dissolved in confusion; the Mobe steering committee feared that a sit-down by thousands would get some people killed, and they were not willing to bear that burden.' Todd Gitlin, *The Sixties: Years of Hope, Days of Rage* (New York: Bantam Books, 1987), p. 396.

85 PARC became one of the key incubators of personal computing. There are several accounts of this extraordinary place and particularly its role in the rise of Steve Jobs's Apple, see Michael A. Hiltzik, *Dealers of Lightning: Xerox PARC and the Dawn of the Computer Age* (New York: HarperBusiness, 1999); Douglas K. Smith and Robert C. Alexander, *Fumbling the Future: How Xerox Invented, Then Ignored, the First Personal Computer* (New York: W. Morrow, 1988); and M. Mitchell Waldrop, *The Dream Machine: J.C.R. Licklider and the Revolution That Made Computing Personal* (New York: Viking, 2001).

86 A film of Hendrix's performance by John McDermott was released in October 2015 as *Jimi Hendrix: Electric Church*. Although the Atlanta event was called 'The Southern Woodstock', the recording was overshadowed by the massive success of the film *Woodstock* released in March 1970 and, therefore, remained unreleased for 45 years.

27 Peggy Caserta was a notable bisexual and partner of Janis Joplin, see Peggy Caserta with Dan Knapp, *Going Down with Janis* (New York: Dell, 1973), a period piece in its own right.

28 See the Digger Archive, at www.Diggers.org.

29 See Joshua Bloom and Waldo E. Martin, *Black Against Empire: The History and Politics of the Black Panther Party* (Berkeley: University of California Press, 2013) for the founding and early years of the Black Panthers.

30 As a result he did not box from 1967 to 1971, when the Supreme Court overturned his conviction by 8–0, and thus Ali lost the best years of his career.

31 Jim Haynes recalled in October 1969, as the Lab closed, 'People flowed through – young, old, fashionable, unfashionable, beautiful, bored, ugly, sad, aggressive, friendly ... They asked, "What's the product? What's its name?" The real answer was Humanity: you can't weigh it, you can't market it, you can't label it, and you can't destroy it'. Quoted in Barry Miles, *London Calling: A Countercultural History of London Since 1945* (London: Atlantic, 2010), p. 240.

32 Members of the Merchant Navy and those serving in the British Armed Forces have been allowed to be open about their sexuality only since 2000, following a ruling by the European Court of Human Rights. Homosexuality was decriminalized in Scotland by the Criminal Justice (Scotland) Act 1980 and in Northern Ireland by the Homosexual Offences (Northern Ireland) Order 1982.

33 On Saturday 1 July the BBC had made the first colour broadcast on television – Wimbledon tennis on BBC 2.

34 Prime Minister Harold Wilson famously said in a ministerial broadcast: 'From now the pound abroad is worth 14 per cent or so less in terms of other currencies. It does not mean, of course, that the pound here in Britain, in your pocket or purse or in your bank, has been devalued.'

35 Having devoted his life to spiritual study in his native India, A.C. Bhaktivedanta Swami Prabhupada (1896–1997) decided to go to America in 1965, at the age of 69, to spread the message of Chaitanya Mahaprabhu, a sixteenth-century Bengali spiritual teacher. He sailed on the freighter *Jaladuta*, with only a suitcase, an umbrella, a supply of dry cereal, about eight dollars of Indian currency, and a few books. The first temple he founded in the US was at 26 Second Avenue, New York. His arrival coincided with growing interest in Eastern religions and mysticism. San Francisco, with its long-established Asian population, had hosted a centre for Zen Buddhism since the 1930s.

36 Scott H. Bennett, *Radical Pacifism: The War Resisters League and Gandhian Nonviolence in America, 1915–1963* (Syracuse University Press, 2003), p. 240

37 The festival was held at the 4,000-seat Sidney B. Cushing Memorial Amphitheatre high on the south face of Mount Tamalpais, on the north side of the Golden Gate. At least 35,000 people were bused up on 'Trans-Love Bus Lines' to the first major event of the Summer of Love and what was, in effect, the world's first rock festival. Profits from a $2 admission fee went to the Hunters Point Child Care Center, a popular cause given the events of the previous September.

38 The song was produced by John Phillips and Lou Adler, who used it over the next month to promote the Monterey International Pop Festival held in June. The song has been called 'the unofficial anthem of the counter-culture movement of the 1960s'. See Scott McKenzie obituary, *Daily Telegraph*, 20 August 2012, available at http://www.telegraph.co.uk/culture/music/music-news/9487213/Scott-McKenzie-1960s-counter-culture-singer-dies-at-73.html

39 In 1967, 16 US states still had laws banning mixed-race marriages. Chief Justice Earl Warren's opinion for the unanimous court held that: 'Marriage is one of the "basic civil rights of man," fundamental to our very existence and survival ... To deny this fundamental freedom on so unsupportable a basis as the racial classifications embodied in these statutes, classifications so directly subversive of the principle of equality at the heart of the Fourteenth Amendment, is surely to deprive all the State's citizens of liberty without due process of law. The Fourteenth Amendment requires that the freedom of choice to marry not be restricted by invidious racial discrimination. Under our Constitution, the freedom to marry, or not marry, a person of another race resides with the individual and cannot be infringed by the State.' See https://www.law.cornell.edu/supremecourt/text/388/1. Alabama only adapted its laws to match this decision in 2000. In June 2007, on the 40th anniversary of the decision, Mildred Loving said: 'I believe all Americans, no matter their race, no matter their sex, no matter their sexual orientation, should have that same freedom to marry ... I am still not a political person, but I am proud that Richard's and my name is on a court case that can help reinforce the love, the commitment, the fairness and the family that so many people, black or white, young or old, gay or straight, seek in life. I support the freedom to marry for all. That's what *Loving*, and loving, are all about.'

40 Monterey International Pop Festival – three day concert event held from 16 to 18 June 1967 at the Monterey County Fairgrounds. See http://montereyinternationalpopfestival.com/festival/

41 Joan Baez served 10 days at the Santa Rita Rehabilitation Center. There were linked protests in many other cities.

42 Transcription available at http://kingencyclopedia.stanford.edu/encyclopedia/documentsentry/ive_been_to_the_mountaintop/

43 http://www.rollingstone.com/music/lists/500-greatest-albums-of-all-time-20120531/the-jimi-hendrix-experience-electric-ladyland-20120524

44 See Robert Poole, *How Man First Saw the Earth* (New Haven, CT; London: Yale University Press, 2008).

45 The film was based on the 1963 book by Nell Dunn.

46 There would be further trouble at a demonstration in October.

47 The explosion caused a wave of public opposition to high-rise housing. Further such projects were abandoned and new buildings legislation introduced, marking the beginning of the end of comprehensive slum redevelopment and, from the early 1970s, sparking a growing interest in restoration rather than demolition of run-down neighbourhoods. Ronan Point was eventually demolished in 1986.

48 The Hayward Gallery was opened on Tuesday 9 July. With the Tate and the Whitechapel London now had four publicly funded art galleries – along with the Royal Academy. The Hayward's first exhibition was a major retrospective of the paintings of Matisse.

49 It eventually became *Time Out*. Also in 1968 John 'Hoppy' Hopkins founded BIT, a spin-off from *International Times*, which provided listings and local information in person and by telephone. The *BIT Guide* passed on travellers' tips from those who had already been on the road.

50 Powers of theatre censorship belonging to the office of the Lord Chamberlain, in place since 1737, were abolished on 26 September by the Theatres Act 1968.

51 It was during the debate on the Act that MP Enoch Powell made his famous 'Rivers of Blood' speech in Birmingham on Saturday 20 April. The ensuing furore led to Powell's dismissal from his shadow Cabinet position by Edward Heath, Leader of the Opposition, and walkouts by London dockers.

52 Following the death of their manager Brian Epstein on 27 August 1967, the Beatles sped up development of a new company, Apple Corps, which would handle their various business interests. Their plan was to have five divisions: records, electronics, film, publishing and retailing. This included the famous Apple Boutique at 94 Baker Street, which was designed (along with a lot of the clothes) by the Dutch design collective The Fool. It opened on 7 December 1967, with Lennon and Harrison attending, and closed a little over seven months later, on 31 July 1968. It was never profitable – partly due to extensive shoplifting.

53 On 31 March President Johnson had said he would not run for re-election, leaving an opening for Senator Robert F. Kennedy. His death left the Democrats in disarray and ultimately gave Nixon a narrow victory later in the year.

54 In May 1970, the California Appellate Court reversed the conviction and ordered a new trial. After two subsequent trials ended in hung juries, the district attorney said he would not pursue a fourth trial.

55 The film starred Jack Nicholson, who had written the screenplay for *The Trip* (1967), exploring the use of LSD, and who then found fame in *Easy Rider* (1969).

56 On Wednesday 21 June, Douglas Englebart at the 'Research Center for Augmenting Human Intellect' at Stanford Research Institute (SRI) had filed a patent for the 'mouse'. The December event, now known as the 'Mother of All Demos', is recognized as a key event in the history of computing. The live demonstration unveiled a hardware and software system called the oN-Line System (NLS) that included almost all the elements of modern personal computing: windows, hypertext, graphics, efficient navigation and command input, video conferencing, the mouse, word processing, dynamic file linking, revision control and a collaborative real-time editor. The demo was filmed by Stewart Brand, editor of the *Whole Earth Catalog*.

57 The single was released on Friday 11 July although it had been written in January following the publication of the Apollo 8 'Earthrise' photograph. It reached number five, giving Bowie his first UK hit. On Saturday 16 August Bowie organized the Beckenham Free festival in south-east London to coincide with Woodstock Festival in the US.

58 The event was planned over three days but ran into a fourth, on the Monday.

59 Paul McCartney had married Linda Eastman on 12 March 1969. On 30 January the Beatles had staged their last public performance on the roof of Apple Corps at 3 Saville Row, recorded for the documentary film *Let It Be*. John Lennon's parting shot as the police stopped the performance was 'I hope we passed the audition'.

60 Concorde's maiden flight was on 2 March, in France. The first scheduled supersonic passenger flights started on 21 January 1976 on the London–Bahrain and Paris–Rio (via Dakar) routes. Concorde was initially banned in the US because of protest against the sonic booms. After the ban was lifted scheduled service from London to New York began on 22 November 1977.

61 The Who had released *Tommy*, their 'rock-opera' album, on 23 May. David Bowie sat in the front row and then went backstage to give Pete Townshend an advance copy of his new single 'Space Oddity' – which had been played over the PA system at Hyde Park.

62 This was the only concert Dylan played between 1966 and 1973. The extraordinary story of how he was attracted to the festival is told in Ray and Caroline Foulk, *Stealing Dylan from Woodstock: When the World Came to the Isle of Wight* (London: Medina, 2015).

63 Poetry was a key component of the counter-culture. Indeed, the International Poetry Incarnation, which attracted 7,000 to the Royal Albert Hall in London on 11 June 1965, is often taken as the start of the counter-culture in the UK. Peter Whitehead filmed the event and released it as *Wholly Communion* (1965). Performers included Ginsberg, Corso, Ferlinghetti, Fainlight, Horovitz, Trocchi, Logue, Voznesensky, Mitchell and Jandl.

64 On 30 September 1968, Diana Ross and the Supremes had released 'Love Child', which became a number one hit in the US. Motown had generally avoided 'message' records but this song raised the issue of unplanned pregnancy and babies doomed to grow up in a ghetto environment. To match the mood of Black Struggle, the group appeared on *The Ed Sullivan Show* in street clothes – Diana in a sweatshirt emblazoned 'Love Child', cut-off jeans and Afro hair – in contrast to their usual elaborate sequinned outfits.

65 The park led to increasingly violent conflict between the protesters and the University of California, Berkeley. California Governor Ronald Reagan had called the campus 'a haven for communist sympathizers, protesters, and sex deviants', as quoted in Christopher Carter, *Rhetorical Exposures* (Tuscaloosa: University of Alabama Press, 2015), p. 85. Eventually, he called in the National Guard to clear the area. On 15 May buckshot and teargas were fired at protesters and student James Rector was killed.

66 Walkouts and strikes preceded a splintering at the *Berkeley Barb*. Ultimately *Berkeley Tribe* was taken over by a feminist faction. Underground newspapers saw many fights over sex advertising revenue, which was usually a key part of overall financing.

67 Charles Manson was eventually convicted of the murders. He had moved to LA in 1967 and attracted a following of dropouts – 'the Family' – establishing a pseudo-religious commune at two ranches near Death Valley. Manson expounded a theory of race war in US cities and claimed this was predicted by the Beatles in messages encoded in the song 'Helter Skelter' on the *White Album*. In August 1969 Manson ordered members of the Family to carry out specific murders with slogans to encourage racial conflict. The trial was a bizarre media event, with Manson saying 'the music is telling the youth to rise up against the establishment.' He was sentenced to death in 1971, but this was commuted to life imprisonment in 1972. Manson is currently incarcerated in Corcoran State Prison, California.

68 Native American protesters stayed for 19 months, leaving on 11 June 1971.

69 The performance by the Rolling Stones at the concert is shown in *Gimme Shelter* (1970) a documentary film directed by Albert and David Maysles and Charlotte Zwerin. The murder of 18-year-old Meredith Hunter, who had pulled out a gun, became a symbol of the decline of hippy idealism at the end of the 1960s. *Rolling Stone* in its 21 January 1970 edition said, 'Altamont was the product of diabolical egotism, hype, ineptitude, money manipulation, and, at base, a fundamental lack of concern for humanity'.

70 A US Department of Defense Program. The first transmission on the ARPANET (Advanced Research Projects Agency Network, the precursor of the Internet) was the logon from UCLA to SRI on 29 October 1969. By 1972 the ARPANET connected 37 computers across the US.

71 Seven editors are credited, including Thelma Schoonmaker, Martin Scorsese (who was also one of the cameramen), and Michael Wadleigh. Schoonmaker was nominated for an Academy Award for Film Editing and Dan Wallin and L.A. Johnson were nominated for Best Sound.

72 The couple on the cover, Bobbi Kelly and Nick Ercoline, married in 1971 and are still together – 'Woodstock was a sign of the times, so many things were churning around in our world at that time: civil rights, the Vietnam War, women's rights. It was our generation.' (*Sydney Morning Herald*, 16 August 2009, available at http://www.smh.com.au/national/the-love-and-peace-live-on-after-40-years-20090815-elpt.html.) '[Jim] "Corky" [Corcoran] is lying on the ground to the right of us. He'd just returned from Vietnam. To me there's something particularly symbolic about that: a festival dedicated to peace with a Vietnam marine on the cover of its album. We remain good friends.' *Guardian*, 7 August 2015, available at https://www.theguardian.com/artanddesign/2015/aug/07/thats-me-in-the-picture-woodstock-bobbi-ercoline.

73 Figures from http://www.earthday.org/about/the-history-of-earth-day. In 1969, at a UNESCO Conference in San Francisco, peace activist John McConnell proposed a day to honour the Earth and the concept of peace, to be celebrated on 21 March, the first day of spring in the northern hemisphere. This was sanctioned in a Proclamation written by McConnell and signed by the UN Secretary General. A separate Earth Day was founded by United States Senator Gaylord Nelson as a day of environmental activism and was first held on 22 April 1970.

74 Quoted in Judith Weintraub, 'Germaine Greer – Opinions That May Shock the Faithful', *New York Times*, 22 March 1971.

75 In April 1966, on Boeing's 50th Anniversary, Pan Am had ordered 25 of these aircraft. Celebrating the signing of the contract, Juan Trippe, the Head of Pan Am, said the plane would be '... a great weapon for peace, competing with intercontinental missiles for mankind's destiny'. (Quoted in Graham Simmons, *The Airbus 380: A History*, Barnsley: Pen and Sword, 2014, p. 31.) Heathrow Airport was booming: Terminal 1 opened in April 1969. Passenger numbers rose from 5 million in 1970 to 27 million by the end of the decade.

76 Margaret Harrison founded the London Women's Liberation Art Group in 1970. In 1971 her exhibition was closed by the police for its 'pornographic' depiction of men, including one of Hugh Hefner as a Bunny Girl. The UK Gay Liberation Front held its first meeting at the London School of Economics on 13 October 1970.

77 This issue, including Rupert Bear in compromising positions, led to the famous *OZ* obscenity trial in 1971, see Geoffrey Robertson, *The Justice Game* (London: Chatto & Windus,1998). It was guest-edited by a talented young group of teenagers who went on to forge successful careers, including: Charles Shaar Murray, writer for *NME*; Peter Popham, foreign correspondent for *The Independent*; Deyan Sudjic, founder of *Blueprint*, editor of *Architectural Digest* and now director of the New Design Museum; Colin Thomas, photographer; and Trudi Braun, who became a senior editor at *Harper's*.

78 It transferred to the West End and ran through to 1980, in 3,918 performances.

79 In J.G. Ballard's novel *Concrete Island* (1974), his version of the Robinson Crusoe character is marooned on an imaginary motorway intersection on the Westway.

80 The audience was estimated at 600,000, on an island with a population below 100,000. This was the last of three consecutive festivals. As a result of the Isle of Wight Act 1971 and three subsequent renewals, gatherings of more than 5,000 people were effectively banned for 32 years. The event was filmed by Murray Lerner but for financial reasons the material was only released in 1997 as *Message to Love*. Three weeks later, on Saturday 19 September 1970, the Piltdown Festival was held at Worthy Farm, Glastonbury – the first incarnation of what would become the UK's longest-running annual festival – a small crowd of 1,500 paid a £1 entry fee which included free milk from the farm. Jimi Hendrix had died the previous day.

81 There had been earlier protests in the US, notably at the Miss America Pageant in Atlantic City on 7 September 1968, coverage of which included the *New York Post* headline 'The Bra Burners' (12 September 1968). Bra-burning connected the feminist protest and anti-war protesters who burned their draft cards. A local paper had reported that 'the bras, girdles, falsies, curlers, and copies of popular women's magazines burned in the "Freedom Trash Can"', though protesters maintain categorically that no bras were burned. The phrase nonetheless became an international trope and was then linked with 'liberated' women who chose to go braless.

82 The event says much about attitudes in the UK in 1970, when Miss World was the most popular programme on television, attracting 24 million viewers. It was already a highly controversial year for competition: South Africa had been allowed two entrants, one black, one white. On the day, the Angry Brigade exploded a bomb under a BBC outside broadcast van in an attempt to prevent transmission. Jennifer Hosten (Miss Grenada) was the first black woman to win Miss World; second place went to the black contestant from South Africa (Miss Africa South); the white representative (Miss South Africa) was fifth. The Prime Minister of Grenada was on the judging panel! Numerous complaints about the result were sent to the press, and accusations of racism were made by all sides, leading the organizing director to resign – all of which helped raise awareness of the Women's Liberation protest.

83 Neil Young composed the song 'Ohio' as a protest anthem in response ('Tin soldiers and Nixon coming / We're finally on our own / This summer I hear the drumming/ Four dead in Ohio'), having seen the photographs in *Life* magazine. He said the event was 'probably the biggest lesson ever learned at an American place of learning'. The song was recorded in Studio 3 at the Record Plant, Los Angeles, on 21 May and rush-released by Atlantic as a single, backed with Stephen Stills' 'Find the Cost of Freedom'. It reached number 14 on the US *Billboard* Hot 100. Crosby, Stills & Nash had 'Teach your Children' in the charts at the same time. The song is ranked 395th in *Rolling Stone*'s Greatest Songs of All Time (2004).

84 'The Mobilization brought over one hundred thousand people to rally in Washington on only ten days' notice, although plans for civil disobedience – around a White House shielded by sixty buses – dissolved in confusion; the Mobe steering committee feared that a sit-down by thousands would get some people killed, and they were not willing to bear that burden.' Todd Gitlin, *The Sixties: Years of Hope, Days of Rage* (New York: Bantam Books, 1987), p. 396.

85 PARC became one of the key incubators of personal computing. There are several accounts of this extraordinary place and particularly its role in the rise of Steve Jobs's Apple, see Michael A. Hiltzik, *Dealers of Lightning: Xerox PARC and the Dawn of the Computer Age* (New York: HarperBusiness, 1999); Douglas K. Smith and Robert C. Alexander, *Fumbling the Future: How Xerox Invented, Then Ignored, the First Personal Computer* (New York: W. Morrow, 1988); and M. Mitchell Waldrop, *The Dream Machine: J.C.R. Licklider and the Revolution That Made Computing Personal* (New York: Viking, 2001).

86 A film of Hendrix's performance by John McDermott was released in October 2015 as *Jimi Hendrix: Electric Church*. Although the Atlanta event was called 'The Southern Woodstock', the recording was overshadowed by the massive success of the film *Woodstock* released in March 1970 and, therefore, remained unreleased for 45 years.

87 Following several legal tussles with the authorities over obscene films, Alex de Renzy (1935–2001) went to Denmark in October 1969 to attend Sex 69, the first porn trade show hosted in Copenhagen after the legalization of adult pornography that year. This resulted in his first adult movie, premiered at the Screening Room, 220 Jones Street, in 1970, and the rapid development of San Francisco as a centre for adult film production – termed the 'smut boom'. After a landmark decision in the *People v. Alex de Renzy*, his *Pornography in Denmark: A New Approach* made for $15,000 went on wider release, grossing $2 million. For a detailed history of the evolution of sexual attitudes, pornography and censorship during the 1960s in the US and UK, see John Heidenry, *What Wild Ecstasy: The Rise and Fall of The Sexual Revolution* (New York: Simon & Schuster, 1997) and Michael Stabile's documentary *Smut Capital of America* (2011), available at https://vimeo.com/15163640.

88 Liberal attitudes in San Francisco had already produced America's first topless bar, the Condor Club. Located at the corner of Columbus and Broadway, just across the road from the City Lights Bookstore, it opened on 19 June 1964. A large lit sign in front of the club featured a picture of dancer Carol Doda with red lights on the image of her breasts, known as 'the new Twin Peaks of San Francisco'. The Condor went fully nude on 3 September 1969 and the Broadway area of Northbeach began to decline as the porn trade took over. In 1972, California banned nude dancing in establishments that served alcohol. In 1970, Amsterdam saw the start of the Wet Dream Festival. In America, porn film production eventually shifted to Los Angeles, where it remains today.

89 NOW was founded by Betty Friedan and 48 other women in June 1966. In 1968 it issued a Bill of Rights seeking to achieve an Equal Rights Amendment to force equality in employment and other areas. In 1969 Ivy Bottini, who was openly lesbian, designed the famous logo, which is still in use today. See, Robin Morgan (ed.), *Sisterhood Is Powerful, An Anthology of Writings from the Women's Liberation Movement* (New York: Random House, 1970), claimed as 'One of the 100 most influential books of the 20th Century' by the New York Public Library. Morgan used the royalties to establish the Sisterhood Is Powerful Fund, America's first feminist grant-giving organization.

90 The concert recording was eventually released in 2013 as *San Francisco 1970: The Classic Radio Broadcast* (Leftfield Media). Other live recordings from this time include *Live at the Fillmore East, March 7, 1970: It's About that Time* (released 2001) and *Black Beauty: Miles Davis at Fillmore West*, recorded on 10 April 1970, when Davis opened for the Grateful Dead (released 1973). At this time Bill Graham was running the two Fillmores as companion music venues on opposite coasts. He shut them in June/July 1971 to move his business focus to 'stadium rock'.

91 It became one of the most popular songs of all time and is ranked 4th in *Rolling Stone*'s Greatest Songs of All Time (2004).

92 On Sunday 15 August 1971 President Nixon announced that the United States was leaving the gold exchange standard of which it had been a part since the 1944 Bretton Woods system. The decision has been blamed for the stagflation (high unemployment and high inflation) of the 1970s. The oil crisis of 1973 was the result of the decision by the Arab members of OPEC, plus Egypt and Syria, to organize an oil embargo following the Yom Kippur War. Oil quadrupled in price with the impact lasting through the 1970s. Nixon's resignation on 9 August 1974 as a result of the Watergate Affair, and the fall of Saigon to the North Vietnamese on 30 April 1975, effectively ending the Vietnam War, contributed to a growing disillusionment and negativity in the US.

93 Data from the US Bureau of Labor Statistics, available at https://www.google.co.uk/publicdata/explore?ds=z1ebjpgk2654c1_&met_y=unemployment_rate&idim=country:US&fdim_y=seasonality:S&hl=en&dl=en.

94 The advance of containerization was greatly helped by its use by the American military to ship supplies during the Vietnam War in the late 1960s. Container ships reduced costs by shifting from manual handling to much faster unloading by crane. The results were a massive decline in dock labour and a demand for new port facilities where containers were stacked in the open air instead of in warehouses. In London and San Francisco the old docks rapidly became redundant.

95 Libby Porter and Kate Shaw (eds), *Whose Urban Renaissance? An International Comparison of Urban Regeneration Strategies* (London: Routledge, 2009), p. 226.

96 There were exceptions. San Francisco-based jeans manufacturer Levi Strauss expanded in the 1960s and '70s, although their factories were located across the US and increasingly overseas. The [Generation] Gap, now one of America's largest clothes retailers, was founded in San Francisco by Donald and Doris Fisher in 1969; there are currently nearly 3,700 Gap, Inc. stores in 400 locations worldwide. However, in June 1971 Stewart Brand held a 'Demise Party' for the *Whole Earth Catalog* – although publication continued sporadically – and on 4 July Bill Graham closed the famous Fillmore West music venue.

97 The 1960s were traumatic years for the Hollywood studios as television continued to erode their markets.

98 The Woolwich site was founded by the German company Siemens Brothers to manufacture submarine cables in 1863. Over the next thirty years Siemens' cables transformed global communications. For 100 years, the Woolwich factory had been a key part of London's manufacturing base. See Hansard, http://hansard.millbanksystems.com/commons/1968/feb/20/gecaei-merger.

99 The LDDC (1981–98) took over responsibility for 8.5 square miles of former dockland, much of it derelict with 95 per cent social housing and poor transportation links.

100 Robert Skidelsky, 'Meeting Our Makers: Britain's Long Industrial Decline', *New Statesman*, 24 January 2013, available at http://www.newstatesman.com/culture/culture/2013/01/meeting-our-makers-britain%E2%80%99s-long-industrial-decline.

101 Thatcher's economic reforms saw the deregulation of UK financial markets in 1986, starting with the 'Big Bang' on 27 October. It coincided with a technological shift, from 'open outcry' trading to electronic, screen-based trading. The result was huge, although contentious: London became one of the most important global financial centres.

102 For early use of the term see Alain Touraine, *The Post-Industrial Society. Tomorrow's Social History: Classes, Conflicts and Culture in the Programmed Society*, translated by Leonard F.X. Mayhew (New York: Random House, 1971) and Daniel Bell, *The Coming of Post-Industrial Society: A Venture in Social Forecasting* (New York: Basic Books, 1973).

103 One side-effect was that housing costs were still reasonable. Returning to London from university in Autumn 1978, I rented a room in a three-bedroom house in East Dulwich just purchased for £17,500. Forty years later, similar houses are now priced at £650,000, over seven times the cost when adjusted for real terms. See http://www.bankofengland.co.uk/education/Pages/resources/inflationtools/calculator/index1.aspx.

104 See Walter Isaacson, *Steve Jobs* (New York: Simon & Schuster, 2011), p. 384.

105 Subsequent meetings were held at SLAC, the Stanford University Linear Accelerator Center. For its history, see Steven Levy, *Hackers: Heroes of the Computer Revolution* (Garden City, NY: Doubleday, 1984) and the television film *Pirates of Silicon Valley* (TNT, 1999).

106 Nick Fletcher, 'Apple Becomes First Company Worth $700bn', *Guardian*, 25 November 2014, available at https://www.theguardian.com/technology/2014/nov/25/apple-first-company-worth-700bn-iphone.

107 In the GLC plan The Strand would have become a major one-way road, with an entirely new road cut east–west along Maiden Lane to the north. In April 1971 the Covent Garden Community Association was founded to oppose the plans, but they were officially approved in 1972. In 1973 Labour won control of the GLC and the plans were stopped. For the broader picture in the UK, see Dan Cruikshank and Colin Amery, *The Rape of Britain* (London: Elek, 1975). The Save London's Theatre Campaign (SLTC) was launched by Equity in 1972 in response to the threat when only three London theatres were listed. Its work led to the founding of the Theatres Trust in 1976. The SLTC's archive is now lodged in the Theatre & Performance Department at the Victoria and Albert Museum.

108 The map artworks were created by joining together 21 online dating sites to create a census of the US 'Based on an analysis of the profiles of 19 million single Americans'.

THE COUNTER-CULTURE (pp. 100–17)

1 A popular misquote attributed to Charles Erwin Wilson, CEO for General Motors, later US Secretary of Defense.

2 Grace Slick, *Somebody to Love? A Rock 'n' Roll Memoir* (New York: Warner Books, 1998), p. 116

3 Ian Dury, 'Sex and Drugs and Rock and Roll' (London: Stiff Records, BUY 17, released 26 August 1977)

4 Martin A. Lee and Bruce Shlain, *Acid Dreams: the CIA, LSD, and the Sixties Rebellion* (New York: Grove, 1985), p. 134

5 Timothy Leary, *Flashbacks: A Personal and Cultural History of an Era; an Autobiography*, with a foreword by William S. Burroughs (Los Angeles: J.P. Tarcher; New York: St Martin's Press, 1990), p.205

6 Timothy Leary in conversation with the author at Millbrook, NY, July 1967 (from journals)

7 Paul McCartney, quoted in Clinton Heylin: *Bob Dylan: Behind the Shades Revisited* (New York: HarperCollins, 2003), p.205

8 Frank Zappa, quoted in Heylin, ibid.

9 Detective Sergeant Norman Pilcher to a friend of the author during a raid in late 1967. Pilcher was sentenced to four years imprisonment for perjury in 1973.

10 The Who/Pete Townshend, 'My Generation' (London: Brunswick 05944, released 29 October 1965)

11 Dennis Hopper, quoted in a booklet accompanying a 4-CD box set, *Monterey International Pop Festival* (UK: Castle Communications, 1983), p. 19

12 Jean-Jacques Lebel, 'Every time he touches you it makes me come', in William Levy (ed.), *Wet Dreams* (Amsterdam: Joy Publications, 1973), p. 144

13 Jacques Hyzagi, 'Robert Crumb Hates You', *American Sniper*, 14 October 2015

YOU SAY YOU WANT A REVOLUTION? (pp. 196–217)

1 Ian MacDonald, *Revolution in the Head: The Beatles' Records and the Sixties* (London: Fourth Estate, 1994), p. 1

2 Of the BBC's Radiophonic Workshop

3 Scott Plagenhoef, 'The Beatles: Revolver', *Pitchfork*, 9 September 2009

4   MacDonald (cited note 1), p. 182

5   'McCartney observes that they usually stayed sober during writing sessions to avoid getting "clouded up".' Barry Miles, *Paul McCartney: Many Years from Now* (1997), p. 272. LSD was still legal in the US during their trip to Los Angeles. Paul McCartney waited another year to try the drug.

6   Barry Miles, *The Beatles Diary Volume 1: The Beatles Years* (London: Omnibus, 2001), 14 October

7   Mike Evans, *The Art of the Beatles*, exh. cat., Walker Art Gallery (Liverpool: A. Blond/Merseyside County Council, 1984), p. 28

8   Ibid.

9   Macdonald (cited note 1), p. 172 footnote 1

10 See Savage, this volume.

11 Nicholas Schaffner, *The Beatles Forever* (London; New York: McGraw-Hill, 1978), p. 53

12 Timothy Leary et al., *The Psychedelic Experience: A Manual Based on the Tibetan Book of the Dead* (New York: University Books, 1964)

13 As quoted by Emily King, 'The Hazy Gang', *Guardian*, 5 June 2006, available at http://www.theguardian.com/artanddesign/2006/jun/05/art

14 Plagenhoef (cited note 2)

15 Derek Taylor, *It Was Twenty Years Ago Today* (London: Bantam, 1987), p. 24

16 MacDonald (cited note 1), p. 249

17 John McMillian, *Beatles Vs. Stones* (New York: Simon & Schuster, 2013), p. 171

18 *The Beatles Anthology* DVD, Episode 6:8 'Sgt Pepper', 00.58

19 See Miles, this volume; Ian Inglis, 'Nothing You Can See That Isn't Shown': The Album Covers of the Beatles, *Popular Music*, vol. 20, no. 1 (January 2001), pp. 83–97.

20 MacDonald (cited note 1), p. 215, note 2

21 The inspiration, according to Lennon, was the *Daily Mail* report on 17 Jan 1967 of the death of Tara Browne, millionaire counter-culture enthusiast, in a car crash in South Kensington at the end of 1966.

22 MacDonald (cited note 1), p. 230

23 Inglis (cited note 19), p. 87

24 Miles (cited note 5), pp. 344–5

25 Adam Bychawski, 'The Night Jimi Hendrix Played Tribute to the Beatles', *New Musical Express*, 1 June 2007, available at http://www.nme.com/news/jimi-hendrix/28660

26 MacDonald (cited note 1), p. 165, footnote 1, cites Giorgio Gomelsky, manager of the Yardbirds, who claims that Jimmy Page introduced Harrison to the sitar around March 1965.

27 Unfortunately there were eventually no profits to share and the tensions created around these ventures added to the stresses and later to the break-up of the band. See Savage, this volume.

28 Evans (cited note 7), p. 31

29 Storm Thorgerson, *Classic Album Covers of the '60s* (London: Paper Tiger, 1989), p. 183

30 Ibid.

31 MacDonald (cited note 1), p. 328

32 As published in *Black Dwarf* (vol. 13, no. 9), 10 January 1969

33 Evans (cited note 7), p. 31

34 MacDonald (cited note 1), p. 27

BRITISH FASHION 1966–70: 'A STATE OF ANARCHY' (pp. 226–43)

The author would like to thank Brigid Keenan for her help during research for this essay.

1   'London: The Swinging City', *TIME* (15 April 1966), cover

2   Mary Quant, *Quant by Quant* (London: Cassell, 1966), p. 34

3   Felicity Green, *Sex, Sense and Nonsense: Felicity Green on the '60s Fashion Scene* (Woodbridge, Suffolk: ACC, 2014), pp. 93–5

4   Quant (cited note 2), p. 75

5   Alexandra Pringle, 'Chelsea Girl' in Sara Maitland (ed.) *Very Heaven: Looking Back at the 1960s* (London: Virago, 1988), pp. 37–8

6   Twiggy, *Twiggy by Twiggy* (London: Hart-Davis MacGibbon, 1975), p. 51. See Twiggy Dresses, minidress, designed by Paul Babb and Pamela Proctor, printed polyester, London, 1967–9. Given by Gillian Saville. V&A: T.15–2007 (not illustrated).

7   Geoffrey Aquilina Ross, *The Day of the Peacock: Style for Men 1963–1973* (London: V&A, 2011), p. 42

8   George Melly, *Revolt into Style: The Pop Arts in Britain* (London: Penguin, 1972), p. 151

9   Kiki Byrne archive V&A AAD/2015/9. Veronica Horwell, John Michael Ingram obituary, *Guardian*, 3 July 2014, available at www.theguardian.com/fashion/2014/jul/03/john-michael-ingram

10 Marion Foale interviewed with Sally Tuffin by Sonia Ashmore and Jenny Lister, 4 April 2006, transcribed extracts available at www.vam.ac.uk/content/articles/i/marion-foale-and-sally-tuffin

11 Ibid.

12 Ritva Ross interviewed by the author, V&A, London, 19 October 2015

13 An RCA graduate, Mike began 'The Ritva Man' label in 1969, designing knitwear for his Hyde Park baseball team of American expats. These 'Home Run' and 'Strike Zone' sweaters included appliquéd motifs, and lower sleeves of a contrasting colour, inspired by the layered shirts worn by baseball players (for example, V&A: T.14–2000, not illustrated). In the early 1970s, Ross collaborated with David Hockney and other ex-RCA students to produce the 'Artists' Collection' and made limited-edition tour sweaters for bands including the Rolling Stones and Simon and Garfunkel.

14 David Gilbert and Sonia Ashmore, 'Mini-skirts, Afghan Coats and Blue Jeans: Three Global Fashion Happenings of the Sixties' in Mirjam Shatanawi and Wayne Modest (eds.), *The Sixties: A Worldwide Happening* (Amsterdam: Uitgeverij Lecturis, 2015), p. 175

15 Jane Ormsby Gore interviewed by Sonia Ashmore and Jenny Lister 1 February 2006, transcribed extracts available at www.vam.ac.uk/content/articles/i/jane-ormsby-gore

16 Ross 2011 (cited note 7), p. 93

17 Ormsby Gore interview (cited note 15)

18 Ross 2011 (cited note 7), p. 88

19 John Pearse, quoted in Max Décharné, *King's Road: The Rise and Fall of the Hippest Street in the World* (London: Weidenfeld & Nicholson, 2005), p. 195

20 Sharon Kane, 'Sweet Jane: The Rise and Decline of the Afghan Coat 1966–197?', blog posting: sweetjanespopboutique.blogspot.co.uk/2012/05/rise-and-fall-of-afghan-coat-1966-197.html, cited by Gilbert and Ashmore 2015 (cited note 14)

21 Mary Quant talks to Alison Adburgham, 'The Permissive Society', *Guardian*, 10 October 1967, available at www.theguardian.com/theguardian/2008/oct/10/3

22 Marit Allen, British *Vogue* (January 1968): 54

23 Lord John, jacket, yellow woven floral furnishing fabric, London, c.1967. Given by Peter Davies. V&A: T.25–2014 (not illustrated).

24 Ross 2011 (cited note 7), p. 100

25 Mr Fish, kaftan or abaya, printed silk, Great Britain, 1973. Given by Mrs Annabel Whitehead. V&A: T.29–1997 (not illustrated).

26 Gilbert and Ashmore 2015 (cited note 14), pp. 163–77

27 Christopher Breward, 'Boutiques and Beyond: The Rise of British Fashion' in Christopher Breward and Ghislaine Wood (eds), *British Design from 1948: Innovation in the Modern Age* (London: V&A, 2012), p. 214

28 Jenny Diski, *The Sixties* (London: Profile, 2009), p. 13

29 Ibid.

30 Barbara Hulanicki, 'Biba' in Breward and Wood (eds), 2012 (cited note 27), p. 222

31 Liz Lightfoot, 'UK Fashion Schools Top Global Rankings, But Are Their Students Ready for Work?', *Guardian*, 24 August 2015, available at http://www.theguardian.com/education/2015/aug/24/fashion-school-ranking-students-central-saint-martins-csm

32 'Tyrannosaurus Rex Is Alive and Well and Living Off Ladbroke Grove', *Honey* (November 1970), transcribed by Liz Eggleston and posted on her blog at https://emmapeelpants.wordpress.com/category/tasty-fellas/marc-bolan/

THE CHROME-PLATED MARSHMALLOW THE 1960S CONSUMER REVOLUTION AND ITS DISCONTENTS (pp. 252–69)

1   For an excellent historiographical overview of the rise of consumer culture and obsolescence in design see Nigel Whiteley, 'Towards a Throw-Away Culture: Consumerism, "Style-Obsolescence" and Cultural Theory in the 1950s and 1960s', *Oxford Art Journal* 10 no. 2 (1987): 3–27.

2   Reyner Banham, *A Critic Writes: Selected Essays by Reyner Banham* (Berkeley: University of California Press, 1996), p. 5

3   Jean Baudrillard, *The System of Objects*, translated by James Benedict (London and New York: Verso, 2005), p. 13

4   Ibid.

5   Ibid., p. 223

6   Christopher Brooker traces the 1960s cultural revolution back to the 1950s prominence of the 'image' in television, advertising and consumer culture, in *The Neophiliacs: A Study of the Revolution in English Life in the Fifties and Sixties* (London: Fontana, 1970).

7   Andrew Blauvelt (ed.), *Hippie Modernism: The Struggle for Utopia* (Minneapolis: Walker Art Center, 2015), p. 11

8 Turner, this volume; Barry M. Katz, *Make It New: The History of Silicon Valley Design* (Cambridge, MA: MIT Press, 2015)

9 Fred Turner, *From Counterculture to Cyberculture: Stewart Brand, the Whole Earth Network, and the Rise of Digital Utopianism* (Chicago: University of Chicago Press, 2006), p. 103

10 Marshall McLuhan, *Understanding Media: The Extensions of Man* [first published New York: McGraw-Hill, 1964], (Berkeley: Gingko Press, 2011), p. 13

11 *The Waste Makers* (1960) was one of Vance Packard's three best-selling books to top the US non-fiction listings, the others being *The Hidden Persuaders* (1957) and *The Status Seekers* (1959). See Daniel Horowitz, *Vance Packard and American Social Criticism* (Chapel Hill: University of North Carolina Press, 1994), p. 133.

12 Vance Packard, *The Waste Makers* (New York: David McKay, 1960), p. 161

13 Ernest Dichter, *The Strategy of Desire* [first published Garden City, NY: Doubleday, 1960] (London and New York: Transaction, 2004), p. 85

14 Ibid., p. 86

15 Ibid., p. 91

16 Fred Turner, *The Democratic Surround: Multimedia and American Liberalism from World War II to the Psychedelic Sixties* (Chicago; London: University of Chicago Press, 2013), p. 215

17 Sam Binkley, *Getting Loose: Lifestyle Consumption in the 1970s* (Durham, NH and London: Duke University Press, 2007); Felicity D. Scott, *Architecture or Techno-Utopia: Politics after Modernism* (Cambidge, MA: MIT Press, 2007)

18 Packard (cited note 12), p. 8

19 Ibid., p. 3

20 CBS, 'At Home, 2001', The 21st Century documentary series (episode premiered 12 March 1967)

21 Victor Papanek, *Design for the Real World: Human Ecology and Social Change* (New York: Pantheon Books, 1971)

22 WNED-TV, Design Dimensions, series of 13 half-hour programmes (première: 28 September 1963)

23 Ibid.; Victor Papanek, 'Pop Culture', *The Raleigh Times*, 17 August 1963, p. 11

24 Tom Wolfe, 'There Goes (VAROOM! VAROOM! That Kandy-Kolored (THPHHHHHH!) Tangerine-Flake Streamline Baby (RAHGHHHH!) Around the Bend (BRUMMMMMMMMMMMMMMMMMM......', in *Esquire* (November 1963), pp.114–15

25 Max Horkheimer and Theodor Adorno, 'The Culture Industry: Enlightenment as Mass Deception', in T. Adorno and M. Horkheimer, *Dialectic of Enlightenment: Philosophical Fragments*, edited by Gunzelin Schmid Noerr, translated by Edmund Jephcott (Stanford, CA: Stanford University Press, 2002)

26 Victor Papanek, 'Do-It-Yourself Murder: Social and Moral Responsibilities of Design', *SDO Journal* (1968), p. 26

27 Alison J. Clarke, 'Actions Speak Louder: Victor Papanek and the Legacy of Design Activism', *Design and Culture* 5 no. 2 (2012): 151–68; Alison J. Clarke, 'Buckminster Fuller's Reindeer Abattoir and Other Designs for the Real World', in *Hippie Modernism: The Struggle for Utopia*, edited by Andrew Blauvelt (Minneapolis: Walker Art Center 2015), pp. 68–75

28 Victor Papanek, 'Actions Speak Louder', *Industrial Design* 15/9 NOV (1968): 41

29 Alison J. Clarke 2012 and 2015 (cited note 27)

30 Paola Nicolin, *Castelli di carte. La XIV Triennale di Milano, 1968* (Macerata: Quodlibet, 2011)

31 Raoul Vaneigem, *The Revolution of Everyday Life*, translated by Donald Nicholson-Smith [first published Seattle: Left Bank, 1983] (London: Rebel Press, 2001), p. 72

32 Wolfgang F. Haug, *Critique of Commodity Aesthetics: Appearance, Sexuality, and Advertising in Capitalist Society*, translated by Robert Bock (Minneapolis: University of Minnesota Press, 1986)

33 Alice Twemlow, 'I Can't Talk to You If You Say That: An Ideological Collision at the International Design Conference at Aspen, 1970', *Design and Culture* 1 no. 1 (2009): 23–50; Greg Castillo, 'Counterculture Terroir: California's Hippie Enterprise Zone', in *Hippie Modernism: The Struggle for Utopia*, edited by Andrew Blauvelt (Minneapolis: Walker Art Center, 2015), p. 96

34 The group included Roger Tallon, Claude Braunstein, Eric Le Comte and Giles de Burre as well as other specialists within geography and economics. See Castillo 2015 (cited note 33), p. 96.

35 Marc Dessauce (ed.), *The Inflatable Moment: Pneumatics and Protest in '68* (New York: Princeton Architectural Press, 1999)

36 Esther Choi, 'Atmospheres of Institutional Critique: Haus-Rucker-Co's Pneumatic Temporality', in *Hippie Modernism: The Struggle for Utopia*, edited by Andrew Blauvelt (Minneapolis: Walker Art Center, 2015), p. 33

37 Castillo 2015 (cited note 33), p. 96; see also Scott 2007 (cited note 17)

38 *Design Journal*, 'Crying Wolfe' (1971): 26, available at http://vads.ac.uk/diad/article.php?title=269&year=1971&article=d.269.25

39 Sheila Levrant de Bretteville's husband Peter, an architect, had worked with radical urban Group X and Giancarlo De Carlo in Milan in 1970. Sheila Levrant de Bretteville interviewed by the author, Warsaw, 25 September 2015. See also Benjamin Tong, 'Interview with Sheila Levrant de Bretteville', August 2012, available at http://www.rosab.net/en/idca-1971-special-edition-of-the/interview-with-sheila-levrant-de.html?lang=fr.

40 Tong 2012 (cited note 39)

41 See Laura Cottingham, *Seeing through the Seventies: Essays on Feminism and Art* (London and New York: Routledge, 2000)

42 Victor Papanek was a short-lived dean of CalArts in 1971 following the resignation of Richard Farson. Sheila Levrant de Bretteville recounts her struggle with Papanek over her ambition to create a separate women's design programme, him describing the proposal as being the equivalent of making a 'ghetto'. Sheila Levrant de Bretteville interviewed by the author, Warsaw, 25 September 2015.

43 Ellen Willis, 'Women and the Myth of Consumerism', *Ramparts* 8 no. 12 (June 1970): 14

44 Ibid.

45 Ibid., 16

46 Alison J. Clarke, 'Ettore Sottsass: The Design Ethnologist', in *The Italian Avant-Garde 1968–1976*, edited by Alex Coles and Catherine Rossi (Berlin: Sternberg Press, 2013), pp.67–78; Clarke 2015 (cited note 27)

47 See 'The Archigram Archival Project' at Westminster University, London, http://archigram.westminster.ac.uk/project.php?revID=4480

48 http://archigram.westminster.ac.uk/project.php?id=145; Peter Cook (ed.), Archigram [first published London: Studio Vista, 1972] (New York: Princeton Architectural Press, 1999), p. 124

49 Ibid.

50 Both Papanek and Haug spoke of the sexualization of products in capitalist culture, using gendered terms to describe the process by which designers transformed commodities into seductive entities.

51 Lane de Nicola, 'The Internet, the Parliament, and the Pub', in *Design Anthropology: Object Cultures in Transition*, edited by Alison J. Clarke (London: Bloomsbury, 2017)

52 Guy Julier, 'Design versus Financial Crisis', lecture presented at the Future of Design series of lectures and workshops organized by Czechdesign at the Academy of Arts, Architecture & Design in Prague (26 November 2015)

53 Francisco Laranjo, 'Critical Everything', *Modes of Criticism* (4 August 2015), available at http://modesofcriticism.org/articles/critical-everything/

'WE ARE AS GODS...' COMPUTERS AND AMERICA'S NEW COMMUNALISM, 1965–75 (PP. 278–95)

1 Judson Jerome, *Families of Eden: Communes and the New Anarchism* (New York: Seabury Press, 1974), pp. 16–18; cited in Timothy Miller, *The 60s Communes: Hippies and Beyond* (Syracuse, NY: Syracuse University Press, 1999), pp. xix–xx

2 Students for a Democratic Society (SDS), 'Port Huron Statement', in Tom Hayden, *The Port Huron Statement: The Visionary Call of the 1960s Revolution* (New York: Thunder's Mouth Press, 2005), pp. 47, 136

3 *Chicago Seed*, quoted in Wini Breines, *Community and Organization in the New Left, 1962–1968: The Great Refusal* (New York: Praeger, 1982), p. 36

4 Theodore Roszak, *The Making of a Counter Culture: Reflections on the Technocratic Society and Its Youthful Opposition* (Garden City, NY: Doubleday, 1969), pp. 50, 240

5 Charles A. Reich, *The Greening of America* (New York: Random House, 1970), p. 136

6 Ibid., pp. 136, 196

7 Gerd Stern, personal communication with the author, 15 September 2005

8 Stewart Brand, ed., *Whole Earth Catalog* (Menlo Park, CA: Portola Institute, Fall 1968), p. 2

9 Ibid., p. 3

10 R. Buckminster Fuller, *Ideas and Integrities: A Spontaneous Autobiographical Disclosure* (Englewood Cliffs, NJ: Prentice-Hall, 1963), pp. 35–43

11 Brand ed. (cited note 8) [p. 2 in 1998 reprint]

12 Peter Rabbit, *Drop City* (New York: Olympia Press, 1971), p. 31; quoted in William Hedgepeth, *The Alternative: Communal Life in New America* (New York: Macmillan, 1970), p. 36

13 Steve Jobs, Graduation Speech, Stanford University, 14 June 2005. Full text available at http://news.stanford.edu/news/2005/june15/jobs-061505.html

14 Douglas Engelbart, Demo, Stanford Research Institute, Menlo Park, 9 December 1968. Film available at http://web.stanford.edu/dept/SUL/library/extra4/sloan/mousesite/1968Demo.html

15 Efrem Lipkin, 'A Public Information Network', *People's Computer Company* 4, no. 1 (1975): 17

16 Lee Felsenstein, interview with the author, 18 July 2001

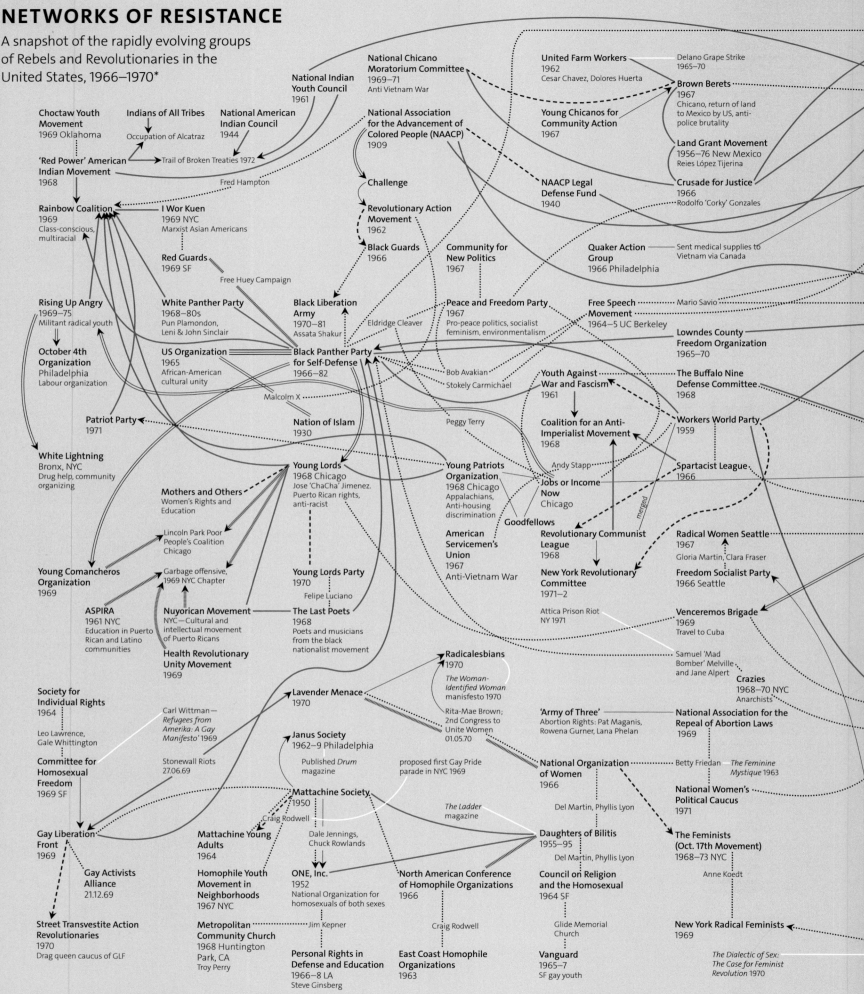

NETWORKS OF RESISTANCE

A snapshot of the rapidly evolving groups
of Rebels and Revolutionaries in the
United States, 1966–1970*

Choctaw Youth Movement
1969 Oklahoma

Indians of All Tribes
Occupation of Alcatraz

National American Indian Council
1944

National Indian Youth Council
1961

National Chicano Moratorium Committee
1969–71
Anti Vietnam War

United Farm Workers
1962
Cesar Chavez, Dolores Huerta

Delano Grape Strike
1965–70

Brown Berets
1967
Chicano, return of land to Mexico by US, anti-police brutality

'Red Power' American Indian Movement
1968

Trail of Broken Treaties 1972

Fred Hampton

National Association for the Advancement of Colored People (NAACP)
1909

Young Chicanos for Community Action
1967

Land Grant Movement
1956–76 New Mexico
Reies López Tijerina

Rainbow Coalition
1969
Class-conscious, multiracial

I Wor Kuen
1969 NYC
Marxist Asian Americans

Challenge

Revolutionary Action Movement
1962

NAACP Legal Defense Fund
1940

Crusade for Justice
1966
Rodolfo 'Corky' Gonzales

Red Guards
1969 SF

Black Guards
1966

Community for New Politics
1967

Quaker Action Group
1966 Philadelphia

Sent medical supplies to Vietnam via Canada

Free Huey Campaign

Rising Up Angry
1969–75
Militant radical youth

White Panther Party
1968–80s
Pun Plamondon, Leni & John Sinclair

Black Liberation Army
1970–81
Assata Shakur

Peace and Freedom Party
1967
Pro-peace politics, socialist feminism, environmentalism

Free Speech Movement
1964–5 UC Berkeley

Mario Savio

Eldridge Cleaver

Lowndes County Freedom Organization
1965–70

October 4th Organization
Philadelphia
Labour organization

US Organization
1965
African-American cultural unity

Black Panther Party for Self-Defense
1966–82

Bob Avakian

Stokely Carmichael

Youth Against War and Fascism
1961

The Buffalo Nine Defense Committee
1968

Malcolm X

Peggy Terry

Coalition for an Anti-Imperialist Movement
1968

Workers World Party
1959

Patriot Party
1971

Nation of Islam
1930

Andy Stapp

Spartacist League
1966

White Lightning
Bronx, NYC
Drug help, community organizing

Young Lords
1968 Chicago
Jose 'ChaCha' Jimenez.
Puerto Rican rights, anti-racist

Young Patriots Organization
1968 Chicago
Appalachians, Anti-housing discrimination

Jobs or Income Now
Chicago

Radical Women Seattle
1967
Gloria Martin, Clara Fraser

Mothers and Others
Women's Rights and Education

Goodfellows

Revolutionary Communist League
1968

merged

Freedom Socialist Party
1966 Seattle

Young Comancheros Organization
1969

Lincoln Park Poor People's Coalition
Chicago

American Servicemen's Union
1967
Anti-Vietnam War

New York Revolutionary Committee
1971–2

Venceremos Brigade
1969
Travel to Cuba

Garbage offensive, 1969 NYC Chapter

ASPIRA
1961 NYC
Education in Puerto Rican and Latino communities

Nuyorican Movement
NYC—Cultural and intellectual movement of Puerto Ricans

Young Lords Party
1970

Felipe Luciano

Attica Prison Riot
NY 1971

Samuel 'Mad Bomber' Melville and Jane Alpert

Health Revolutionary Unity Movement
1969

The Last Poets
1968
Poets and musicians from the black nationalist movement

Crazies
1968–70 NYC
Anarchists

Society for Individual Rights
1964

Radicalesbians
1970

The Woman-Identified Woman manisfesto 1970

'Army of Three'
Abortion Rights: Pat Maganis, Rowena Gurner, Lana Phelan

National Association for the Repeal of Abortion Laws
1969

Leo Lawrence, Gale Whittington

Carl Wittman—
Refugees from Amerika: A Gay Manifesto' 1969

Lavender Menace
1970

Rita-Mae Brown;
2nd Congress to Unite Women
01.05.70

Committee for Homosexual Freedom
1969 SF

Stonewall Riots
27.06.69

Janus Society
1962–9 Philadelphia

Published *Drum* magazine

proposed first Gay Pride parade in NYC 1969

National Organization of Women
1966

Betty Friedan *The Feminine Mystique* 1963

National Women's Political Caucus
1971

Gay Liberation Front
1969

Mattachine Society
1950

Craig Rodwell

The Ladder magazine

Del Martin, Phyllis Lyon

Daughters of Bilitis
1955–95
Del Martin, Phyllis Lyon

The Feminists (Oct. 17th Movement)
1968–73 NYC

Anne Koedt

Gay Activists Alliance
21.12.69

Mattachine Young Adults
1964

Dale Jennings, Chuck Rowlands

North American Conference of Homophile Organizations
1966

Council on Religion and the Homosexual
1964 SF

Homophile Youth Movement in Neighborhoods
1967 NYC

ONE, Inc.
1952
National Organization for homosexuals of both sexes

Craig Rodwell

Glide Memorial Church

New York Radical Feminists
1969

Street Transvestite Action Revolutionaries
1970
Drag queen caucus of GLF

Metropolitan Community Church
1968 Huntington Park, CA
Troy Perry

Jim Kepner

Personal Rights in Defense and Education
1966–8 LA
Steve Ginsberg

East Coast Homophile Organizations
1963

Vanguard
1965–7
SF gay youth

The Dialectic of Sex: The Case for Feminist Revolution 1970

*This network is not a snapshot of a single moment in time, nor is it possible to include in a single spread every group that existed in five years of such intense protest. The groups shown have been chosen not only for importance but also to represent the since unparalleled breadth of those liberation struggles happening contemporaneously. Beyond direct rivalries, the wide spectrum of mutually exclusive positions on vision and strategy between groups has not been marked. Some groups also run either side of 1966–1970 so as to situate these years in their broader context. It is the connections partially illustrated here that both created and sustained the zeitgeist of making change.

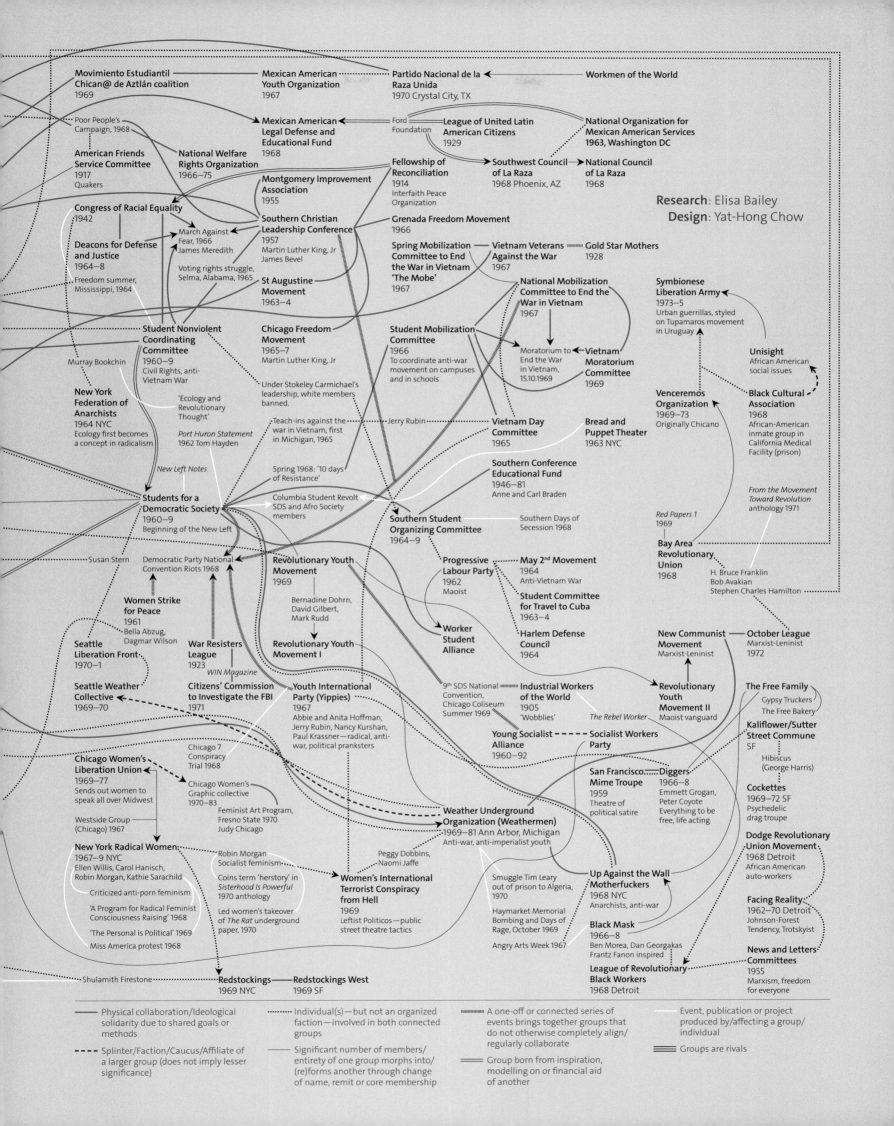

Movimiento Estudiantil Chican@ de Aztlán coalition 1969

Mexican American Youth Organization 1967

Partido Nacional de la Raza Unida 1970 Crystal City, TX

Workmen of the World

Poor People's Campaign, 1968

Mexican American Legal Defense and Educational Fund 1968

Ford Foundation

League of United Latin American Citizens 1929

National Organization for Mexican American Services 1963, Washington DC

American Friends Service Committee 1917 Quakers

National Welfare Rights Organization 1966–75

Montgomery Improvement Association 1955

Fellowship of Reconciliation 1914 Interfaith Peace Organization

Southwest Council of La Raza 1968 Phoenix, AZ

National Council of La Raza 1968

Congress of Racial Equality 1942

March Against Fear, 1966 James Meredith

Southern Christian Leadership Conference 1957 Martin Luther King, Jr James Bevel

Grenada Freedom Movement 1966

Research: Elisa Bailey
Design: Yat-Hong Chow

Deacons for Defense and Justice 1964–8

Voting rights struggle, Selma, Alabama, 1965

Spring Mobilization Committee to End the War in Vietnam 'The Mobe' 1967

Vietnam Veterans Against the War 1967

Gold Star Mothers 1928

Freedom summer, Mississippi, 1964

St Augustine Movement 1963–4

National Mobilization Committee to End the War in Vietnam 1967

Symbionese Liberation Army 1973–5 Urban guerrillas, styled on Tupamaros movement in Uruguay

Student Nonviolent Coordinating Committee 1960–9 Civil Rights, anti-Vietnam War

Chicago Freedom Movement 1965–7 Martin Luther King, Jr

Student Mobilization Committee 1966 To coordinate anti-war movement on campuses and in schools

Moratorium to End the War in Vietnam, 15.10.1969

Vietnam Moratorium Committee 1969

Unisight African American social issues

Murray Bookchin

'Ecology and Revolutionary Thought'

Under Stokeley Carmichael's leadership, white members banned.

Jerry Rubin

Vietnam Day Committee 1965

Bread and Puppet Theater 1963 NYC

Venceremos Organization 1969–73 Originally Chicano

Black Cultural Association 1968 African-American inmate group in California Medical Facility (prison)

New York Federation of Anarchists 1964 NYC Ecology first becomes a concept in radicalism

Port Huron Statement 1962 Tom Hayden

Teach-ins against the war in Vietnam, first in Michigan, 1965

Southern Conference Educational Fund 1946–81 Anne and Carl Braden

New Left Notes

Spring 1968: '10 days of Resistance'

Columbia Student Revolt SDS and Afro Society members

Red Papers 1 1969

From the Movement Toward Revolution anthology 1971

Students for a Democratic Society 1960–9 Beginning of the New Left

Southern Student Organizing Committee 1964–9

Southern Days of Secession 1968

Bay Area Revolutionary Union 1968

H. Bruce Franklin Bob Avakian Stephen Charles Hamilton

Susan Stern

Democratic Party National Convention Riots 1968

Revolutionary Youth Movement 1969

Progressive Labour Party 1962 Maoist

May 2nd Movement 1964 Anti-Vietnam War

Women Strike for Peace 1961 Bella Abzug, Dagmar Wilson

Bernadine Dohrn, David Gilbert, Mark Rudd

Student Committee for Travel to Cuba 1963–4

New Communist Movement Marxist-Leninist

October League Marxist-Leninist 1972

Seattle Liberation Front 1970–1

War Resisters League 1923

Revolutionary Youth Movement I

Worker Student Alliance

Harlem Defense Council 1964

The Free Family

Gypsy Truckers
The Free Bakery

WIN Magazine

9th SDS National Convention, Chicago Coliseum Summer 1969

Industrial Workers of the World 1905 'Wobblies'

The Rebel Worker

Revolutionary Youth Movement II Maoist vanguard

Kaliflower/Sutter Street Commune SF

Seattle Weather Collective 1969–70

Citizens' Commission to Investigate the FBI 1971

Youth International Party (Yippies) 1967 Abbie and Anita Hoffman, Jerry Rubin, Nancy Kurshan, Paul Krassner—radical, anti-war, political pranksters

Young Socialist Alliance 1960–92

Socialist Workers Party

Hibiscus (George Harris)

Chicago 7 Conspiracy Trial 1968

San Francisco Mime Troupe 1959 Theatre of political satire

Diggers 1966–8 Emmett Grogan, Peter Coyote Everything to be free, life acting

Cockettes 1969–72 SF Psychedelic drag troupe

Chicago Women's Liberation Union 1969–77 Sends out women to speak all over Midwest

Chicago Women's Graphic collective 1970–83

Feminist Art Program, Fresno State 1970 Judy Chicago

Weather Underground Organization (Weathermen) 1969–81 Ann Arbor, Michigan Anti-war, anti-imperialist youth

Dodge Revolutionary Union Movement 1968 Detroit African American auto-workers

Westside Group (Chicago) 1967

Robin Morgan Socialist feminism

Peggy Dobbins Naomi Jaffe

Smuggle Tim Leary out of prison to Algeria, 1970

Up Against the Wall Motherfuckers 1968 NYC Anarchists, anti-war

Facing Reality 1962–70 Detroit Johnson-Forest Tendency, Trotskyist

New York Radical Women 1967–9 NYC Ellen Willis, Carol Hanisch, Robin Morgan, Kathie Sarachild

Coins term 'herstory' in Sisterhood Is Powerful 1970 anthology

Women's International Terrorist Conspiracy from Hell 1969 Leftist Politicos—public street theatre tactics

Haymarket Memorial Bombing and Days of Rage, October 1969

Black Mask 1966–8 Ben Morea, Dan Georgakas Frantz Fanon inspired

News and Letters Committees 1955 Marxism, freedom for everyone

Criticized anti-porn feminism

'A Program for Radical Feminist Consciousness Raising' 1968

Led women's takeover of The Rat underground paper, 1970

Angry Arts Week 1967

'The Personal is Political' 1969

Miss America protest 1968

Shulamith Firestone

Redstockings 1969 NYC

Redstockings West 1969 SF

League of Revolutionary Black Workers 1968 Detroit

Physical collaboration/Ideological solidarity due to shared goals or methods

Individual(s)—but not an organized faction—involved in both connected groups

A one-off or connected series of events brings together groups that do not otherwise completely align/ regularly collaborate

Event, publication or project produced by/affecting a group/ individual

Splinter/Faction/Caucus/Affiliate of a larger group (does not imply lesser significance)

Significant number of members/ entirety of one group morphs into/ (re)forms another through change of name, remit or core membership

Group born from inspiration, modelling on or financial aid of another

Groups are rivals

INDEX

Page numbers in *italic* refer to
the illustrations

A

Abbey Road Studios, London
140, 147, 196, 206, 214–15
ABC-Dunhill 178
Abernathy, Ralph 69
Abolafia, Louis 117
abortion 70, 76
Abortion Act (1967) 28
'Abortion Is a Personal Decision'
poster 88
acid *see* LSD
Acid Tests 101, 103, *104*, 144, 169,
198
Adler, Lou 178
Adorno, Theodor, 'The Culture
Industry' 258
Adron, Ralph *270*
advertising 174
Afghanistan 236
'Afro-American Solidarity with the
Oppressed People of the World'
poster *91*
Albers, Josef 108
Albin, Peter 172
Albrecht, Bob 294
album sleeves 108–11
Alcatraz 40, *41*
Aldermaston marches 101, *102*
Aldridge, Alan *6*, *200*, 217
Space Race 274
Aldwych Theatre, London 22
Ali, Muhammad 26
Ali, Tariq 34
Alice in Wonderland (BBC film)
148, 149
Allen, Marit 230, *231*, 237
Alpert, Richard *104*, 115, 116
alternative communities 152, 153
Amboy Dukes 112
'America Is Devouring Its Children'
poster *81*
Amin, Idi 52
Anders, William (Bill) *275*
Earthrise 32, 286, *286*
Andrews, Ed ('Punch') 183
Angry Brigade 154
The Animals 179
Ant Farm 261–3
Antonioni, Michelangelo 22, 138,
233, 263
Apex Novelties 108
Apollo 8 mission 32, *275*
Apollo 11 mission 38
Apple boutique, London
205, 206, 237
Apple Computer 51, 52, *294*, 295
Apple Corps 153, 206
Apple Tailoring 237
'Aquarian Age' 115
Archigram
Electronic Tomato 268, *269*
Info Gonks 268, 269
Architectural Review 258
'Armée ORTF Police' poster *85*
Armstrong, Neil 38
Art Deco 236, 243
Art Nouveau 200
art schools 228
Arts Council 52
Arts Lab, London 28
Artworkers Coalition *84*
Asher, Jane 205
Asher, Peter 205
Ashmore, Sonia 241
Aspen 259, 260–64
Aspen Times 263, 264

Atelier populaire *85*
Atlanta International Pop
Festival 46
Atlantic City 70
Atlantic Records 178
Aubert, Jean 261
Augmentation Research Center
(ARC) 290
Autumn Records 174
Avalon Ballroom, San Francisco
28, 112, 145, 170, 172
The Avengers (television series)
226

B

Baader Meinhof Group 217
Babbs, Ken 103
Babitz, Mirandi *248*
badges *131*, *301*
Baer, Steve 294
Baez, Joan 28, 46
Bailey, Kofi *62*, *89*
Baker, Ginger 153
Balin, Marty 169
Ballard, Hank 183
Baltimore 181
Ban the Bomb marches *102*
Banham, Reyner 252, 263
Barbarella (film) 253
Barrett, Syd 112, *142*, 148, 149, 153
Bash Street School Magazine 120
Bates, John 226
Baudrillard, Jean 258, 260–61
The Consumer Society 260
The System of Objects 253
Bauhaus 263
Bay Area 51, 100, 105, 147, 168, 170,
174, 254, 279, 294
Bayer, Herbert 263
BBC 4, 22, 28, 34, 38, 40, 139,
148, 150
Beach, Sylvia 105
The Beach Boys 111, 179, *179*, 196
Beardsley, Aubrey 108, 200, *200*
The Climax 127
beat generation 100, 101, 105,
168–9, *170*
The Beatles 22, *23*, 100, 111, 138–9,
140, 143, 144, 147, 148, 153, 168,
196–217, 237–8
Abbey Road 40, 214–15, *214–15*, 216
Let It Be 46, 216–17, *216*
Magical Mystery Tour 150, *207*
'Revolution' *6*, *33*, 34, 217
Revolver 20, 147, 198, 199–200,
199
Rubber Soul 144, 147, 197–8, *197*,
206
*Sgt. Pepper's Lonely Hearts Club
Band* 19, 26, 108–11, 140, 149,
183, *196*, 202–10, *202–9*, 212,
213, 236
White Album (The Beatles) 151,
206, 212–13, *212*, 215
Wonderwall 220
The Beau Brummels 174
Beck, Julian 28
Beckett, Samuel 46
Bee Gees 28
Beirut 238
Belloli, Jay *81*
Beriano, Luciano 196
Berkeley 290
Berkeley Barb 40, 105, *105*
Berkeley Vietnam Day
Committee 101–3
Berry, Chuck 179
Biba 226, 227, 233, 241–3
Big Bang 52

Big Brother & the Holding
Company 22, 28, 112, 115, *159*, *163*,
172, *176*, 178, 284
Cheap Thrills 108
Birtwell, Celia 241, *242*
Black, Cilla 238
Black Dwarf 213
Black Lives Matter 75
Black Panther Party 22, 34, *66*, 67,
69, 170, 186
Black Power 44, 56, 64–7, 69, 75
Blackboard Jungle (film) 182
Blackburn, Tony 28
Blackhill Enterprises 153
Blades, London 238, *239*
Blake, Peter 108–11, *202*, 204,
205, 212
Blake, William, 'London' 13, *14*
Blauvelt, Andrew 254
Blind Faith 153
Blossom Toes 149
Blow-Up (film) 19, 22, 138, *233*,
233, 236
blow-up structures 261, *262*
Blue Cheer 187
Blues Magoos 112
Blues Project 112
BOAC 19
Boeing 19, 46
Bolan, Marc 154, 243
Bonzo Dog Doo Dah Band 149
Boston 116
Boulting, Ingrid 241
boutiques 228–30, 233–7
Bowart, Walter 105
Bowen, Michael 22, *133*
Bowie, David 38, 236, *237*
The Man Who Sold the World
238
*The Rise and Fall of Ziggy
Stardust* 204
Boyd, Joe 28, 147
Boyle, Mark 22
Brand, Lois 280, 284, 294
Brand, Stewart 144, 198, 254,
280–81, 281–7, 290, 294, *301*
Bretteville, Sheila Levrant de
263, 264, *264*
British Defence Science and
Technology Laboratory, Porton
Down 143
British Fashion Council 228
British Home Stores 227
Brook, Peter, *US* 22, *23*
Broughton, Edgar 153
Brown, Arthur 112
Brown, Charles 178
Brown, David *191*
Brown, H. Rap 67
Brown, James 185
Browne, Tara 205
Brutalism 252
Buck, Paul 145
Buffalo Springfield 28, 181–2
Burgess, Anthony, *A Clockwork
Orange* 252–3
Burrell, Kenny 183
Burroughs, William 100, 144, 168
Bush, George W. 75, 77
The Byrds 38, 111, 112, 138, 143, 178,
179–81, *181*, 183
Byrne, Kiki 228

C

Cage, John 196, 205, 279
California 179, 215
California Institute of Arts
(CalArts) *262*, 263–4
Cambodia 46, *47*, 68–9, 117, 294

Campaign for Nuclear Disarmament
(CND) 101, *102*
Camus, Albert 64
Can You Pass the Acid Test 101
Capitol Studios 178, *179*
Captain Beefheart 111
Carey, Martin *62*
Carmichael, Stokely 22, 28, *29*, 64–7,
65, 69
Carnaby Street, London 22, *23*, 226,
228, *228*, 238
Carroll, Lewis 139, 149, 204
Carson, Rachel, *Silent Spring* 72,
263
Carter, Ernestine 227
Carter, Ron 183
Caserta, Peggy 22
Cash, Dave 28
Cashman, John, *The LSD Story* 145
Cassady, Neal 103, 116, 169
Castell, Luria 103
CBS 256
Celestial Arts *96*
Centre for Alternative
Technology 253–4
Chalk, Warren 268
Chandler, Raymond 183
Chaplin, Charlie 138
The Charlatans 112, 169, *173*
Charles, Ray 178
Cheetah discotheque, New York 145
Chelsea Antiques Market 241
Chicago 61, 67–8, *68*, 69, 77, 279
Chicago, Judy 264
Chicago Blues Band *177*
China 20, 64
The Chocolate Watch Band 182
Choi, Esther 261
Christian Right 76
City Lights Bookstore, San Francisco
105, 168, *170*
civil rights movement 59, 61, 64,
67, 69, 70, 75, 76, 100, 156, 253,
279
Clapton, Eric 153
Clark, Gene 181
Clark, Ossie 241, *245*
Cleave, Maureen 147
Cleaver, Eldridge 67, 68
Cleaver, Kathleen *92*
Clendinning, Max *270*
Clifford, Clark 68
Clinton, Bill 75–7
Clinton, Hillary 76–7
A Clockwork Orange (film) 252–3,
254
clothes *161*, *192–3*, *273*
The Beatles 206, *206*, *208–9*,
218–19
counter-culture 100, 103
London fashion 226–43, *227–49*
CND *78*, 152
Cobb, Ron *123*
Cochran, Eddie 179
Cocker, Joe 190
Les Cockettes paper doll book *83*
Cohen, Leonard 40, *41*, 46
Cohen, Sheila 236
Cohen, Dr Sidney 143
cold war 290
Coleman, Ray 140
Colorado 278
colour supplements 227
comics 105–8, 169
Commoner, Barry, *Science and
Survival* 72
communes 278–87, 294, 295
Communism 20, 60
'Community Memory' 294

Compendium, London 105
Compton, Gene 22
computers 34, 46, 51–2, 278, 287,
290–95, *294*
Concorde 40, *41*
Conklin, Lee 174
Conservative Party 46
consumerism 100, 101, 252–69
Cook, Peter 268
Coon, Caroline 116, 152
Cooper, Michael 111, *119*, 204,
204, 205
Copland, Aaron 196
Corso, Gregory 104
counter-culture 100–35
Country Joe & the Fish 40, 112, 172
Courrèges, André 226
Covent Garden, London 52
Cowan, John 22
CP-1 Cube 259
Cream 112, 150, 153, 186
Disraeli Gears 150
Crittle, John 237
Cronkite, Walter 256
Crosby, David 111, 181
Crosby, Stills, Nash & Young 40
Crumb, Robert 105–8, 117
Fritz the Cat 108
Cruz, Ted 76
Cuba 64
Cybernetic Serendipity, London
(1968) 34, *35*

D

Daily Mirror 226, 241
Daltrey, Roger *193*
Damascus 238
Dandelion Records 158
Darcy, Tom Francis, 'Chopping Block'
poster *74*
Davis, Angela *81*
Davis, Bette 204
Davis, Miles 46, *47*
De Carlo, Giancarlo 260, 264
de Gaulle, Charles 26, *85*
de Renzy, Alex 46
Debord, Guy, *The Society of the
Spectacle* 260
DeCrow, Karen 70
Democratic National
Convention 34, 57, 64, *68*
Democratic Party 56, 60, 67, 68, 69,
75, 76–7
Derbyshire, Delia 196
DeRosa, Tony *84*
Design Dimensions (television
series) 258
Design Journal 263
Detroit 56, 61, *61*, 112, 181, 183–7,
187
The Deviants 153
Dichter, Ernest 255, 265
The Strategy of Desire 255–8
Dickens, Charles 18
Diddley, Bo 159
Dig ('happening') 22
The Diggers 28, 115, 116, 152, 153
Dirty Harry (film) 51
Disc and Music Echo 138, 139–40
Diski, Jenny 241
Domino, Fats 179
Donahue, Tom 174
Donovan 112, 138, 144, 153
The Doors 28, 46, 111, 112, 140, *177*,
297
Douglas, Emory *91*
The Dovers 143
Drop City, Colorado 278, *278*, 281,
287, 294

drugs
  counter-culture 100, 101
  laws 19
  marijuana 19, 117, 139, 154
  police action against 116, 139
  see also LSD
Dunaway, Faye 238
Dunbar, John 22, 205
Dupree, Simon 149
Durkee, Steve 294, *301*
Dury, Ian 100
Dylan, Bob 32, 40, 56, 69, 100, 111, 148, 168, 181, 196, 197
  'Mister Tambourine Man'
  poster *9*

E
The Eagles, *Hotel California* 50
Eames, Charles and Ray 261
Earth Day 44, 72, *73*, *90*
East Side Books, New York 105
East Totem West *146*
East Village Other (EVO) 105, 108
Eastwood, Clint 51
Easy Rider (film) 38
École des Beaux-Arts *85*
Ed Sullivan Show 20, *181*
Edgar Broughton Band 153
Education Act (1944) 101
Eero, Aarnio, *Globe* chair 253
Eighth Street Bookshop, New York 105
Electric Train *163*
Elektra Records 187
Elizabeth II, Queen 34, 226
Elliott, Tony 34
Emerson, Lake & Palmer 46
EMI 111, 139
Engelbart, Douglas 34, 290–94, *291*
English, Bill 294
English, Michael 108, *109*, *119*, *235*, *247*
  Summer Sadness for John Hopkins *155*, *156–7*
environmental movement 44, 72, 117
Environmental Protection Agency (EPA) 44, 72, 75
Epic Records 178
Epstein, Brian 206
Esam, John *104*, 144
Esquire magazine 258
Establishment 100, 117, 154, 213, 217, 278
Eurovision Song Contest 28
Euston Station, London 19, 34
Evening Standard 34, 147
Everett, Kenny 28
Everly Brothers 147
'Exorcise the Pentagon' poster *63*
Exploding Plastic Inevitable 111, 145, *145*
Expo '67, Montreal 26, 256, *298–9*

F
The Factory, New York *110*, 111
Fainlight, Harry *104*, 144, 152
Fairbrother-Roe, David, *Polypops* *270–71*
Fairport Convention 153
Faithfull, Marianne 205, 226
Family 153, 156
  Music in a Doll's House 213
Family Dog 103, 108, 112, *159*, *163–5*, 169–70, *172*, 174, *176*
Fanon, Frantz 67
Farmer, Bob 140
Farren, Mick 116
fashion *see* clothes
Federal Bureau of Investigation (FBI) 69

Feilding, Amanda 117
Felsenstein, Lee 294, 295
feminism 44, 46, 56, 70, 76, 117, 243, 264
Ferguson, Michael, *The Seed* 173
Ferlinghetti, Lawrence 103, 104, 144, 168
Field, Marcus *104*, 144
Fields, Danny 187
Fifth Estate 105
Fillmore Auditorium, San Francisco 22, 145, 170, 172, 183
Fillmore East, New York 112
Fillmore West, San Francisco 46, 112
films 19, 50, 51, 182–3
Filo, John Paul *47*
Fish, Michael 238
Fleetwood Mac 150
Florida 75, 77
Flower Pot Men 149
Floyd, Clem *248*
Fluxus 205
Foale, Marion 228–30
Foale & Tuffin 228–30, *230–31*
Fonda, Jane 46
Fonda, Peter 38, 147
The Fool 205, 206, *209*, *222–3*, 237
Fortuny, Mariano 238
Four Tops 46
14-Hour Technicolor Dream 28, *29*, 112, *113*
France 115–16
Frankfurt School 258
Franks, Bill 228
Fraser, Robert 139, 204, 205
Fratini, Gina 228
Free Clinic 116
Free Speech Movement 279, 290, *292–3*
Freeman, Bobby 174
Freeman, Robert 198
Freiberg, David 172
French, Gordon 51
French Group 261
Freud, Sigmund 199–200
Friedan, Betty, *The Feminine Mystique* 70
Friends magazine 105, 154
Friends of the Earth *96*
Front, Charles 198
Frost, David *206*
The Fugs 112, 147
Fulbright, William J. 60
Fuller, R. Buckminster 100, 254, 256, 286, *287*
Fulson, Lowell 178

G
Galahad 116
Gallup polls 76
Garcia, Jerry 172
Gates, Larry 87
'Gay Liberation' poster *82*
gay liberation movement 51, 56, 71, 76, *84*, 117
Gaye, Marvin 46
General Electric Company 50
General Motors 77, 100
geodesic domes 254, 278, 286, 287, *287*
Getty, Paul, Jr *241*
Getty, Talitha 238, 241, *241*
Gibb, Bill 229
Gibb, Russ 183–5
Gibbs, Christopher *236*
Gilbert, David 241
Ginger Group 237
Ginsberg, Allen 62, 100–104, *104*, 115–17, *116*, 144, 168, 169, *170*, 202, *303*
Ginsburg, Ruth Bader 76
Girl on a Motorcycle (film) 226

'GIRLS SAY 'YES' to boys who say "No"' poster *87*
Gleason, Ralph J. 174
  The Jefferson Airplane and the San Francisco Sounds 170
Global Tools initiative 265
Gold brothers 238
The Good Time Manual 51
Google 269, 290, 295
Gordon, Dexter 178
Gordon, Harry *234*
Gordon, John 139
Gordy, Berry, Jr 183
Gore, Al 77
Graham, Bill 112, 116, *162*, 170, *171*, 174, *175*, *177*, 183–5
Grande Ballroom, Detroit *183*, *184*, 185–7, *186*
Granny Takes a Trip, London 236, *236*, 237, *247*
graphic design 108–11
Grass Eye (magazine) 154
The Grass Roots 178
Grateful Dead 22, 28, 40, 108, 112, 115, 152, *164*, *169*, 170, *175*, *177*, 178, 186
  The Grateful Dead 111
Great Society 56, 60, 75
The Great Society (band) 169, 174
Greater London Council (GLC) 52
Grech, Ric 153
Green, Felicity 226
Green Party (US) 77
Greenberg, Stanley 76
Greene, David *268*
Greer, Germaine, *The Female Eunuch* 44, *94*
Greer, Maretta 115
Gregory, Dick 68, 112
Grey, Camille, *Lipstick Bathroom* 264, *265*
Griffin, Rick 108, *159*, 174
Grimshaw, Gary *184*, 185
Grogan, Emmett 28, 116
Grosvenor Square demonstration (1968) *79*, 213
Grunwick strike (1976–8) 52
Guardian 236–7
Guevara, Che *80*
Guthrie, Woody 56, *86*

H
Haeberle, Ron *84*
Haight-Ashbury 28, 40, 51, 62, 144, 152, 183, 284
Hair (musical) 34, *35*
HALO (Haight-Ashbury Legal Organization) 116
Hamilton, Richard 34, 212–13
  The Beatles 221
  Kent State 69
  Swingeing London 67 – poster *141*
  Swingeing London 67 (a) 140
Hapshash and the Coloured Coat 108, *109*, *119*, *235*, *247*
Hare Krishna 28
Harlem Peace March (1967) *79*
Harper, Roy 153
Harperin, Danny *132*
Harris, Rufus 116
Harrison, George 116, 153, 154, 197, 198, 206, *206–7*, 216
  see also The Beatles
Haug, Wolfgang, *Critique of Commodity Aesthetics* 260
Haworth, Jann 108–11, *202*, 204, *205*
Hayden, Tom 64
Haynes, Jim 28
Hayward Gallery, London 34, 46
The Head Shop *126*
Heartbeat in the Brain (film) 117
Heath, Edward 46

Hell's Angels 28, *41*, 115, 169, 170
Helms, Chet 103, 169, 174
Help! (film) 198
Hemmings, David 22
Hendrix, Jimi 28, 38, 46, 100, *102*, 108, 112, 115, 150, *151*, *160–61*, 178, *180*, 206
  Are You Experienced 140
  Axis Bold As Love 150
  Electric Ladyland 150–51
  'Purple Haze' 138
The Herd 149
Herrman, Bernard 147
Heseltine, Michael 46
Hewlett Packard 286
Hill, Vince 138, 139
Hillman, Chris 181
Hills, Joan 22
HIP Job Co-op 116
Hipgnosis *118*, 148
hippies 62, 103, 238, 284
Hitchcock, Billy 104
Hitler, Adolf 85
HIV/AIDS 76
Hoffman, Abbie 62, 115, 116–17
Hoggart, Richard, *The Uses of Literacy* 252
Hollingshead, Michael 144
Hollo, Anselm *104*
Holly, Buddy 147
Hollywood 50, 182
Holmes, John 44
Homebrew Computer Club 51, 295
homosexuality 19, 100
  decriminalization 28
  gay liberation movement 51, 56, 71, 76, *84*, 117
  Stonewall Inn Rebellion 70–71, *71*
Hooker, John Lee 183
Hoover, J. Edgar 69
Hope, Bob 46
Hopkins, John 'Hoppy' 28, 112, 116, 144, 147, 152, *153*, 154, *155*, *156–7*, *302–3*
Hopper, Dennis 38, 115
Horkheimer, Max, 'The Culture Industry' 258
Hornby, Charles 238, *239*
Hornsey College of Art 213
Horovitz, Michael *104*, 144
  Children of Albion: Poetry of the Underground in Britain 40
Hoskyns, Barney, *Waiting for the Sun* 181
Hotpoint 255
Huckleberry's 116
Hujar, Peter *81*
Hulanicki, Barbara 226, 241–3
Human Be-In, San Francisco (1967) 28, 115, *116*, *133*, 152, 284, *285*
Humperdinck, Englebert 138
Humphrey, Hubert H. 67–8
Hung on You, London 233–6, *235*, *236*, *248*
Hunt, Ron *120*
Hunter, George, *The Seed* 173
Hurford, John, *Dandelion* 158
Huxley, Aldous, *The Doors of Perception* 143–4

I
ICL 51–2
if i 92
The Illustrated Paper 105
immigration 76
The Incredible String Band 112
Independent Group 252
Indiana, Robert, *Love* 189
Indians of All Tribes 40
Indica Books, London 105
Indica Gallery, London 22, 205

Industrial Design magazine 259, 261
inequality, economic 75–6
Ink 105
Institute of Contemporary Archaeology (ICA) 22
Institute of Contemporary Arts (ICA) 34, *35*
International Days of Protest 101–3, 198
International Design Conference in Aspen (IDCA) 259, 260–64, *263*
International Poetry Congress (1965) *302*
International Poetry Incarnation 104–5, *104*, 144, 152, 198
International Times (IT) 22, 28, 105, *106*, 112, 116, 147, 152–3, 154, *155*, 205
Iron Butterfly 111, 187
Ironside, Janey 228
Isle of Wight Festival 40, *41*, 46, *47*, 154, *158*
Italy 260, 265
ITN 140

J
Jackson, Milt 183
Jackson State College 69, 117
Jagger, Mick 40, *41*, 139, 152, 154, 236, 238, *245*
Jan & Dean 179
Jandl, Ernst *104*
Jaws (film) 50
Jefferson Airplane 40, 112, *150*, 152, 169, *175*, 284
Jeger, Lena 46
Jenkins, Roy 22
Jenner, Peter 147–8, 149, 153
Jethro Tull 153
Jim Kwesin Jug Band *163*
Jimi Hendrix Experience
  see Hendrix, Jimi
Jobs, Steve 51, 52, 290, 295
Johnson, Lyndon B. 56–61, 64, 67, 68, 148
Johnson, Matthew 22
Johnson, Philip 256
Jones, Allen 213
Jones, Brian 28, 40, 139, 153, 154
The Jones Brothers 183
Joplin, Janis 40, 112, 115, *178*, 284
Joy, Eric 238

K
Kaleidoscope 149
Kaleidoscope (film) 228
Kandel, Lenore 115
Kantner, Paul 169–70, 172
Kaufmann, Edgar, Jr 258
Kaukonen, Jorma 172
Keenan, Brigid 227
Kelley, Alton 103, 108, *159*, *163*, *164*, 174
  'Zig-Zag Man' poster *176*
Kennedy, John F. 38, 253
Kennedy, Robert F. 34, 56, 67, 69
Kent, Corita 92
Kent State University 46, *47*, 69, *69*, 117
Kerouac, Jack 40, 168
Kerry, John 69
Kesey, Ken 101, 103–4, 116, 144, 168–9, 198, 284
  One Flew Over the Cuckoo's Nest 168
Khanh, Quasar *262*
Kinetics, London (1970) 46
King, Andrew 153
King, Coretta 28
King, Martin Luther, Jr 28, 32, 56, 59, 61, 64, 67, *67*, 69, 213, 253

King's Road, London 226, 227, 228, 230, 233–6, *246*
The Kinks 111
Kiromiya, Kiyoshi, 'Fuck the Draft' poster *59*
Kissinger, Henry 117
Kitchen Sink Press 108
Klarwein, Mati, *Grain of Sand 296*
Klossowki de Rola, Stash 145
Koch brothers 77
Koger, Marijke *209*, *222*, 237
Korda, Alberto *81*
Kramer, Wayne 185
Krugman, Paul 75
KSAN 174
Kubrick, Stanley 34, 252–3, *254*
Kunkin, Art 105
KYA 174

L
Labour Party 19, 22
Laine, Denny 112
Laing, R.D. *29*, 144
Lama Foundation 294
Lambert Studios *93*
Lapidus, Ted *219*
Laslett, Rhuane 152
Last Gasp 108
Laurel, Alicia Bay, *Living on the Earth 300*
LaVigne, Robert *170*
Leary, Timothy 28, 100, 101, 104, 105, 115, 116, *116*, 144, 148, 215, 284
The Psychedelic Experience 147, 200
Lebel, Jean-Jacques 115–16
Le Pavé 87
Quelques indications supplémentaires sur la mort 123
Lee, Martin A. 103
Leeger, Josje *209*, *222*, 237
Lennon, John 22, 40, 46, *53*, 112, 147, 148, 151, 154, 198, 199, 200, *201*, *203*, 205, *206*, *210–11*, 213–16, *213*, *218–19*, 236, 237
see also The Beatles
Leon, Jim, *The Politics of Experience 125*
Leone, Dave 183
'Let Us Discover the Love in Each Other' poster *88*
Levy, Bill *106*
Lewis, John 67
liberalism 56, 75, 76
Liberty Union Party 68
Libre commune, New Mexico 294
Life magazine 32, 145
Lincoln, Abraham 77
Lindsay, Norman *107*
Lipkin, Efrem 294
Little Richard 179
Little Willie John 183
Loach, Ken 34
Cathy Come Home 22
London 18–52
counter-culture 100, 152–4
economic problems 50, 51–2
fashion 226–43
population 50, 51
Swinging London 199
underground clubs 112
London Docklands Development Corporation (LDDC) 50, 52
London Fashion Week 228
London Free School 147, 152
London Model House Group 228
London School of Economics (LSE) 40
London Street Commune 153
The Long Hair Times 152
Lord John, London 238
Los Angeles 50, 56, 100, 111, 112, 116, 140, 143, 144, 147, 178–83

Los Angeles Free Press 105
Love (band) 111, 147, 178
Love Pageant Rally (1966) 22
Loving, Mildred and Richard 28, *29*
LSD (acid) 156, 281, 284
Acid Tests 101, 103, *104*, 144, 169, 198
in British underground 152
criminalization of 22, 138
effects of 143–4
influence on music 138–43, 147–50, 197, 199–200
legality 10, 19, 169
spread through youth culture 144–5
Lycett-Green, Rupert 238, *239*

M
McCann, Gerald 228
McCarthy, Eugene 67, 69
McCarthy, Joseph 60, 100
McCartney, Paul 46, 111, 116, 140, 153, 198, 199, 204–16
see also The Beatles
McClaren, Malcolm 236
McClure, Michael 115
MacDonald, Ian 202–8, 205, 213, 217
McDonough, Jack, *San Francisco Rock* 169–70
McGovern, George 69, 76
McGowan, Cathy 227
McGrath, Tom *106*
McGuinn, Jim 181
McInnerney, Michael 108, 111, *113*
McKenzie, Scott *27*, 28, 149
Maclean, Bonnie 174
McLuhan, Marshall 145, 254, 265
MacMillan, Iain 214, *214*
McNair, Archie 226
McNamara, Robert 60
McQueen, Alexander 243
magazines 19, 152–3, 154, 227
Maharishi Mahesh Yogi 206
Mailer, Norman, *The Armies of the Night* 62
Malcolm X 67
The Mamas and the Papas 28, 178
Manson, Charles 117, 215
Mantra Rock Dance, San Francisco (1967) 28, *29*
Mao Zedong 20, 64
Little Red Book 20
The Marbles 169
'March Against Fear' (1966) 64
Marcuse, Herbert 100
marijuana 19, 117, 139, 154
Marquee Club, London 152
Martin, George 196, 214
Martin, Peter D. 168
Marvel Comics 169
Matrix Club, San Francisco 108, 169
Medicaid 75
Medicare 75
Melanie 46
Melly, George 19, 200, 228
Merry Pranksters 101, 103–4, 144, 169, 284
Metzner, Ralph, *The Psychedelic Experience* 147
Michael, John 228
Michael X 152
Middle Earth Clothing *130*
Milan Triennial 260, 261, *261*, 263
Miles, Barry 152, 153, 205
Miles, Trevor 236
Milk, Harvey 51
Miller, David 59
Miller, Herbert 261
Miller, Jeffrey *47*
Miller, Jonathan 148

Miller, Larry 174
Milton Keynes 50
Miss America 70
Miss World Contest 46
Mr Fish, London *41*, 238, *240*
Mitchell, Adrian 104, *104*, 144
Mitchell, Joni *39*, 46
Mitchell, Mitch *102*
Mlinaric, David 236, 238
'The Mobe' 46, 62
Moby Grape 112, 152
Moe's, Berkeley 105
Mole Express (magazine) 154
The Monkees (television show) 22
Monterey International Pop Festival (1967) 19, *114*, 115, 140, 154, 178, 183, *192*
Montreal Expo '67 26, 256, *298–9*
Monty Python's Flying Circus 40
The Moody Blues 112
Moon landings 38, *275*
Moore, Fred 51
More, Thomas, *Utopia* 13, *13*
Morocco 238, 241, *241*
Morris, William 236, 237, *249*
Moscoso, Victor 108, *159*, 174, *297*
Mothers of Invention 112
Freak Out! 111–12
Motor City 5 (MC5) 112, *184*, 185–6, *185*, 187
Motown 149, 183
Mouse, Stanley 108, 111, *159*, *164*, 174
'Zig-Zag Man' poster *176*
The Move 28, 112, 148, 149
Moynihan, Daniel Patrick 60
Mucha, Alphonse 108, 200
Job 163
Muhammad, Elijah 67
Muir, Jean 227
Mungo Jerry *162*
murders, San Francisco 50–51
Museum of Modern Art, New York 258
Mystic Eye *144*

N
Nader, Ralph 77
Unsafe at Any Speed 258
NASA 38, 286
Nasty Tales 122
Nation of Islam 67
National Guard (US) 22, *23*, 46, 62, 69, 117, 186
National Organization for Women (NOW) 46, 70, *70*
National Security Agency 295
Native Americans 40, *41*, 236
Natural Resources Defense Council 72
Navarre, General Henri 60
NBC 34
Nelson, Gaylord 72
Nelson, George 261
Nelson, Ricky 179
Neville, Richard *29*, *47*, *107*, *122*, 154
New Communalists 279–87, 290, 294
New Deal 60, 75
New Left 64, 67, 70, 75, 101, 213, 264, 279, 290, 294
New Musical Express 138, 198
New Scientist magazine 286
New York 100, 111, 112, 147
New York Radical Women 70
New York Stock Exchange 116
New York Times 44, 67, 72
Newark 56, 181
The News Chronicle 143
The News of the World 139, 144
newspapers 105, 227
Newton, Huey P. 34, 67, 69
The Nice 150

Nicholson, Jack 38
Nixon, Richard M. *33*, 34, *35*, 44, 46, *47*, 50, 57, 68–9, 72, 75, 117
Northern Ireland 40
Notting Hill Carnival 152
Notting Hill Gate, London 152
Nova magazine 227, *232*, 233
nuclear weapons *78*, 101, *102*, 143, 156, 279, 280
Nudist Party 117
Nutter, Tommy 238

O
Obama, Barack 75, 76, 77
O'Brien, Desmond 144
Observer 108, 227
obsolescence 255
Occupy 269
Ochs, Phil 56–7, *57*
Oh! Calcutta (revue) 46, *47*
oil crisis (1973) 50, 156
Oldham, Andrew Loog 139
'On vous intoxique!' poster *85*
Ono, Yoko 22, 40, 112, 205, 213, *213*, 215, 216
Ceiling Painting (Yes Painting) 205
'An Open Letter to the People of a Dying Planet' poster *96*
Open University 40
Ops Veda (magazine) 154
The Oracle of the City of San Francisco 22, 105
Ormsby Gore, Jane 233, 236
Oscars 44
Osiris Visions *81*
Our World (television broadcast) 140, 206
Ovshinsky, Harvey 105
Owsley, Augustus Stanley III 28, 115
Oxford Circle *159*, *164*
OZ magazine 28, *29*, 46, *47*, 105, *107*, *119*, *126*, 152–3, 154

P
Packard, Vance 264–5
The Hidden Persuaders 255
The Waste Makers 255–8, *256*, 269
Palo Alto Research Center (PARC) 290
Pan Am 46
Pan-Scandinavian Design Students Organization *257*, 259
Panton, Verner 253
Papanek, Victor 253, 258, *258–9*, 261, 264, *266–7*
Design for the Real World 259, *268*, 269
Paradox 263, 264
Paris 230
1968 protests 34, *35*, 115–16, 205, 213, 253, 260
Pariser, Alan 178
Parkinson, Norman 241, *242*
Peace and Freedom Party 68
Peace Eye, New York 105
Peacock Revival 238
Peanut Butter Conspiracy *297*
Pearls Before Swine 112
Pearse, John 236
Peel, John 28, 153, *158*
Pentagle 46
People 144
People's Computer Center 294
People's Computer Company 294
'People's Park', Berkeley 40, 46
Pereira, Dunstan *88*
Perkins, Carl 179
Perry, Charles 144
Peter Rabbit 287
Petticoat magazine 227
Phillips, John 28, 178

Pink Floyd 22, 28, 38, 105, 112, 139, 147–8, *148*, 149, 150, 153, 236, 238
Piper at the Gates of Dawn 149
UmmaGumma 118
pirate radio stations *5*, 150
Plagenhoef, Scott 196
Play Power 122
Plunket Greene, Alexander 226
Poco 162
Poe, Edgar Allan 204, *205*
Poiret, Paul 233, 238
Polanski, Roman 40, 144
politics, US 56–97
Pollock, Alice 241
pollution 44, 72
Poor People's Campaign (1968) *62*, *89*
Pop Art 212
Pornography in Denmark (film) 46
'Port Huron Statement' 13, *14*, 64, 279
Porter, Thea 238–41, *248*
Post Office Tower, London 19
Posthuma, Simon *209*, *222*, 237
Potter, David, *People of Plenty* 256
poverty 60–61, 75
Powell, Aubrey *118*, *148*
Presley, 34, 40, 179
The Pretty Things 112
Pringle, Alexandra 227
Print Mint 108
Procol Harum 112, 140, 148, *162*
protests 56–7
Aldermaston marches 101, *102*
in Paris 34, *35*, 115–16, 205, 213, 253, 260
Selma march 59
see also Vietnam War
Psych-Out (film) 34
psychedelia
British music 147–51
drugs 138–45
posters 108, 174
Psychedelic Shop, Haight-Ashbury 144
Psychedelicatessen, New York 111
Pulitzer Prize 47
punk 50, 156

Q
'Q. And babies? A. And babies' poster *84*
Quant, Mary 226, 227, *227*, 228, 230, 236–7, 241, 243, *249*
Queen magazine 227
Quicksilver Messenger Service 112, 115, *165*, 172, *176*
Quintessence 153, 154

R
race relations
Black Panther Party 22, 34, *66*, 67, 69, 170, 186
Black Power 44, 56, 64–7, 69, 75
inequality 75, 76
Race Relations Act (1968) 34
racial discrimination 19, 28, 61
riots 59–60, 61, *61*
radio stations 150, 174
Radio Times 46
The Rag 105
Rainey, Michael 233–6, *236*
Ramparts magazine 264
The Rationals 186
Rauschenberg, Robert *90*
Raven, Mike 28
Ready Steady Go! (television programme) 227
Reagan, Ronald 56, 57, 75, 76, 215
Red Brigade 217
Red Crayola 112
Red Desert (film) 263
Red Dog Saloon, Virginia City 169

316

Red Guard (China) 20
Red Mole (magazine) 154
Redding, Noel *102*
Redding, Otis 115, 149
Redgrave, Vanessa 22, 34
Reich, Charles A., *The Greening of America* 280–81
Reid, Terry 154
Release 116, 152
Renoma *218*
Republican Party 61, 68, 75, 76, 77
Resource One 294
Richards, Keith 139, 154
Richter, Dan *104*
Ricks, Willie 64
Rigg, Diana 226
Riley, Bridget 108
 Drawing 121
Riot on Sunset Strip (film) 182–3
riots 59–60, 61, *61*, 181–2, 186, *187*
Rip Off Press 108
Ritva 230–33, *232*
Roberts, Tommy 236
Rodriguez, Spain 108
Roe, Dave *158*
Roe v. Wade (1973) 70, 76
Rolling Stone magazine 28, 32, 144, 152, 154, 174
Rolling Stones 40, 111, *128*, 139, 147, 153, 179, 185, 198
 Their Satanic Majesties Request 111, *119*, 150
 see also Jagger, Mick
Ronan Point, London 34
The Ronettes 22
Roosevelt, Theodore 72
Ross, Diana 149
Ross, Mike 230
Roszak, Theodore, *The Making of a Counter Culture* 279–80
Roundhouse, London 46, 105, 112, *129*, 147
Royal College of Art (RCA) 227, 228
Rubin, Barbara *104*
Rubin, Jerry 62, 115, 116
Ryder, Mitch 186

S
Sadler, Staff Sgt Barry, 'The Ballad of the Green Berets' 20
Saigon, US Embassy evacuation *97*
Saint-Exupéry, Antoine de, *Terre des hommes 26*
St Laurent, Yves 241
St Marks Bookshop, New York 105
St Pancras Station, London 19
Salinger, J.D. 100
Samberg, Paul, *Fire!: Notes from the Counterculture* 40
The San Diego Door 105
San Francisco 18–52
 alternative communities 51, 279, 281–4
 counter-culture 101, 103, 115, 116
 drugs 103, 144
 economic problems 50
 murders 50–51
 music 168–78, 179–80, 183
 population 50
 Silicon Valley 51
 underground bands 112
San Francisco Chronicle 174
San Francisco Mime Troupe 170
San Francisco State University 34
Sanders, Bernie 68, 77
Sandersons 237
Sandison, Ronnie 143
Sandoz 143
Santana, Carlos 40, *191*

Sassoon, Vidal 226
Sätty (Wilfried Podreich), 'Listen Sleep Dream' poster *134*
Savile, Jimmy 46
Scalia, Antonin 77
Schaffner, Nicholas 200
Schapiro, Miriam 264
Schneemann, Carolee 28
Schumacher, E.F., *Small Is Beautiful* 156
Scientific American magazine 286
Scott, Ridley 295
Scott Richard Case 186
SDO 257
Seale, Bobby 67
Seed (newspaper) 279
The Seeds 179
Seegers, George *258*
Seger, Bob 183, 186
Seidemann, Bob *159*
Selma, Alabama 59
Senate Foreign Relations Committee 60
sexuality 100, 117
 see also homosexuality
Shaftesbury Theatre, London 34
Shakespeare & Co. 105
Shankar, Ravi 28, 148, 196, 197, *207*
Shapiro, Benny 178
Sharp, Martin *9*, 108, *122*, *129*
 Headopoly 124
 'Legalise Cannabis: The Putting Together of the Heads' poster *135*
Shaw, Sandie 28, 227, *249*
Sheldon, Gilbert 108
Sherr, Max 105
Shrimpton, Jean *246*
Sierra Club 72, 170
Silicon Valley 51, 254, 290
Sinclair, John 112, 185–7
Singer, David *162*
Sirhan, Sirhan 34
Skolnick, Arnold H. *188*
Slick, Darby 169
Slick, Grace 100, 169, *192*
Slick, Jerry 169
Sly and the Family Stone 40, 46, 174, *191*
The Small Faces 138, 139, 143, 149
Smart, Larry, 'Jimi Hendrix' poster *160*
Smashing Time (film) 19
Smith, Fred 185
The Smoke 139
Snatch (comic) 105
Snyder, Gary 100, 115, 116
Social Deviants 116
Soft Machine 22, 105, 112, *180*
'Solidarity with the African American People' poster *91*
Sons of Adam *159*
Sons of Champlin 172
Sorbonne, Paris 115
Sottsass, Ettore, *Valentine* typewriter 252
The Sound of Music (film) 198
Southbound Freeway 186
Southern, Terry 38
Southern Christian Leadership Conference (SCLC) 61, 69
Spector, Phil 216
Spiegelman, Art 108
Spirit 111
Squires, Eddie *272–3*
The Standells 179, 182
Stanford Research Institute (SRI) 40, 290
Stanford University 51, 290
Star Wars (film) 50
Starr, Ringo 147, 148, 216, *302*
 see also The Beatles

Status Quo 150
Stephen, John 226, 228, 238
Steppenwolf 38
Stern, Gerd 279, 281
Stewart, Ed 28
Stills, Stephen 111, 181–2
Stollman, Steve 152
Stonewall Inn Rebellion (1969) 56, 70–71, *71*, 117
The Stooges 187
'Stop Police Brutality and Entrapment of Homosexuals' poster *84*
Streisand, Barbara 238
Student Mobilization Committee to End the War in Vietnam 84
Student Non-Violent Co-ordinating Committee (SNCC) 64–7, 69
Students for a Democratic Society (SDS) 13, *14*, 57, 59, 64, 67, 69, 279
Sullivan, Edmund Joseph 108
Summer of Love (1967) 115, 140, 183, 197–8
The Sun Trolley 28
The Sunday Times 227
Sunset Strip 179, 181, *182*, 186
Supreme Court (US) 22, 70, 71, 75, 76, 77
The Supremes 149
surfing 179
Swinging London 19, 22, 199, 226

T
Tantric Lovers 119
Tate, Sharon 40, *41*
Taylor, Derek 178
Taylor, Mick 153
Tea Party 76
television 227
Terré, Nathan *130*
 'Zodiac-Terré' poster *125*
terrorism 69, 154
Tet Offensive (1968) 32, 60, 213
Thatcher, Margaret 50
theatre censorship 19
13th Floor Elevators 112
Thorgerson, Storm *118*, *148*
TIME magazine 22, 26, 72, 183, 199, 226
The Times 204
Tin Can Radio *258*
Tomorrow 149, 150
Top 10 138, 139, 149
Top of the Pops 46
Townshend, Pete 112, 174
Traffic 148, 149, 153
 Dear Mr Fantasy 150
A Tribute to Dr Strange (1965) 103, *103*, 169, 174
Trips Festival (1966) 22, *23*, 144, 198, 284
Trocchi, Alexander *104*, 144
 Sigma Folio 13, *15*
The Troubadour, Los Angeles 112
Trump, Donald 76, 77
Tuffin, Sally 228–30
Tulloch, Courtney 152
Tunisia 238
Turnbull & Asser 238
Turner, Fred 256
 From Counterculture to Cyberculture 254
The 21st Century (television series) 256
Twiggy 22, 227–8, *228–9*
2001: A Space Odyssey (film) 34, *35*, 252
Tynan, Kenneth 46, 204
Tyner, Rob 185
Tyrannosaurus Rex 153

U
UFO, London 28, 108, 112, 147
Ugandan Asians 52
Uncle Russ Travel Agency *184*, 185, 186
Underground Press Syndicate 154
'Uneasy Riders ("We Blew It")' poster *96*
unemployment 50, 75
UNESCO 259
Union Oil Company 72
United States of America (band) 111
University of California, Berkeley 51, 144, 294
University of London 40
University of Michigan 59
Up the Junction (film) 34
US Marines *58*, 59
USCO 280, 281–4, *282–4*, 294, *301*
The Utah Free Press 105
Utopie: L'Architecture comme problème théorique 261

V
Valens, Ritchie 179
Valentine, Penny 138
Van Hamersveld, John *180*
Vaneigem, Raoul, *The Revolution of Everyday Life* 260
Vanguard 22
Vanilla Fudge 112
Vecchio, Mary Ann *47*
Velvet Underground 22, *110*, *145*, 147
 The Velvet Underground and Nico 111
 White Light/White Heat 111
The Ventures 179
Veruschka 236
Viet Cong 26, 32, 60, 62, 213
Vietnam Moratorium Committee 68
Vietnam War 22, 40, 44, 75, 148, 156, 253
 anti-war protests 28, *29*, 34, 59, *59*, 62, 67, 68–9, 76, 77, 101–3, *102*, 117, 213, 236, 279
 casualties 20, 59, 100
 as catalyst for youth movement 174
 Johnson escalates involvement in 56, *58*, 59, 60, 100, 143
 Muhammad Ali refuses to fight in 26
 Nixon and 68
 Tet Offensive 32, 60, 213
Village Voice 105
Vincent, Gene 179
Vogue 227, 230, *231*, 233, 237, *241*, *242*
Voorman, Klaus *199*, 200
Vostell, Wolf, *Moon Landing 275*
Voting Rights Act (1965) 59, 61

W
Wadleigh, Michael 44
Wallace, George C. 68
'War Is Good Business' poster *93*
'War Is Hell' poster *84*
War on Poverty 56, 60–61
Warhol, Andy 22, *110*, 111, *145*, *244*
Warner Bros 178
Washington, Dinah 183
Washington DC 62, 67, 68, 69
Watergate scandal (1974) 75
Watts riots (1965) 59–60, 61
Waymouth, Nigel 108, *109*, *119*, *235*, 236, *247*
Weathermen 69
Wedge, James 228–30
Wells, Junior *177*
Wenner, Jann 28
West, Keith 149

West Coast Pop Art Experimental Band 111
Westmoreland, General William 60
Westwood, Vivienne 243
The Wha 185
Where It's At (magazine) 34
The Whisky, Los Angeles 112
White Panther Party 112, 116, 186–7
'White Rabbit' poster *146*
Whitehouse, Mary 139
The Who 28, 40, 46, 112, 115, 174, 178, *186*, 197
 Tommy 111
 The Who Sell Out 150
Whole Earth Catalog 34, 144, 253, 254, 284–7, *288–9*, 290, 294, 295
Wiener, Norbert 286–7
WikiLeaks 117
Wilcock, John 152
The Wild Ones (film) 182
Wilde, Oscar 204, *205*
Wilkes, Tom *114*
Williams, Danny 22
Willis, Ellen 264–5
Wilson, Brian 111, 196
Wilson, Harold 22, 148
Wilson, S. Clay 105–8
Wilson, Wes 108, *159*, 174, *177*, 185, 198
Winwood, Stevie 153
Wolfe, Tom, *The Kandy-Kolored Tangerine-Flake Streamline Baby* 258–9
Womanhouse project 264
Women Strike for Equality demonstration, New York (1970) *94*
Women's Graphics Collective *88*
women's liberation movement *see* feminism
Women's Strike for Equality (1970) 46
Woodstock (documentary) 44, 154
Woodstock Festival 38, 44, 115, *188*, 190–91, *193*
World Cup 22, 46
World Psychedelic Centre 144
Worthy Farm 154
Wozniak, Steve 51, 52, 290
Wright, Rick 149

X
Xerox 46, *47*, 290

Y
The Yardbirds 112, 179, 197
York, Susannah 228
Young, Jimmy 28
Young, Neil 181
Young, Ron 46
Youth International Party (Yippie) 116–17

Z
Zap Comix 105
Zappa, Frank 111–12, *132*
'Zappa on the Toilet' poster *132*
Zigzag (magazine) 154
The Zombies, *Odessey and Oracle* 150

PICTURE CREDITS

1 By permission of the Master and Fellows of St John's College, Cambridge
5 Jean-Philippe Charbonnier/Gamma-Legends/Getty Images
7 Courtesy of FoundSF.org
8 © Shinko Music/Premium Archive/Getty Images
9 © Wes Wilson
10 © Francis Miller/The LIFE Picture Collection/Getty Images
11 © Harvey W. Cohen
12 © Feliks Topolski/Huton Archive/Getty Images
13 © Ralph Crane/the LIFE Picture Collection/Getty Images
14 © Daily Mail /REX/Shutterstock
16 © Georges Melet/Paris Match Archive/Getty Images
18 © Bettmann/Getty Images
19 Franciszka Themerson, courtesy of the Themerson Archive
20 MGM/Stanley Kubrick Productions/The Kobal Collection
21 Charles Everest © Cameron Life Photo Library
22 20th Century Fox/Moviepix/Getty Images
23 Rolls Press/Popperfoto/Getty Images
24 New York Daily News/ Getty Images
25 Ralph Crane/the LIFE Picture Collection/Getty Images
26 The Estate of David Gahr/Premium Archive/Getty Images
28 David Redfern/Redferns/Getty Images
29 Leonard Burt/Hulton Archive/Getty Images
30 Courtesy of PARC, a Xerox company
31 STF/AFP/Getty Images
32 © Bettmann/Getty Images
34 © Larry Burrows/The LIFE Picture Collection/Getty Images
36 Courtesy of the Library of Congress, Washington DC
37 © Rolls Press/Popperfoto/Getty Images
39 Bettmann/Getty Images
40 © Bentley Archive/Popperfoto/Getty Images
42 © Joseph Louw/The LIFE Images Collection/Getty Images
43 Paul Sequeira/Premium Archive/Getty Images
44 © Rita Donagh
45 © Bettmann/Getty Images
46 © Bettmann/Getty Images
47 Fred W. McDarrah/Premium Archive/Getty Images
48 © Hulton Archive/Getty Images
49 © Newsday, Inc. 1970
50 © Estate of John Victor Lindsey Hopkins
51 © Estate of John Victor Lindsey Hopkins
52 Clive Limpkin/Hulton Archive/Getty Images
53 © Builder Levy
54 © Alberto Korda
55 © Jay Belloli/Courtesy of the Center for the Study of Political Graphics
57 Courtesy of the Center for the Study of Political Graphics
58 Courtesy of Jon Savage
61 ©Tony DeRosa/Courtesy of the Center for the Study of Political Graphics
65 © Lester Balog. Courtesy of the Woody Guthrie Archive/Woody Guthrie Center, Tulsa, OK, USA
66 © Jean-Jacques Lebel
67 Collection of the Oakland Museum of California

68 Courtesy of the Center for the Study of Political Graphics
69 Courtesy of the Center for the Study of Political Graphics
71 © Robert Rauschenberg Foundation/DACS, London/VAGA, New York 2016
72 © Emory Douglas
73 © Emory Douglas
74 © Corita Art Center, Immaculate Heart Community, Los Angeles, CA. Photograph by Arthur Evans
75 © Alan Copeland
76 Courtesy of the Center for the Study of Political Graphics
77 © Michael Abramson/The LIFE Images Collection/Getty Images
78 Reprinted by permission of HarperCollins Publishers Ltd © 1970 Germaine Greer
79 Courtesy of Pennebaker Hegedus Films
80 Courtesy of the Center for the Study of Political Graphics
81 Courtesy of the Center for the Study of Political Graphics
82 © Bettmann/Getty Images
83 © Mary Ellen Mark Library
84 © Estate of John Victor Lindsey Hopkins
85 © The Evening Standard/Hulton Archive/Getty Images
86 © GLOBE/REX/Shutterstock
88 © Wes Wilson
89 © Ted Streshinsky/Corbis Historical Collection/Getty Images
90 © Estate of John Victor Lindsey Hopkins
94 © Robert Crumb
95 © Nigel Waymouth and Michael English
96 Photo © Billy Name/Lid Images
98 © Tom Wilkes
99 © Jim Marshall Photography LLC
100 Photography Aubrey Powell/Storm Thorgerson at Hipgnosis. © Pink Floyd Music Ltd.
101 © Nigel Waymouth and Michael English
102 © Michael Cooper
103 © Ron Hunt
104 © Bridget Riley 2016. All rights reserved Courtesy Karsten Schubert, London
105 © The Estate of Martin Sharp/DACS 2016
107 © Ron Cobb
108 © Jean-Jacques Lebel
109 © The Estate of Martin Sharp/DACS 2016
110 © Nathan Terré
114 Iconic Images/Terry O'Neill
115 © The Estate of Martin Sharp/DACS 2016
116 © Nathan Terré
120 © Sätty
121 © The Estate of Martin Sharp/DACS 2016
122 © Rita Donagh
123 © Rita Donagh
124 Baron Wolman/ Hulton Archive/Getty Images
125 Photo by Bernie Cochrane owner of The Psychedelic Eye
126 © Steve Schapiro/ Corbis Premium Historical/ Getty Images
127 © East Totem West
129 © H. Greene/Everett/REX/Shutterstock
130 Photograph by Gered Mankowitz © BOWSTIR Ltd/2016/Mankowitz.com
131 © Estate of John Victor Lindsey Hopkins
132 © Michael English
133 Photograph by Brian Walker
134 Lawrence Schiller/Premium Archive/Getty Images
135 © Estate of John Victor Lindsey Hopkins
137 Courtesy of Ray Foulk
138 © Bob Seidemann
140 © Larry Smart
141 Courtesy EMP Museum, Seattle, WA
148 © Paul Ryan/Michael Ochs Archive/Getty Images
149 © Dale Smith

150 © Jon Brenneis/The LIFE Images Collection/Getty Images
151 © Jim Marshall Photography LLC
155 © Wes Wilson
156 © Everett Collection Historical/Alamy Stock Photo
157 © Fox Photos/Hulton Archive/Getty Images
158 © John Van Hamersveld
159 Michael Ochs Archives/Getty Images
160 Michael Ochs Archives/Getty Images
161 Julian Wasser/The LIFE Collection/Getty Images
162 Courtesy of the Burton Historical Collection, Detroit Public Library
163 © Gary Grimshaw
164 © Leni Sinclair/Michael Ochs Archives/Getty Images
165 Tom Copi/Michael Ochs Archives/Getty Images
166 © Tom Weschler
167 © Declan Haun/The LIFE Picture Collection/Getty Images
168 © Arnold H. Skolnick
169 © Robert Indiana
170 © Elliott Landy/Premium Archive/Getty Images
171 Baron Wolman/Hulton Archive/Getty Images
172 Ralph Ackerman/Hulton Archive/Getty Images
173 Tucker Ranson/Hulton Archive/Getty Images
174 Michael Ochs Archives/Getty Images
176 © Moviestore Collection/REX/Shutterstock
178 © 1967 Paul McCartney/Photographer: Linda McCartney
179 © Apple Corps Ltd
180 © Apple Corps Ltd
181 Iconic Images/Alan Aldridge
183 © 1966, Reproduced by permission of Sony/ATV Music Publishing (UK) Ltd/Sony/ATV Tunes LLC
184 © Apple Corps Ltd
185 © 1967, Reproduced by permission of Sony/ATV Music Publishing (UK) Ltd/Sony/ATV Tunes LLC
186 © Apple Corps Ltd
187 © Jann Haworth and Peter Blake. All rights reserved, DACS 2016
188 © Yoko Ono/Graham Keen
189 © ITV/REX/Shutterstock
191 © Apple Corps Ltd
192 © Bettmann/Getty Images
194 © Yoko Ono
195 © Apple Corps Ltd
196 © Apple Corps Ltd
197 Keystone/Hulton Archive/Getty Images
198 © Apple Corps Ltd
199 © 1969 Paul McCartney/Photographer: Linda McCartney
200 © Apple Corps Ltd
201 © Alan Aldridge/Iconic Images
204 © Apple Corps Ltd
205 © Apple Corps Ltd
207 © Apple Corps Ltd
208 © Hulton-Deutsch Collection/Corbis Historical Collection/Getty Images
209 Jean-Philippe Charbonnier/Gamma-Legends/Getty Images
211 © The Bill Gibb Trust
212 © Ronald Traeger
216 MGM/The Kobal Collection
219 © Nigel Waymouth and Michael English
220 Courtesy Paul Gorman Archive
221 © 2001 Topham/Colin Jones
222 © Kent Photonews
225 © Condé Nast Archive/Corbis Historical Collection/Getty Images

226 © Norman Parkinson Ltd./courtesy Norman Parkinson Archive
229 Iconic Images/Terry O'Neill
230 © Michael English
235 WARNER BROS/Hawk Films/The Kobal Collection
236 Reproduced by permission of The Random House Group Ltd
237 Copyright Timo Aarniala. Courtesy of Yrjö Sotamaa Archive
238 Courtesy Victor. J. Papanek Foundation, University of Applied Arts Vienna
239 Courtesy Victor. J. Papanek Foundation, University of Applied Arts Vienna
240 Courtesy Archivio Fotografico © La Triennale di Milano
241 Courtesy of the California Institute of the Arts Institute Archive
242 Photo by Maurice Hogenboom/Condé Nast via Getty Images
243 © Sheila Levrant de Bretteville
244 © Sheila Levrant de Bretteville
245 Courtesy of the California Institute of the Arts Institute Archive
246 © Victor J Papanek Foundation, University of Applied Arts Vienna
247 © Victor J Papanek Foundation, University of Applied Arts Vienna
248 © Archigram 1969
249 © Archigram 1966
250 Courtesy Victor. J. Papanek Foundation, University of Applied Arts Vienna
252 © Max Clendinning & Ralph Adron
255 © Iconic Images/Alan Aldridge
256 © DACS 2016
257 © Ullstein Bild/Getty Images
258 © Carl Iwasaki/The LIFE Images Collection/Getty Images
259 Courtesy of Gerd Stern
260 Ted Streshinsky/Corbis Historical Collection/Getty Images
261 © Yale Joel/The LIFE Picture Collection/Getty Images
263 Robert R. Mc Elroy/Archive Photos/Getty Images
264 © bil paul www.sixtiespix.com
265 © NASA 2013
266 Bettmann/Getty Images
267 © Stewart Brand
268 Apic/Hulton Archive/Getty Images
269 Collection of the Oakland Museum of California
270 © Kim Kulish/Corbis Historical/Getty Images
271 © Klarwein Family
274 © Alicia Bay Laurel
275 Courtesy Gerd Stern
276 © Stewart Brand
277 © Estate of John Victor Lindsey Hopkins
278 © Estate of John Victor Lindsey Hopkins
279 © Estate of John Victor Lindsey Hopkins

Cover and chapter openers:
Twiggy: Photograph by Bert Stern. © Estate of Bert Stern. Used with permission; Martin Luther King, Jr: Christian Science Monitor/Getty Images; Andy Warhol: Greg Gorman/Contour by Getty Images; John Lennon: Courtesy of Sam Smart; Jimi Hendrix: © Joe Roberts Jr; Germaine Greer: © Estate of Keith Morris/ Redferns/ Getty Images; Che Guevara: © Alberto Korda; Chairman Mao: © Photo 12/Contributor/ Universal Images Group/ Getty Images; Stewart Brand: Corbis; Timothy Leary: © UPPA/Photoshot; Buckminster Fuller: Bettmann/Getty Images; Allen Ginsberg: © Estate of John Victor Lindsey Hopkins; Kathleen Cleaver: Corbis

ACKNOWLEDGEMENTS

The years from 1966 to 1970 could be considered a watershed moment when the world changed from the 'Modern' into the 'Contemporary'. Fifty years ago is not quite history, as it is within the present lived experience, nor is it still 'current', as social and political attitudes and practice have continued to evolve. This is what makes now such a special time to look at those years, as so many individuals who lived through them can still reflect on what has changed and in what way, and how, indeed, the Sixties changed them. Barry Miles, Stewart Brand, Yoko Ono, Craig Sams, Twiggy, Joe Boyd, Caroline Coon, Gustav Metzger, Jim Haynes, Jean-Jacques Lebel, Jonas Mekas, Nigel Waymouth, Michael Lang and D.A. Pennebaker are just a handful of such individuals who have shared their thoughts with us, and in so doing have enriched the exhibition standpoint of examining 1966–70 from 2016. It is not just these better-known names from whom we have received intellectual, practical and personal assistance, though; everybody we meet has a memory, a thought, an opinion – and sometimes even a thesis! – on what those years have meant for the world of today. We would therefore like to thank these many old and new contacts and friends, within and outside the V&A, who have been incredibly generous in supporting our efforts.

Profound thanks go to Elisa Bailey, the project's Research Assistant, whose contribution has been both extensive and crucial. We similarly recognize the incredible work of the core project team: our designers Pippa Nissen, Alex Sprogis and the team at Nissen Richard Studios, our video designer Finn Ross of FRAY, and sound, lighting and graphic designers Carolyn Downing, Zerlina Hughes and Candy Wall respectively; Curatorial Project Assistant Corinne Jones, and Robyn Earl, Catherine Sargent, Kate Drummond, Olivia Bone, Rachel Murphy, Sarah Scott and their colleagues in the V&A Exhibitions department; our external advisers Jon Savage, Sean Wilentz, Howard Kramer and Barry Miles; and our quality surveyors Sorlan Tan and Keith Flemming.

Alongside our wonderful editor Philip Contos and the team at V&A Publishing, especially Tom Windross and Clare Davis, and book designers Julia Woollams and Michael Johnson at johnson banks, we would like to thank all the contributors to this book, whose individual research interests and expertise make this publication valuable not only as a record of the exhibition and the extraordinary gathering of objects on show, but also in its own right. Thanks also go to the photographers, artists and designers of all natures who have allowed us to show their work.

Countless external people have contributed: the Peel family and James Leeds for the fabulous loans and assistance from the John Peel record collection, which forms the backbone to the exhibition and which provided the albums illustrating the first chapter of this book, Carl Williams with his exceptional counter-culture knowledge and artefacts, the John 'Hoppy' Hopkins Archive and trustees for allowing us access to Hoppy's fantastic work, Woodstock film-maker Michael Wadleigh, Ian Rakoff and his comic collection, our exhibition text editor Maria Blyzinsky and artist Suzanne Treister, from whom we commissioned a new work for the exhibition, are just a few of those to whom we are grateful. At the V&A others have also contributed hugely to the project. Space does not permit us to mention everyone, but we would particularly like to thank: Emily Harris for her inspirational film work with Nick Gordon-Smith, Richard Davis, Lara Flecker, Clair Battisson, Anne Bancroft, Liz Edmunds, Fred Caws, Sophie Hargroves, Joanna Hanna-Grindall, Lucy Hawes, Pandora Ryan, Vanessa Eyles, the Technical Services and Visitor Experience teams; also our colleagues who have since moved on to pastures new but played a vitally important role during their time on the project: Rosie Wanek, Tom Grosvenor and Mark Eastment.

We benefited greatly from the assistance of the following throughout the project: Otone Doi, Gareth Wilson, Catriona Macdonald, Sophy Thomas, Jule Rubi, Christen Ericsson Penfold, Natasha Smith, Philippine Vernes, Ben Levy, Edith Brown, Matteo Walsh Augello and Eleanor Rees.

The V&A Research and Theatre & Performance Departments have been stimulating environments in which to develop such a project, and we are grateful to our colleagues for their advice and support. On behalf of everyone at the V&A we would like to thank Martin Roth, Director, who supported throughout while pushing us to further efforts all the way, and Bill Sherman, Head of Collections and Research – both showed great support in committing the museum to the project and in its development.

CONTRIBUTORS

Victoria Broackes is Senior Curator in the Department of Theatre & Performance, and Head of the London Design Festival at the V&A. She has produced several major V&A exhibitions relating to music, culture and design, including *David Bowie Is* (2013 and touring), and edited and contributed to the best-selling book associated with the exhibition – the first to be authorized by and permit full access to the David Bowie Archive. Previous exhibitions include *Kylie* (2007), *The Story of the Supremes* (2008), *Top of the Pops* (2009), *Diaghilev and the Golden Age of the Ballets Russes 1909–1929* (2010) and *The House of Annie Lennox* (2011).

Alison J. Clarke is professor of design history and theory and director of the Papanek Foundation at the University of Applied Arts Vienna. As a design historian and social anthropologist, her research considers the intersections of design and social relations. A regular contributor to media including *The Genius of Design* (BBC), her book *Tupperware: The Promise of Plastic in 1950s America* was turned into an Emmy Award nominated film-documentary. Recent edited publications include *Émigré Cultures in Design and Architecture* (2016) and *Design Anthropology: Object Cultures in Transition* (2017). Alison is presently completing a monograph titled *Design for the Real World* (MIT) exploring 1960s design activism.

Howard Kramer is an independent museum consultant, curator and writer. He is the former curatorial Director of the Rock and Roll Hall of Fame and Museum (1996–2014) and was lead curator on numerous major exhibitions surveying artists including the Grateful Dead, the Rolling Stones, Hank Williams, the Clash and the Who's *Tommy*. He is the author of *The Rolling Stones: 50 Years of Rock* (2011) and has written for the *Cleveland Plain Dealer*, *Rolling Stone* and *Gadfly Magazine*. Other published contributions include the *Cambridge University Press Companion to the Beatles* (2009) and *Bruce Springsteen: Cultural Studies and the Runaway American Dream* (2012). Recent curatorial contributions include *Bill Graham and the Rock and Roll Revolution* (2015), *Elvis at the O2* (2014) and the National Music Centre of Canada (2016). Kramer previously worked with the V&A on the exhibition *The Story of the Supremes* in 2008.

Jenny Lister has been a curator of Fashion and Textiles at the V&A since 2004. Previously she worked at the Museum of London and Historic Royal Palaces. At the V&A, she has co-curated the exhibition *Sixties Fashion* with Christopher Breward (2006) and *Grace Kelly: Style Icon* (2010), and has contributed to other exhibitions and displays including the 2012 refurbishment of the Fashion Gallery. Her publications include *The V&A Gallery of Fashion* (with Claire Wilcox, 2013) and *London Society Fashion: The Wardrobe of Heather Firbank, 1905–1925* (with Cassie Davies-Strodder and Lou Taylor, 2015).

Geoffrey Marsh is the Director of the V&A's Department of Theatre & Performance and co-curator of *David Bowie Is* currently touring from the V&A. Past exhibitions at the museum include *The Story of the Supremes* (2008) and *Diaghilev and the Golden Age of the Ballets Russes* (2010). Previously, he ran the London office of AEA Consulting and was Director of Development at the Imperial War Museum, which included the project team for the new IWM North in Manchester. Geoffrey has often worked as a consultant for the planning of cultural developments including projects in Australia, Canada, Italy, Belgium and Iraq.

Barry Miles has written extensively on the Beat Generation and the Sixties counter-culture including biographies of Allen Ginsberg, William Burroughs, Jack Kerouac, Charles Bukowski and Frank Zappa, as well as *London Calling: A Countercultural History of London Since 1945*. He was the co-founder of Indica Bookshop and Art Gallery (1965) and of *The International Times* (*IT*, 1966), Europe's first underground newspaper. He lives in London.

Jon Savage is the author of *England's Dreaming: The Sex Pistols and Punk Rock* (1991), *Teenage: The Creation of Youth 1875–1945* (2007), and *1966: The Year the Decade Exploded* (2015). His film credits as writer/consultant include: *The Brian Epstein Story*, *Joy Division* and *Teenage*.

Fred Turner is Harry and Norman Chandler Professor of Communication at Stanford University and the author of *From Counterculture to Cyberculture: Stewart Brand, the Whole Earth Network, and the Rise of Digital Utopianism* (2006), among other books.

Sean Wilentz is George Henry Davis 1886 Professor of American History at Princeton University. He received his PhD in history from Yale University (1980) after earning bachelor's degrees from Columbia University (1972) and Balliol College, Oxford University (1974). His major work to date, *The Rise of American Democracy: Jefferson to Lincoln* (2005), was awarded the Bancroft Prize and was a finalist for the Pulitzer Prize. His most recent books are *The Age of Reagan: A History, 1974–2008*, a reconsideration of US politics since the Watergate affair, and *Bob Dylan in America*, a consideration of Dylan's place in American cultural history.